CONTEMPORARY
AMERICA

A HISTORY OF THE CONTEMPORARY WORLD

General Editor: Keith Robbins

This series offers an historical perspective on the development of the contemporary world. Each of the books examines a particular region or a global theme as it has evolved in the recent past. The focus is primarily on the period since the 1980s but authors provide deeper context wherever necessary. While all the volumes offer an historical framework for analysis, the books are written for an interdisciplinary audience and assume no prior knowledge on the part of readers.

Published

Contemporary Japan
Jeff Kingston

Contemporary America
M.J. Heale

Contemporary Global Economy
Alfred E. Eckes, Jr.

In Preparation

Contemporary Latin America
Robert H. Holden & Rina Villars

Contemporary South Asia
David Hall Matthews

Contemporary Africa
Tom Lodge

Contemporary China
Yongnian Zheng

CONTEMPORARY
AMERICA

POWER, DEPENDENCY, AND GLOBALIZATION SINCE 1980

M.J. HEALE

WILEY-BLACKWELL

A John Wiley & Sons, Ltd., Publication

This edition first published 2011
© 2011 M.J. Heale

Blackwell Publishing was acquired by John Wiley & Sons in February 2007. Blackwell's
publishing program has been merged with Wiley's global Scientific, Technical, and Medical
business to form Wiley-Blackwell.

Registered Office
John Wiley & Sons Ltd, The Atrium, Southern Gate, Chichester, West Sussex, PO19 8SQ, United
Kingdom

Editorial Offices
350 Main Street, Malden, MA 02148-5020, USA
9600 Garsington Road, Oxford, OX4 2DQ, UK
The Atrium, Southern Gate, Chichester, West Sussex, PO19 8SQ, UK

For details of our global editorial offices, for customer services, and for information about how
to apply for permission to reuse the copyright material in this book please see our website at
www.wiley.com/wiley-blackwell.

The right of M.J. Heale to be identified as the author of this work has been asserted in
accordance with the UK Copyright, Designs and Patents Act 1988.

Library of Congress Cataloging-in-Publication Data
Heale, M. J.
    Contemporary America : power, dependency, and globalization since 1980 / M.J. Heale.
        p. cm. – (A history of the contemporary world)
    Includes bibliographical references and index.
    ISBN 978-1-4051-3640-2 (hardcover : alk. paper) – ISBN 978-1-4051-3641-9 (pbk. : alk.
paper)   1. United States–Politics and government–1945–1989.   2. United States–Politics and
government–1989–   3. United States–Foreign relations–1945–1989.   4. United States–Foreign
relations–1989–   I. Title.
    E839.5.H43 2011
    973.92–dc22

                                        2010043500

A catalogue record for this book is available from the British Library.

This book is published in the following electronic formats: ePDFs 9781444396867;
ePub 9781444396874

Set in 10.5/13pt Minion by Toppan Best-set Premedia Limited
Printed in Malaysia by Ho Printing (M) Sdn Bhd

1   2011

For Lesley, again, with love

Contents

Series Editor's Preface

The contemporary world frequently presents a baffling spectacle: "New world orders" come and go; "Clashes of civilizations" seem imminent if not actual; "Peace dividends" appear easily lost in the post; terrorism and "wars on terror" occupy the headlines. "Mature" states live alongside "failed" states in mutual apprehension. The "rules" of the international game, in these circumstances, are difficult to discern. What "international law" is, or is not, remains enduringly problematic. Certainly it is a world in which there are still frontiers, borders, and boundaries, but both metaphorically and in reality they are difficult to patrol and maintain. "Asylum" occupies the headlines as populations shift across continents, driven by fear. Other migrants simply seek a better standard of living. The organs of the "international community," though frequently invoked, look inadequate to deal with the myriad problems confronting the world. Climate change, however induced, is not susceptible to national control. Famine seems endemic in certain countries. Population pressures threaten finite resources. It is in this context that globalization, however understood, is both demonized and lauded.

Such a list of contemporary problems could be amplified in detail and almost indefinitely extended. It is a complex world, ripe for investigation in this ambitious new series of books. "Contemporary," of course, is always difficult to define. The focus in this series is on the evolution of the world since the 1980s. As time passes, and as the volumes appear, it no longer seems sensible to equate "the world since 1945" with "contemporary history." The legacy of the "Cold War" lingers on but it is emphatically "in the background." The fuzziness about "the 1980s" is deliberate. No single year ever carries the same significance across the globe. Authors are therefore establishing their own precise starting points, within the overall "contemporary" framework.

The series treats the history of particular regions, countries, or continents but does so in full awareness that such histories, for all their continuing distinctiveness, can only rarely be considered apart from the history of the world as a whole. Economic, demographic, environmental, and religious issues transcend state, regional, or continental boundaries. Just as the world itself struggles to reconcile diversity and individuality with unity and common purpose, so do the authors of these volumes. The concept is challenging. Authors have been selected who sit loosely on their disciplinary identity – whether that be as historians, political scientists, or students of international relations. The task is to integrate as many aspects of contemporary life as possible in an accessible manner. There is scarcely any aspect of contemporary world history which has not felt, in one way or another, the impress of the United States, whether perceived as champion of freedom or agent of oppression. In its interaction with the world beyond its borders it has experienced, in bewildering combination, both the advantage of military strength and its limitations. It has sometimes found itself operating in lonely eminence, both feared and admired, as the supposed arbiter of the universe. Yet, alongside displays of power, have come moments of self-doubt. Hope has had to be reborn in circumstances of economic uncertainty. It is this sometimes bewildering mixture which this volume captures. Moreover, it does not merely reflect on America's place *in* the world. It captures the sense in which, as no other, the United States is *itself* a world of astonishing diversity. It is this combination that ensured for this book a central place in any consideration of "the contemporary world."

Preface

The quarter-century after World War II is sometimes remembered as a "golden age" for the United States. Its power was without parallel in history and its economy was growing steadily and sometimes strongly. Most, if not all, Americans could avail themselves of the comforts of what J. Kenneth Galbraith called the "affluent society." As a superpower very aware of its awesome responsibilities, the United States played a commanding role on the world stage. Yet in some respects a mightily armed America seemed to insulate its citizenry from foreign influences. In the middle years of the twentieth century the American economy was to a significant degree self-sufficient, and its success reinforced confidence in the American way. As it was purring along, largely oblivious to the wider world, the number of foreigners allowed to settle within American borders was limited. Americans mostly socialized and did business with one another. Ronald Reagan as an actor only once left American shores. Americans – like other peoples – have sometimes been accused of being parochial, of being relatively immune to outside influences, and if this was ever true there was some excuse for it in these years.

Yet the United States could never be truly isolationist, even in the 1950s, and the golden age did not last. By about 1980 it was clear to most Americans that they were part of a world that they could not wholly control, that they were not undisputed masters of their own destiny. The Vietnam War had already delivered a mighty psychological blow, rendering political leaders wary of succumbing again to what Senator William Fulbright had called "the arrogance of power," and now Soviet influence seemed to be on the march. American economic might was also being challenged. Some companies, rendered complacent by their postwar profits, had failed to innovate sufficiently and were ill prepared for the foreign competition that was sending them reeling. Modern technology was increasingly allowing vast amounts of capital, images, and information to swill around the world at the touch of a button, largely outside the control of government. Immigrants from many lands were pouring into the country, simultaneously multiplying global connections while transforming the nature of the population. Major technological and natural disasters, in the United States and elsewhere, also carried the message that Americans were fellow passengers along with the rest of humanity aboard Spaceship Earth. It was during the 1980s that some American scientists began to issue serious warnings about global warming.

This is not to say that the United States was a hapless and innocent victim of these unsettling processes. The United States would exert more influence in this changing world, economically, militarily, and culturally, than any other country, though it could not act as if others did not exist. Ronald Reagan was elected to the presidency with the ambition of restoring American strength and freedom of action, but his policies tended to make the United States yet more dependent on others. When he entered the White House the United States was the largest creditor nation in the world; during his second term it became the largest debtor nation, and it stayed that way. In a variety of ways the United States found that it could not retreat into the haughty isolation that some Americans seemed to favor after Vietnam. While Reagan seemed to hanker for a lost autonomy, Bill Clinton as president tried to persuade his fellow Americans of the virtues of interdependence.

Increasing interaction with the world may have done something to enhance the importance of the presidency, in which national leadership resided. But incumbents, or at least their aides, had also learned how to manage the modern media, though good fortune played its part too. The last president to have served two full terms had been Dwight Eisenhower in the 1950s, but after 1980 three managed to do so. Ronald Reagan was "the Great Communicator," adept after a career in show business at speaking to camera. It was a role he approached with reverence, his respect for the presidency showing in the formal suit he invariably wore in the Oval Office. The son of a feckless shoe salesman and devout mother, Reagan was a true believer in the American dream, which he seemed to personify in his journey from modest Illinois origins via Hollywood to the White House. He was the only president to have been divorced, but traditionalists were reassured by his endorsement of family values and his unquestioning if unobtrusive religious faith – God was "the Man Upstairs." He could swear when angry but he never blasphemed; at weekends he enjoyed watching old-fashioned movies with his wife. Confident, optimistic, amiable, Reagan often broke awkward moments by telling stories, and he liked to swap jokes with his visitors. His easy charm gave him greater popularity than his policies, which reflected deep ideological convictions not often seen in professional politicians. The elderly Reagan could not always command detail, but he knew what he wanted, and the limited number of his goals allowed him to drive toward them. He won public respect as a strong president, and his stubborn determination helped him secure one of the greatest foreign policy coups in American history. His successor, George Bush, served only one term, for which there was a range of reasons, among them his lack of interest in public relations and his downgrading of the White House's celebrated speech-writing operation.

More sensitive to the public mood was Bill Clinton, whose acute antennae and ferocious ambition had lifted him while still a young man from a modest small-town background to a state governorship and then the presidency. He and his talented lawyer wife Hillary seemed to personify the arrival into American politics of the "yuppies," young, upwardly mobile professionals who had attracted attention as a rising social class during the expansion of the Reagan era. A consummate campaigner, Clinton somehow contrived to combine a rare empathy for ordinary folk with a laid-back charm once illustrated by the playing of the saxophone in a late-night television show, complete with shades. A student during the 1960s, Clinton admitted that he had once smoked marijuana ("I didn't inhale it"), and his reputation as a womanizer also associated him with permissive values. But the American public proved tolerant of such peccadilloes. African American writer Toni Morrison called him "our first black president," with his fondness for jazz and junk food, someone that black Americans could identify with when affronted conservatives tried to put the upstart in his place. Clinton also possessed an intellect rarely equaled among American presidents, and he consumed contemporary studies of the state of the nation as avidly as he consumed hamburgers. White House discussions could become like academic seminars. If he never managed a foreign policy triumph to match Ronald Reagan's, he reversed policies on the economy, which under his guidance achieved a dynamism it had not experienced in decades. The inheritor of this strong economy was George W. Bush, the easy-going son of Clinton's predecessor, who was said to be the kind of man Americans would like to have a drink with, except that he himself had forsaken alcohol after the excesses of his youth. A canny enough politician, it was as a war president that Bush secured re-election, though before his term was over historians were debating whether he was the worst president ever. That discussion was premature, though it reflected something of the disenchantment that many Americans felt about the condition of the United States in the modern world.

By conventional measurements the United States grew considerably richer in the decades after 1980 – but periods of great social and economic change bring both winners and losers. Economic growth made some communities and individuals very rich; Americans of the 1980s could marvel at the life of the affluent in such television shows as *Dynasty*. However, partly because of the increasing immersion in a global economy, the distance between the richest and poorest Americans was growing. Continuing suburbanization, spurred on by an unquenchable consumer culture, tended to segment the population, as like settled with like and different social groups increasingly became strangers to one another, a feature exemplified by the emergence of "gated" communities. The unanticipated flood of Third World immigrants further undermined any sense of homogeneity, and, together with the heightened awareness of ethnicity unleashed by the civil rights movement, promoted perceptions of the United States as a multicultural society. The growing diversity of urban America was reflected in the host of crime shows on television, from *Hill Street Blues* to *The Wire*, with their mixed racial and ethnic casts. The eruption of the so-called "culture wars" moved historian Arthur Schlesinger in 1991 to warn of "the fragmentation, resegregation, and tribalization of American life."

The social and cultural divisions, while deepened by economic and demographic transformation, were important though should not be exaggerated. The various culture wars attracted media attention, but were not the most fundamental forces shaping American society and politics. The "mood of the nation," as captured in opinion polls as well as in presidential approval ratings, quite closely followed economic performance, though was also vitally affected by major international events. As had long been the case, American politics was primarily structured by economics, and there was some evidence in the decades after 1980 that economic considerations were coming to loom larger. "It's the economy, stupid!" was famously said to explain the election of Bill Clinton as president in 1992, though it could equally be applied to the presidential elections of 1980 and 2008, and indeed to others in between. The film *Falling Down*, which focused on the plight of a white-collar worker rendered redundant in the "downsizing" of the 1990s, spoke to aspects of an America caught up in painful social and economic change. Such tensions periodically awakened the populist impulse in American politics, as established authorities were attacked in the name of the powerless.

The period since 1980 has often been treated as a predominantly conservative era, and so it was, though this characterization tends to overlook the degree to which American liberalism survived, albeit in new forms. Business pressure groups may have exerted disproportionate influence in Washington during these decades, but progressive and ethnic pressure groups carried some weight too. Environmentalism joined civil rights as the favored social movement of many liberals and became a force to be reckoned with. Conservatism had its limits, and liberals had successfully institutionalized many of their previous gains. While Ronald Reagan made it his mission to "take government off the backs of the people," Americans were not prepared to forego some of the benefits that government brings. Government was still "big" 30 years after Reagan's election, though no more popular.

Such features as massive immigration, increased international competition, and environmental crises tended to break down the boundaries between "domestic" and "foreign." The mid-twentieth century had bequeathed a heritage of "big government," and it was this government that was exposed to the strains associated with the interaction of a fragmented society and a volatile international milieu. Washington was the buffer between the two. It has often been noted that, notwithstanding the capacity of some presidents to secure re-election, the late twentieth century recorded a marked drop in the confidence of Americans in their leaders and in their political institutions. Some of this reflected the impact of these processes, since the federal government often seemed the helpless victim of forces it could not control. The American diplomat George Kennan once recalled of his early boyhood days in the Midwest that "when times were hard, as they often were, groans and lamentations went up to God, but never to Washington." In the aftermath of the creation of the New Deal in the 1930s, the national security state in the 1940s, and the Great Society in the 1960s, however, when times were hard lamentations did go up to Washington, even from those committed to reducing federal power. When times are hard Washington gets blamed, though in a globalized world there are limits to what Washington can do. This would be one of the lessons of the decades that followed the election of Ronald Reagan in 1980.

Acknowledgments

Several friends and scholars have helped to make this book possible. John Ashworth and Iwan Morgan steadfastly read almost the entire typescript; Gareth Davies and John Thompson scrutinized a number of chapters; and Michael Coyne offered his expertise on film history. Their suggestions are greatly appreciated, as are those of the anonymous reviewers and of the series' editor Keith Robbins. Playing important roles too have been the academic hospitality of the Rothermere American Institute, Oxford, and the financial assistance of the Leverhulme Trust.

Chapter 1

Losing Control: The United States in 1980

The Americans were not a happy people as the 1970s ended. The Gallup Poll in January 1979 reported that some 55 percent of respondents expected the coming year to be "worse" than the preceding one; only 33 percent anticipated something "better." In March the same organization found that 69 percent of Americans were "dissatisfied" with "the way things are going in the United States"; by August the figure was up to a record 84 percent. That year *Business Week* published a special issue on the theme of "The Decline of US Power." Another set of polls in 1980 found that Americans believed that their lives "five years ago" had been better than "at the present time," and a *Newsweek* cover asked "Has America Lost Its Clout?" A few years later Ronald Reagan would be credited with restoring American self-confidence, but at the end of the 1970s pessimism rather than optimism was the prevailing sentiment among the public at large.[1]

The decade of the 1970s may not have witnessed the tumult of the "Sixties," but these years had offered Americans scant reason to rejoice. The traumatic war in Vietnam had ended ingloriously, the most powerful nation on earth forced into shameful retreat. Not just the whole of Vietnam, but Cambodia too fell to the communists. International rebuffs to the United States had continued through the decade. There were pro-Soviet governments in Portugal's former African colonies, and in 1979 left-wing groups seized power even in the Americas, in Nicaragua and Grenada. It was communism rather than capitalism that seemed to be winning the battle for the soul of humankind. The Soviet Union, believing that history was moving in its direction, was encouraging developing nations and nationalist forces around the world to join it in resisting capitalist

Contemporary America: Power, Dependency, and Globalization since 1980,
First Edition. M.J. Heale.
© 2011 M.J. Heale. Published 2011 by Blackwell Publishing Ltd.

imperialism. Only a generation earlier a victorious United States had seemed to have the globe at its feet.

In those happy years following World War II, too, the American economy had been truly redoubtable, and its managers were confident of maintaining full employment and an improving standard of living. But in the 1970s an exceptional inflation juddered upward through the decade, remorselessly eroding the savings and living standards of millions. For decades the United States had been able to rely largely on its own resources, but no longer. Bewildering events in the Middle East (together with rapidly increasing world demand) quadrupled the price of oil on the world markets in 1974 and sent it soaring again in 1979, and the consequent shortages forced motorists waiting in gas lines to contemplate the sobering truth that the United States was no longer self-sufficient in energy. The political system offered little comfort. Since the 1960s public confidence in Washington had generally been falling. Richard Nixon had exited the presidency gracelessly and in disgrace, the only president to have had to resign his high office. The Watergate scandal had rendered a massive blow to public confidence in government. As many as 70 persons, including cabinet members and White House aides, had pleaded guilty to or were convicted of crimes associated with Watergate. It was by no means irrational in 1979 to expect the worse of the future. John Updike caught the mood in his novel set in that year, *Rabbit Is Rich*, which begins with: "Running out of gas, Rabbit Angstrom thinks ... The fucking world is running out of gas ... the people out there are getting frantic, they know the great American ride is ending."[2]

* * *

In 1941 *Time* publisher Henry Luce had spoken of "the American Century," anticipating an era in which American values would pervade the world. While the Cold War soon destroyed the optimism of that vision, the postwar era in many ways proved a golden one for the United States, indeed a "Golden Age" in Eric Hobsbawm's phrase for the developed capitalist world in general. In 1945, Norwegian scholar Geir Lundestad has written, that the United States "was really unique in history": "In the overwhelming size of its economy, in its superior military strength, and in its popular message to the world, its soft power, the United States was in a league of its own."[3]

The American economy grew steadily and at times powerfully – Gross Domestic Product (GDP) almost doubled in real terms between 1947 and

1970. Increases in real wages allowed most if not all Americans to partake of the material rewards of what Harvard economist John Kenneth Galbraith ironically dubbed the "affluent society." Historians and social scientists sometimes described American society in the 20 years after 1945 in terms of abundance, homogeneity, consensus, and conformity. To historian David Potter, Americans were a "people of plenty." Sociologist David Riesman spoke of Americans becoming more "other-directed," anxiously taking their cues from their peers, in contrast to the "inner-directed" behavior of their forebears. The political historian Godfrey Hodgson argued that virtually all those in public life in those years, Democrats and Republicans alike, were exponents of "consensus liberalism," agreed on the need for an anti-communist foreign policy abroad and a mixed economy and a modest welfare state at home.[4]

By the 1970s these characterizations were wearing thin, partly because of the political convulsions of the 1960s, which helped to expose the class, racial, and ethnic divisions in American society, and partly because the economy was no longer performing miracles. Demographic changes were also subtly reconfiguring the social landscape. The liberal consensus of postwar America was disappearing into the past; neither liberalism nor consensual values were much favored by these changing circumstances. There were vigorous liberal and progressive causes animating the 1970s, among them feminism and environmentalism, but these were matched by a range of conservative movements, such as anti-abortion and anti-tax crusades. It was neither a liberal nor a conservative era, but one character-ized by a growing awareness of limits and an unease that the outside world was uncomfortably intruding on the American way of life. Broadly, however, the economic, social, and demographic changes served to weaken further the "big government" liberalism associated with the Democratic Party, which had generally enjoyed electoral dominance since the 1930s.

One such influence was the growth of the Sunbelt, that great swath of western and southern states stretching from California to Virginia. As a "postindustrial" economy shifted to light industry, science and medicine, high technology and services, the old industrial centers of the North – the "rustbelt" – shed jobs and people. Many new enterprises were located in the South, some of them attracted by the availability of non-unionized labor and others by the federal contracts consequent upon the Cold War investment in the US military. Lavish Cold War spending also benefited the West, whose fabled climate and lifestyle proved attractive to many. During the years of heady defense expenditure occasioned by the Vietnam War, the rate of capital formation and income growth in the Sunbelt reached twice that of the Northeast. The populations of such cities as New York, Cleveland, Detroit, and Pittsburgh actually dropped in the 1970s; the Sunbelt boom cities of Los Angeles, Houston, Miami, and Atlanta gained people. Houston was said to be the "golden buckle" of the Sunbelt, and in 1982 it became the nation's fourth largest city. In 1970 the Northeast and Midwest together still commanded a majority of US population, but by 1980 the South and the West constituted 52.4 percent of American residents, a proportion that continued to grow. The South alone was home to a third of American population, allowing it considerable electoral clout. Its emerging prosperity worked to the political advantage of the Republicans, who began to challenge the Democrats as the dominant party of the region – although if business values brought some into the Republican fold the party was also helped by white men apparently switching from a Democratic Party overwhelmingly supported by the recently energized black vote.

Broadly favoring conservative causes, too, was the growth of suburbs across the nation, not least in the Sunbelt but also in other regions too. In a sense Sunbelt suburbanization tended to undermine the distinctiveness of the South, for suburbs everywhere promoted what one historian has called an "ethos of middle-class entitlement." While it was mainly white families who moved to suburban homes, in search of housing, good schools, and a safe environment, their outlook was shaped in significant degree by class and property considerations even if these could not be entirely divorced from racial concerns. By 1980 suburbs accounted for 60 percent of urban dwellers, an expanding constituency to which politicians were sensitive. A high proportion of new jobs were being created in the suburbs, many of which were not dormitories but complex communities in their own right, with an array of businesses, schools, churches, medical centers, and shopping and entertainment malls. They had become the characteristic places in which Americans had come to "live, learn, work, shop, play, pray, and die," what one author in 1991 dubbed "edge cities." By that date they housed two-thirds of American office facilities. Many of them were also prosperous, particularly those close to major cities like New York and Washington. Of the 21 counties in the country with the highest per capita incomes in 1985, 20 were suburban.[5]

Suburbs may have had some common characteristics but they varied greatly from one to another. Each social group, whether upper-middle-class white professionals or self-made ethnics, tended to seek out their own kind, a process often abetted by developers, real estate agents, and municipal officials, so that suburbs became class-segmented, each reflecting the predominance of a particular income or racial group. As early as 1970 one regional planner was lamenting that "vast areas of New York's suburbs are now one-class, one-race (often one-religion) in residential composition." The very poor tended to be left behind in the city centers as the jobs fled, among them blacks and other minorities, often unable to articulate a political voice. Suburban taxpayers did not always give high priority to the educational and welfare services of the inner cities, an agenda that tended to accentuate the contrast between decaying cities and their affluent outskirts. This spatial fragmentation militated against political mobilization, and the political influence of the traditional urban machines diminished. Suburban voters tended to look to politicians to protect their interests as homeowners, taxpayers, and consumers. Entrepreneurial values, self-help philosophies, and Christian evangelicalism flourished in many if not all of the well-to-do suburbs of the South and West, receptive territory for conservative politics.[6]

Paralleling the rise of the Sunbelt and the suburbs was the "deindustrialization" of the old manufacturing centers of the North and Northeast. Between 1967 and 1987 Philadelphia lost 64 percent of its manufacturing jobs and Chicago 60 percent. Such traditional industries as textiles and steel were suffering massively from foreign competition, and the auto industry too was in serious trouble. By 1980 Japanese cars had won 22 percent of the American market. Hundreds of thousands of workers in the old industrial cities were laid off, and many of them remained there, unable to relocate to the areas where new jobs were being created, perhaps because they lacked the requisite skills. The decline in the populations of the industrial cities was paralleled by declining union memberships, with long-term implications for the Democratic Party, which counted urban conurbations and labor unions among its core constituencies. In time the suburbs of the North would follow the Sunbelt in developing light, high-tech and service industries. A manufacturing company would be displaced as the largest employer in a community by a high-tech park or a health complex. But at the end of the 1970s it was urban decay that commanded worried attention.

As some northern cities deteriorated into decidedly bleak environments, fears were expressed about the emergence of an "underclass." *Time* magazine in 1977 talked about "the unreachables," who generated a high proportion of "the nation's juvenile delinquents, school dropouts, drug addicts and welfare mothers." The mass poverty of earlier eras had disappeared, and the number living below the "poverty line" had dropped dramatically in the 1960s, but discussions of the underclass evoked images of a permanent, irreducible minority beyond the reach of social and political institutions. The term served the interests of conservatives scornful of the effects of Great Society reform while also carrying the message that politically the truly wretched were powerless, unable to mobilize in their own interests. Most poor people could not be categorized as an underclass, though its imputed existence, suggestive of a black hole into which others might tumble, helps to account for the surly disquiet felt by many American wage earners in the later decades of the century. The poor were helpless too because they were scattered across the immensity of metropolitan and small-town America, and they were divided between themselves in another way. Among them were displaced family farmers and farm workers, forced off their homesteads in the Midwest, Great Plains, and the West as they too encountered foreign competition and declining prices. A high and increasing proportion were African Americans or recent immigrants, often harboring mutual animosities in the scramble for survival. These migrants were arriving in the cities as jobs were leaving them.[7]

American urban society was being reshaped by the extraordinary numbers of foreigners pouring into the country. Mass immigration, it had been thought, was a thing of the past, cut off by barriers erected in the 1920s. As striking as the numbers was its unfamiliar character, Third World rather than reassuringly European. Most immigrants were Hispanics, fleeing the poverty and political regimes of Mexico, the Caribbean, and parts of South America, but a rising number were Asians. Americans generally had been taught by the civil rights struggles of the 1960s to value ethnic diversity, and this understanding was reinforced by the increasing racial and ethnic variety of urban America. If some authors had lamented a perceived homogeneity in American society in the 1950s, in the 1970s it became fashionable to celebrate multiculturalism.

The encouragement of ethnic identity and the return of mass immigration were occurring at a time when the economy was no longer performing at the gratifying level a generation of Americans had come to expect. The historian Arthur Schlesinger suggested that the two were related, attributing the cult of ethnicity to a waning optimism in the American future in an age of straitened circumstances. Each group, perhaps, sensed the need to fend for itself. Demoralized ghetto residents in particular chafed at the seeming unresponsiveness of the economic and political systems, and racial and ethnic hostilities on occasion flared into violence. Miami blacks vented resentments against Cuban refugees in 1980 in riots that took 18 lives.[8]

The straitening circumstances that worried Schlesinger were reflected in the sobering economic figures. GDP had increased by a fraction over 50 percent in the heady 1960s; in the 1970s growth slowed to under 36 percent.

Unemployment, just 4.5 percent in 1965, had jumped to 8.3 percent in 1975. Inflation was savaging the economy. No one could miss the escalating costs of everyday goods – hamburger meat up from 88 cents a pound in 1970 to $1.86 in 1980, milk up from 28 to 59 cents a quart, gasoline from 37 cents to $1.60 a gallon. The higher job losses, unnerving price rises, and decaying urban centers sent home the lesson that the good years were over. For economists this depressing conclusion was confirmed by the productivity figures, which had slowed to anemic annual rates of increase, and in some years actually registered a decline. It was becoming evident that American resources were limited; the panacea of endless economic growth was no longer there to perform its magic. As President Jimmy Carter observed in 1979, "we cannot afford to live beyond our means." Banker Paul Volcker, the new head of the Federal Reserve Board, echoed him: "We have lost that euphoria that we had fifteen years ago, that we knew all the answers to managing the economy." In Congress, journalist Thomas Edsall noticed, debate was shifting "from the relatively peaceful arguments over the cutting up of a growing pie to a bitter fight over which groups will be forced to take smaller shares."[9]

These demographic, social, and economic changes, with their tendency to accentuate differences and disunity, could not but have implications for American politics. Academics were beginning to discern the emergence of a "new American political system" by the end of the 1970s. It was a system in which power was diffused and politics more fragmented, in which political parties, although still prominent, were not the integrative forces they had once been, and in which presidents found their authority frustratingly constrained. Political scientist Anthony King spoke of the "atomisation" of politics, of a situation in which "fewer and fewer cohesive blocs are to be found in the American polity." Further, the holders of elective office, such as presidents and congressmen, seemed to have yielded some of their authority to professional elites, bureaucrats, judges, and interest groups, non-elected bodies who nonetheless were often intimately involved in policy making.[10]

The electorate itself was less dependable. Voters were becoming less partisan, less inclined to back a particular party through thick and thin; the proportion of voters designating themselves "independent" was increasing markedly, and voters were also showing less enthusiasm about actually going to the polls. There had been a postwar high in voter turnout of 63 percent in the presidential election of 1960, but by 1980 the figure was down to 53 percent. As the electorate was becoming less engaged and less partisan it was also growing more suspicious of Washington. While 42 percent of Americans had expressed a "great deal" of confidence in Congress in 1966, by 1981 the figure had plunged to 16 percent. A disenchanted electorate, however, could represent an opportunity for a presidential candidate who was not closely identified with Washington.[11]

Paradoxically, while the electorate was becoming more volatile, professional politicians were tending to become more partisan. Partly this was a consequence of the low voter turnouts in primary elections and other features of the electoral environment, which allowed committed activists to exert pressure in the choice of candidates. For a complex blend of reasons too, each party was tending to lose its restraining wing. Through much of its history, the labor and northern liberal elements in the Democratic Party had been countered by its highly conservative southern bloc, but in the aftermath of the civil rights revolution southern Democrats were having to accommodate themselves to black voters, and some lost their seats to Republicans. While the Democrats were shorn of their conservative bloc, the Republicans were losing their liberal wing, as grassroots activists grew dissatisfied with those leaders who seemed too ready to bow to the discredited consensus politics of the postwar era. As each party became somewhat less heterogeneous in terms of its constituent elements, the ideological gulf between them tended to grow, intensifying the adversarial character of party politics. Where opinion polls showed that the public at large was mostly of middling disposition on many issues, reformist elements tended to tug the Democratic Party to the left of center while conservative activists nudged the Republicans to the right.

Partisanship in national politics was also encouraged by the phenomenon of divided government. In most years after 1968 one major party held the White House while the other controlled Congress, which meant that each branch flexed its muscles against the other. Not only did this internecine branch warfare underline the lack of comity in Washington, serving further to erode popular trust of politicians, it also accentuated a tendency to recruit the criminal justice system to the political process. Between the early 1970s and the mid-1980s the number of indictments brought by federal prosecutors against national, state, and local officials multiplied 10 times. Many were low-level officials, but cabinet officers and White House aides found themselves targets too. The "consensual" style that some political leaders at least had attempted to cultivate in the 1960s would be largely replaced by the 1990s by "attack politics," a process abetted by the rise of the 24-hour news cycle.[12]

The cost of election campaigns escalated prodigiously as television became their principal medium, and money talked. The 1970s and 1980s witnessed the rapid multiplication of Political Action Committees (PACs), through which interest groups channeled funds to politicians. Business, somewhat on the defensive during the liberal advances of the 1960s, was determined to recover its political clout. In 1974 there had been about 200 labor and only 90 corporate PACs; by 1980 the figures were 290 and 1153 respectively. The objective, said a leading advocate of the corporate drive, was to "increase business leverage in politics relative to labor and other groups." The desperate need for campaign funds, and the lack of prudence with which they were often accepted, is one reason for the increasing number of criminal indictments of politicians. Congress and the state legislatures tended to become forums in which lobbyists, mostly representing business, commercial, and professional bodies, and often dripping with cash, pursued their highly specific goals, colliding and colluding with one another. Yet the 1970s were also "boom years for the liberal groups," such as environmental, consumer, and good government bodies, several of them well funded and employing their own teams of lobbyists. One study found that in 1979 citizen groups constituted over a quarter of those testifying at congressional hearings, an impressive proportion. In these years too liberals also increased their institutional strength, and were able to exert some influence from their relatively secure positions in the universities, the media, and the federal and state bureaucracies.[13]

It was not only interest groups that seemed to be usurping the responsibilities of the elected branches of government. American presidents were sometimes frustrated by a sense that the White House had lost control of the bureaucracy. Lyndon Johnson's Great Society programs had spawned a new generation of government agencies, staffed by administrators seemingly eager to push outward the boundaries of their authority, and the regulatory thrust continued into the 1970s. Such regulations added significantly to business costs, and do much to explain the increase in business lobbying. Judges as well as bureaucrats were exerting an influence on public policy. The judiciary had always played a significant role in the American system of government, but its authority rose as that of the parties diminished and as gridlock paralyzed the legislative arena. The growth of rights consciousness in the wake of the civil rights movement of the 1960s encouraged individuals and groups to turn to the courts to establish their rights. Court decisions on culturally divisive issues such as abortion served to inject those issues into party politics. The increasing political salience of the courts meant that nominations to the judiciary, particularly to the Supreme Court, became highly fraught matters, the occasion of epic battles between White House and Senate.

The divers roles of interest groups, the bureaucracy, and the courts in policy making meant that decisions were often being made by bodies outside the control of voters. At the same time the intellectual climate was turning against government. Conservative intellectuals were able to use the growing public distrust to fashion a critique of the political order of the previous generation.

The intellectual move to the right was driven largely by the gloomy economic experiences. In the 1960s economists had boasted of their ability to "fine tune" the economy, but the economy no longer seemed responsive to their ministrations. "Stagflation" – the combination of miserly economic growth and high inflation – was not supposed to happen, and served to undermine confidence in "big government" or Keynesian solutions. The Chicago economist Milton Friedman argued that government spending and budget deficits encouraged inflation and disrupted the free market. Business schools, often the beneficiaries of corporate grants, gave headroom to his monetarist theories. Some formerly liberal intellectuals, several of them Democrats, also moved to the right, questioning the social engineering in government programs that did not seem to work. These "neo-conservatives," together with the monetarists, helped to promote a change in the intellectual climate. They were soon joined by scores of defiantly conservative intellectuals, several of whom found refuge in the flourishing research institutes, such as the Heritage Foundation and the American Enterprise Institute.

A new conservative movement was being consciously created. From the 1970s there was a proliferation of highly partisan "think tanks," often handsomely supported by business corporations and rich entrepreneurs, a part of the larger process by which business was mobilizing on behalf of conservative causes. The Heritage Foundation, for example, described by Ronald Reagan as that "feisty new kid on the conservative block," was established in 1973 with a grant from the Colorado brewer Joseph Coors, and by 1985 it had an annual budget of over $10 million. Conservative journals were also appearing. The right-wing think tanks and journals in turn supplied a stream of articulate contributors to the radio and TV talk shows and newspaper opinion columns, and research papers to congressional staff. The free market conservatism boosted by such sources excoriated not only big-spending Democrats but also the compromises made with liberalism by moderate Republicans. The Republican right, once dismissed as anachronistic cranks by consensus liberals, was coming to draw on considerable intellectual resources. As Democratic Senator Patrick Moynihan observed, "in the course of the

1970s, without anyone quite noticing, the Republicans became a party of ideas."[14]

The right-wing think tanks were part of the New Right, an informal collection of conservative organizations that emerged by the late 1970s. Groups like the Conservative Caucus sought to mobilize grassroots support for right-wing candidates and target liberal office holders. The New Right embraced anti-government libertarians, traditional hard-line anti-communists, and enthusiastic groups of religious moralists. Among the latter was Jerry Falwell's Moral Majority, formed in 1979 to promote a range of "pro-God, pro-family" causes. Abetting their cause was a remark-able evangelical awakening. The kind of evangelical and fundamentalist Protestantism long associated with the South was spreading out across the land. Protestant evangelicals expanded the number of local TV and radio stations they controlled, and several "televangelists" won massive follow-ings. One was Pat Robertson of the Christian Broadcasting Network; by 1979 this was a $50-million-a-year enterprise and its talk show was reach-ing five million viewers. Such television and radio broadcasts helped to fashion an unlikely nascent alliance, mobilizing both urban Catholics and small-town, evangelical and fundamentalist Protestants in defense of tra-ditional family structures and a traditional morality. The Democratic Party in its heyday had reached into the masses with the help of the labor move-ment; the evangelical churches gave Republicans the opportunity to create a grassroots network of their own, complementing their support among the higher income groups.

The Democratic Party was by no means destined to electoral failure, for the proportion of the electorate identifying themselves as Democrats in 1980, around 40 percent, was still substantially larger than the number of Republicans. But the convulsions within the party triggered by the Vietnam War and the unease over the welfare and racial policies it had adopted in the 1960s had served to erode some of its core constituencies. Organized labor, long a force for a liberal agenda, was losing members with the decline of traditional industries. Further, some working- and middle-class urban ethnics deserted the Democrats over "law and order" and what they per-ceived as indulgent attitudes toward black Americans. Suburban growth meant that more Democrats were elected representing a white middle class less interested in the party's traditional agenda. Rather than the "party of the people," the Democrats risked being seen as a party of special interests such as blacks, feminists, and a shrunken organized labor. Liberalism, and with it the Democratic Party, thought one journalist, had "degenerated into an alliance of civil rights activists, trade unionists and feminists with wealthy social liberals from Hollywood and Wall Street." Still, the party benefited from some new influences. The postwar "baby boom" generation was reaching maturity, and many of its members had been inspired by the activism of the 1960s. Some of these retained liberal sensibilities as they made careers in education, social work, law, and even finance, remaining close to the Democratic Party and strengthening its commitment to the kind of "social" liberalism represented by civil rights and environmentalism, if not the labor issues of old.[15]

As the economy failed to produce the largesse on which a growing standard of living depended, government found itself caught uncomfortably between the insistent demands of interest groups and the suspicious gaze of the voters. The political process did not seem to be providing much of an answer to the problems of the 1970s. The major parties themselves were each deeply racked by dissension. In 1976 the new conservative hope, Ronald Reagan, had tried and failed to win the leadership of the Republican Party from a sitting incumbent, Gerald Ford. For the Democrats, in 1980 the liberal champion Edward Kennedy tried and failed to wrest the presidential nomination from an incumbent president, Jimmy Carter. On both occasions, the centrist incumbents, with all the advantages that office brought, saw off these insurgencies from the wings. But these revolts of the right and the left suggested that the consensual style of politics of the postwar era had had its day. The 1976 movie *Network* captured something of the popular mood, with its protagonist's repeated refrain: "I'm as mad as hell, and I'm not gonna take it any more!" Economic, social, and demographic change was undermining the bases of the old political order, deepening the disheartening sense that the United States was drifting out of control.

* * *

The election of Ronald Reagan to the presidency in 1980 is sometimes treated as a repudiation of "the Sixties," the tempestuous decade which conservatives equated with an assault on traditional moral values and the burgeoning of meddlesome government. Certainly Reagan's popularity with American conservatives owed something to his reproofs of student activism and Great Society social engineering, but his eventual elevation to the White House is better explained in terms of the history of the 1970s, particularly its last years. The movements of the 1960s had been inspired by a spirit of activism, by a conviction that individuals and groups could make a difference and that government could effect change for the better.

That sense that Americans were in some measure masters of their own destiny was dispelled by the experiences of the 1970s. Americans turned to Ronald Reagan not so much in a rejection of the 1960s as in an attempt to restore the feeling of empowerment that the 1960s had offered.

By the mid-1970s the successive crises associated with Watergate, Nixon's abdication, the oil shock and the faltering economy had already shaken the public's confidence in government down to an unaccustomed low. According to one poll, public trust in government dropped from 61 percent of those surveyed in 1964 to 22 percent in 1976. Jimmy Carter, a born-again Christian and wealthy peanut farmer who had been governor of Georgia, was the beneficiary of this disaffection, as he was later to be the victim. He was able to campaign for the presidency as an outsider, untainted by the corruption and incompetence associated with Washington. As he liked to boast: "I'm not a lawyer, I'm not a member of Congress, and I've never served in Washington." Jimmy Carter, promising that he would not lie to the American people, rode to the White House on the back of this distrust, berating the "lack of competence and integrity" of the existing political leadership.[16]

Carter's temperamental earnestness might have seen him through good times, but circumstances conspired against him. He was one of the unluckiest presidents ever. Within months of his assuming office his Director of the Budget was obliged to resign over allegations of mismanagement and corruption in his previous career as a banker, calling into question both Carter's judgment and his assumption of the moral high ground, and his approval rating promptly dropped. As one aide put it, the public began to think he "was just like every other president." But it was the last two years of Jimmy Carter's administration that led many Americans to believe that he was not up to the job.[17]

For a period Carter had been able to point to some successes, such as a reasonable economic performance, the prospect of peace in the Middle East following his brokering of the Camp David Accords between Israel and Egypt in 1978 (which indeed brought a lasting settlement between those two countries), and his securing of a treaty to pass control of the Panama Canal Zone to Panama. This last measure, however, angered a portion of the right. Conservative columnist George Will saw it as presaging the "vanished mastery" of the United States. The Democrats did lose seats in both houses of Congress in November 1978, but the numbers were not large for a mid-term election. The years 1979–1980, however, constituted an era of virtually unending crisis. Three phenomena in particular combined to convey the impression to Americans that their government was helpless in the face of events. The economy, especially inflation, was behaving spectacularly badly, immigrants were pouring at will over the country's borders, and an Islamic state was holding American citizens hostage. The government in each case, it seemed, had no effective response.[18]

With the approach of the 1980 election the weaknesses of the economy came to a head. The annual inflation rate was running at about 12 percent and the prime interest rate peaked at 21.5 percent. Real wage rates were declining and about eight million were unemployed. As incumbent governments tend to do when they are beset by deteriorating economic conditions, the Carter administration attributed some blame to external factors, such as the escalating price of oil. Its Republican opponents insisted that America's ills were home grown and within the power of leadership to solve. Further, the Republicans believed they had the answer.

Through the Carter administration the global economy had been recoiling from the massive oil price hike of 1974, though thereafter the supply of oil had eased and with it the price. But any American tempted to think that his gasoline was safe once more was rudely disabused by the experiences of 1979, when supplies on the world market were disrupted following the fall of the Shah of Iran. At the end of June about 60 percent of gas stations were actually closed. "Nothing else," Carter's chief domestic policy adviser told him, "has so frustrated, confused, angered the American people – or so targeted their distress at you personally." Scuffles between motorists sometimes broke out in the long and surly lines that formed at the filling stations that summer; in one fight 40 people were injured. These mortifying scenes underlined the helplessness of government, and taught the hard lesson that the American way of life was at the mercy of obscure events in a far-off country. One bumper sticker read "Send the Marines for Oil Now."[19]

Reinforcing the message about the uncertainty of the energy supply was a crisis at the nuclear power plant at Three Mile Island, Pennsylvania, in March 1979, when the possible meltdown of a reactor threatened the lives of the half-million people living in the region, from which over 130 000 fled. If nuclear energy could not fuel cars, it could replace oil in power plants, but the Three Mile Island crisis stalled the development of the nuclear alternative and over a hundred reactor orders were cancelled. The United States was to be even more dependent on the supply of foreign oil, the main reserves of which were located in a notoriously unstable part of the world.

"One failure could cause the downfall of this administration – inflation," Jimmy Carter privately remarked on one occasion: "Almost everything is subservient to it in political terms." And so it proved. As the inflation rate intensified, Carter's approval rating diminished, reaching a mortifying low of 29 percent according to Gallup in June 1979. With high inflation went high interest rates, as the Federal Reserve Board under Paul Volcker severely contracted the money supply. This represented a dramatic shift in monetary policy. Some economic historians see Volcker's appointment to "the Fed" in August 1979 as a transformative moment in modern history, as he inaugurated a blistering war on inflation at the cost of rising unemployment. But inflation could not be killed overnight, and by the turn of the decade prices were rising at the fastest rate ever recorded in American history. No issue worried – scared – Americans more than the snowballing cost of living, which was destroying savings, negating wage increases, killing the dreams of many of buying their own homes or sending their children to college, and facing the elderly, the poor, and those on fixed incomes with the prospects of hunger and homelessness.[20]

If the government had lost control of the economy, it also seemed to have no control over American borders. Immigration, much of it illegal, had been rising fast, a phenomenon made graphic by the Mariel episode beginning in April 1980. Thousands of Cubans had sought refuge in the Peruvian embassy in Havana, and Cuba's president, Fidel Castro, eventually announced that they (and others wishing to join them) were free to leave the country via the port of Mariel, where their American relatives could collect them. This was an irresistible invitation to the excited Cuban communities in Florida, which dispatched thousands of small boats, and within weeks 125 000 Cubans had been boatlifted to safety. Much of this was at odds with US procedures, and Castro in effect was inciting a defiance of American immigration laws. After some prevarication, Carter promised that the United States would welcome the Marielitos with "an open heart and open arms." But the story did not end there. Popular sympathy for the Marielitos began to evaporate with press reports that Castro was opening jails and mental institutions so that he could dump their inmates on the good-hearted American public. The Marielito crisis, played out in television pictures and insistent headlines, underlined both the porous nature of American borders and the helplessness of government.

Both the energy crisis and the Marielito episode illustrated the United States' vulnerability to changing circumstances in the outside world. In the Middle East Iran had been its strongest ally, one that might preserve some kind of stability in the region, but through 1978 Iran was aflame. "The disintegration of Iran," Carter's National Security Adviser wrote to him, "would be the most massive American defeat since the beginning of the Cold War, overshadowing in its real consequences the setback in Vietnam."

Toward the end of 1979 and throughout 1980 this vulnerability was brought home to Americans in a singularly humiliating way. Carter had given permission for the deposed Shah of Iran to come to the United States for medical treatment. There were angry anti-American demonstrations in Iran, where the Ayatollah Khomeini had become the effective leader of a revolutionary fundamentalist regime, and in November the US Embassy in Tehran was invaded by hundreds of Islamic "students," who proceeded to hold 52 American diplomats hostage while demanding the return of the Shah. Intense anti-American feeling in the country kept the American captives walled in the embassy for week after week. The richest and most powerful nation on earth found itself helpless in the face of a bunch of foreign "students," who nightly tormented American television audiences by abusing the hostages or burning the American flag. "When I see what they do to that flag," said a longshoreman, "it just gets me in the heart."[21]

The Cold War was shading into the Age of Oil. Plotting American policy in the Middle East was made no easier by the historic commitment of the United States to the state of Israel, an immense burden in its dealings with the "Arab world." By the New Year the issues of Middle Eastern stability and containment of the Soviets had become intertwined.

Not that the Soviet Union was being contained. The Nixon and Ford administrations had sought a relaxation of tensions with the Soviet Union, and the Carter White House had struggled to maintain the principle of détente. An agreement with the Soviets on limiting strategic arms had been reached in June 1979 (SALT II), but public faith in the policies of détente was eroding, largely because of a massive Soviet defense build-up and Soviet adventures in Africa and Asia. During the 1960s the left had revolted against US foreign policy, but now a revolt came from the right, conservatives believing that the Soviets were taking advantage of the US reluctance to act forcefully in the aftermath of Vietnam. Jimmy Carter, who had hoped to reduce defense spending, felt obliged to raise it after all.

What was seen as Soviet adventurism in the 1970s was capped in December 1979 when the Soviet Union invaded Afghanistan, where a regime respectful of Soviet interests was facing unrest. Control of that harsh land would put the Soviets within striking distance of the Gulf, with its huge reserves of oil. The action seemed further evidence that American Cold War policies were failing, and again underlined the helplessness of the United States, which had no effective means of responding. The invasion provoked widespread condemnation in the United States, doomed approval of the SALT II treaty, and aroused fears of Soviet incursions into the Gulf at a point when Americans had become highly aware of their dependence on it. "The Soviet invasion of Afghanistan is the greatest threat to peace since the Second World War," said Carter. Any attempt to gain control of the Gulf region, he somberly warned in announcing the Carter Doctrine, would be "repelled by any means necessary, including military force."[22]

The Carter Doctrine designated the secure flow of Gulf oil as a "vital interest" of the United States. But for the moment at least the doctrine was little more than rhetoric. There was little the United States could actually do to expel Soviet troops from Afghanistan. Carter imposed a grain embargo and called for a boycott of the Olympic Games, to be held in Moscow in July 1980, and the US Olympic Committee duly agreed. Banning farmers from selling grain to the Soviets and stopping athletes from going to Moscow, however, hardly suggested that the United States was calling the shots with respect to the Soviet Union, and meant that private American citizens were paying the price for governmental helplessness.

By the beginning of 1980, as the Soviet invasion of Afghanistan and the plight of the US hostages in Tehran competed for the headlines, Carter's dilemmas had not abated. At first the hostage crisis had rescued him from the unpopularity the raging inflation had brought, but firm words and tortuous negotiations failed to release the hostages. As the months ticked by and as a presidential election loomed, Carter was under intense pressure to attempt some kind of military action. In April an attempt to rescue the hostages in Tehran with the use of helicopter gunships went tragically awry, photographs of the burnt bodies of American crewmen surviving as grim mementos of the failed mission. The hostage crisis was a humiliation from which the Carter administration could not recover. "Can you imagine how helpless we must look to the world right now?," muttered Zbigniew Brzezinski, the National Security Adviser. The negotiations over the hostages dragged on agonizingly through the presidential campaign of 1980, which could well have turned in favor of Carter had the hostages been flown home before election day. "It's a hell of a note being the President of the United States and going into the homestretch of a close race that will be decided not in Michigan or Pennsylvania or New York – but in Iran," sighed Carter on the eve of the election. The negotiations were eventually concluded successfully on the last day of Carter's term, by which time he had lost the presidential election.[23]

Even before the hostage crisis and the invasion of Afghanistan, a demoralized Carter had taken to television in his so-called "malaise speech" of July 1979, when he seemed to attribute the nation's ills to "growing doubt about the meaning of our own lives and in the loss of a unity of purpose for our Nation." But any president could have been doomed by the misfortunes that befell Jimmy Carter – the oil shortages, the escalating prices, the porous American borders, the Soviet adventurism, the hostages. "Poor bastard – he used up all of his luck in getting here," reflected the 1980 Democratic campaign chairman of Carter's presidency: "We've had our share of victories and defeats, but we've not had a single piece of good luck in the past three years." Moreover, these domestic and foreign afflictions were being visited on a country already pessimistic about its outlook. It was hardly surprising that in July 1980 some 77 percent of those polled disapproved of Carter's handling of his job, the worst rating of any president in the history of such polling.[24]

Carter's political stock was such that he could not even be sure of being renominated by his party. In the summer of 1979 only 34 percent of Democrats supported his conduct of the presidency, the lowest endorsement of a president by his party ever recorded. Rather conservative in fiscal policy, during his presidency Carter had sought to tug his party away from its big spending past, but New Deal liberals had not disappeared and many had been outraged at his policies. With Carter's popularity plummeting in 1979, in the autumn Senator Edward Kennedy announced himself a candidate for the Democratic nomination, and for a time he held a massive lead in the polls. On one occasion he dismissed Carter as a "clone of Reagan." At the end of the year, however, the seizure of the hostages precipitated a patriotic rally behind the president. While Carter's standing suffered during the travails of 1980, his position as president and his rival's own tarnished past enabled him to see off the liberal insurgency.[25]

Seeing off the Republican Party, however, was another matter. Long-term political, sociological, and intellectual trends were beginning to work to the advantage of conservative forces. Nonetheless, the Democrats still held handsome majorities in both houses of Congress; there were many more registered Democrats than Republicans in the electorate; and in the right circumstances the party could have retained the White House. Further, the Republican leadership, decimated by the fallout of the Nixon years, had few outstanding candidates to offer.

There was no shortage of unexceptional candidates. There was serious competition for the nomination in – for the Republicans – a promising year. In January 1980 as many as seven men competed in the early Iowa caucuses, although by the time of the national convention in July most had dropped out. One of the stronger contenders was George H.W. Bush, who entered the race trailing clouds of offices – as a former congressman, Ambassador to the United Nations, chief of the US Liaison Office in China, chair of the Republican National Committee, and Director of the CIA. It had been years, however, since he had campaigned for electoral office, and his opponents teased him for his celebrated "resumé." Another hopeful was John Anderson, an Illinois congressman whose reputation for integrity was an asset at a time when professional politicians were held in low esteem. But better placed to profit from the anti-Washington sentiment was the one-time movie actor Ronald Reagan. In fact George Bush led in Iowa, but by mid-March Reagan's bandwagon was rolling and he thereafter won most of the Republican primaries. John Anderson pulled out of the Republican race to launch a campaign for the presidency as an independent and Bush withdrew at the end of May.

Reagan had not always been a conservative; indeed, he admitted he had been guilty of "hemophiliac liberalism." That was an exaggeration, but he had voted four times for Franklin Roosevelt, inheriting the allegiance of his Irish Catholic father. Born in a small Illinois town in 1911, Reagan attended a small church-related college, distinguishing himself as an athlete, and after graduation found a position as a sports announcer for an Iowa radio station. Moving to Hollywood, his easy articulacy and good looks carried him to some acting success. Defective eyesight kept him out of combat during the war, which he spent in California making army morale films. Respected by his fellow actors, he became president of the Screen Actors Guild in 1947. Still a Democrat, he was a relatively conservative labor leader, deeply suspicious of communist machinations in local union politics, quietly sharing his knowledge of the Hollywood left with the FBI. When his screen career flagged he turned to television, from the mid-1950s becoming host of CBS's popular General Electric Theater. As he completed his transition from union to corporate spokesman he also moved politically to the right. He formally switched to the Republican Party in 1962 and won the admiration of conservatives for a resounding television speech shortly before the 1964 presidential vote, and two years later his celebrity swept him into the governorship of California. Reagan's spectacular victory in the biggest state in the union made him a major political figure, and he used the media attention he now commanded to further his rhetorical campaign against big government, high taxes, and 1960s-style permissiveness. He failed to win the Republican nomination against the incumbent Gerald Ford in 1976, but promptly turned his sights to the next presidential election.

By the spring of 1980 it was evident that Reagan would win the Republican nomination. The prospect of a Reagan–Carter contest was a bemusing one for political commentators. Reagan's rhetoric placed him well to the right of the electorate as a whole, and, in terms of popular perception, he was not yet the avuncular figure he would become. Some of his actions in the campaign had given pause to many, such as formally opening it in Philadelphia, Mississippi, where three civil rights workers had been notoriously murdered in 1964, and announcing "I believe in states' rights." Carter for his part was encumbered with the failings of his presidency. An article in *The Nation* joked that, "the Democrats seem intent on nominating the only candidate Ronald Reagan could possibly beat," while the Republicans were nominating "the only candidate Jimmy Carter could possibly beat." It was a mark of Reagan's limitations as a candidate that, despite the administration's travails, the president remained very much in the race. In October Carter was narrowly ahead in some polls.[26]

In his acceptance speech Reagan characterized Carter's economic policy as an "indigestible economic stew": "one part inflation, one part high unemployment, one part recession, one part runaway taxes, one part deficit spending and seasoned by an energy crisis." This was to be the central theme of his campaign, in which he linked Carter's handling of the economy with the evils of government. Reagan promised that as president he would trim the budget, and he strongly espoused a 30 percent reduction in income tax. This "supply-side" doctrine, which insisted that a tax cut would reinvigorate the economy as more resources were made available for investment, had the backing of many congressional Republicans and provided the party with a positive agenda for overcoming the celebrated economic "malaise." As the campaign drew to a close Reagan and Carter met in a televised debate. Carter efficiently demonstrated his command of the issues, but it was Reagan's confident poise that perhaps most impressed viewers, as he presented a persona far removed from the dangerous extremist of Democratic rhetoric. "There you go again," he gently responded to Carter's parries. In the final moments he looked directly at the television audience to ask: "Are you better off than you were four years ago?"

A significant number of wavering voters seem not to have made up their minds until the last week of the campaign, a particularly fraught time in the administration's frustrating negotiations with the Iranians. In many states the difference between the two major candidates was close, and it needed only a relatively small number to swing to Reagan to clinch the election, which he took with 51 percent of the popular vote. Although this was only a bare majority, he led Carter by a formidable 10 points. The independent, John Anderson, polled 7 percent, the best outcome for a third party candidate since 1968. The congressional elections also reflected disillusionment with the governing party. The Democrats' losses in the House of Representatives were their largest in a presidential year since 1920, although they did retain control. The senatorial elections were even more disappointing for the Democrats, with a loss of 12 seats, for which there was no Democratic precedent in the twentieth century, and the Republicans took command of that chamber.

Reagan's victory was decisive, although was not conclusive proof that the country had turned smartly to the right. In the popular vote he secured only three percentage points more than Gerald Ford had in 1976, and in an exit poll only 11 percent said they had voted for him because he was a conservative. Most striking was the scale of Democratic defections. A formidable 29 percent of those who had voted for Carter in 1976 actually plumped for Reagan in 1980. Others defected to John Anderson, among them such lifetime Democrats as Franklin D. Roosevelt Jr, and President Kennedy's widow, Jacqueline Onassis. Among those groups who would normally expect to give majority support to the Democratic candidate were blue-collar workers, who split 47 to 46 percent for Reagan; these "Reagan Democrats" were vital to his election. Some were perhaps swayed by the evangelical revival and the campaign activities of the Moral Majority, which succeeded in mobilizing some Catholics as well as Protestants for "pro-God, pro-family" policies. But the economy was uppermost in the public mind. About a third of the electorate thought they were "worse off" financially than a year before, and these broke to Reagan by 64 percent to 25 percent for Carter, and Reagan performed particularly well among blue-collar workers who believed their economic position to be declining. To adapt a phrase that Bill Clinton's team made popular in the 1992 presidential election, "it was the economy, stupid."[27]

*   *   *

The outcome of the 1980 presidential election owed more to disarray in the Democratic Party and the unhappy coincidence of a number of domestic and foreign crises than to a resurgent conservatism. The unnerving inflation, the agonizingly long crisis over the imprisoned hostages, and the perception of a helpless and incompetent administration doomed Carter's bid to retain possession of the White House. There was a yearning in the public at large for deliverance from the sense that the nation had lost control of its destiny and for a restoration of happier times. Reagan was credited with being "a strong leader" by some voters, and perhaps they glimpsed in him some potential to be a savior. Pollsters found that a majority believed that he was the candidate most likely to "make America feel good about itself again."[28]

Chapter 2

Borrowing as a Way of Life: A Dependent Economy and a Fragmenting Society

Most Americans at the outset of the 1980s had memories of what in retrospect was an economic "golden age." The United States had emerged from World War II with a supercharged economy, in which not a minority but a solid majority of citizens enjoyed the largesse of a consumer society. Most Americans, it seemed, had become comfortably "middle class." A car worker or a truck driver (then usually male) might expect to own his own home and automobile and see his children off to college. Indeed, the rising living standard of blue-collar workers was seen as one of the great triumphs of the American economy, decisively seeing off the doctrines of Karl Marx. There were still some Americans in poverty but their numbers were declining, and, while a few were immensely rich, the inequality in family incomes was tending to wane. This great economic juggernaut, fueled by a seemingly inexhaustible supply of cheap oil, remorselessly ploughed ahead through these postwar years, providing ever more goods and services and allowing government to maintain not only the mightiest peacetime military establishment ever known but also welfare services which, however patchily, provided protection for many and ensured that the luckless at least survived. Virtual full employment and regular economic growth seemed the hallmarks of a supremely healthy economy, one which nurtured expectations of even better times ahead.

It had become evident by 1980 that this promise was not being fulfilled, one reason why Ronald Reagan proved such a seductive presidential candidate. Within a few years Reagan's cheerleaders were able to claim that the economy had recovered from the travails it had suffered in the 1970s. By 1984 it was "morning again in America." Superficially at least, this was the

Contemporary America: Power, Dependency, and Globalization since 1980,
First Edition. M.J. Heale.
© 2011 M.J. Heale. Published 2011 by Blackwell Publishing Ltd.

case – employment was rising, inflation falling, the national product increasing smartly, the poverty numbers declining. Yet the sunny statistics camouflaged the fact that the American economy was undergoing far-reaching change, and not all Americans were benefiting. Between 1980 and 1995, President Clinton would point out in the latter year, better-educated Americans generally prospered, but "the rest of our work force have seen their incomes either stagnate or fall. An America that, in our finest moment, has always grown together, now grows apart." His Council of Economic Advisers attributed this growing apart to the pressures of "rapid techno-logical shifts and a changing global economy." The American economy had become increasingly entangled with that of the world.[1]

* * *

Growing international competition and the revival of large-scale immigra-tion were among the forces transforming American life between the late 1970s and the early 1990s. The "golden age" had in some respects been an insular age. The United States might have assumed a towering position on the world stage, with its military scattered liberally across the earth, but during the middle decades of the twentieth century its economy was to a remarkable degree self-sufficient and its people did not have to make room for many new arrivals. Assured of virtually full employment, and safe-guarded by a range of welfare services, particularly after the Great Society had added its portion, the citizens of this society enjoyed a high degree of security, at least if they could disregard the risk of nuclear war. But these comfortable years were not to last. During the later decades of the twentieth century the general standard of living continued to rise, but increasing interaction with the outside world also brought economic insecurity, a chipping away of welfare benefits, an accentuating gulf between rich and poor, and hard times for the most deprived. Other Western economies, also subject to internationalizing pressures, underwent similar processes.

The vibrant economy over which John Kennedy had briefly presided could almost be compared with the famously "closed" system of the Soviet Union. Thanks to its size and geographical remoteness, the United States relied less on foreign trade than almost any other developed nation. Americans primarily did business with one another. Raw materials were extracted from American mines and wells, they were turned into products in American factories, and American businessmen sold their goods and services to American citizens, corporations, and governments. The United States was not isolated from the world economy, of course, although much of its international commerce was with a limited number of other advanced nations, such as Canada and Britain.

By the 1970s the American economy was beginning to lose its comfortable self-sufficiency, and the process continued. In 1996 a pair of Harvard economists remarked: "Thirty years ago Americans could act as if the U.S. economy existed in a vacuum. Today they clearly cannot." Americans had become dependent on the outside world in a number of respects, as was illustrated by the celebrated "twin deficits" that characterized the economy from the 1980s. One was the foreign deficit, occasioned as the country began importing much more than it was exporting. The dollars that foreigners thus earned were mostly reinvested in the United States. The other was the budget deficit of the federal government, as its expenditures came vastly to exceed revenues. The government had to borrow the difference, and much of this was also supplied by foreigners prepared to buy US Treasury bonds. Continuing economic growth and technological innovation were inevitably bringing considerable change to the American economy, but the twin deficits helped to shape the direction of that change.[2]

The budget and foreign deficits were intimately intertwined, as was shown by the Reagan administration's success in 1981 in securing a major tax cut, which reduced the government's revenue but left more money in the pockets of Americans, many of whom spent it on attractive imported goods. Partly because of the tax cut and partly because of increased military expenditures, the federal government was itself soon running a large budget deficit. This policy of "spend and borrow" was followed by a jump in the economy's performance after a few lackluster years in the early 1980s. As more people found jobs, and as the federal government reduced its tax take, Americans were able to spend more, as they also decided to save yet less. The return of vigorous economic growth was in significant degree driven by this rising personal consumption, which in turn sucked in imports. At the same time, the high budget deficit obliged the government to borrow more, although it could not raise enough from spendthrift Americans disinclined to save. This meant pushing up interest rates and enticing overseas investors, which in turn served to increase the value of the dollar. The dollar effectively appreciated by over a third between 1980 and October 1985, so that each dollar bought a lot more foreign currency – or goods. A stronger or overpriced dollar meant that exports became more expensive and imports cheaper, adding powerfully to the forces widening the trade gap. The consequent increased competition for American industry ravaged some traditional manufacturing sectors. While imports shot up, exports only inched up.

But the high domestic spending and the effective overdraft allowed by foreign financiers at least lifted the economy out of the doldrums inherited from the 1970s. Assisting its revival was the decline of inflation, thanks to the strict monetary policy of the Federal Reserve Board and to the fortuitous but dramatic drop in the international price of oil. In the second half of the 1980s the real price of oil fell to well below its 1979–1980 peak and even to below its peak in the 1973–1974 shock. The celebrated "Reagan boom" was not achieved without considerable outside help.

A large part of this help was the huge amount of foreign capital sucked in by the foreign deficit, over a trillion dollars' worth between 1980 and 1995, although at the beginning of that period the United States had been a net exporter of capital. Senator Patrick Moynihan in 1986 remarked that, "we borrowed a trillion dollars from the Japanese and gave a party." Sums of this size carried implications for the global economy. The high US interest rates, according to investment banker Jeffrey Garten, "attracted so much foreign money to the United States that the rest of the world was being decapitalized." The British economist Sam Brittan complained that, "The U.S. is conducting a raid on world savings." Other countries were often unhappily obliged to follow the American lead, creating what the West German Chancellor called "the highest real interest rates since the birth of Christ." But as government supporters liked to point out, foreigners would not have put their money into the American economy unless they had confidence in it, and there were few other economies that offered the advantages of both security and the relatively high interest rates found in the United States.[3]

It was not only foreign credit that made possible these relatively flush times. The American economy was awash with debt, without which it could not have expanded as it did. The American government, as noted, spent more than it earned; American consumers went on a credit card binge, while businesses took out loans in order to restructure or to invest in new technology. The extraordinary increase of debt of all kinds sustained employment and kept the economy moving, and other economies too.

It was not unusual for the federal government to owe money, but never before in peacetime had it resorted to borrowing as it did in the 1980s. In 1986 alone, for the first time ever, the US government borrowed $200 000 000. It was in these years that the national debt began to grow faster than the economy; as one budget deficit followed another, the debt remorselessly increased, becoming "the greatest peacetime accumulation of government debt in history." In the 1960s the public debt had dropped markedly as a proportion of GDP, and in 1981 represented a fairly modest 26.5 percent, yet by 1993 it had roughly doubled to 51.9 percent, in significant measure because of tax cuts. Americans could party in the 1980s, noted a Harvard economist, because they had "billed the tab to the future," that is, the escalating debt had been largely used to finance current consumption rather than investment in infrastructure or productive capacity. Further, the government faced an immediate cost in interest payments on the debt, which became one of the larger items in the federal budget. (Conservative pundit George Will recognized that such payments to domestic and foreign investors would swallow a high proportion of income tax receipts, by 1988 constituting "a transfer of wealth from labor to capital unprecedented in American history.") As early as 1984 foreign funds paid for 40 percent of the budget deficit. "Fed policy is now increasingly influenced and even dictated by the needs of our foreign creditors," explained the Mellon Bank's chief economist in 1987. Fed chief Paul Volcker gloomily conceded that "we have mortgaged our future." The nightmare that Japanese investors might not show up at a bond auction was said to make the Secretary of the Treasury "sit upright in bed in the middle of the night." These loans enabled the government to go about its business, and it could be said that foreign investors made possible Reagan's defense build-up. But the resulting tightness of the federal budget limited its flexibility. When the recession of 1991 loomed, President George H.W. Bush did not feel able to give the economy a boost by increasing federal spending and borrowing yet further.[4]

Many American citizens, too, seemed to subscribe to the philosophy of "spend, spend, spend," and corporations joined in the bonanza. Consumer debt, as a proportion of personal income after taxes, climbed from 63 percent in 1970, to 75 percent in 1980, and to 97 percent in 1990. This was arguably good for the economy – increased consumption accounted for over two-thirds of the growth during the expansion of 1982–1990. Credit cards were not new, but by the 1980s they had become readily available and were tempting Americans into greater debt. In 1969 total credit card debt had been a reasonable $2.7 billion; in 1980 it was $22 billion; and by 1994 a thumping $74 billion. Hardly surprisingly, savings accounts, already weak by international standards, shrank yet further. The number of families with savings accounts fell from 61.7 percent in 1983 to 43.5 percent in 1989. (One reason for the decline was the stagnation of wages for many workers, which meant raiding savings to pay for such increasing costs as housing and health care.) The plummeting of saving meant that there was little domestic money left for investment, particularly after the thirsty federal government had exacted its share, leaving it to foreign resources to plug this gap. Businesses too became more indebted. Diminishing profits meant that firms had increasingly to borrow money for new investment. Interest payments on their debts in the 1980s were over three times what they had been in the 1950s. Servicing these became a significant part of company costs, reducing funds for new investment and creating pressure to downsize the workforce and curb wages. In short, if Americans were spending more, they were investing less, and underinvestment boded ill for the economy. Between 1950 and 1980, the value of the plant and equipment behind the average American worker increased from \$26 000 to \$43 100; by 1987 the figure had barely inched up to \$45 900, not exactly a recipe for sustained competitiveness.[5]

If government spending and foreign investment helped the economy to grow, the exposure to outside forces obliged American industry to adapt in order to survive. The loss of both foreign and domestic markets to international competitors compelled action. Economists pinpointed the most fundamental of the economy's problems – a slowing of the rate of increase in productivity (or output per hour worked) since the late 1960s. During the "affluent" years of 1957 to 1969, labor productivity had increased on average by 2.9 percent a year, which meant that American workers were producing 40 percent more per hour of work at the end of that period than at the beginning; between 1969 and 1979 the rate slowed to 1.5 percent a year, and between 1979 to 1990 to a feeble 1.0 percent. Virtually every other advanced economy posted better rates of productivity growth in the 1970s and 1980s, Japan perhaps five times as much. To a degree, the United States could cope with this because its actual productivity still led the world, and its rivals were narrowing the gap rather than leaping into the lead. Nonetheless the slowing rate of productivity increase did not augur well. Without increasing productivity there could be no sustained increase in the standard of living (unless foreigners financed it), and stagnant productivity could only expose the country to yet more international competition.

Various answers were given to the question why American productivity was lagging or – to put it another way – why American industry was now apparently so inefficient. A frequent charge was that manufacturers in at least some major industries had grown complacent during the golden age and had failed adequately to invest in new technology. Much attention was paid to the allegedly torpid market reactions of the giant conglomerates that had emerged in the 1960s, when corporations had often acquired subsidiaries doing business in a range of unrelated areas, partly in an attempt to avoid the American anti-trust laws (which discouraged mergers within industries). Conservatives were tempted to blame poor performance on the high labor costs in such highly unionized industries as steel and automobiles, stemming from wage settlements reached in the halcyon postwar years, and contrast them with the low wage rates in competitor countries. Businesses also pointed to the proliferation of laws in the 1970s regulating consumer products, the environment, and workplace conditions, encumbering them with substantial costs that international competition prevented them from passing on to consumers. With the onset of the large budget deficits in the Reagan years, economists argued that the government's need to borrow meant that it absorbed a high share of national saving, leaving little for private domestic investment, with adverse implications for productivity. Government policies, particularly the budget deficit, also meant that the dollar was overvalued, at least in the first half of the decade, so that American industry could not readily compete with "artificially" cheap imports. Initially, many American businesses had reacted to intensified foreign competition by greater investment in their traditional products, thus exacerbating global overcapacity. In this context, the overvaluation of the dollar hit American manufacturing particularly hard.

The threat of foreign competition was a relatively novel one for American industry. Occasionally the trade balance reached into the black, but for most of the three decades after 1980 the current account of the balance of payment (the broadest measure of US trade) showed a yawning deficit. Aggravating the deficit occasioned by the booming importation of consumer goods was the decline in foreign markets for farm products, as both Third World and European countries succeeded in greatly increasing their agricultural output. The United States lurched from being the world's largest creditor to being the world's largest debtor, indeed "the largest debtor nation ever known to mankind," a reversal it accomplished in just four brief years between 1982 and 1986. Between 1980 and 1985 the trade balance stumbled from a modest surplus of $30.6 billion to a stunning deficit of $145.4 billion. "This is the greatest unilateral transfer of wealth in the history of the world," wrote one economist.[6]

Such American industries as steel and textiles had been in retreat to foreign competitors in the 1970s. Companies went bankrupt, workers lost jobs, whole regions succumbed to depression. European and Far Eastern manufacturers were successfully selling motor cars, consumer electronics, and computers in the American market. Among the Asian success stories was that of the "Gang of Four," South Korea, Taiwan, Singapore, and Hong Kong, which between 1980 and 1987 doubled their collective share of American imports to 15.3 percent, more than that of all the European economies combined. By the late 1980s the United States was importing more industrial products than it exported. German cars and Japanese televisions often seemed good value for money, calling into question not only the efficiency but also the quality of American industry.

One component in the deteriorating trade deficit was the price of oil, thrust spectacularly upward by the "shocks" of 1973–1974 and 1979–1981, as OPEC (Organization of the Petroleum Exporting Countries) countenanced large price increases. The very functioning of the economy had become critically dependent on certain overseas supplies, not least of oil in which it had ceased to be self-sufficient. Each year, one economist explained in 1980, "the United States transfers to OPEC a substantial percentage of attainable growth." Petroleum imports accounted for nearly half of the trade deficit in 1989, the year in which the Berlin Wall was pulled down. The United States had also increasingly to import such vital minerals as aluminum, nickel, zinc, chromium, and tungsten. Bauxite is needed for aluminum, and whereas the United States had once produced most of the bauxite it needed, by 1988 it was importing 94 percent of it. At the same time as the country was "winning" the Cold War it was becoming dependent on foreign suppliers of strategically important materials, one reason for the deep interest of its administrations in the political stability of far-flung parts of the planet.[7]

By the time the oil price dropped again in the mid-1980s the advanced industrial economies, including the United States, had been jolted into accelerating the movement of their capital and labor away from energy-intensive industries and toward those that used less energy, such as light industry, high tech, and services. The American manufacturing labor force dropped by 1.1 million between 1979 and 1990 while service employment grew by 20 million. Investment in finance, insurance, and real estate soared. In the 1980s McDonalds boasted a larger workforce than the basic steel industry. Ronald Reagan later claimed some credit for the widening trade gap over which he had presided: "Our difficulties accelerated the modernization and restructuring of our industrial base and in the end helped make America more productive and more competitive."[8]

This restructuring was a response to major structural change in the world economy. Not only Japan and West Germany but even some Third World countries had become major manufacturers not only of low-value consumer items but also of sophisticated products, exploiting their natural advantages of low wages and sometimes access to cheap raw materials. For many Americans the astonishing rise of the Japanese economy represented a threat to US supremacy. The semiconductor chip, a crucial component of computers, for example, was initially an American creation, but in the course of the 1980s Japan replaced the United States as the dominant producer for the international market. Long-term strategies had to be devised by American business if it was to restore its profitability. One, as noted, was to shift resources away from the ailing "smokestack" industries, with their heavy reliance on foreign fuel and its volatile price. Another was to drive down costs, which often meant curbing wages and benefits. Yet another was to transfer production to low-wage countries overseas. If ailing companies failed to take some kind of action they risked being taken over, for the 1980s witnessed an unprecedented wave of takeovers and mergers, as entrepreneurs discerned potential profits to be made in revamping firms for the changing times.[9]

And foreign investors increasingly invaded the United States directly. They sometimes bought up whole corporations or built their own plants on American soil. Between 1980 and 1988 Japanese investment in the country multiplied roughly six times. In 1982 Honda started to make cars in the United States and was soon followed by five other Japanese firms. Sony decided to make color television sets in southern California, and by 1987 Japanese companies were making six million color television sets in the United States, over four times the number imported from Japan. The famous ice-cream maker Baskin-Robbins was bought by a British firm. The Canadians and the Dutch were also major investors. The scale of this invasion was staggering. In 1980 there had been only about $83 billion in the United States in foreign direct investment; by 1992 it was $420 billion. A September 1987 *Time* cover story was entitled "For Sale: America," comparing the United States to "a huge shopping mart in which foreigners are energetically filling up their carts." By 1987 nearly half of the commercial real estate in downtown Los Angeles was owned by foreigners and almost a quarter of that of New York. It could almost be said that Americans were on their way to becoming a nation of tenants.[10]

Though there was unease at the scale of the foreign invasion, and periodic hostile comments directed in particular at the Japanese, the decaying communities that were being revitalized were mostly very grateful. The opening of a Japanese factory in the Midwestern "rustbelt" was usually the occasion of a great reception. One example was the Illinois town of Ottawa, where the Japanese opened a typewriter factory in 1989. The local dignitaries dressed up in Japanese robes to welcome them, including the state governor, the mayor, and the local beauty queen. Economists Edward Graham and Paul Krugman pointed out that other advanced countries had long experienced a significant foreign presence and that "the United States is simply becoming more normal – that it is becoming, like other countries, a host as well as a home for multinational firms." Americans, they seemed to be saying, had to learn to be less parochial.[11]

American government broadly abetted the attempts to make American industry more competitive, despite business fury at the "strong" dollar. The high interest rates imposed by the Fed from 1979 to combat inflation also had the effect of precipitating a serious recession in the early 1980s, which wiped out many inefficient businesses. Administrations repeatedly confirmed their commitment to free trade, and under Presidents Reagan and Bush they championed a number of initiatives, most notably the North American Free Trade Agreement (NAFTA) with Canada and Mexico. (Nonetheless, the relentless pressures on American industries triggered protectionist demands from both labor organizations and corporations, to which governments sometimes succumbed – by the end of the 1980s around a third of goods enjoyed some protection.) Government also generally accepted that the regulatory regimes introduced in the late 1960s and 1970s were hampering industry's attempts to compete internationally. Talking of the potential of the economy in 1979, Jimmy Carter anticipated Ronald Reagan: "Let's reduce government interference and give it a chance to work." During the late 1970s the Carter administration embarked on a major deregulation drive, and by 1989 the share of the economy subject to tight regulation was reduced by about two-thirds. These efforts were rewarded by the resurgence of a number of vital industries. With the deregulation of the airlines competition increased and fares dropped. Some airlines went out of business, but altogether the sector prospered during the Reagan era, when passenger traffic increased by over 50 percent. The deregulated railroads, too, increased in efficiency. Telecommunications had also come under scrutiny in the 1970s, especially the role of AT&T. The outcome of an anti-trust suit saw the breaking up of AT&T's local services into seven new regional companies in 1984. With new companies also offering long-distance service, rates dropped substantially. New technology and fiber optics cable were being introduced, ushering in further transformations in the industry. By the 1990s the booming telecommunications industry bore little resemblance to the business once arthritically controlled by AT&T. A beginning was also made to the deregulation of petroleum, natural gas, and finance.[12]

The break-up of large corporations was also a favored strategy of the finance markets in the 1980s. Some of the relative sluggishness of the American economy was attributed to the earlier tendency for large companies to develop as conglomerates, acquiring interests in an array of activities unconnected with their original core business. As they grew into unwieldy giant bureaucracies, they tended to lose touch with their customers and were particularly ill suited to respond to the growing international competition. The Reagan administration eased the rules on mergers within industries, encouraging firms to combine in new ways. "Merger mania" became one of the features of the 1980s.

The wave of takeovers, mergers, and leveraged buyouts, reaching its peak in the middle of the decade, was one of the greatest in American history, generously lubricated by new forms of financing and now facilitated by high-speed computers. The exploding financial sector was displacing manufacturing at the center of the economy. Both takeovers and buyouts (where a group of investors acquired controlling shares in the business) usually involved borrowing money, and corporate indebtedness increased dramatically. Financiers proved skilful in devising innovative methods to fund mergers, and junk bonds and mortgage-backed securities turned some finance houses into business giants. The huge turnover of junk bonds (offering high returns at high risk) reflected the borrowing by companies to finance restructuring or new acquisitions. Many takeovers were of a speculative nature, tempted by the prospect of short-term gains, leading one economist to characterize the United States as a "casino society," epitomized by the high-stakes maneuverings on Wall Street. "A hyperactive stock market," warned the financial pundit Warren Buffet, "is the pickpocket of enterprise." Others saw virtue in the speculative ethic. "Greed … is good …," explained Gordon Gekko in the 1989 film *Wall Street:* "Greed – mark my words – will save America." Once taken over, many conglomerates were broken up as firms returned to more specialized activities. Workforces, both blue- and white-collar, were often downsized too. Inefficient plants were closed as companies absorbed the message that their survival depended on innovation, efficiency, and the quality of their products.[13]

Another strategy adopted by major corporations was to join their competitors in foreign locations. Plants could be established abroad, allowing companies similar advantages to their rivals in access to cheap labor. Some firms had long deployed foreign subsidiaries, but corporate investment abroad grew rapidly in the 1970s and even more dramatically in the following decade. During the 1980s American companies increased their spending on factories, equipment, and research abroad at a faster rate than their investments in the United States. What has been called the "deindustrialization of America" was in part the outcome of decisions by multinational corporations to shift their manufacturing operations to developing countries. By the late 1980s the greater part of the operating profits of many US multinationals came from sales made by their foreign affiliates. Its overseas profits enabled Ford to survive the recession of the early 1980s, when its domestic performance was disastrous. For many years AT&T had assembled standard telephones in Shreveport, Louisiana, but mounting competition from abroad prompted the company to switch production to Singapore, where it could pay lower wages; in 1989 AT&T made another switch to the yet cheaper labor force of Thailand. This was part of a more complex strategy. Between 1984 and 1992 AT&T eliminated 21 000 blue-collar jobs in the United States, added 8000 to their white-collar workforce, and created 12 000 factory jobs abroad. The very threat of exporting jobs served to keep wages down in the United States.[14]

The loss of such jobs also meant a decline in union membership, and some labor spokesmen (and subsequent scholars) believed that the weakening of organized labor was yet another deliberate strategy by managers and government to further economic restructuring. In 1978 Doug Fraser, president of the Union of Automobile Workers (UAW), disturbed by the increasingly confrontational attitude of employers in collective bargaining, charged the business community with conducting a "one-sided class war" against working people. During the 1980s the UAW, one of the strongest unions in the golden age, lost 500 000 members. The long-term evolution away from heavy industry was likely to erode union membership anyway, but in their desperate quest to reverse the trend toward lower profits many companies did seek to weaken unions or to operate without them. Manufacturing jobs were relocated not only to developing countries but also to non-unionized communities in the South or other parts of the United States. The decline of the large conurbations and the dispersal of industry into smaller plants, suburbs, and rural areas allowed employers to recruit more non-union labor.[15]

The National Labor Relations Board, established under Franklin Roosevelt to regulate industrial relations, became less accommodating to labor interests. In 1985 its Reagan-appointed chairman equated collective bargaining with "the destruction of individual freedom." In the mid-1980s unions often settled for security when contracts were renegotiated rather than for higher pay. A third of the workers covered by new collective-bargaining agreements in 1985 submitted to a freeze or even wage cuts. Labor organizations were disappointed by the support they received from the Carter administration, but under Ronald Reagan and George H.W. Bush the White House proved even less sympathetic. In 1981, when the air traffic controllers went on strike, President Reagan summarily fired them, so wrecking the union. This was "brutal overkill," protested Lane Kirkland, president of the AFL-CIO (American Federation of Labor and Congress of

Industrial Organizations). "Reagan made it respectable to bust unions," said labor lawyer Robert M. Baptiste, and other employers felt encouraged to use similar tactics. A number of unions lost strikes as their members were displaced by permanent replacements, a feature that obtained of about 20 percent of strikes in the second half of the 1980s. When Greyhound bus drivers struck in 1990, the company quickly trained hundreds of new drivers. With the ending of the Cold War, labor spokesmen believed, pressures on the unions intensified as corporations portrayed them as "outmoded relics of a bygone age." The federal government also showed limited interest in sustaining the value of worker protection measures. Federal unemployment insurance and AFDC ("welfare") provisions were reduced in the 1980s. The federal minimum wage was not raised during the Reagan presidency, the longest period it had ever gone without an increase. Buffeted by economic restructuring and employer and governmental policies, the proportion of union members in the non-farm workforce, which had peaked in 1945, fell from 27 percent in 1970 to 12 percent in 1991, less than in any other advanced industrial economy.[16]

The American labor movement's traditional limitations left it vulnerable in this increasingly hostile environment. Its historical weaknesses had always been in part related to the divisions within the wage-earning classes, and the resumption of large-scale immigration not only increased competition for jobs but also accentuated the ethnic diversification among workers, while the growing employment of women, temporary and part-time workers furthered the workforce's fragmentation. This growing "segmentation" militated against any sense of solidarity, though economists saw advantages in the job market's increasing "flexibility." If the falling union membership eased the economic transformation, more jobs were being generated, though often poorly paid. During the Reagan years new jobs were created at the fastest rate ever recorded in peacetime history.

In many respects the restructuring of American industry served the larger economy well. Deregulation and the new modes of finance allowed capital to be located in parts of the economy where it could be used more productively. In the years 1979–1986 labor productivity gains in manufacturing (though not in other sectors) reached about 3.5 percent a year, impressively up from around 1.4 percent a year in 1973–1979. By the mid-1980s manufacturing was recovering the profitability it had lost after 1979, and profits increased further in the second half of the decade with the falling value of the dollar (and helped by the containment of wages). Many companies now found that profits were to be made in high-quality and specialized goods or services – electronics, microprocessors, electrogalvanized steel, computer software, customized videos – often designed for niche markets, and for which highly skilled employees were necessary. The Carter and Reagan defense build-ups expanded the aerospace and defense industries, further enriching such flourishing Sunbelt states as Texas and California, and commercial aircraft remained a major business. The American chemical industry enjoyed world leadership in chemical technology and a healthy trade surplus, and in the 1980s several of its firms sharpened their competitive edge by turning to pharmaceuticals, biotechnology, and specialty chemicals. High-tech industries increasingly replaced traditional plants in such states as Massachusetts and New Jersey, while California's "Silicon Valley" became internationally renowned for its state-of-the-art IT companies. Service industries like entertainment, telecommunications, marketing and consultancy, tourism and health care fast expanded their payrolls. The world of finance in particular was expanding its influence throughout the economy. The number of employees on Wall Street doubled between 1979 and 1987.[17]

While the revitalization of parts of manufacturing industry and the continued growth of the service sector helped to sustain the post-1982 boom, this restructuring had its human and other costs. Broadly, while the changing economy provided the better educated and skilled with good jobs, those in relatively low-skill occupations fared less well. The real income of most American workers – the 80 percent of the workforce not counted among the privileged higher executive, managerial, and technical categories – declined by about 12 percent between 1973 and 1995, even as their bosses enjoyed raises. Only the increasing participation of women, especially wives, in the workforce sustained the living standards of many families. Incomes also tended to become more volatile, with many families finding that their income varied significantly from year to year, both up and down, increasing their sense of insecurity. According to a *New York Times* report in 1996, some 65 percent of workers who lost their jobs but eventually found others did so at lower rates of pay.[18]

A variety of influences combined to produce wage stagnation: the declining number of skilled blue-collar jobs, the expansion of low-wage service occupations in firms like McDonalds, the downward pressure on costs in companies racked by increasing competition and high debts, the weakening of unions, the growing supply of cheap immigrant labor. The proportion of men with "good jobs" (those offering at least the median wage, health insurance, and a retirement plan) fell from 37.7 percent in 1979 to 31.8 percent in 1989. Real wages for low-pay workers declined during the 1980s and early 1990s to the point where, according to one bank economist, "low-paid workers in the U.S. have lower living standards than do low-paid workers in many other economically advanced nations." What was especially striking was the erosion of wages for male workers, which helps to explain the decline in savings and the escalating credit-card debts. The median income for a 40-year-old male (in 2006 dollars) was $45 446 in 1974 and $41 310 in 1994. Adding to the insecurity of many families was the declining provision of health insurance for permanent workers by private sector employers. The disproportionate rise in the costs of such items as health care, child care, education, and public transportation meant that debt became a way of life for many.[19]

It was those with limited education who suffered most. In 1980 the typical male college graduate earned about 80 percent more than the man who had not advanced beyond high school; by 1990 the gap had nearly doubled. The average real wage of male high school dropouts declined by over a quarter in the 20 years after 1973, while the best educated, often in occupations insulated from foreign competition, maintained their earning power. A great educational divide was opening up. One effect was to make it harder for those born into poor families ever to make their way up into the middle class, for they were never likely to receive the necessary schooling. Among the hardest hit were members of minorities. Affirmative action helped some black Americans, and a black middle class grew, though middle-income black Americans were mainly in public sector occupations. But the evidence also suggested that as black males were shaken out of blue-collar jobs they moved into lower-paid jobs in the service sector, more than was the case with their white peers. The median income of black families as a proportion of white family income edged down in the 1980s, and for Hispanic families the decline was even greater. Some minority groups suffered poverty and ill-health rates that were high by international standards. According to one 1990 study, black men in Harlem had a poorer life expectancy than men in Bangladesh.[20]

There were some parallels in the experience of women, some of whom prospered in the changing economy while others were edged into poverty. Aided by affirmative action, a vigorous feminist movement, and the fast growth of the service sector, more women entered the job market and some were very successful. The proportion going to college rose inexorably and more entered the professions. In 1970 women had represented just 4.9 percent of lawyers; by 1990 the figure was 21 percent. But the ratio of poor women to poor men was also tending to increase. The "feminisation of poverty" was a long-term process; in 1950 some 54 percent of all poor adults had been women; by 1989 the proportion was about two-thirds. The reasons were complex, though included changing family structures and the increasing proportion of female-headed households (accentuated by the disappearance of jobs for men from the old industrial centers). Poverty was by no means confined to young women struggling to bring up children on their own, but it was disproportionately concentrated on them.

It was not only the poorest Americans who had to tighten their belts, but many in the middling income groups too, as politicians began uneasily to realize. Households in the middle income category slid from a share of 16.1 percent of household income in 1970 to 14.0 percent in 1980 and to 13.8 percent in 1990. Actually these figures are somewhat misleading, for the number of people in the higher income groups was rising fast while that in the middle income groups was falling – there were people successfully moving up, which helps to explain the consumer boom. In one analysis which divided families into "lower," "middle" and "upper" in terms of income groups, the proportion in the middle class dropped from 57.1 percent of families in 1976 to 53.0 percent in 1986, while the upper class mushroomed from 9.7 percent to 15.3 percent. The proportion in the lower class remained around a third. Thus, many middle income Americans joined the wealthy, but not all did. For those who remained in the middle-class, median family income tended to remain stagnant or even to decline. A few tumbled into the lower income category. The blue-collar workers that the Cold War era had rewarded with middle-class lifestyles were finding that the best times were behind them.[21]

Even more striking than the stagnation or decline in incomes for those in the lower and middle reaches of the scale were the phenomenal gains made by the most fortunate. The wealthiest 1 percent of families owned about 22 percent of all wealth in 1975; by 1995 their share had rocketed to 42 percent. In an increasingly open economy, senior executives were able to demand awesomely high rewards for their services. Top earners benefited from President Reagan's tax cuts, while those with large investments, that is the already well-to-do, enjoyed the returns on high interest rates, and the booming stock market added to the fortunes of many. Highly skilled professionals, even if they did not join the ranks of the very wealthy, were often able to move up from middling to the higher income categories. The highly visible "yuppies" of the upper middle class seemed proof of a kind that the American dream was still alive. As the rich prospered and increased their distance from the poor, their connections with the larger society became more tenuous. The upwardly-mobile – and those who inherited wealth – frequently married one another, thus boosting their household incomes, and sent their offspring to private schools and then to the more prestigious universities. Even the more able children of the less privileged could often aspire to no more than the two-year community colleges, which in 1990 contained over half of the country's freshmen. Ivy League universities conscientiously recruited minority students like African Americans and Hispanics, but otherwise their rising costs meant that for the most part they were institutions for the rich. Many rich and cosseted families lived in the gated communities that were proliferating in these years, protected from contact with the hoi polloi. Historian Christopher Lasch described a new meritocratic and cosmopolitan elite, largely detached from the society that enriched it, connected to corporations or other bodies with interests beyond the country's borders, whose loyalties were "international rather than regional, national, or local." Journalist Michael Lind also identified a distinct elite, though saw it as a "white overclass" that divided and ruled: "the white elite is separated from the masses in taste and value, and the masses are divided among themselves along racial lines." In both formulations, an influential elite uncoupled from the larger society inevitably clove to its own interests rather than those of the bulk of Americans.[22]

The straitening circumstances of many Americans created conditions in which a populist suspicion of the powerful could take hold. A survey by the Democratic Party in 1991 found that rather than thinking the economy had improved under the Republicans, more voters believed that "the rich have gotten richer while the middle class got stuck paying the bill." One study after another in the late 1980s and 1990s testified to an increase in income inequality over the previous two decades, which was often attributed to some combination of technological change and global competition. In 1978 the heads of major companies had earned 35 times more than an average worker; by 1992 it was 126 times as much. During the middle decades of the twentieth century there had been some attempt to recruit a significant part of the workforce into the consumer society through relatively high wages and benefits, but this strategy in effect was abandoned as the economy came more to depend on high levels of consumption by the upper middle classes. There was talk of an "hourglass economy," with those in work tending to concentrate in either the best-paid or the worst-paid jobs. The inequality of income experienced by the American workforce was more pronounced than in other advanced economies. Not entirely coincidentally, as some scholars have noticed, American politics tended to become more polarized as the income gap widened.[23]

The central promise of American life – the opportunity for getting on – was being withdrawn, the yuppies not withstanding. Social mobility was declining. There had been some mild improvement in the 30 years after

1950, as more Americans moved up the social scale, but statistics indicate that this came to a halt around 1980, after which mobility declined. Further, intergenerational mobility – where children moved up to higher income groups than their parents – apparently declined in the decades after 1980. The geographical segregation of rich and poor also increased, paralleling the ethnic and racial segregation intensified by the massive immigration. The poor were becoming increasingly concentrated in particular neighborhoods, with implications for the quality of schools, standards of health, and crime rates. In societies characterized by marked and increasing inequality, of which the United States was but one – though a prime – example, studies indicated that infant mortality tended to be relatively high, working hours long, and the prison populations large. When President George H.W. Bush was told by Hillary Clinton in 1989 that the United States held nineteenth place among industrial countries for infant mortality he could not believe it, though later discovered "she was right."[24]

The growing disparity in incomes could conceivably be seen as a mark of the resilience of the American economy, or at least an adaptation to new circumstances. Other economies proved less flexible. If some of America's problems were rooted in the relative insularity it had enjoyed during the golden age, these were nothing compared to the problems faced by the Soviet Union and its successor states. Even more than the American economy, the Soviet economy had been sealed off from the international system, and by the 1980s seemed like an industrial dinosaur in an age when silicone and software were revitalizing other advanced economies. Seriously exacerbating the problems of the Soviet Union was the marked drop in the price of oil (its major export) after 1982, depriving its exchequer of yet further income, including the foreign currency needed to acquire Western technology. The Soviets might be capable of producing five times as many tractors as the United States, but it was information technology that was becoming essential to economic progress. Soviet premier Mikhail Gorbachev admitted as much: "We are encircled not by invincible armies but by superior economies." Failure to innovate combined with the immense scale of Soviet arms expenditures placed crippling strains on the system, and when the Soviet Union dissolved in the early 1990s its economy was close to ruins.[25]

The countries of Western Europe, though they fared better than the Soviet Union, also encountered greater problems than the United States in adapting their economies to the modern world. European unemployment multiplied five times between 1973 and 1985; hardly any new jobs were created. For several years in the 1980s British unemployment was in double percentage points, a proportion virtually unknown in the United States. In 1989 the unemployment rate was 5.3 percent in the United States, while in the United Kingdom it was 7.3 percent, in France 9.3 percent, and in Spain 17.2 percent. The mass and persisting unemployment that appeared in many Western European countries, in significant part because of global economic forces, was avoided by an American economy that managed to keep expanding and that created new jobs, however lowly paid. And while the soaring of the Japanese economy in the 1980s jangled nerves in the United States, in the early 1990s the "Japanese miracle" imploded, a belated proof to some Americans that there was no economic model better than their own free enterprise system.

The American economy, then, was successful in generating new jobs, no mean accomplishment when the postwar baby boom was still supplying new entrants to the labor force in the 1980s, when immigrants were pouring into the country, and when women were embracing the world of paid work in unprecedented numbers. The administrations of these years could also congratulate themselves on beating inflation, though the general abating of inflation around the world in the late twentieth century was also the product of other forces, such as the falling price of oil and increasingly competitive international trade.

The resilience and adaptability of the American economy may have allowed it to outlast the Soviet economy, but there were contrasting lessons that could be learned from the experience. For those who identified with the conservative revival personified by Ronald Reagan, the steady growth of the American economy and the collapse of the Soviet Union were proofs of the transcendent virtues of the free enterprise system. The conservative Republicans who surged into Congress in the 1990s demanded the further deconstruction of government, less regulation and lower taxes, and offered the same prescriptions to other countries. But if a messianic urgency came to characterize the economic philosophy of the right wing, many main-stream economists and social scientists were viewing the American eco-nomic performance with unease. They accepted that the kind of "command economy" represented by the Soviet system had been discredited, and they recognized that there had to be a vital role for the market, but they dis-cerned serious dysfunctions in the American political economy and feared for its future.

If the ferocious geopolitical competition of the Cold War was eventually resolved by the bankrupting of the Soviet Union, the cost to the United States included a massive national debt and a massive trade deficit. High military spending, according to some analysts, had distorted the American economy and diverted resources from more productive areas, contributing to the country's poor productivity record. The obsession with the Soviets also distracted American policy makers from other potential threats to the United States, or so some argued. Over the previous quarter-century West Germany and Japan in particular had emerged as major economies, their productivity increases shaming that of the Americans. It was not too far-fetched to believe, on the statistics then available, that the Japanese economy would overtake that of the United States, a situation made even less palatable by the fact that the United States was already dependent on Japan for much sophisticated electronic equipment, particularly semiconductor chips, including some used in its defense industry. (A Japanese scholar suggested that the Cold War had actually ended because both the United States and the Soviet Union had come to realize how much each depended on advanced Japanese technology, and had concluded that they should settle their differences in the face of this common potential enemy.) For some analysts, the transformation from a manufacturing to a service economy was a matter for grave concern, for they doubted whether American political and economic supremacy could long survive without a strong base in manufacturing industry, with its capacity to develop advanced technology. It was ironic that as Ronald Reagan's admirers were crediting the president with restoring American dignity, a growing academic and popular literature focused on the theme of "decline." "The fundamental power of the American corporation to compete has been called into question," admitted a former Reagan economic adviser in 1989. According to a special report in the *New York Times* in May 1992, the consensus among economists was that "the United States consumes so much and invests so little that it is jeopardising its future." In the late 1970s there had been a preoccupation with America's relative military decline; now the focus was on the economic. The theme flavored the election campaign of 1992, when the American people arguably concluded that Ronald Reagan had not delivered an economic miracle after all.[26]

*   *   *

For good or ill, the American economy had become increasingly open since the election of Ronald Reagan, and was intricately bound up with that of the outside world. How far the increasing income inequality and residential segregation could be attributed to growing international competition and burgeoning immigration has been much debated, though it can hardly be doubted that they played a part. Americans responded to their eroding economic insularity with contrasting perspectives. Some in the early 1990s lamented the passing of American economic independence, the new status of the United States as the biggest debtor nation in the world, the increasing foreign ownership of American businesses and real estate. Others pointed out that the economic and financial interconnections with the outside world had helped the United States transform its economy, which was stronger than it had been 15 years earlier. The frustrations experienced by some Americans, such as the stagnating of middle-class incomes, could provide the bases for nativist or populist reactions against American governmental policies by the 1990s, and there were indeed periodic explosions of outrage. But there could be no turning back to the relatively autonomous economy of the mid-twentieth century. International pressures like the oil shocks and increasing business competition may have powerfully influenced the restructuring of the American economy, but it was still the largest in the world and during the 1980s it enjoyed rather better growth than most. In 1980, for example, the combined GDP of 12 West European countries was greater than that of the United States; by 1990 the American GDP had overtaken the 12. If the United States was in hock to the rest of the world, its exuberant spending was also the engine that was pulling the global economy. Populist unease there may have been at the perceptions of American dependency, but as the United States emerged from the Cold War its political leadership in the 1990s decided that the salvation of the economy lay in yet further immersion in the wider world.

Chapter 3

Strangers in the Land: Open Borders and American Identity

In the late twentieth century several global influences were impacting on the United States. The restructuring of the American economy was in no small part driven by international competition and eased by foreign investment, and the high American standard of living owed much to the willingness of others to lend to the United States. American society, too, was being reshaped by currents originating beyond American borders. These same decades witnessed massive movements of people around the world. Many of them targeted the United States.

British historian Eric Hobsbawm has remarked that the most fundamental change of the twentieth century was the extraordinary doubling of world population between 1950 and 1990. This was an unprecedented phenomenon, made possible in part by the plummeting of death rates consequent on modern medicine. Population had grown particularly fast in the Third World, with the result that there was an increasing gap between rich and poor countries. During the "golden age," world population had soared, while that of the Third World in particular had grown spectacularly. Generally, however, food production had increased at an even faster rate, so most people were more-or-less fed, but in the 1980s the agricultural revolution slowed. Yet in that decade alone the world acquired 842 million more people. In many countries populations were expanding faster than their economies could support them. There had been a growing migration from poor countries to richer ones since World War II, but the harder times of the 1970s sent many more in search of a better life, and the volume mounted steeply from the mid-1980s. In addition to economic migrants, the political instability in much of the world – the revolutions, military

Contemporary America: Power, Dependency, and Globalization since 1980,
First Edition. M.J. Heale.
© 2011 M.J. Heale. Published 2011 by Blackwell Publishing Ltd.

coups, ethnic strife – spurred yet others to flee their homelands, and a seemingly endless refugee crisis haunted the globe.[1]

By the 1980s the United States was receiving more immigrants than all other countries combined. This represented an enormous human influx. Not since before the barriers went up in the 1920s had such huge waves of peoples swept into the United States. The foreign-born percentage in the population, which had been dropping for decades, began to rise again in the 1970s. Immigration had been edging up since World War II, and it rose to 4.5 million in the 1970s and yet further to 7.3 million in the 1980s, when the rate in relation to the American population was over twice what it had been in the 1950s. Further, huge, and increasing numbers of illegal immigrants, accumulating into millions, found their way to the country.[2]

It was not only the sheer scale of this migration but also its novel composition that had profound implications for American society. Traditionally immigration to the United States had been overwhelmingly European, but now its character shifted dramatically toward the Third World. The largest contingent were the mostly poor Hispanics escaping the distressed societies of Mexico and Central America for the succor hopefully to be found to the north. The United States shared the longest land border of any developed nation with a developing one, Mexico, the disparity of income between such contiguous nations being the greatest in the world. Asians too arrived in force, large numbers of Vietnamese, Koreans, and Chinese making their often hazardous way from the troubled countries of Southeast Asia. The political instability in the Middle East also served to augment the Muslim population of the United States. Over 100 000 Iranians arrived in the 1980s.[3]

* * *

For the most part the newcomers settled in the expanding Sunbelt states of the South and the West, most notably California, Texas, and Florida, though large numbers found their way to the urban Northeast, especially New York and New Jersey. The Rio Grande river between Texas and Mexico represented the world's busiest border, as countless numbers crossed it daily. Much of Texas was being repossessed by Mexicans. Asians were making their way to the state too, such as the Vietnamese who came to dominate the shrimping business in the Gulf of Mexico. The ethnic heterogeneity of American cities was once more refreshed. New York City neighborhoods were colonized by Koreans, Haitians, Russians, and Chinese. Soviet Jews found a haven in Brooklyn's Brighton Beach section, and Dominicans colonized parts of Manhattan's Upper West Side. Brooklyn's

East Flatbush neighborhood became the home of many Trinidadians and Jamaicans. In the Midwest the Detroit area had the largest concentration of Arabic speakers outside the Middle East, while the Middle Atlantic's Jersey City attracted middle-class families from India. But it was Los Angeles that became the quintessential immigrant city. About a fifth of the newcomers who had arrived in the United States since 1970 lived in southern California by the mid-1980s. "Away from its affluent pockets Los Angeles is like a booming Third World city," wrote one journalist: "'Koreatown,' 'Little Saigon' and a host of little Philippines, Irans, El Salvadors, Cambodias, Taiwans and Israels stretches for miles." Ethnicity as well as economics was furthering the nation's residential segmentation.[4]

In many cities foreign-language television broadcasts catered to these new populations, as did multilingual election booklets, while, following civil rights-style legislation and court decisions, school-teaching came to be provided in a variety of foreign languages. These services publicly underlined the presence of the new immigrants; globalism had come to America. Many city centers were already decaying, and tensions sometimes flared between groups competing for housing and jobs. Hospitals and schools in poor towns near the Mexican border struggled to cope. Yet there were also neighborhoods that were revitalized by immigration. Tensions in the inner cities would have been greater but for the fact that many new immigrants bypassed them and made directly for the suburbs. A significant proportion of immigrants also found that they were eligible for some affirmative action programs, a feature that irked poor whites (who could not claim such benefits) and American-born minorities. Given the various racial entitlements and multiculturalist teachings generated by the civil rights movement, the new immigrants arguably had less reason than earlier generations to assimilate quickly. "Replacing the old, assimilationist view is a competing ethnic-cultural pluralism," noted the New York State Education commissioner in 1989. At the end of the twentieth century over 28 million of the people in the United States had been born abroad, a little over half of them in Latin American countries and a quarter in Asian. Both because of the scale of the immigration, and because of high birth rates among the newcomers, the very identity of the American nation was arguably under threat – it would become increasingly difficult for Americans to see themselves as the inheritors of a Western European civilization.[5]

Most of these immigrants did find gainful employment. Many took jobs that American-born workers often spurned, such as agricultural labor and domestic service. The mass arrival of poor immigrants tended to keep down wage rates and worked to the disadvantage of American workers with poor schooling and few skills, and while the effect in this respect does not appear to have been pronounced, their presence meant that poor whites and minorities not unnaturally feared for their jobs. On the other hand, skilled, scientific, and professional immigrants also found jobs in the expanding high-tech economy. A high proportion of the technical work-force in California's booming Silicon Valley was foreign-born. By the 1980s the profile of immigration resembled an hourglass – there were bulges both at the bottom and at the top of the occupational hierarchy (although that at the bottom was expanding faster). A *Business Week* analysis of immi-grants who had arrived in the five years prior to 1992 found that a slightly higher proportion were college educated than were native-born workers; at the same time more than twice as many were high school dropouts. While some immigrants became college teachers, engineers, IT workers, medical scientists, and economists, others – in much larger numbers – became agricultural laborers, gardeners, janitors, fast food and restaurant workers, and domestics. Arguably this bifurcation served the economy well, providing it with both cheap labor (thus reducing the price of goods and services for American consumers) and skilled labor (thus advancing tech-nological and managerial efficiency). Harvard economist George Borjas argued that immigration was "an income redistribution program, a large wealth transfer from those who compete with immigrant workers to those who use immigrant services or buy goods produced by immigrant workers"; consumers benefited if low-pay workers did not. Simmering conflicts between blacks, Latinos, and Asians in Los Angeles had been noted before the major race riot broke out there in May 1992. Over 50 people died in the riot, which was precipitated by the acquittal of white policemen accused of beating a black American, although Korean shopkeepers were among those whose property suffered and Latinos constituted a high proportion of those arrested.[6]

Overall the American economy probably gained more than it lost from the return of mass immigration, but the sheer numbers were unnerving. The tidal wave that swept into the country had not been foreseen. It was composed of at least three fairly distinct strands, each of which was growing. There were refugees seeking security in a land that had traditionally wel-comed the oppressed. There were those arriving under regular immigrant visas, making their lives in the United States like so many before them. And there were the "illegals," undocumented aliens who either somehow smug-gled themselves into the country or arrived on legitimate visas and simply outstayed their welcome.

There had been immigration quotas for most of the twentieth century, but they had been manipulated episodically to permit the entry of refugees. While the Soviet Union and the People's Republic of China were mostly able to keep a hold on their populations, the aftermath of the Vietnam War opened new refugee streams. Between 1975 and 1979 presidential parole programs brought 400 000 Vietnamese and other Asians to the United States. As Cubans, Vietnamese, and Cambodians pressed their claims to American asylum, the United States in 1980 passed the Refugee Act, which – in an accommodation to global standards – accepted the general international definition of refugees as those fleeing any country, "because of persecution, or a well-founded fear of persecution." The numbers could be large. During the first year of the act nearly 500 000 were admitted under the new process, and hundreds of thousands of refugees from Vietnam, Cambodia, and Laos followed. In the early 1990s refugees constituted about 15 percent of all immigrants.

Dwarfing the refugee numbers were those thronging into American ports and airports on legitimate immigrant visas. The irony was that in 1965 the United States had tried to rationalize its immigration policy and set an overall limit at about 300 000 a year, with quotas of 170 000 for eastern hemisphere immigrants and 120 000 for western hemisphere. But, critically, the 1965 act had also allowed the immediate relatives of American citizens and permanent residents, notably their spouses and children, entry without limit. It was not widely anticipated that the new law would greatly affect the composition of American society. The "ethnic mix of this country will not be upset," promised one of its sponsors, Senator Edward Kennedy of Massachusetts, who was also confident that "our cities will not be flooded with a million immigrants annually." At the time the total number of immigrants was not particularly high, and the preferences in the 1965 law accorded to the relatives of American residents might be expected to reinforce the existing ethnic makeup of the population. Such complacent expectations were to be rudely shattered. Journalist Theodore White called the 1965 law "noble, revolutionary – and probably the most thoughtless of the many acts of the Great Society," one that "probably changed the future of America." On the one hand, burgeoning population pressures multiplied the numbers clamoring to enter the United States beyond anything anyone had imagined. On the other, once migrants had established permanent residence or citizenship, the preferences accorded to relatives meant that they were able to reel in other family members behind them, and they in turn could reel in yet others seemingly ad infinitum. This multiplier or "pyramiding" effect on the scale that materialized had not been foreseen.

While there were fluctuations, in the later decades of the twentieth century around two-thirds of legal immigrants were admitted on the basis of family ties. Similarly unexpected was the rather abrupt replacement of European migration by that from the Third World, particularly the sheer volume of human beings escaping the poverty of Central and Southern America and the Caribbean. Senator Kennedy reflected in 1988 that there had been two unintended consequences of the 1965 revisions, specifically that a few countries had come to dominate the legal immigration system and that numbers had risen dramatically: "Neither result was intended, and both have occurred because of the emphasis on family connections."[7]

Then there were the large numbers of undocumented or illegal immigrants, which had begun to excite alarm only in the mid-1970s (the phenomenon had hitherto been modest), when the Commissioner of the Immigration and Naturalization Service warned that, "we're facing a vast army that's carrying out a silent invasion of the United States." Most of these were Mexicans dodging the border controls, but there were also large numbers who had entered the country legally, perhaps on tourist visas, and stayed. The number of "apprehensions" of illegal immigrants by the Immigration and Naturalization Service soared to over a million a year in the late 1970s, about three times what it had been at the beginning of the decade, and these presumably were just the tip of the iceberg. The illegal immigrants aroused greater concern than the refugees or legal immigrants, partly because their true numbers could not be known and because, after all, they were illegal, though there were also suspicions that the exposés focused on them owed something to racial prejudice.[8]

The return of mass immigration and what many perceived as its alien nature raised two major questions. One focused on American sovereignty and carried implications about the competence of government. If an attribute of a nation's sovereignty is the control over admission to it, this swelling flood threatened the capacity of the United States to determine both residency and citizenship. Secondly, the nature of the new immigration seemed to threaten a makeover of the American character, wrenching it away from its historic roots. Around four-fifths of the American population in the mid-1980s was of European descent, roughly the reverse of the proportions found among recently arrived immigrants. The new immigration prompted renewed concerns about American identity.

During the course of the 1970s anxieties about immigration increased as the numbers rose, but, as noted in Chapter 1, it was the Marielito crisis that set the alarm bells ringing. Following press reports that Castro was using the opportunity to offload his island's undesirables, public opinion turned against the refugees brought to the United States by the celebrated "freedom flotilla." Public suspicions seemed confirmed when Cuban criminals were involved in a prison riot in Atlanta and when others destroyed a Louisiana immigration center. Like the Carter White House, the succeeding Reagan administration also vacillated between tough and softer stances, Reagan worrying about "what to do with 1000's of Cubans – criminal & the insane that Castro loaded on boats & sent here," though eventually almost all the Marielitos were allowed legal residence. The perception of these immigrants as criminal was reinforced by the 1983 film *Scarface*, which depicted Al Pacino as a Marielito turned drug baron.[9]

The Marielito crisis, played out in television pictures and insistent headlines, had underlined the degree to which the United States no longer controlled its admissions. Further, it was not just people who were being illicitly imported, but crime and disease too, or so it seemed. American vulnerability had been exposed. It hardly helped that the crisis blew up at a time when there were serious worries about the American economy. The Marielitos were not the only refugees, as others were arriving from Vietnam, Haiti, and elsewhere, but they helped to promote the message that such refugees were mostly unskilled and impoverished, would not be easily assimilated, and that there could be no end to their influx. The United States might have been able to take in refugees from Hitler's Third Reich, but could it forever absorb the dispossessed of the Third World?

The incoming tide continued to swell remorselessly in the 1980s, and there was no sign of migration reverting to its traditional channels. By the mid-1980s about 85 percent of immigration was Latin American, Caribbean, Asian, or Middle Eastern in composition, raising questions about how well these strangers could be accommodated in a society without undermining what many saw as its essentially Anglo-European character. Public sentiment was turning against immigration. In 1965 only 33 percent of those surveyed had favored reducing immigration; the figure rose to 42 percent in 1977 and to 49 percent in 1986.[10]

With evidence of the unintended consequences of the 1965 act mounting, in 1978 Congress set up the Select Commission on Immigration and Refugee Policy, a bipartisan body chaired by educationist Father Theodore M. Hesburgh, who struggled to find a humane strategy that nonetheless would allow the United States to "regain control of its borders." Most members of the Commission were basically sympathetic to immigrants. Senator Edward Kennedy, as in 1965, spoke to their interests. At the other pole was Senator Alan Simpson of Wyoming, who was strongly restrictionist, though the two came to agree that the key to effective reform was controlling illegal immigration. The Commission's 1981 report broadly supported continuing the liberal policies of the 1965 act, with its priority of family reunion, while urging stronger border controls and an amnesty to allow those illegals already in the country to regularize their status and in due course qualify for citizenship. Huge numbers would thus be welcomed into the American polity. The Commission was worried that rising sentiment against illegal immigration would spill over into resentment of legal immigration and hoped to draw the poison from the issue. As its director Lawrence Fuchs later explained, "the central strategy was to take xenophobia, race, and even economic conflict out of the debate." While there were aspects of the report that annoyed liberals, notably a proposal for national identity cards, broadly it set a fairly progressive agenda for immigration reform in the new decade. In a sense it was an elitist document, responding less to grassroots resentments and more to the recommendations of scholars and pro-immigrant politicians like Kennedy.[11]

Debate continued as immigrant numbers mounted. The integrity of the American state and the composition of American society were recurrent motifs. "Immigration to the United States is out of control and it is so perceived at all levels of government by the American people – indeed by people all over this world," warned Senator Simpson in 1982. He insisted that "uncontrolled immigration" was "one of the greatest threats to the future" of the United States, one that served to undermine "American values, traditions, institutions, and … our way of life." Senator Lloyd Bentsen of Texas fretted that "we are the only nation that has virtually abdicated control of our borders and is unable to account for millions of aliens – legal and illegal – living, studying, and working in this country." Democrat Lawton Chiles of Florida stressed the need for a policy that would unequivocally put the American government in a "position in which we, not other governments, or the people of other nations, control immigration to this country." Although opinion polls conventionally showed disapproval of the high levels of immigration, for most Americans the issue was not a burning one and it fell to a number of lobbies, local citizens' groups, and individuals to try to mobilize the public. A determined restrictionist movement emerged with the formation of the Federation for American Immigration Reform (FAIR) in 1979, followed by the American Immigration Control Foundation, formed in 1983, and from 1985 the Center for Immigration Studies, a think tank which sought "fewer immigrants but a warmer welcome for those admitted." These pressure groups avoided racist rhetoric, generally arguing that they did not want to end immigration but rather to restrict it to manageable levels, so that American communities would not be overwhelmed, resources depleted, or wages undercut. But, vocal as they were, they faced an uphill task. There were already well-entrenched interests, such as agricultural employers and Hispanic groups, with good access to Congress and ready to resist every proposal for reform. The major party leaders were not eager to tangle in an issue that might lose them votes, and it was these interests that tended to prevail, to the exasperation of the new restrictionist bodies.[12]

The Reagan administration gave the Hesburgh report little attention. But it did fret over the civil wars and political unrest in Central America and the large numbers of refugees making for the US border. While it continued to admit large numbers of Cuban refugees, it was less friendly toward those peoples fleeing right-wing or other authoritarian regimes, notably Salvadorans and Haitians. When a number of religious groups formed the Sanctuary movement to aid refugees from Central America, particularly from El Salvador, it was harassed by the federal authorities for operating this "new underground railroad." But even refugees from communism represented dangers to American well-being, it seemed, and Reagan himself advanced a doctrine of pre-emptive intervention to avert unwanted asylum seekers. Urging Congress to supply more aid to the Nicaraguan Contras, who were fighting against a left-wing government, he argued: "If we allow Central America to be turned into a string of anti-American dictatorships the result would be a tidal wave of refugees – and this time they'll be "feet people" and not "boat people" – swarming into our country seeking safe haven from communist repression to the south." Conservative Republican Senator Jesse Helms also worried about the "havoc" caused by Soviet expansion in Central America, adding that to accept those fleeing as refugees would be to bail out communist regimes.[13]

The White House set up a Task Force on Immigration and Refugee Policy, but the cabinet members on it increasingly sent their deputies or even their "deputy's deputies" to its meetings. Its eventual proposals to the cabinet included a conditional amnesty for illegal immigrants who had long been residents, and, as Hesburgh had urged, a national identification card to allow illegal aliens to be distinguished from authentic residents. When a skeptical aide suggested that it would be cheaper to tattoo an identification number on everyone's arm, evoking the image of Nazi concentration camps, Interior Secretary James Watt trumped him with a biblical reference, denouncing the scheme as "the mark of the Beast." Reagan closed the discussion with the joke that "Maybe we should just brand all the babies." Eventually the administration did formulate some half-hearted proposals that Congress ignored. In 1984 the president repeated a now familiar refrain when he worried that "we have lost control of our own borders." By the mid-1980s there were estimated to be between three and five million illegal aliens in the United States, and they were variously accused of undercutting American labor, burdening welfare programs, and smuggling in drugs. One congressman charged that aliens were "preying on our schoolchildren by stealing their lunch money."[14]

With the Reagan administration for the most part indifferent to the problem of immigration, but anti-immigration lobbies becoming more active, it fell to members of Congress to take up the cause. Not that party leaders were especially keen to embrace it. House Speaker Tip O'Neill tended to use his influence to delay or block proposals, on one occasion claiming that reform had "no constituency." In the Senate Alan Simpson spearheaded a bill modeled on the Hesburgh Commission's report and personally emphasized the need for cultural homogeneity, arguing that a "substantial proportion" of recent immigrants did not "assimilate satisfactorily into our country." This and other proposals were shunted around Congress for years, as opposing lobbies ambushed one another. Business groups feared they were being expected to enforce the immigration laws and Hispanic groups feared foreigners would be discriminated against in seeking jobs. Labor unions were divided, some welcoming the prospect of less immigrant competition, others uneasy about the impact of the amnesty for illegals. Arguably the new immigration did something to encourage US citizens to emphasize their common identity. The 1970s-style cherishment of ethnicity had passed; a poll conducted by the Roper Organization in 1986 found that instead of thinking of themselves as Irish Americans or Polish Americans or whatever, 86 percent said they were "just American."[15]

As Congress failed to act decisively, the voices railing against the foreign invasion became more strident. In 1985 the former governor of Colorado, Richard Lamm, with his co-author Gary Imhoff, published *The Immigration Time Bomb: The Fragmenting of America*. This assailed uncontrolled immigration for undermining American cultural identity and for intensifying social problems, not least crime (for which the Marielitos served as a prime example). Others too were increasingly uneasy about the cultural implications. The Hispanic population was the fastest growing group in the United States. "The United States is a nation without meaningful borders," said columnist Carl Rowan: "So many Mexicans are crossing U.S. borders illegally that Mexicans are reclaiming Texas, California, and other territories that they claim the Gringos stole from them." The Center for Immigration Studies reported projections that indicated that the California workforce could consist largely of immigrants and their descendants by 2010, and pointed out that they would be "mostly nonwhite" workers who would be supporting "mostly white pensioners with their payroll contributions."[16] The sheer size of this population, together with its high birth rate and the incessant arrival of yet more, created visions of the Hispanic reconquest of a region that had once belonged to Mexico. The birth rate of the American-born population had been dropping since the 1960s and in the 1970s it fell below replacement level, while the millions of new immigrants, together with the children they begat, had become a major source of population growth. Some seemed darkly to suspect that the fecundity of Latino migrants was part of a strategy to overwhelm the Anglo majority. "Perhaps this is the first instance in which those with their pants up are going to get caught by those with their pants down?," complained FAIR's John Tanton.[17]

The various bodies calling for tighter controls were resisted by lobbies sympathetic to immigrants, among them Mexican American and Latino groups, civil liberties organizations, cultural radicals, and especially agricultural employers. *The Immigration Time Bomb* complained of the obstructive power in Congress of an "unlikely coalition of the far right and the far left, fueled by a coalition of big business and Hispanic pressure groups."[18]

The debate in Congress focused primarily on the problem of illegal immigrants, although it was difficult to envisage life without them. "Throughout the Southwest, and to a lesser extent in such Northern cities as New York and Chicago, illegal aliens have become an integral part of the economic fabric," observed one newsman: "They bus tables and wash dishes in restaurants, work in foundaries, empty bedpans in hospitals, mow lawns, clean houses and make shoes in Los Angeles." A rational response was to legalize them. Finally a bill became law in 1986, the year that marked the hundredth anniversary of the Statue of Liberty. As one of its supporters put it, "Everyone wanted a bill." By "everyone," he had his fellow legislators in mind, exhausted by the lobbying of the special interest groups who had a major role in fashioning policy in an area largely abdicated by the party leaderships. The president too was ready to acquiesce, indicating his willingness to sign the bill that he saw as Senator Simpson's: "It's high time we regained control of our borders & his bill will do this."[19]

Given the "turn against immigration" the Simpson–Rodino Act of 1986 was surprisingly liberal. The restrictionists had helped raise the salience of the issue, but the pro-immigrant groups were able to ensure that the new act was one they could live with. It was primarily an attempt to stem the tide of illegal aliens. The "front door" could be opened more widely once the "back door" had been closed. A major provision offered amnesty to illegal immigrants who had arrived before 1982 and been in continuous residence since. The "shadow society" of illegal aliens living in poverty and subject to exploitation were thus given a route to permanent legitimate residence and ultimately perhaps to citizenship. The quid pro quo was a provision that for the first time made it an offense knowingly to employ undocumented aliens, and employers faced fines or even imprisonment for disregarding the law. Agricultural and other business lobbies disliked this provision, though the most vigorous opponents in Congress were Hispanic members who feared that employers would not hire foreign workers. While this provision garnered a lot of publicity and gave the act an aura of toughness, in reality the enforcement procedure was weak. To win the votes of legislators representing farm interests primarily in the western states there was also a controversial provision to make it easier for growers to import agricultural workers as temporary residents. In Congress, both Republicans and Democrats were divided on the bill, although it won somewhat greater support from Democrats. There was unease among Republicans both about the extra responsibilities placed on business and about the poverty of the immigrants admitted, which could mean a drain on public aid. Many restrictionists were unhappy with the final bill. "We wanted a Cadillac, we were promised a Chevy, and we got a wreck," complained the head of FAIR.[20]

The amnesty provision recognized reality, although, as critics pointed out, once legalized immigrants would be able to bring in other family members after them. Eventually over three million aliens were accepted into the amnesty program, most of them Mexicans. It was assumed that this would be a one-off measure, since with better border security and strong penalties for employing illegal immigrants the problem would not recur. In this the act was a hopeless failure, for the numbers were mounting again by the 1990s. While chain-link fences and eventually a 14-foot ditch were among the obstacles intended to stop the flow of illegals across 2000-plus miles of the Mexican border, they had little effect. Ten years after passage of the act the Immigration and Naturalization Service estimated that there were as many as five million undocumented aliens in the country and that 275 000 more were arriving each year. They chanced detection and deportation because they could after all find work in an expanding American economy – as farm laborers, domestics, and the other menial jobs that citizens often spurned. Sometimes employers were fined for hiring aliens without proper papers, but these were the exceptions that proved the rule that the authorities were willing to tolerate the supply of Third World workers whose illegal status rendered them disinclined to make trouble.

The 1986 act also did nothing to curb legal immigration, with its inbuilt "pyramiding" effect.

If the restrictionists had failed to erect effective barriers against the alien invasion, they could at least hope that the newcomers might be Americanized. This was the aim of some groups that feared that the traditional Anglo-American culture was being undermined. "Our language embodies every-thing we believe, every aspect of our concepts and our culture. English is the glue," Lamm and Imhoff concluded in their *cri de coeur*: "It holds our people together; it is our shared bond." They envisaged a diminished stream of immigrants successfully Americanized through learning the English lan-guage. Others were already thinking the same, and a vigorous movement developed to make English the official language of the United States. In April 1981 Senator S.I. Hayakawa, a conservative Republican from California, introduced into Congress a constitutional amendment to this effect. The amendment would have changed little, since English was the normal language of official discourse (although voting ballots and the like were bilingual where needed) and immigrant groups over time had always adapted to it, but the proposal precipitated considerable controversy. One supporter, Kentucky Senator Walter Huddleston, insisted that the common language was the key to the nation's success as a "melting pot," that it had "allowed us to develop a stable and cohesive society that is the envy of many fractured ones," but that in recent years immigrants had been refusing to learn it and were threatening to turn the country into "another Tower of Babel."[21]

Among Hayakawa and Huddleston's targets were the bilingual programs that had been introduced into American schooling since the late 1960s to assist non-English-speaking pupils. Initially seen as a way of assimilating immigrant children, affirmative action pressures had multiplied bilingual programs throughout the country, and by 1980 they were being conducted in 80 different languages. What had begun as a modest remedial program seemed to some to have spiraled out of control, transformed into a mon-strously expensive device for perpetuating cultural differences. Often poorly taught in their own language, critics claimed, many children never learned English. Irksome to many conservatives too were laws mandating multilingual ballots and voting materials. Such devices, it was held, served to deepen rather than bridge ethnic divides.

In 1983, after retirement from the Senate, Hayakawa, along with John Tanton of FAIR, founded U.S. English as a lobbying organization "In Defense of Our Common Language." Hayakawa himself took particular exception to what he saw as the aggressive claims of Hispanic groups, some of whose spokespersons on occasion insisted that all American children should be taught Spanish as well as English. "One official language and one only," was his cry, "so that we can unite as a nation." Conservative columnist William F. Buckley, Jr. agreed on the need to quell the separatism of the "militant Spanish-speaking minority." Richard Lamm told a congressional committee in 1986: "We should be color blind but not linguistically deaf. We should be a rainbow but not a cacophony." In that year U.S. English claimed 200 000 members; by 1988 it boasted 400 000. Some critics espied a racist intent in the Official English movement, and while Hayakawa's amendment was regularly presented, a wary Congress never passed it.[22]

But the cause did take off in several states. One group in 1986 warned: "Hispanics in America today represent a very dangerous, subversive force that is bent on taking over our nation's political institutions for the purpose of imposing Spanish as the official language of the United States." The Virginia legislature had declared English the state's official language in 1981, and Indiana, Kentucky, and Tennessee followed suit in 1984. That year California voters approved Proposition 38, sponsored by members of U.S. English, demanding that voting materials should be in English only, in defiance of the provisions of the federal Voting Rights Act. In 1986 some 73 percent of voters approved Proposition 63 making English the state's official language, and making it possible to sue state or local governmental bodies if they failed to comply. Nonetheless California officials did not dismantle minority-language services. Elsewhere the cause was gaining momentum by the mid-1980s. In 1986 Larry Pratt, president of Gun Owners of America, founded a new hard-line lobby, English First, and in 1987 five state legislatures adopted Official English. In the following year voters added Official English amendments to their state constitutions in Arizona, Colorado, and Florida, and in 1990 Alabama voters adopted English as their official language. Passage of measures was sometimes followed by reports of anti-Hispanic incidents, such as employees being sacked for not speaking English. "I ♥ English" bumper stickers appeared in Florida. Most official language provisions were more symbolic than coercive. It was one thing for a state to make English its "official" language much in the way that it might designate a state flower; it was quite another for it to pursue an "English only" policy, which could threaten bilingual education and other multi- and bilingual services.[23]

Some states turned back the demands of the Official English groups, and U.S. English itself was rocked in 1988 when a private memorandum written by Tanton surfaced imputing corruption and political apathy to Latin American immigrants. It also subsequently transpired that he believed that population and immigration control might be achieved through forced sterilization. A number of the group's prominent sponsors resigned, as did Tanton himself. By this date opponents of Official English were themselves organizing a lobby. In 1987 they formed the English-Plus Information Clearing-house (EPIC) in Washington, supported by a range of ethnic, educational, and civil liberties groups, which generally sought to promote educational policies which would help all residents master English while protecting other languages and maintaining multilingual public services. Part of EPIC's concern was the need to expose students to the outside world, to enable them to function properly in a globalized society. New Mexico, Washington state, Michigan, and Oregon endorsed English Plus policies at the end of the decade.[24]

* * *

Divisions over Official English tended to reflect the same forces as the immigration debate. While some kind of support for immigration restriction and Official English could be found throughout American society, it tended to be stronger at lower income levels and among trade unionists, and attracted too those concerned with preserving the national culture. Conversely, opponents of such policies were found in much of the business community, and among civil libertarian and ethnic associations. The relative if largely symbolic success of the Official English campaign at state level served to obscure the extent to which the formulation and enforcement of immigration policy in the 1980s reflected the strength of those interests that aligned themselves with immigrants.

The return of mass immigration had further undermined any wistful hope that Americans might maintain a decorous distance from the rest of humankind. People as well as goods and capital were pouring into the country. Attempts to stem the flow and to impose a measure of cultural conformity on the new arrivals were for the most part unsuccessful. Immigration policy was fashioned more by pressure groups and interested elites than by public opinion or by party leaders, and largely symbolic measures, such as the penalties loudly threatened but not enforced against businesses employing illegal immigrants, were used to assuage the fears of those who complained that the United States had lost control of its borders. There were indirect political repercussions. Immigrants came to form a significant part of the low wage-earning groups, but many of them were not qualified to vote or chose not to do so, weakening the pressures on politicians for progressive policies. By the end of the 1980s demands for reforming immigration policy were mounting again, when a public uneasy about the rising numbers found itself confronted by energetic lobbies calling for further liberalization. With Cold War anxieties disappearing and renewed concerns being expressed about the state of the American economy and its capacity to compete internationally, business lobbies and financial journalists were urging the necessity of improving the supply of skilled workers, and if education could not do the job, perhaps the immigration laws could be refashioned to poach the brains and skills of other countries. Eventually the immigration act of 1990, although limited by the usual need to compromise, did allow for the entry of larger numbers of workers with the skills needed by the American economy. The unexpected reappearance of mass immigration since the 1970s had increased the ethnic diversification of American society, had multiplied connections with the wider world, and had generated debates about what it meant to be American. The sponsors of the new immigration act hoped that it would help the United States to survive and prosper in an age of globalization.

Chapter 4

Glad Morning Again: A Reagan Revolution?

Ronald Reagan, it has been said, was an ordinary Joe who got to be president. Frances Fitzgerald called him the "American Everyman," and like other authors compared him to the character played by James Stewart in the film *Mr Smith Goes to Washington*, the homely, idealistic if somewhat naïve small-town American who confronted the corruption in the US Senate. Reagan at 69 was the oldest man ever to be elected president, but he was physically energetic and impressively fit, and his thick head of hair retained its brown-red sheen, although he was occasionally suspected of dozing off when policy details were discussed. "I have left orders to be awakened in case of a national emergency," he riposted, "even if I'm in a Cabinet meeting." His amiability served him well with the press and the public, yet he was only truly close to his wife Nancy. A surprisingly large number of his aides were to publish memoirs of their experiences, not all of them friendly, an attitude which seemed to reflect in part the distance this genial man kept from them, leaving them the sense that they were simply hired hands. It was ideas that were important to Reagan, not people, even if his ideological crusade did not seem to be driven by intellectual curiosity. But intelligent, assured, and temperamentally buoyant, he knew how to project himself and his ideas, a process helped by the narrow range of his personal agenda.

Reagan's biographer Lou Cannon used the phrase the "citizen-politician," as he did himself: "I was a citizen-politician," he observed in his Farewell Address, "and it seemed the right thing for a citizen to do." If so, he had been a citizen-politician for over 30 years before he was elected president,

Contemporary America: Power, Dependency, and Globalization since 1980,
First Edition. M.J. Heale.
© 2011 M.J. Heale. Published 2011 by Blackwell Publishing Ltd.

ever since his emergence as an activist in the Screen Actors Guild in the mid-1940s. But if this was a role consciously adopted for a political career, it was a persona he could comfortably inhabit. "We Republicans have to show people we're not the party of big business and the country-club set," he said during the 1980 campaign: "We're the party of Main Street, the small town, the city neighborhood; the shopkeeper, the farmer, the cop on the beat, the blue-collar and the white-collar worker." Reagan aligned himself smoothly with the populistic impulses in American political culture. His lower middle-class origins were authentic enough, and he reflected that his small-town boyhood gave him "the standards and values that would guide me for the rest of my life." The Hollywood roles that he was assigned were not suave sophisticates but the boy-next-door, and he himself hankered – mostly in vain – for parts in western pictures. He never played a character who was not American. For Reagan, the United States was "a beacon of hope, a shining city," assigned a providential mission to uphold and extend "the sacred fire of human liberty." This vision, rooted in the origins of the American experiment, presumed that America was exceptional, and that all that was needed, as Reagan said in his First Inaugural, was "to renew ourselves here in our own land." In this scenario, there was little to be gained by looking abroad. Americans had to look within, to their own traditions, their own willpower.[1]

* * *

There was an aspect of Ronald Reagan's mentality that seemed to reflect the optimism of a more confident age. By the 1980s many Americans had come to lose faith in the science and technology that had spearheaded the remarkable growth of the mid-twentieth century. Economists of the 1960s had boasted of their capacity to "fine-tune" the economy; scientists had assured their contemporaries that they could send Americans to the moon and back. The economic shoals that the country had experienced in the following decade had contributed mightily to a loss of confidence in the experts. But Reagan at least retained a belief that his economic prescriptions would deliver, as he almost alone was also confident that scientists would deliver his cherished goal of a "space umbrella," the Strategic Defense Initiative. As Garry Wills noted, he was "the first truly cheerful conservative." Conservatives had tended to be pessimists, distrustful of human nature. Reagan, however, took an optimistic view of humankind, and the alliance of his conservative principles with a conviction in the essential goodness of human nature helps to explain his extraordinary appeal. "One of my dreams," he said in 1983, "is to help Americans rise above pessimism by renewing their belief in themselves."[2]

Through his years as an actor Reagan had only once left the United States, when he briefly made a film in Britain. His press secretary often heard him say: "I long for the days when the President never left the continental United States, when it was traditional that he never travelled abroad." While far from uncommon in his generation, Reagan's formative influences were exclusively American; there was something parochial in his makeup. In an era when professional Washington politicians were held in unusually low regard, such attributes served him well.[3]

Reagan's campaign for the presidency had reflected these characteristics. Although once an FBI fink who had told stories to federal investigators about his leftist colleagues in Hollywood, Reagan did not attribute American problems to fell foreign influences or to factors beyond the control of Americans themselves. As an opposition candidate it was natural enough to find fault with the current administration; if the causes of the nation's ills were internal, then government could do something about them. Reagan was convinced that the solution lay largely in the hands of government, even if it consisted of government divesting itself of the responsibilities it had accumulated over the years. Reagan did not promise more government, rather the reverse, but he did promise action. In his speech announcing his candidacy he rejected the notion that the United States was in decline: "If there is one thing we are sure of it is that history need not be relived; that nothing is impossible, and that man is capable of improving his circumstances beyond what we are told is fact." The outside world was largely irrelevant to Reagan's agenda.[4]

Of course, it was not wholly irrelevant. Reagan was highly critical of détente. He harked back to an earlier Cold War position in insisting that there was no alternative to maintaining the military strength of the United States and to treating the Soviet Union as its mortal enemy. "The ideological struggle dividing the world is between communism and our own belief in freedom to the greatest extent possible consistent with an orderly society," he said in a radio address in 1978, concluding: "Détente – isn't that what a farmer has with his turkey – until thanksgiving day?" Reagan was not going to flinch from confrontation with the Soviet Union, but his primary strategy was to build up US military might (a commitment that fortuitously advantaged the growing Republican constituencies in the South and the West). This was a unilateralist vision – it would be nice to have allies, but they did not figure particularly large in Reagan's thinking.[5]

The restoration of American self-reliance was also central to Reagan's plans for the economy, the mismanagement of which by the Democrats had been the dominant issue of his recent campaign. The solution was simple: "The key to restoring the health of the economy lies in cutting taxes." Sophisticates sometimes dismissed Reagan as simplistic, but in broad policy terms it was clear what he stood for: a strengthened defense, lower taxes, reduced government, and less federal regulation. His range of interests was narrow, and Reagan paid little attention to detail or to policy areas unconnected with these objectives. One congressional ally discovered that Reagan was "a very quick study," adding: "A lazy man, but still very bright."[6]

Yet those who followed Reagan's campaigns knew what he wanted. More than most presidents, he was an ideologue. "As much as anyone I have known," said his long-time associate Mike Deaver, "Reagan attaches himself to a cause rather than people." Over 30 American Enterprise Institute fellows were recruited to the new administration, and the ready access of the conservative think tanks to the White House meant that, in Sidney Blumenthal's phrase, Reagan's victory "was the victory of an ideological elite." Reagan's appointees knew that they had to adhere to the conservative views of the president, which at least gave his administration a measure of coherence.[7]

Reagan's cabinet appointments revealed the extent to which he prioritized values. For the most part he selected conservatives who were committed to his policy agenda, rather than, say, representatives from different parts of the Republican Party. His cabinet and White House appointments also reflected his inner confidence. He had no hesitation in surrounding himself with powerful personalities, whether Al Haig as Secretary of State, Caspar Weinberger as Secretary of Defense, Don Regan as Secretary of the Treasury, Jim Baker as Chief of Staff and later as Secretary of the Treasury, or William Casey as Director of the CIA. Some of these, such as Baker, were pragmatic rather than ideological conservatives, fortunately for the running of the White House. This conservative near-consensus had to substitute for clarity in decision making. Don Regan dubbed the early Reagan years "The Guesswork Presidency." "The President seemed to believe that his public statements were all the guidance his private advisers needed," he explained. This did not always make for harmonious counsels, and in time the administration became notorious for its internal chaos, which was to be exacerbated in Reagan's second term, but Reagan himself rose serenely above the infighting of his subordinates.[8]

Reagan's self-confidence was to serve him well. Political scientists might bewail the fragmented character of American politics, but Reagan's remarkable persona provided Americans with at least an appearance of leadership. He could not be sure of controlling Congress, where the Democrats held handsome majorities in the lower house throughout his presidency, but when his popularity was riding high he could use it to gain his political objectives. In his first term in particular he was well served by his closest aides, with the skilled political operator Jim Baker as Chief of Staff, an old Californian associate Ed Meese as counselor to the president and keeper of the conservative flame, and Michael Deaver, the deputy chief of staff who handled the media. Between them they somehow overcame the decision-making confusion with which the administration was beset. In addition to this "troika," there was the young David Stockman as Budget Director. Democratic chieftain and House Speaker Tip O'Neill said of this group that "they knew where they were going and they knew how to get there," adding that in 1981 at least they were "probably the best-run political operating unit I've ever seen." Reagan also showed himself to be a fairly flexible conservative – a "pragmatic ideologue" – sometimes prepared to accept half a loaf rather than none. The conservative agenda could also be furthered in ways that did not involve legislation. Conservatives could be appointed to federal agencies and the courts, programs disliked by the right could be starved of funds, and bureaucratic rules could be rewritten to reflect the values of the White House.[9]

Once elected, Reagan was swift to take action. With the election won, the economy came first. "We ought to have three goals," said Jim Baker, "and all three of them are economic recovery." Reagan himself reflected: "If we get the economy in shape, we're going to be able to do a lot of things. If we don't, we're not going to be able to do anything." The greater part of Reagan's Inaugural Address, which he wrote himself, was devoted to the need to restore a "dynamic economy," and he equated "our present troubles" with the "intervention and intrusion in our lives that result from unnecessary and excessive growth of government." His very first official act was to sign a freeze on the hiring of federal employees. After the woes of the 1970s, the Reagan administration was promising sustained economic growth, and this would be secured by freeing up market forces. David Stockman even wanted Reagan to declare "a national economic emergency" soon after his inauguration to ram through a shock program that would transform the political culture.[10]

Reagan did not do that, but just four brief weeks into his presidency he presented his historic paper to Congress, *America's New Beginning: A Program for Economic Recovery*. It contained four key elements: cutting the rate of growth in federal spending, with a view to reaching a balanced budget within a few years; slashing personal income tax rates by a stunning 30 percent over three years; deregulation to liberate business; and, in conjunction with the Federal Reserve Board, a strict anti-inflationary monetary policy. "We're in control here," he insisted: "There's nothing wrong with America that together we can't fix." This daring combination of policies became known as "Reaganomics." In no other area of domestic policy would the Reagan presidency have such a far-reaching impact, undoing the conventional wisdom of the previous generation. It decisively pointed a direction for the Reagan administration, and in securing the passage of its main elements by a suspicious Congress Reagan demonstrated his mastery of the political process – in 1981.[11]

Fate intervened to strengthen Reagan's political hand less than six weeks after his economic plan had been unveiled. On March 30, 1981, outside the Washington Hilton hotel, a disturbed young man, John W. Hinckley, opened fire on the presidential party, permanently disabling Press Secretary James Brady. Reagan himself was hit and was rushed to hospital where emergency procedure saved his life. The seriousness of the president's condition was not revealed to the public, which instead was treated to his insouciant response. "Honey, I forgot to duck," he told his wife, invoking a line of heavyweight boxer Gene Tunney when he once lost a championship fight, and while in his hospital bed he repeated an old W.C. Fields gag: "All in all, I'd rather be in Philadelphia." Chroniclers have speculated on the psychological impact on Reagan of this near brush with death – that, for example, the experience encouraged him to adhere more closely to his own firmly held beliefs or that it contributed to his determination to make peace with the Soviet Union. The immediate political effect was dramatic. Reagan's standing in the polls had been a modest 59 percent two weeks earlier; after the assassination attempt it soared to 77 percent. "This is a long-term plus for Reagan," reflected the Democratic congressman Morris Udall: "There is an aura there that wasn't there before." Just four weeks after the shooting, while still recovering, Reagan made his first public appearance – a televised address on behalf of his economic program before a joint session of Congress, which greeted him exuberantly. Steering the tax cut and the budget through Congress remained a complicated process, but Reagan's newfound popularity undoubtedly eased it. By June 1981 polls indicated broad public support for Reagan's handling of the economy.[12]

Reaganomics represented a clear repudiation of Keynesianism. Market incentives rather than government manipulation of demand, the argument went, were most likely to raise productivity and increase supply, that is to say production. This was the solution to the stagflation of the 1970s. By the time Reagan took office there was widespread support for some revamping of the tax system, the spiraling inflation having greatly added to the tax burden experienced by many families. In 1978 a celebrated "taxpayers' revolt" in California decisively approved Proposition 13, which drastically cut the state property tax and ignited similar movements in other states. Two leading Republicans, Representative Jack Kemp and Senator William Roth, had been advocating a large reduction in federal income taxes since 1977, influenced by the ideas of economist William Laffer, whose celebrated Laffer Curve showed that tax revenues disappeared as the tax rate approached either zero or 100 percent. Reduce the tax rate, it was concluded, and people would work harder and save more, business would be reinvigorated, and ultimately more tax revenues would flow in. "Frankly, it is my belief that at lower, more efficient rates of taxation we'll get more revenue," Jack Kemp said in 1980. Critical to supply-side thinking was the undoubted need to increase productivity, and incentives to work and invest were the means to achieve this. While the serious supply-siders were careful not to claim that a whopping tax cut could be rapidly self-financing, the theory possessed seductive qualities. The most vital federal expenditures, such as on defense, could remain untouched. With the economy deteriorating in the late 1970s, the Kemp–Roth formula became the favored economic strategy of the Republican leadership, and journalist Jude Wanniski of the *Wall Street Journal* enthusiastically promised that the Republicans would be "reborn as a party of economic growth."[13]

The president himself did not need much convincing. In 1976 he had published an article entitled "Tax Cuts and Increased Revenue," citing precedents for this happy equation in the administrations of Warren G. Harding and John F. Kennedy, and in July 1981 he again invoked the Kennedy precedent, suggesting that "our kind of tax cut will so stimulate our economy that we will actually increase government revenue." There were mainstream economists who agreed that the tax system did militate against investment, although supply-side theory, at least in its most unqualified form, had only a limited following among professional economists. Nonetheless a group of devoted supply-siders won access to the White House, and while their views were not uncontested even there, the president was drawn to a strategy that seemed to offer a relatively painless solution to the country's ills. The highest marginal federal income tax rate was actually 70 percent, and Reagan himself had once paid tax at the 90 percent wartime rate. In his Budget Director's words, on hearing of the Laffer Curve he "knew instantly that it was true and would never doubt it a moment thereafter." Not all of Reagan's advisers possessed the same faith in the Kemp–Roth formula as a miracle cure, but it offered a route to cutting back on welfare and other government expenditures and allowing market forces freer rein. "Pray God it works," one Republican reportedly muttered: "If this economic plan doesn't jell, where are we going to get the money for anything?"[14]

In fact Budget Director Stockman grew increasingly skeptical about supply-side theory as he wrestled to reduce government spending, and he came to recognize that the numbers did not add up. Too much of it, notably Social Security and defense, had to be shielded from cuts. "He joined the administration with the enthusiasm of a young puppy," recalled a colleague of the young Stockman, "eager and urgent, bounding and leaping through the federal budget with wild-eyed fashion." But where Reagan himself was primarily interested in the tax cut, Stockman's target was the array of governmental programs that had burgeoned since the New Deal – the "federal dragon" – and that he believed had been captured by interest groups. With the use of optimistic forecasts about economic growth – the "Rosy Scenario" – and with an unrivaled mastery of the complex budgetary process, Stockman put together a bill that seemed to give Reagan what he wanted. Stockman was unable to make the sweeping cuts in domestic programs he yearned for, but he privately hoped that these would follow when an alarming budget deficit became "a powerful battering ram" and "force[d] Congress to shrink the welfare state." But Congress would not prove so obliging – and Stockman also found his cabinet allies digging in their heels when he tried to pare their departmental funds and his White House colleagues shrinking from strategies that imperiled electoral support.[15]

The budget bill that eventually passed Congress was a political victory for the administration. Since the 1960s forms of social welfare spending had increased dramatically, and to Stockman the federal budget had become a "'coast-to-coast soup line' that dispenses remedial aid with almost reckless abandon." While the spending cuts were much less than what he had initially anticipated, AFDC (welfare) rolls, food stamps, and other relief programs were cut back significantly. Journalist William Greider figured they were "the biggest package of budget reductions in the history of the republic." But to Stockman's disgust there were White House capitulations to special interests too and he was obliged to make more resources available for defense, a Reagan priority. In May the House of Representatives passed the budget with the help of "boll weevil Democrats," southern conservatives who for the moment were prepared to throw in their lot with the popular president. "I'm getting the shit whaled out of me," admitted the Democrats' congressional chieftain, Tip O'Neill.[16]

On the separate tax bill Reagan reluctantly agreed to reduce his 30 percent tax cut goal to 25 percent, but the resulting act nonetheless secured the largest federal income tax cut in American history. It also indexed tax brackets (thus eliminating the hated "bracket creep" whereby incomes raised to match inflation were relentlessly pushed into higher brackets), improved depreciation allowances for business, and provided for the creation of Individual Retirement Accounts, which, with the prospect of tax benefits, led to the mushrooming of so-called 401(k) savings plans and wider share ownership. The accelerated depreciation allowance reflected the influence of the business lobby – the "hogs were really feeding," said Stockman. But of the elements of his economic plan, it was the income tax cut that was closest to the president's heart. Secure that, he seemed to believe, and the remaining components of the Reagan Revolution would somehow fall into place. "My faith was in those tax reforms," Reagan was to explain in his memoirs, "and I believed we could have a balanced budget within two or three years – by 1984 at the latest." David Stockman knew better – the tax cut and the tightening budget, remarkable political victories though they were, were not going to make the deficit go away.[17]

How far the massive tax cut was designed in turn to force spending cuts – to "defund" the welfare state – has been a matter of controversy. "Starving the beast" could be a means of shrinking big government. Stockman himself seemed genuinely to be searching for ways of moving the budget toward balance, though he evidently hoped that the prospect of high budget deficits would have a sobering effect on other office holders. "The Reagan Revolution, as I had defined it, required a frontal assault on the American welfare state," he explained in his memoir: "That was the only way to pay for the massive Kemp–Roth tax cut." Reagan himself, in a major speech to the nation in February 1981 explaining the need to prioritize cutting taxes before cutting federal spending, mused on the analogy of curing children's extravagance "by reducing their allowance." Fed chief Paul Volcker later sardonically commented on the novel idea that "the way to keep spending down was not by insisting taxes be adequate to pay for it but by scaring the Congress and the American people with deficits." But the budget deficits continued to prey on Reagan's mind, even if his other priorities prevented him doing much about them, and defunding the welfare state was probably less a deliberate strategy than a side effect of Reagan's policies. As long as the deficit remained, new social programs could not be seriously contemplated. Conservatives could be relieved at the outcome, a Cato Institute analysis in 1991 finding that "one of the central budgetary achievements of the Reagan years was to halt the creation of new domestic spending programs."[18]

The 1981 tax cut became the abiding symbol of Reaganism, even a turning point in American political history, for later Republicans made tax cutting the raison d'être of their party. But the Reagan administration was soon obliged to seek ways to plug tax loopholes and even conjure certain tax increases as the budget deficit yawned, including large increases in 1982. Though Reagan sometimes contemplated temporary ad hoc measures, he was not prepared to retreat on his dramatic income tax cut. "I think it's time for you and me and the American people to stand together and tell the Congress," he said to a business group on one occasion, "'No, you may not touch our tax cut.'" The deficit, however, ensured that the federal budget would be a central issue in American politics for years to come. "Put plainly, under Ronald Reagan, big government became a bargain," said Senator Pat Moynihan sarcastically: "For seventy-five cents worth of taxes, you got one dollar's worth of return." One legacy of the accumulating debts, Stockman later remarked, was an appalling financial position "and a political system that became so impaired, damaged, fatigued, and bloodied by coping with it year after year that it now functions like the parliament of a banana republic."[19]

Reagan's political ascendancy was confirmed in the summer of 1981 by his handling of the air controllers' strike. Government employees were forbidden by law to participate in strikes against the public safety, and the air traffic controllers had formally accepted that when they took their jobs. They were skilled middle-class employees, represented by the Professional Air Traffic Controllers Organization, which had actually backed Reagan in the 1980 campaign. As a former union president, indeed one who had led a strike, Reagan emphasized that he respected the right of workers in the private sector to strike, but that government could not tolerate serious disruption of vital public services. A mere seven months into his presidency, Reagan made a stand. He gave the strikers 48 hours to return to work, and any that failed to do so, as he crisply put it, "They're terminated." And so his position adamantly remained. Reagan summarily fired the strikers, imposed a lifetime employment ban on them, and used supervisors and military personnel to keep the planes flying. Public opinion supported the president's decisive action, some 71 percent backing him in one poll. The *Washington Post*'s David Broder expressed a widely held perception: "The message is getting around: Don't mess with this guy." Even the Soviet leaders took note – they were struck by a photo of the strikers' leader being led away to jail in handcuffs. The union was wrecked and

Reagan's message was unmistakable. He won the public relations battle, and other employers felt encouraged to use similar tactics. Fed chief Paul Volcker was reported as believing that "the most important single action of the administration in helping the anti-inflation fight was defeating the air traffic controllers' strike." Some years later a British observer in Washington remarked: "I've asked so many leading European financiers when and why they started pumping money into this country, and they all said the same thing: when Reagan broke the controllers' strike." Reagan was at the height of his authority in August 1981, and his action reverberated down the years.[20]

Nonetheless during that year the administration did experience a major setback. The Social Security system had been heading for serious financial trouble, and a report of 1980 had predicted that the trust fund for old-age insurance would be exhausted imminently. Conditioned by Stockman's budget-cutting drive, the administration submitted a plan to reduce Social Security costs by a mammoth $45 billion, including sweeping benefit cuts for those taking early retirement (nearly two-thirds were doing so.) This proposal, admitted a White House aide, became "the broken vial of poison in the proposal." During a ferocious political firestorm the Democrats represented the plan as "a breach of contract" with the American people and the Republicans as the party that was out to "cut your social security benefits," at a time when they were giving big tax breaks to the rich. "They were absolutely taken to the cleaners," recalled one Democratic aide: "It was after that when the 'fairness' question became serious." The White House was forced into an embarrassing retreat, and in December 1981 Reagan, as a means of depoliticizing the issue, appointed a National Commission on Social Security Reform. The relatively poor showing of Republican candidates in the mid-term elections of 1982 was attributed in part to the success of the Democrats in pinning the label of unfairness on the administration. One Democratic advert declared: "It's not fair, it's Republican." Eventually, in 1983, after members of both parties held secret meetings to thrash out a bipartisan solution, Congress agreed to a package of Social Security amendments that restored the system's viability (partly by raising both the payroll tax and, in the distant future, the normal retirement age). Reagan obligingly signed the act, though it contained a large tax hike and negated the gains for many working Americans of the 1981 tax cut. In this instance the Reagan agenda had been frustrated and the White House had been forced to compromise. The affair also illustrated the political difficulty of making hard decisions under the American electoral system – the actual loss of benefits was postponed for decades.[21]

Reagan's gutsy responses to the assassination attempt and the air controllers' strike conspired to give him a prolonged honeymoon period in 1981, when he also successfully embarked on his dramatic defense build-up, but by the end of the year his magic was fading. The embarrassment over Social Security was followed by an economic downturn, though the recession of 1981–1982 at least achieved one goal: bringing inflation down. The rocketing inflation of 1979–1980 was the domestic issue that more than any other had undermined confidence in the Carter administration. Reducing inflation was actually more the product of the shock therapy brutally administered by the Federal Reserve Board under Paul Volcker than of any action of the White House. The "Fed" was independent of the executive – economic adviser Martin Anderson repeated the line that the Fed "reports first to Congress and then to God" – and Volcker so prized his independence that he even declined to come to the White House for his first meeting with the new president, which had to be arranged on neutral territory. Appointed by Carter in 1979, Volcker had embarked on a draconian monetary policy to squeeze out inflation, and maintained high interest rates into the Reagan years, despite rising joblessness. (An IMF official subsequently observed that to establish its credibility the Fed "had to demonstrate its willingness to shed blood, lots of blood, other people's blood.") Relations between the Fed and the White House cooled somewhat as the Volcker prescription produced the recession that hurt the Republicans in the mid-term elections of 1982, although Reagan himself punctiliously abided by the convention of non-interference in monetary policy and reappointed Volcker as Fed chief in 1983, thus reaffirming his commitment to the anti-inflation drive. Whoever or whatever deserves the credit for defeating inflation (and the declining world price of oil helped significantly), the Consumer Price Index dropped dramatically during Reagan's first term. The administration naturally claimed the credit, although whipping inflation came at significant cost, unemployment rising above 10 percent during the recession, and more than twice that in parts of the traditional manufacturing sector. The massive shedding of jobs and of unprofitable plant accelerated the relative decline of manufacturing and its consequent restructuring, as discussed in Chapter 2, and the movement of capital to the financial sector. Real wages dropped too, and did not begin rising again until the 1990s. Still, inflation was beaten. "By bringing down the rate of inflation in the mid-1980s," business historian Louis Galambos has written, "the government opened the way for the private sector to fund the transformations essential to U.S. competitiveness."[22]

Rolling back taxes may have been Reagan's first priority, but he had other objectives too. Other than militarily he wanted to roll back the functions of the federal government, thus freeing industry from regulation (which would also diminish federal bureaucracy), reducing welfare programs, and turning over some functions to the states. After 1981, however, Reagan found Congress less cooperative. His attempt to restructure federalism and slim down the central government in 1982 by transferring many functions to the states was rebuffed. By the late spring of 1982 Gallup polls showed that more Americans disapproved than approved of Reagan's conduct as president, and his approval rating reached a nadir of 35 percent in January 1983.

Reagan was never again to achieve the mastery over Congress he had enjoyed in 1981, and for much of his administration he sought where he could to further his agenda without resort to legislation. (The Iran–Contra scandal discussed in Chapter 5 was to represent the most notorious attempt to bypass Congress.) One technique was to staff the federal agencies and the courts with conservatives. Reagan scriptwriter Peggy Noonan was bemused by the rather intense "movement conservatives" she encountered in the administration, often idealistic young people devoted to "a cause, a belief." The new Secretary for Education, Terrel Bell, found himself at war with the "movement conservatives" when he tried to staff his department with "experienced educators." According to one early analysis, "The primary qualification for appointment – overshadowing managerial competence and experience or familiarity with issues – appeared to be the extent to which an appointee shared the president's values." The most significant of these conservative appointments were those made to the courts. By the time he left office Reagan had appointed about half of the federal judiciary. As his Attorney General, Edwin Meese, put it, the intention was "to institutionalise the Reagan revolution so it can't be set aside no matter what happens in future presidential elections."[23]

Deregulation was a major component of the Reagan agenda. At virtually every early cabinet meeting, according to one participant, Reagan told "some regulatory horror story." He was continuing a process begun by Jimmy Carter, for by the end of the 1970s the sluggishness of the economy was widely attributed to excessive regulation. The Carter administration had substantially dismantled obstructions to competition in the transportation and communication industries, notably in the airline, trucking, and railroad industries, and had begun deregulating natural gas and financial services. This was not strictly a matter of political ideology, for liberals like

Senator Edward Kennedy supported parts of Carter's deregulation drive. But the more fervent Reaganites itched to go much further, although their main legislative accomplishments were limited to deregulating savings and loan banking (with unhappy results) and cable television. Preferring to rely on executive action in changing federal rules rather than legislation (which would have to be shepherded through an obstreperous Congress), the administration got off to a determined start. On his third day in office Reagan established the Presidential Task Force on Regulatory Relief, which slashed some 181 federal regulations in the first three months. After the first year it was claimed that *The Federal Register*, which provided a regulations checklist, had been reduced in size by a third; some 32 regulations affecting the automobile industry were lifted or eased. The administration further liberalized federal regulations governing such sectors as telecommunications. The objective was also pursued through funding cuts. Staff positions in the Consumer Product Safety Commission were reduced by 38 percent during Reagan's first term, and within about a year the Solid Waste Bureau's staff numbers were slashed from 74 to just one! Agencies that enforced the civil rights laws were also put under pressure, the Equal Employment Opportunity Commission losing 10 percent of its funding in the first two years. The deregulatory cause was particularly driven by the appointment of officials committed to the Reagan agenda, who eased the enforcement of anti-trust laws and health and safety regulations. Nonetheless, the appointment of ardent Reaganites to the agencies had its political downside – their lack of regulatory expertise meant that their actions were sometimes successfully challenged in the courts.[24]

The environment had not featured significantly in the 1980 campaign, and became subordinate to Reagan's deregulation drive. Conservative think tanks, most notably the Heritage Foundation, helped to reinforce White House skepticism about the value of environmental regulation. Reagan's priorities were evidenced in the appointment as Interior Secretary of James Watt, who assumed office promising that: "We will mine more, drill more, cut more timber to use our resources." (Watt divided his fellow citizens into "Liberals and Americans.") "I will build an institutional memory that will be here for decades," he said as he appointed like-minded individuals to key positions. He was determined on such a wholesale blitz on his department's regulations that no successor "would ever change them back because he won't have the determination that I do." He secured the removal of employees whose views he thought unduly environmentalist, rejigged procedures in ways that advantaged corporate interests, allowed mining exploration on public land, and stopped the enlargement of national parks. "This is now a captive agency," said one disillusioned Interior Department bureaucrat in 1983: "It is totally a captive of the mining interests." The Environmental Protection Agency (EPA) head, Anne Gorsuch, possessed a similar outlook, telling officials of the United Nations Environment Program in 1982 that the free market was the best way to solve environmental problems, and the number of hazardous waste prosecutions dropped markedly. The EPA's operating budget was cut by about a third in the early 1980s.[25]

Nonetheless the administration's deregulatory assault disappointed its champions. There was resistance in Congress, the courts, much of the bureaucracy itself, and among the public, and the pro-business favoritism of some officials led to scandals. A toxic waste controversy precipitated Anne Gorsuch's departure in 1983, as did James Watt's indiscretions. Congressional committees probed EPA actions, and by 1984 over 20 of its officials had resigned or been fired. While Reagan's appointment of his Californian friend William P. Clark to replace Watt hardly pleased environmentalists, at least the new Secretary adopted a less provocative profile, and the appointment of the moderate William D. Ruckelshaus, the first head of the EPA, to his old post was widely welcomed. The Reagan administration, committed to improving the economy and to removing what it deemed to be unnecessary regulations, never became a champion of the environment, but after the early controversies exposed the degree of public support for environmental protection, it pursued its agenda with greater circumspection. By 1984 Reagan was even arguing for an extension of the Superfund (created at the end of the Carter presidency to clean up toxic waste) and also for an increased budget for the EPA, although not to the level it had once enjoyed.

One reason for the administration's modest retreat was that the attack on environmentalism had provoked powerful resistance from a wide array of lobbies, and environmental organizations actually grew in membership. Denied access to the administration (even in the Nixon years they had had some involvement in environmental policy making), they took their causes to the courts and into election campaigns. With many environmental aims strongly supported by public opinion, Congress frustrated several administration initiatives and exposed agency circumvention of regulations. In 1986 it passed a water-pollution control bill over a pocket veto and reauthorized and expanded the Superfund. The Reagan administration's appointments and policies had made the environment a hotly contested political issue, though broadly speaking a standoff was reached. None of the principal pan-industrial regulatory laws affecting industry or the environment introduced in the 1960s and 1970s was repealed, though the environmental movement was unable to secure major new programs. In one sense, the 1980s were a wasted decade, the administration's early attacks on environmental regulations giving way to inaction rather than to attempts to modernize them, such as by introducing market incentives to reconcile environmental protection with economic growth. Even the Heritage Foundation thought that the administration had "squandered" the opportunity "to reform America's flawed environmental protection programs."[26]

The wider deregulatory drive also stalled. Beset by bureaucratic, interest group, and legislative opposition and sobered by the complexity of their mission, the Task Force's drive soon ran out of steam. Its most significant achievement was to discourage the adoption of new regulations; the growth of spending on the federal regulatory agencies slowed appreciably during Reagan's first term. The regulatory regime was so woven into the fabric of this complex society that it was able to withstand the offensive directed against it. By the end of Reagan's first term, deregulation had largely disappeared from the administration's agenda. During his second the budgets and personnel of the federal regulatory agencies were increasing again.

Much as he believed in deregulation, Reagan knew when to make tactical political retreats. Reagan's reverses over Social Security and the environment might have damaged him more had the economy not revived quite strongly after the 1981–1982 recession, partly thanks to the "military Keynesianism" of his defense build-up, and with it Reagan's popularity. At the end of 1983 the veteran columnist Joseph Kraft judged that "Ronald Reagan has made the country feel good about itself." The emerging boom ensured the president's re-election.[27]

The Republican campaign was built around the theme that it was "Morning Again in America." Reagan gleefully distinguished between Republican and Democratic psychology, claiming the two parties represented "two fundamentally different ways of governing – their government of pessimism, fear, and limits, or ours of hope, confidence, and growth." He also retained his populist touch, exploiting the perception that "liberal Democrats" had displaced "traditional Democrats" and had reduced their party to a collection of self-interested lobbies: "You know, national Democrats used to fight for the working families of America, and now all they seem to fight for are the special interests and their own leftwing ideology." Reagan was further boosted by his foreign policy foray into Grenada, the success of American athletes at the Olympic Games in Los Angeles, and not least by his highly personable television performances. "America is back, standing tall," boasted Reagan. As economic growth reached an exceptional 6 percent during 1984 there was a sense that the good times had returned. "You ain't seen nothing yet," was the jubilant White House line.[28]

For the Democrats, Jimmy Carter's former vice-president, Walter Mondale, conducted a traditional presidential campaign and made much of the accelerating budget and trade deficits that Reaganomics appeared to have spawned, even insisting that he would raise taxes if elected (arguing that Reagan too would be forced to do so). But Mondale's earnestness was of little avail. While running behind in the polls, Mondale did score well against an uncomfortable Reagan in the first of two television debates, but in the second the canny 73-year-old bested his opponent with the promise: "I will not make age an issue in this campaign. I am not going to exploit, for political purposes, my opponent's youth and inexperience."

Reagan won with 59 percent of the popular vote, carrying every state except Minnesota (Mondale's home state) and the District of Columbia. The flourishing economy seemed evidence that Reaganomics had worked. During the 1970s usually about a third of the electorate had said they identified with the Republicans; in 1984 the figure jumped to 43 percent. Reagan led among almost all class, religious, and ethnic groups, including Catholics and blue-collar workers. Around 40 percent of voters polled revealed that what they liked most about the president was that he was a "strong leader." Reagan's 1981 victories over Congress and the air traffic controllers had left a lasting impression, and the good times of the mid-1980s seemed further evidence of his adroit leadership. Also, Reagan's devotion to "Star Wars," however ridiculed by sophisticates, appears to have persuaded many Americans that he was not a war hawk – in offering security from nuclear attack, the space shield seemed to promise a lasting peace. The Republicans' invocation of vague, feel-good emotions, rather than clearly formulated policies, allowed them to sidestep the ballooning budget deficit that they had promised to eliminate. It also meant that there was no clearly defined agenda for Reagan's second term. One newsman said that, "unlike 1980," Reagan had achieved "a landslide without a mandate."[29]

But the victory was more one for Reagan personally than for the Republican Party. The Democrats actually made a net gain of one in the Senate, reducing the Republican majority there to six, while they easily retained control of the House of Representatives. Although their majority in the latter was somewhat reduced (from the high point reached during the recession year of 1982), it was larger than after the 1980 election. In 1980 Reagan's coattails had helped the Republicans win control of the Senate, but in 1984 he seemed to have lost them. The Democrats also held about two-thirds of both the state governorships and legislative chambers.

The Republicans had not won unequivocal control of American government. As Tip O'Neill put it: "the American people supported this president
without necessarily endorsing his programs." The Reagan Revolution,
whatever it now was, was unlikely to be advanced through the new Congress.
Nonetheless, the loss of yet another presidential election was mortifying
for the Democrats, intensifying soul-searching over their image as "the
party of the past and status quo" and their need to articulate a "post-welfare
program." One veteran tried to look on the bright side: "life does send up
flowers through the manure pile."[30]

* * *

Actually the Reagan Revolution had largely stalled after the halcyon year of
1981. Reagan's battles with Congress and other agencies had contributed
to the emergence of a somewhat more pliable attitude before the end of
his first term. Some conservative hard-liners, such as Al Haig and James
Watt, had left the administration, for the most part to be replaced by more
pragmatic conservatives. On the foreign front, Reagan had dropped his
fiercely anti-Soviet rhetoric and was signaling a desire for dialogue with the
Soviet Union. Domestically, the administration had retreated over Social
Security and the environment, while the recession of 1981–1982 encouraged some rethinking of economic policy. The White House began to place
emphasis on grants to upgrade math and science teaching and the expansion of retraining programs. "The challenge of government is to identify
the things we can do now to ease this massive economic transition for the
American people," Reagan said in 1983, now conceding both a role for
government and an awareness of the debate over the declining competitiveness of American industry. The marketplace alone, it seemed, would not
solve the country's economic problems. Journalist David Broder noticed
Reagan's repeated insistence "that government policy must assist – and not
resist – the 'great transition' of the American manufacturing base from
heavy industry to high technology." As the White House came to reveal a
greater pragmatism on domestic policy, it was also discovering limits to
economic autonomy: "We must also recognize that our own economic
well-being is inextricably linked to the world economy. We export over 20
percent of our industrial production, and 40 percent of our farmland pro-
duces for export." Reagan would enter his second term confident that the
economic boom had vindicated his policies, yet ready to negotiate with
congressional opponents and to engage more fully with the wider world.
Henceforth, for the Reagan White House, foreign issues would take precedence over domestic policy.[31]

Chapter 5

Reviving and Winning the Cold War

Ronald Reagan was elected to the presidency at a time of widespread public pessimism about the state of the nation. But the perception of governmental helplessness was not confined to domestic matters. To many Americans the international stature of the United States was also in decline. In a speech at Harvard in June 1980, the former Secretary of State Cyrus Vance spoke of the "disturbing fear in the land that we are no longer capable of shaping our future."[1]

"Wandering without aim" was the charge that Ronald Reagan had directed at American foreign policy in 1976, and the continued growth of the Soviet military and Soviet intrusions in several parts of Africa, Asia, and Central America in the late 1970s seemed further proof that the USSR was bent on establishing global superiority. During the 1980 campaign Reagan attacked Jimmy Carter's foreign policy as "bordering on appeasement." He was determined to rescue the United States from the humiliating condition to which he believed that the policy of détente had reduced it. By the end of his presidency he had achieved more than even he could have expected. Both domestic and foreign commentators acknowledged that Reagan had restored America's international prestige. Even more stunningly, this most ardent of anti-communist Cold Warriors had presided over the ebbing of the Cold War.[2]

There was irony in Reagan's foreign policy successes. Elected as an anti-Soviet hard-liner, he left office with the title of peacemaker. His fierce resolve to restore American strength and dignity was married to a strongly unilateralist instinct, a belief that the United States could rely on its own resources and often act alone, but his various policies served in many

Contemporary America: Power, Dependency, and Globalization since 1980,
First Edition. M.J. Heale.
© 2011 M.J. Heale. Published 2011 by Blackwell Publishing Ltd.

respects to increase American interaction with the outside world and to make the country more dependent on others. Reagan's celebrated defense build-up, for example, the greatest in American peacetime history, was made possible in significant part by Japanese and Saudi Arabian investors prepared to buy US Treasury bonds. In asserting American authority, Reagan discovered more of the world. He was an ideological warrior, supremely confident of the superiority of the American way. As the economy gained momentum after 1982, Reagan regularly associated its performance with political freedom and saw free enterprise and democracy as progressing in tandem around the world. "These democratic and free-market revolutions are really the same revolution," he said on one occasion: "They are based on the vital nexus between economic and political freedom." Long wary of the United Nations like other conservatives, after Reagan retired from the presidency he actually called for the creation of a new UN army, an "army of conscience."[3]

*   *   *

Reagan had been inveighing for years against what he saw as the weakness of American foreign policy, a charge cruelly pointed up by the hostage crisis in Tehran. "Well, so far détente's been a one-way street the Soviet Union has used to pursue its own aims," said the president in signaling a new direction in his first press conference. Reagan's stance was underlined by his foreign policy appointments. The Secretary of State was Alexander Haig, a former NATO commander, whose offer to reduce Cuba to "a fucking parking lot" apparently disturbed even the president. As Ambassador to the UN Reagan appointed Jeane Kirkpatrick, who had publicly argued for a distinction between "authoritarian" (mostly right-wing) regimes, which might evolve in a democratic fashion and which the United States might support, and "totalitarian" (mostly communist) regimes, in which there was little hope of nurturing freedom. At the Defense Department was Reagan's fellow Californian Caspar Weinberger, a skilful bureaucrat strongly committed to the military build-up. Reagan's foreign policy team, however, was hardly harmonious. The Defense and State departments were often at furious odds, a situation that did not much improve when the tempestuous Haig was replaced with the phlegmatic George Shultz in 1982.[4]

It was Soviet intentions that obsessed the incoming Reagan administration. "The Russians have told us over & over again their goal is to impose their incompetent and ridiculous system on the world," Reagan had said in a radio address in 1975. By the fall of 1980, according to Robert M. Gates, then a senior CIA official, "the sense that the soviets and their surrogates were 'on the march' around the world was palpable in Washington and elsewhere." "Moscow is the greatest source of international insecurity today," the new Secretary of State concurred. Reagan's aide Ed Meese was later to impute a prophetic ingredient to the president's conviction, claiming that he "was more than simply 'anticommunist'; he was an anticommunist with a game plan."[5]

If so, the first part of the game plan was massively to expand American military power. In that honeymoon year of 1981, despite an uncertain economy, Reagan persuaded Congress to commit to a five-year defense plan costing a phenomenal $1.36 trillion dollars. The Soviet Union "has been engaged in the greatest military buildup in the history of man," Reagan explained in August, "and it cannot be described as necessary for their defense." There had indeed been a Soviet build-up, though it was questionable whether the Soviets had established the military superiority often imputed to them, and in any case it owed a lot to the same rationale as Reagan's: regarding themselves as the underdog, Soviet officials wished to strengthen their military so that they too could negotiate from strength. But what to them was a defensive strategy could seem offensive to American eyes and called for an energetic response. During Reagan's first term military spending duly soared by about 50 percent, and it did not stop there, the Pentagon's annual budget almost doubling in the course of his presidency. Reagan was truly horrified by the prospect of nuclear war, but his exploding defense budget reflected a decision to develop a new generation of nuclear arms. There were new Trident missile submarines and the new MX/Peacemaker ICBM, with its 10 warheads, as well as thousands of new tanks, aircraft, and a larger navy.[6]

There was considerable public unease at the sky-rocketing military spending, and a popular "nuclear freeze" movement took off, demanding that both sides stop manufacturing weapons. At points in 1982–1983 as many as 70 percent of those polled expressed reservations about the nuclear build-up; an estimated 750000 people turned out in a protest demonstration in New York's Central Park. Senator Edward Kennedy characterized Reagan's argument as saying that "we have to build more nuclear bombs today … in order to reduce the number of such bombs tomorrow," in other words, "voodoo arms control." In October 1982 a media hubbub followed the revelation that the Roman Catholic bishops were preparing a pastoral letter challenging the morality of American nuclear policy, and on subsequent publication it insisted that "the arms race poses a threat to human life and human civilization which is without precedent." In the November

1982 elections voters in eight states approved a nuclear freeze. The renewed arms race also provoked strong anti-nuclear movements in Europe, where concerns were being deepened by the deployment of intermediate-range nuclear missiles in Britain and on the continent, something that had been agreed in the Carter years but was now being implemented.[7]

But while Reagan believed it essential to negotiate from strength, time was to prove that he was no warmonger. Defense Secretary Caspar Weinberger combined tenacious support for a huge escalation in defense spending with a dogged reluctance actually to use military force. His caution was matched by that of the president. Reagan's fiery rhetoric served to disguise his reluctance to commit to military or provocative action. "I've always recognized that ultimately there's got to be a settlement, a solution," he said of the rivalry with the Soviet Union in December 1981. When the Soviets shot down a Korean airliner in 1983, Reagan flew back from his Californian ranch to hold a crisis meeting with his foreign policy and defense chiefs, who outlined various US responses before Reagan concluded: "Fellas, I don't think we need to do a damn thing." Congress too was wary of military intervention that might escalate into another Vietnam. The administration's belief in a strong military, along with its unwillingness to use it, helps to explain the emergence of the Reagan Doctrine. "Our mission is to nourish and defend freedom and democracy, and to communicate these ideals everywhere we can ...," said Reagan in 1985, adding that "Support for freedom fighters is self-defense." This seemed to mean that while large numbers of troops would not be sent abroad, the United States would support insurgencies against communist regimes, particularly in the Third World. A journalist dubbed this the Reagan Doctrine; its general thrust was loudly promoted by the right-wing Heritage Foundation. If the public would not support military action abroad, local forces would have to do the front-line fighting, with economic and military aid and covert support provided by the United States. The Reagan Doctrine could be seen as the counterpart of the administration's promotion of market economics abroad; in neither case did the United States have to commit extensive resources of the kind that had once been swallowed up in the swamps of Vietnam. Reagan's admirers would later persuade themselves that the Reagan Doctrine too was part of his master "game plan."[8]

Implementing the Reagan Doctrine implied unleashing the Central Intelligence Agency, which had been severely bruised during the 1970s by the exposure in the post-Watergate era of some of its activities. The CIA, which Carter had made some attempts to rein in, was given its head again under its gung-ho director Bill Casey. The CIA's budget grew at an even faster rate than the defense budget between 1981 and 1986; within a few years its covert operations more than doubled. By 1983, suspected *Newsweek*, the CIA was funding activities in Central America, Afghanistan, Iran, Libya, Ethiopia, Mauritius, and Cambodia. Reagan was sympathetic to Casey's view that supplying anti-communist groups around the world with arms would further stretch an already over-extended Soviet empire. If the United States resisted the Soviet challenges, and managed to defeat the Soviets even once, that "will shatter the mythology ... and it will all start to unravel."[9]

To shatter Soviet mythology, however, it would first be necessary to challenge it. Secretary Haig considered it imperative that the United States confront the Soviet Union after "the Carter experiment in obsequiousness." Opportunities to display American determination and – more quietly – to make use of the CIA soon afforded themselves in Eastern Europe and Central America. In March 1981 Reagan explained the communist threat to CBS's Walter Cronkite: "They have told us that their goal is the Marxian philosophy of world revolution and a single one-world Communist state and they're dedicated to that," and even after his first year he accused the Soviets of "acting more like international brigands than ever." Soviet–American trade declined as relations between the two superpowers became acrimonious.[10]

An early test of American resolve came in Poland, where in 1981 the communist regime was threatened by the Solidarity trade union movement led by Lech Walesa. Under Soviet pressure the Polish government imposed martial law, which at least vindicated Reagan's harsh warnings about the Soviets' fell intentions. The administration introduced sanctions against the military dictatorship in Poland, thus demonstrating to the world, in Reagan's words, "that America will not conduct 'business as usual' with the forces of oppression." But the sanctions were of modest effect without the support of America's NATO allies in Europe. The Polish issue also gave Reagan's hard-line colleagues an opportunity to block construction of the projected Siberian natural gas pipeline to West Germany, which would have allowed the Soviets to increase their foreign earnings. The White House eventually abandoned its stance on the pipeline, perhaps in part because Reagan had become aware of the value of covert action to Polish workers. Money and communications equipment were quietly supplied to Solidarity, partly through the cooperation of the Pope (a Pole), the AFL-CIO, and even leaders of the Socialist International. According to journalist Carl Bernstein, who uncovered much of this activity: "The American embassy in Warsaw became the pivotal CIA station in the communist world and, by all accounts, the most effective." Years later the unrest in Poland would be seen as an early sign of the unraveling of the Soviet bloc.[11]

But it was Central America that provided the main testing ground for the Reagan Doctrine. The Reagan White House was all but obsessed with signs of Soviet interference in what it regarded as its own backyard. In 1979 the Marxist-inspired Sandinistas had seized power in Nicaragua, and in the same year the left-wing New Jewel Movement took control in the small island of Grenada, where it was soon receiving assistance from Fidel Castro's Cuba. By 1980 the right-wing military government in El Salvador was at war with left-wing guerrilla groups, a brutal conflict infamously illustrated in March when death squads assassinated Archbishop Oscar Romero during mass. The Carter White House, its attitude toward the Soviet Union hardening in 1979–1980, sent Pentagon advisers to Central America. For the incoming Reagan administration, it was time to take a stand. Jeane Kirkpatrick argued that Central America and the Caribbean had become "the most important place in the world for us," because Soviet interference could disproportionately divert American resources.[12]

Failure to resist Soviet expansion in Central America from the outset, insisted Alexander Haig, "would result in a loss of credibility in all our dealings with the Soviets." He even reportedly said that at some point the United States would have to invade Cuba, that is, "go to the source" of the poison in the region. As it happened, the first confrontation came over El Salvador, for which Reagan proposed military and economic aid within weeks of taking office. But combating communist influence there was not for the sake of the El Salvadorans alone: "What we're doing … is [to] try to halt the infiltration into the Americas by terrorists, by outside interference and those who aren't just aiming at El Salvador but, I think, are aiming at the whole of Central and possibly later South America – and, I'm sure, eventually North America." Socialist guerrilla activity was continuing in El Salvador, but the supply of CIA and military aid to its government seemed only to provoke a greater rebel offensive. Through the 1980s the United States also provided aid for the military regimes of Guatemala.[13]

The Reagan administration also perceived Soviet influence in the small Caribbean island of Grenada, a former British colony and member of the Commonwealth of Nations. For once there was a military option that would not invoke fears of another Vietnam. The reform regime of Maurice Bishop was overthrown in October 1983 by a more militant Marxist faction backed by Cuba. "Hey, fuck it, let's dump these bastards," advised Bill Casey. Reagan sent in troops to protect US citizens on the island during the unrest and to ensure the exclusion of Marxists from a reconstituted regime. Several

Latin American governments and NATO allies, including Britain (angry at not being properly consulted about the invasion of a Commonwealth country), condemned this military invasion, but it secured its objective, the Americans on the island were safe, and the troops were soon withdrawn. The action won popular approval, partly because of memories of the long agony that followed the seizure of US citizens in Iran in 1979. Although the tiny size of Grenada meant that the action could hardly be accounted a glorious victory, the operation was important in strengthening the hand of the more militant members of the Reagan administration. "Grenada showed that it could be done," one of them later told historian Odd Arne Westad; it "proved that boldness and determination could defeat the Communists." It also contributed to Reagan's image as a strong president, as did other minor military operations, such as the shooting down of two Libyan jets in 1981 and an air attack on Syrian positions in Lebanon in 1983.[14]

The success in Grenada may have encouraged the White House to deepen its involvement in Nicaragua, which it saw as at the heart of the instability in Central America. Nicaragua became the focus of its covert activities in the region, and, when these were exposed, in the words of historian John Patrick Diggins, "Nicaragua became the most controversial issue in American politics since the Vietnam War." In 1979 the moribund Somoza dictatorship had collapsed before the revolutionary forces of the Sandinistas, whose new government Jimmy Carter had modestly aided. Within about a year, however, the Sandinista regime under Daniel Ortega was establishing friendly relations with the Soviet Union. Ortega was turning Nicaragua into a "Soviet ally on the American mainland," as Reagan put it. His overthrow became a priority, and the CIA was authorized to assist Nicaraguan elements who were fighting the government. These Contras, or "freedom fighters" as Reagan would call them, operated in part from Honduras, where they were trained by the CIA. While Congress accepted the legitimacy of CIA activity to intercept the supply of weapons from Nicaragua to the El Salvadoran rebels, it objected to operations to overthrow the Nicaraguan government, which it prohibited in December 1982. For some years the administration kept the full extent of its involvement more or less covert, although in 1984 a political storm erupted when it was discovered that the CIA had mined three Nicaraguan harbors, a breach of international law. Even Senator Barry Goldwater, who as chair of the Senate Intelligence Committee had a right to be informed of covert operations, was furious when he discovered the extent of CIA responsibility. "I've pulled Casey's nuts out of the fire on so many occasions," he fumed, "I feel like such a fool." The United States withdrew from the jurisdiction of the World Court when it learned that the Court was about to rule that it had violated international law, while Congress prohibited further military aid to the Contras. But Reagan was not one to abandon his freedom fighters. He devoted his very first major television address from the Oval Office after his 1984 re-election to trying to persuade the public of the need to fund the Contras. His attempts to provide them with succor in defiance of Congress would come close to destroying his presidency.[15]

Yet as the Reagan White House insistently and mostly surreptitiously took the fight to what it regarded as the communist enemy in such places as Poland, Nicaragua, and Afghanistan, it was also beginning to court the masters of the Kremlin. The regimes in Poland and Nicaragua might conceivably be overthrown, but Reagan knew that the Soviet Union could not be thus subverted. As a true believer in free enterprise, he was confident that the Soviet Union must one day collapse under its own inadequacies, and this assumption perhaps also contributed to his reluctance to use military force. He was happy to apply pressure to the Soviet Union, but there is no evidence that he anticipated a Soviet implosion on his watch. In the meantime, armed with his enhanced military, he reasoned that he could do business with it (although his build-up counter-productively triggered fears in the Soviet Union that he was planning a first strike). When Deputy National Security Adviser Robert McFarlane recruited diplomat Jack Matlock to the National Security Council in 1983 he told him that when Reagan first came to office "he felt we were too weak to negotiate effectively with the Soviets," but after two years of defense growth "he feels it is time to pursue negotiations aggressively." In particular, Reagan hoped to win Soviet support for his own dream of abolishing nuclear weapons.[16]

An early indication of a softer line came in Reagan's 1983 State of the Union Address, in which he deplored the "wasteful arms race" and looked to the Soviets to join a mutual "search for greater security and major arms reductions." As journalist Don Oberdorfer noticed, "Gone were 'the Soviet regime,' 'the Soviet empire,' 'the shadow of Soviet power' and other such anti-Soviet phrases of the past." A few weeks later, Reagan secretly met with the Soviet ambassador to assure him of his willingness to engage constructively with the Soviets. By this date Al Haig had been replaced as Secretary of State by George Shultz, a respected businessman, academic, and veteran of Nixon's cabinet, who encouraged the president's accommodating instincts. One observer said of him, with some relief, that he "made the making of foreign policy dull again." Nonetheless, the seeds of the administration's change of tone probably lay in the president himself, even though that same year he would famously describe the Soviet Union as an "evil empire," no less than the "focus of evil in the modern world." One sign of a softening attitude, though partly a response to pressure from American farmers, was the signing of a five-year treaty with the Soviet Union in August 1983 guaranteeing the supply of American wheat. The Secretary of Agriculture anticipated that the "power of food – if you use it" could part "the tight Soviet Iron Curtain." US–Soviet trade was soon increasing again. "I would not say that again," Reagan said only nine months after his reference to the "evil empire," and he never did.[17]

What helps to explain Reagan's effort at dialogue with the Soviets was his revulsion at the doctrine of Mutually Assured Destruction (MAD), which underlay the defense strategies of both superpowers, and his discovery of a miraculous alternative. Almost alone among his generation of political leaders, he nurtured a vision of a nuclear-free world. The doctrine of MAD horrified him, as he told his aides during his first year in office. He had spoken movingly of the need to avoid nuclear war at the 1976 Republican convention, and his friend Martin Anderson testified that "the concern about nuclear war, and the challenge to diminish the threat of that war was always foremost in his mind," both before and throughout his presidency. This personal conviction was to open a fissure between the president and his conventionally minded defense advisers, but he was not deterred. He told the Japanese Diet in November 1983: "I know I speak for people everywhere when I say our dream is to see the day when nuclear weapons will be banished from the face of the Earth."[18]

In the spring of 1983 he announced the Strategic Defense Initiative (SDI, or "Star Wars" as its opponents soon derided it), a huge research program to create a defense shield or umbrella, mounted from space, which would ensure that hostile missiles did not reach the United States. This fantastic conception implied a fundamental rethinking of nuclear strategy – MAD could be dispensed with since the shield would make nuclear missiles "impotent and obsolete." Most scientists seriously doubted whether such a system could work, but the administration pressed ahead with the research, and, just as Reagan found recruits among economists to support his controversial supply-side policies, there were scientists too who gained access to the White House to stoke his enthusiasm for Star Wars. Defense Secretary Weinberger happily joined the president in developing an arms strategy that would shift the emphasis from offensive to defensive systems. In his 1984 State of the Union Address Reagan even appealed directly to the Soviet people to support his vision of ensuring that nuclear weapons would never be used: "But then would it not be better to do away with them entirely?"

In a major address that January he clarified his intentions: "Reducing the risk of war – and especially nuclear war – is priority number one." In contrast to his first Inaugural Address, in which defense and foreign issues had gone unmentioned, his second made world peace a priority: "We seek the total elimination one day of nuclear weapons from the face of the earth." Making clear his revulsion at the logic of MAD, Reagan insisted that the way forward was his program to find "a security shield that would destroy nuclear missiles before they reach their target," which would serve to "demilitarize the arsenals of Earth" and "render nuclear weapons obsolete." Nonetheless, to the Soviets SDI was deeply unsettling, a bid at a first-strike capability which would upset the balance of terror, or, as premier Yuri Andropov put it, "disarm the Soviet Union."[19]

Paralleling its rhetorical championing of freedom and democracy, which it professed to see spreading through the world, was the Reagan administration's enjoinment of free market economics on other countries. Secretary of State George Shultz argued that it was "time for democracies to celebrate their system, their beliefs, and their success ... Opinions are being revised about which system is the wave of the future ... History is on freedom's side." Investment banker Jeffrey Garten noted that the Reagan team "defined the nature of [America's] global responsibility in unilateral terms," expecting the American economy to serve as an example for humankind. Allies complained about the harmful impact on their economies of the high US interest rates, to little avail. The Reagan White House's unilateralist trait was also reflected in its suspicion of such bodies as the United Nations (UN) and the World Bank. In 1984 the United States enforced a 25 percent reduction on funding for the International Development Agency, a branch of the World Bank providing programs for the poorest countries, as it also withdrew from UNESCO (United Nations Educational, Scientific, and Cultural Organization), an action one student has attributed to "an ideologically motivated campaign to achieve the punitive humiliation of a major UN agency." Such agreements as the Law of the Sea Treaty were rejected as being expressions of a "collectivist ideology." When the Reagan regime did engage with the major international agencies, it tended to set conditions in agreeing to economic assistance, although its prescriptions for austerity measures and balanced budgets for Third World countries hardly sat well with its own practices. Thus as the Reagan administration trumpeted the values of "free enterprise" through the 1980s, stricken governments around the world retreated from what could be seen as socialist agendas when they sought assistance from the IMF (International Monetary Fund) or other international sources. As time passed, the Reagan administration did try to cooperate more with other nations on economic issues, but it could never free itself entirely from its unilateralist instincts. When Reagan's term ended, the United States owed the UN nearly $520 million in unpaid dues, though this was a measure of congressional as well as White House disapproval.[20]

Neither free market ideology nor the Reagan Doctrine, however, was able to supply the administration with much of a guide for policy in the Middle East, where it proved no more successful than its predecessors in fashioning a constructive strategy. American objectives, as ever, could not be readily reconciled: protecting the West's essential oil supply, resisting Soviet influence, safeguarding Israel's borders, accommodating the homeless Palestinians displaced by the creation of Israel, finding a reliable ally able to sustain order in the region. The new fundamentalist regime in Iran was fiercely hostile to the United States, and during the long 1980s war between Iran and Iraq the United States quietly lent aid to the latter, controlled by the ruthless Saddam Hussein. In 1988 Saddam resorted to chemical warfare against the Iraqi Kurds, a gruesome offensive which included the reported use of US-made helicopters, precipitating a strong condemnation by the US Senate and calls for tough sanctions. This the administration refused, clinging to its diplomatic overtures toward Iraq. Before this date, as discussed below, the United States had bizarrely found itself supplying arms to the hated Iranians. The terrain of the Middle East was proving exceptionally treacherous, but gradually the United States came to look more to Saudi Arabia for a strong ally in the region, and in his second term Ronald Reagan presided over a great expansion of arms sales to the Saudis. Perhaps Saudi Arabia and Israel could together protect American interests in the region and fend off threats from international communism and Islamic fundamentalism. Given the Arab world's intense resentment of Israel and the fundamentalists' detestation of what they saw as a corrupt and pro-American Saudi regime, the strategy was fraught with danger.

The Reagan White House did recognize that fundamental to the instability in the Middle East was the Israeli–Palestinian conflict. It advanced an unsuccessful "peace plan" in 1982, though it was premised on the assumption that it would be possible to secure peace in Lebanon, which by this date had become a focus of rival pressures. Its government was virtually disintegrating in the face of occupations of parts of the country by the Palestine Liberation Organization (PLO) and Syria. Israel was vulnerable to PLO attacks from Lebanon, and was also worried about its northern neighbor Syria (where the Reagan team suspected Soviet influence). The Israelis tried to end the Palestinian threat in 1982 with a military invasion of Lebanon and an aerial bombardment of West Beirut, and did succeed in expelling the PLO. American marines were dispatched to Lebanon as part of a multinational force to restore order, but with little success. Rival militias competed between themselves and with the precarious Lebanese government, and the peacekeeping forces returned after the Christian militia of Lebanon (apparently with Israeli complicity) horrifically slaughtered at least 1700 men, women, and children at the Palestinian refugee camps of Sabra and Shatila. In April 1983 a car bomb smashed into the US Embassy in Beirut, causing 63 deaths, over a quarter of them American. Reagan responded by allowing American ships and planes to use their firepower on behalf of the regime of President Amin Gemayel, so positioning the United States as the enemy of the militia groups. In October a suicide truck crashed into the US marine barracks and exploded, killing 241 Americans. Reagan vowed that the United States "must be more determined than ever" to protect that "strategic area of the earth," but the marines could not be defended and by April 1984 had been pulled out. The anarchic country became a no-man's-land for Americans and other Westerners, who from time to time were taken hostage by fundamentalist groups.[21]

Ronald Reagan, like his predecessor, discovered the near helplessness of a superpower when its citizens were taken hostage in hostile territory. The White House publicly proclaimed the impossibility of negotiating with terrorists, but secretly was more pliable. President Carter's political demise was a lesson they did not want repeated. Further, Reagan himself keenly felt his responsibility for the safety of American citizens: "The American people will never forgive me if I fail to get those hostages out." Seven Americans were held by Shi'ite groups by 1985. The Shi'ites were closely connected with Iran, with its fiercely anti-American leadership, but through intermediaries some kind of understanding was reached that a supply of arms to the Iranian regime could secure the release of hostages. In August 1985 Reagan approved the provision of anti-tank missiles in order to secure the freeing of four of them, with Israel acting as middleman (Congress having banned arms sales to Iran), but only one American was released. Nonetheless National Security Council (NSC) officials persisted, adding anti-aircraft missiles to the weapons sold to the Iranians. The cornucopia of missiles did little to dislodge the hostages. One was freed in July 1986 but three more were taken prisoner a couple of months later. An opinion poll in December 1986 revealed that, "more people approve of the way Jimmy Carter handled Iran than approve of Mr. Reagan's performance." Carter may have lost an election thanks in part to a hostage crisis, but he had at least refused to pay a "ransom" and had eventually secured the hostages' return.[22]

But the arms-for-hostages initiative had become fatally coupled with the White House's fixation with Nicaragua. Reagan was still determined to sustain the "freedom fighters" against what he saw as the Soviet-backed regime of Daniel Ortega, and his massive re-election victory had added to his confidence. Reagan worked hard to win new funds from Congress for the Contras, but there was a possible substitute. From 1984, when Congress was moving to cut off aid to the Contras, National Security Adviser Robert McFarlane, with his deputy Oliver North and with the president's blessing, had been working to find alternative funds. "We cannot break faith with the contras," insisted McFarlane, echoing the president's sentiments, the obligation to respect Congress apparently being less compelling. McFarlane, his successor John Poindexter, North, and the CIA's Casey were overseeing both of these covert operations – arms-for-hostages and aiding the Contras – and North hit on the idea that surplus funds from the arms sales could be diverted to the latter. This was done, but in October 1986 a cargo plane carrying arms was shot down over Nicaragua. An American survivor admitted to being part of a CIA-sponsored operation. The United States was revealed to be involved in the resupply of the Contras despite the explicit ban by Congress. And supplying arms to a country as reviled by Americans as Iran seemed scarcely credible to many members of the public. "It's like suddenly learning that John Wayne had secretly been selling liquor and firearms to the Indians," said one Reagan appointee.[23]

The stunning crisis that became known as Iran–Contra exploded on the American public in the autumn of 1986, ending a year in which Reagan's personal approval rating had been at its height. Richard Nixon had been ejected from the presidency by the exposure of a covert operation run from the White House, but now an even more extensive covert operation was being masterminded within the NSC staff, a part of which became a kind of secret government within the government. Yet exposure of Iran–Contra did not bring down the Reagan administration. Reagan not only survived the possibility of impeachment but in some measure recovered his authority.

The Reagan White House realized that a "cover-up" was likely to drag it down further. At the end of November 1986 Attorney General Ed Meese revealed the diversion of Iranian funds to the Contras and a major constitutional crisis erupted. President Reagan flatly denied trading arms for hostages and insisted that he knew nothing of the diversion of funds. His approval rating dropped by over 20 points in a month, and a *Newsweek* poll showed that 90 percent did not believe Reagan was telling the truth. In another poll, which asked, "Whom do you trust more to make the right decisions on foreign policy – Ronald Reagan or Congress?," Congress won out by an astonishing 61 to 27 percent. North was quickly fired, Poindexter resigned, several investigations were set in train, and something of the secret government within the government was exposed. "I told him I wasn't sure that was legal," said a senior official of North's operation.[24]

In his 1987 State of the Union Address, Reagan fessed up to a "major regret": "I took a risk with regard to our action in Iran. It did not work, and for that I assume full responsibility." Having accepted responsibility, he swiftly sidestepped blame: "We will get to the bottom of this, and I will take whatever action is called for," an exculpatory stance that did nothing to placate his Democratic critics in Congress. He was still plagued by the plight of Nicaragua: "Nicaraguan freedom fighters have never asked us to wage their battle, but I will fight any effort to shut off their lifeblood and consign them to death, defeat, or a life without freedom." As the *Washington Post* put it: "For the president, dismantling the Nicaraguan 'second Cuba' in Central America is more than a goal; according to close associates, it's a personal obsession." A joint committee of Congress held televised hearings in the summer of 1987, and while it became clear that administration officials had engaged in illegal actions, destroyed files, and lied to Congress, the degree of Reagan's complicity was never fully established, while Oliver North's feisty performance, playing the part of a wronged patriot, made him something of a folk hero. It seemed that while the American public had no wish to see US involvement in Central America, it had some sympathy for efforts to free the hostages in the Lebanon and it more or less trusted the president to do what was right. It could not be conclusively demonstrated that Reagan had wittingly broken the law, and, with Reagan entering the last year of his term, the prospect of impeachment receded.[25]

Iran–Contra could have destroyed Ronald Reagan, but at the same time events were unfolding which were to give him a reputation as one of the greatest American presidents. During his early years in the White House, with his anti-Soviet rhetoric and his arms build-up, Reagan's relationship with the Kremlin could hardly have been worse, and he never met a Soviet leader during his first term. Yet during his second, Reagan met the Soviet premier on five occasions, and the relationship warmed. Reagan's emerging personal mission to secure a nuclear-free world in part explains this rapprochement, but even more important were profound changes in the Soviet Union.

There was no easy path to the rapprochement. Quite apart from the harsh rhetoric of its early days, the Reagan regime never let up on the support it gave to various anti-communist forces outside the Soviet Union. As well as its largely covert operations in Latin America and Poland, it was also increasingly implicated in supporting the anti-Soviet forces in Afghanistan. From 1984 it helped to manage training camps for the Mujahidin in Egypt. CIA Director Casey compared American involvement with the support given to organized resistance to Hitler during World War II. "Here is the beauty of the Afghan operation," he told his colleagues: "Usually it looks like the big bad Americans are beating up on the natives. Afghanistan is just the reverse. The Russians are beating up on the little guys. We don't make it our war. … All we have to do is give [the Mujahidin] help, only more of it." At the same time as Reagan was making overtures to the Soviets in the mid-1980s, the supply and training of the Mujahidin was stepped up. In 1986 Reagan agreed to send hundreds of Stinger surface-to-air missiles, which were soon destroying Soviet helicopters. As historian Donald Critchlow has observed: "This was the largest covert operation in American history." In the same period the United States was also increasing its support for rebels in Nicaragua and Angola.[26]

But important change was taking place in the Soviet Union, where a younger generation was moving into positions of power. In 1985 the premiership was assumed by Mikhail Gorbachev, who was willing to admit the stagnancy of the Soviet economy and the inadequacy of the traditional Soviet method of central planning. The Cold War was hemorrhaging the Soviet economy, a process exacerbated in the mid-1980s by the dramatic fall in oil prices (and thus Soviet revenues), and Gorbachev wanted desperately to reduce defense costs and to secure greater access to modern technology. Soviet ideology had once held that its brand of Marxism would conquer the world, but in 1986 Gorbachev publicly abandoned the notion of an inevitable conflict between communism and capitalism. He had come to view internal decay as a greater threat to the Soviet Union than Western military power. His attempts at reform seemed to make the Soviet Union more acceptable to Western eyes. As it happened, by the mid-1980s the hard-liners of the Reagan administration had mostly left, to be replaced by moderates such as Shultz at the State Department and Colin Powell at the NSC. Less inclined to be deeply suspicious of every Soviet move, the new men around Reagan were reinforced by his wife Nancy, who, assisted by her astrologer, had apparently come to the conclusion that her husband's place in history would be best served by the title of peacemaker. But Reagan himself had begun looking for a new relationship with the Soviets at least as early as 1983 (he had been privately writing friendly letters to Soviet leaders since 1981). Within two or three years a revolution was in the making as both the Soviets and the Americans profoundly changed their stances toward one another.

Building on his friendly overtures of 1983–1984, confident of the increased strength of his military, and assured of a more responsive Soviet Union, in his second term Ronald Reagan embarked on a remarkable course of personal diplomacy with the Soviet leadership, convinced that his affability could soften Kremlin attitudes. His previously expressed "forthright" views about the Soviets, he explained in a major foreign policy address in January 1984, did not mean that "we can't deal with each other." Gorbachev proved even more committed to the process. Although the United States consulted its allies, for the West it was Ronald Reagan who was in the driving seat, personifying the unilateralist impulse that American military dominance made possible. Britain's Margaret Thatcher assured Reagan that Gorbachev was someone they could do business with, and, after meeting him at Geneva in November 1985, Reagan agreed. The explosion at the nuclear power plant in Chernobyl in April 1986, with its release into the atmosphere of an immense radioactive cloud, underlined for everyone the dangers of nuclear war. At Reykjavik in October 1986 the president even unnerved his advisers by impetuously agreeing to the abolition of all nuclear weapons, although that summit collapsed because Reagan was not prepared to give up his cherished SDI. A frustrated Gorbachev subsequently told his Politburo that Reagan was "a feeble-minded cave man."[27]

But Reykjavik was to prove a "psychological turning point" as Gorbachev and Reagan determined to intensify their efforts to reach accord, and Gorbachev himself became very popular in the West. "He's one of us – a political animal," exclaimed one congressman when Gorbachev visited Washington in December 1987. Congress itself had played a part by reducing Reagan's budget request for SDI by a third and limiting the tests that could be conducted in space, and Gorbachev no longer raised objections to the program, which he now seemed confident would not work. It was at this Washington summit that a historic accord was signed, the precise timing of its signing apparently being chosen for auspicious effect by Nancy Reagan's astrologer. Gorbachev saw it as "a date that will mark a watershed separating the era of a mounting risk of nuclear war from the era of a demilitarization of human life." The INF (Intermediate-Range Nuclear Forces) treaty provided for the elimination of both intermediate- and short-range ballistic missiles, and, critically, the two superpowers agreed to mutual and extensive inspections to confirm that the missiles were being dismantled. Opponents to the treaty surfaced in both countries, in the United States Reagan being assailed by right-wing Republicans and New Right groups, but by the late 1980s, for the first time ever, the nuclear arsenals held by the superpowers in Europe were actually being reduced. Soviet and American strategic missiles would no longer be directly facing one another. In the summer of 1988 Reagan visited Moscow, where he too discovered his popularity with the people. In December Gorbachev announced at the United Nations a dramatic reduction of conventional arms in Europe, without any reciprocal actions from the West, confirming that Soviet military strategy was geared to defense rather than offence. The Cold War eased further as the Soviet Union began withdrawing its troops from Afghanistan.[28]

The Soviet Union was not to implode until 1991, but as he left the presidency Ronald Reagan could reflect that he had played a role in ending the Cold War. "Psychologically and ideologically, the Cold War was over before Ronald Reagan moved out of the White House," US Ambassador to Moscow Jack Matlock has written. When asked by a journalist in 1988 whether the Soviet Union was still an "evil empire," Reagan responded "No, that was another time, another era." There is little evidence that Reagan's defense build-up did much to force a change in Soviet strategy, but once negotiations began, Reagan's vision of a nuclear-free world drove him on. His immunity to the conventional wisdom of the Cold War, his resilient optimism about the future, and his confidence in communication made possible his historic engagement. Gorbachev told his colleagues that at the Washington summit he had understood "probably for the first time ... how much the human factor means in international politics." Reagan never doubted it. He fervently believed in his capacity to make a personal breakthrough. Further, his domestic popularity helped him to carry most Americans with him. It may be doubted whether any other American politician who might have been elected president in the 1980s, steeped in Cold War verities, could have secured this historic accord. Margaret Thatcher generously said of her friend: "He won the Cold War without firing a shot."[29]

* * *

If Reagan's personal diplomacy was important, so was the larger context in which the Cold War ended and the Soviet Union dissolved. Western prosperity contrasted with the austerity of the communist-bloc countries, meaning that not only did the West have greater resources, but its opulence conspicuously testified to the success of the capitalist system while serving to undermine the confidence of Eastern Europeans in communism. The Western values of both individual liberty and consumerism were power-fully seductive. Socialist ideology was further undermined by the dramatic rise of capitalist countries in East Asia, as well as by China's embrace of market economics from 1983 ("the most momentous international event of the Reagan years," according to one scholar). During the 1980s the IMF and the World Bank, reflecting the "Washington Consensus" with its emphasis on free markets, insisted on "structural reform" in the several countries to which aid was offered, further enlarging the global reach of capitalism. The democratic regimes of the United States and Western Europe, and their (mostly reasonable) respect for civil liberties allowed their governments to boast of freedom, while the communist regimes spent energy and resources in trying to control the increasingly restless peoples over which they presided. (A private joke of Russian insiders was that theirs was the only country in the world "surrounded by hostile Communist countries.")[30]

Ultimately the Soviet leaders could not contain nationalist resistance to their authority, a condition that does more to explain the dissolution of the Soviet empire than any specific US policy. The rapid advances in high technology in the Western world in the 1970s and 1980s, illustrated by the multiplication of space satellites and the spread of personal computers and ever more sophisticated means of communication, seemed to leave the Soviet empire marooned in an earlier age. Even in such an old-fashioned device as telephone connections, in 1985 the Soviet Union had only about one-sixth as many as the United States, and many did not work. Secretary of State Shultz told Gorbachev that the Soviets "would need to be part of the information age if they were to be part of the modern world." But the peoples of Eastern Europe, or at least many of them, could see and hear something of the marvels of the West on their television and radio sets. "In the end," Odd Arne Westad has written, "Mikhail Gorbachev's *perestroika* project was about being included into the world that the satellite channels represented while upholding a degree of challenge to the system that had created them." The communist system was losing credibility with both its leaders and its peoples, and this is a major explanation for its mostly peace-ful demise, and, more immediately, for Gorbachev's fervent determination to reach an accord with the West.[31]

Chapter 6

The Morning After: The Limitations of Conservatism

In retrospect the figure of Ronald Reagan seems to preside over the 1980s like a benign colossus, but there was more to the era than this remarkable man, and the Reagan Revolution itself met with as much failure as success. During the decade Music Television (MTV) soared into noisy prominence, Madonna became a fashion icon as her albums became global hits, and Donald Trump erected the monumental Trump Tower on New York's fashionable Fifth Avenue. Mike Tyson became the world's youngest ever heavyweight champion in 1986, and Michael Jordan's speed, style, and acrobatic skills made him a phenomenal basketball star. Celebrity culture expanded as the mass media rode the entrepreneurial currents, and modern communications turned such celebrities into global figures. Perhaps Ronald Reagan, with his gift for the public stage, was not an unfitting personification of the era.

But the style of conservatism that he represented had its limits. The old-fashioned morality that the Reagan White House endorsed was not conspicuously upheld in the wave of teen and dance movies, such as *Dirty Dancing*, released by Hollywood in these years (even if many of their protagonists proved wholesomely American). The permissive currents that flowed from the 1960s lived on in popular culture and social attitudes. Economically, the administration might point to the impressive growth of the financial, health, and high tech sectors, though it was less clear that it had answers to the social maladies that erupted into the headlines in the mid-1980s, notably the growth of homelessness, the spread of AIDS, and the proliferation of crack cocaine in the cities. Further, liberal movements had not abandoned the field. A range of pressure groups successfully

Contemporary America: Power, Dependency, and Globalization since 1980, First Edition. M.J. Heale.
© 2011 M.J. Heale. Published 2011 by Blackwell Publishing Ltd.

defended and sometimes advanced progressive causes. The Democratic Party made some accommodation to Reaganomics, but it also regrouped, and it increased its representation in Congress during the Reagan years. Reagan can be credited with promoting a laissez-faire or neoliberal economic philosophy, which advanced inexorably around the world, yet after 1981 he was remarkably unsuccessful in securing new conservative measures from Congress, although he did resort to other means to further his agenda. Had it not been for his stunning role in reaching a rapprochement with the Soviet Union, the balance of his presidency would likely have been remembered as unexceptional.

* * *

The Democratic Party's losses in the 1980 and 1984 presidential elections were sobering experiences. During Reagan's first term some Democratic leaders began to discuss how to reform the Democratic Party to stem the hemorrhage of voters to the Republicans. A Democratic task force in 1982 suggested that economic growth rather than redistribution could be a basis for the party's economic policy, and a number of so-called neoliberals urged policies to move the economy away from traditional smokestack industries to the high technology sector. The demoralizing defeat of Walter Mondale in 1984 intensified efforts to fashion a larger electoral coalition than the "interests" with which the party was traditionally identified. The need, a former Carter administration official said, was for the Democrats to give precedence to economic policy and "become the party of growth, productivity, opportunity and hope" rather than the party of social policy. The outcome was the formation in 1985 of the Democratic Leadership Council (DLC) to explore "new ideas," which came to include measures to foster economic growth and competitiveness, rather than the big government prescriptions of old. The DLC was not altogether welcomed by party liberals, and some African American politicians were suspicious of its apparent attempt to diminish the visibility of minority groups in the Democratic Party, dismissing it as the "southern white boys' caucus." But even some traditional Democrats had come to support aspects of laissez-faire economics. As far back as 1978 Edward Kennedy had played a lead role in airline deregulation, and the Democrats' willingness to consider deregulation in certain industries won some respect from business. In 1984 corporate donations to the Democratic Party for the first time exceeded those of organized labor. After the 1984 election, while not a member of DLC, Kennedy agreed that his party needed to dispel the notion "that all the Democrats have to give is more programs," that the Democrats "must do more with less."[1]

Also having some impact on the Democratic Party was the energy of progressive interest groups. After the fracturing of the electoral coalition that had sustained the reform administrations of Franklin Roosevelt and Lyndon Johnson, and with Republicans usually in command of the White House after 1968, it had made some sense for liberals to abandon electoral politics for interest group politics and seek favorable action from legislative committees and the courts. Some did so. In a sense, liberalism fragmented into its constituent parts, and continued quite successfully as disparate movements devoted to feminism, consumer protection, environmentalism, and so on. There were conservative citizen groups too, but by the 1980s several progressive groups were well established and were the more successful in commanding media attention and securing responses from government. Such citizen organizations as the National Organization of Women, Greenpeace, and Common Cause had memberships in the hundreds of thousands. For the most part formally non-partisan, they might direct their attentions to Republican lawmakers as well as Democratic, but they usually found greater sympathy for their causes in the Democratic Party. Such groups enjoyed their greatest support among the middle and upper-middle classes, and at a time when labor groups were contracting, their influence also edged the Democratic Party's agenda away from the working-class issues of old and toward the quality-of-life issues important to many in suburban America. "The best one can say about the bulk of these organizations," concluded one analysis, "is that they sing with an upper-middle-class accent." With the decline of labor unions and the increasing attenuation of party ties with individual voters, too, the Democrats were coming to tilt their general fundraising efforts toward the middle classes most likely to vote. Some in the party, particularly the "baby boom" centrists who were rising to influential positions during the 1980s, were able to subscribe both to the neoliberal economic ideas that Reagan had helped to popularize and to the liberal positions on social and environmental matters of the progressive citizen groups. The old labor issues of union rights, redistribution of income, and the rebuilding of cities did not figure highly on this agenda.[2]

The Democrats could take some consolation from the congressional elections of 1984, when they retained a substantial majority in the House of Representatives and narrowed the Republican lead in the Senate. In the mid-term elections of 1986 they regained the Senate, with a healthy majority of 10, although several of their successful candidates had "supported government policies to encourage economic growth and traditional American family values." Ronald Reagan might have been gratified by this accommodation, but he was unlikely to achieve significant new legislation without the cooperation of congressional Democrats.[3]

Ronald Reagan began his second term by reshuffling his White House management team, a questionable action by someone who relied so heavily on a strong staff to protect him from his limitations. He amiably acceded to a request from Chief of Staff Jim Baker and Treasury Secretary Don Regan that they swap jobs. Gone was the reasonably competent troika of Baker, Ed Meese (who became Attorney General), and Mike Deaver, and in its place the tough ex-marine Regan instituted a centralized command structure. This system did not work well, and eventually the abrasive Regan was ousted early in 1987, the victim of his own hubris and the enmity of the First Lady. He complained to Vice President George Bush, "I'm being fired like a shoe clerk."[4]

Reagan's own priority after re-election was to make the tax system "more fair, and bring the rates down for all who work and earn." Irked by Democratic charges that his policies lacked "fairness," he hoped to turn tax reform – as opposed to tax reduction as such – into a popular crusade. Promising to end the various tax breaks that allowed many companies and individuals to pay little tax, Reagan proposed a system that would be "a model of fairness, simplicity, efficiency, and compassion." If the tax base could be widened, so that more people and companies paid their fair share, there would be less need for high rates. The Tax Reform Act of 1986 was a major measure. It abolished or reduced a range of tax credits and concessions, increased capital gains taxes for those with the highest incomes, but reduced individual tax rates across the board, dramatically lowering the marginal rate at the highest incomes from 50 percent to 28 percent. It also removed six million poor Americans from the system. Reagan took to television to sell the plan, aligning himself with the average citizen: "There is one group of losers in our Tax Plan – those individuals and corporations who are not paying their fair share, or, for that matter, any share. From now on, they shall pay a minimum tax. No more free rides!" Jim Baker later claimed that the new act was "the greatest domestic achievement of the president's second term." Nonetheless, it was more a bipartisan than a Republican product, to which prominent Democratic Senators Pat Moynihan and Bill Bradley and Congressman Richard Gephardt made vital contributions. When the tax bill came to the House of Representatives, the Republican members initially voted overwhelmingly against it, though eventually the president prevailed on enough of them to join with the Democratic majority in passing it.[5]

When Reagan took office the top marginal rate had been 70 percent; he took considerable satisfaction at reducing it to 28 percent in the course of his presidency. "With the tax cuts of 1981 and the Tax Reform Act of 1986," he reflected in his memoirs, "I'd accomplished a lot of what I'd come to Washington to do." In signing the 1986 law he boasted that it gave the United States "the lowest marginal tax rates ... among the major industrialized nations." Reagan had indeed flattened the tax system, and the top rate would remain low by mid-twentieth-century standards; other countries moved in the same direction. While the very rich – the top one percent of earners – greatly benefited from the tax changes, more generally the changes did not have the effect of making the system more regressive. In 1990, for example, in terms of family income, the top 20 percent of families paid 27.3 percent of their income in federal taxes, compared to 26.8 percent in 1980. The proportions that other income groups paid in federal tax also changed only very marginally, although those in the middling categories were paying somewhat more, leading to complaints about a squeezed middle class. Overall, taxes had been redistributed rather than reduced, increases in payroll taxes for Social Security and Medicare offsetting the income tax cuts. The vaunted tax cuts, however, had succeeded neither in increasing productivity, as the supply-siders had promised, nor in generating economic growth in such a way as to increase tax revenues and thereby close the deficit.[6]

During his second term Reagan also amplified his commitment to family values, which became a familiar theme in his public statements. Leaders of the Christian right enjoyed conspicuous access to the Reagan White House. Nonetheless Reagan did little to advance their agenda, despite his regular and occasionally bizarre invocations of God. "You might be interested to know that the Scriptures are on our side on this," he said in 1985 in resisting cuts to the defense budget. He early backed anti-abortion legislation, which may have reassured the evangelical constituency but did not convince Congress. The courts, strengthened by Reagan's appointees, chipped away at abortion rights, as in reducing access to abortion for Medicaid recipients, but the abortion rate did not abate. Yet if Reagan was able to deliver little of substance to his evangelical supporters, his friendliness seemed to earn political rewards. In the 1980 presidential election, some 63 percent of white born-again Christians had cast their ballots for Reagan, but so had white Protestants generally. But in 1984 support from the white born-again Christians jumped to 78 percent, and when George H.W. Bush ran as the Republican candidate in 1988 he scooped 81 percent from this group (against 66 percent of white Protestants). During the course of his administration the Christian right became an important and growing part of the Republican coalition. Reagan was setting his face against the permissive moral values that had erupted in the 1960s, as well as against atheistic communism, and evangelical Americans rallied to this cause. "Ronald Reagan saved the country," rejoiced Moral Majority leader Jerry Falwell in 1988.[7]

Helping to consolidate the Christian right behind the Republican Party was the huge controversy triggered by Reagan's nomination of the conservative jurist Robert H. Bork to the Supreme Court in 1987. This row also inaugurated the long-term contestation over judicial nominations that would become a regular feature of American politics. Since Reagan's accession the White House had taken particular care to screen possible appointees to the federal judiciary to ensure that they took conservative positions, particularly on abortion, what some called an "ideological litmus test." The Solicitor General's office was encouraged to pursue conservative positions before the Supreme Court, and administration officials regularly made speeches criticizing liberal judges. In 1986 Reagan nominated the Supreme Court's most conservative member, William Rehnquist, as Chief Justice, and Senate liberals mobilized a large though insufficient vote against his confirmation. The affair was a dress rehearsal for a greater confrontation over the judiciary the following year.

The new controversy was precipitated by the retirement in June 1987 of Justice Lewis Powell, who had been the swing vote on the bench between the conservative and liberal wings, and his departure finally gave the administration the opportunity to secure the safely conservative Court it craved. Patrick Buchanan, the former White House communications director, once predicted a justice like Bork would "do more to advance the social agenda – school prayer, anti-pornography, anti-busing, right-to-life and quotas in employment – than anything Congress can accomplish in 20 years." Bork was a well-qualified conservative jurist with a reputation for attacking the Supreme Court's enlargement of civil and individual rights in the 1960s and 1970s. New Right fundraiser Richard Viguerie was ecstatic: "This is the most exciting news for conservatives since President Reagan's re-election." Opposition to Bork's nomination from both liberal lawyers and politicians was immediate, and went well beyond questioning his legal qualifications. Senator Edward Kennedy charged Bork with subscribing to views on civil rights and the First Amendment worthy of a "Neanderthal."

He conjured a lurid vision of Bork's America, in which "women would be forced into back-alley abortions," blacks "sit at segregated lunch counters," and "rogue police … break down citizens' doors in midnight raids."[8]

The controversy over Bork, which journalist Haynes Johnson described as "the most telling political incident of the Reagan presidency," developed into an extraordinarily passionate battle between lobbies on both sides. "This guy is a symbol for a lot of what has been going on since 1980," explained one civil liberties activist. The White House felt similarly, summoning extensive resources on Bork's behalf. When the confirmation hearings of the Senate Judiciary Committee opened, 23 spotlights were trained on Bork's face, with its beard that looked as if it had been stuck on. During five grueling days Bork repeated his belief in "judicial restraint," grounding individual rights in those clearly identified in the Constitution. But his attempts to distance himself from some of the more conservative stands in his record led to charges that he was undergoing a "confirmation conversion," and even some conservatives began to back away from him. Pat Robertson, the celebrated television evangelist and a candidate for the Republican nomination for president, complained that Bork had "gone before the television cameras and said he is in the mainstream and wouldn't do anything different from anybody else." In the eventual Senate vote, Bork was defeated by 58 to 42, the largest margin ever for a Supreme Court nomination. Six Senate Republicans voted against the nomination.[9]

The seat eventually went to Anthony Kennedy, a restrained mainstream conservative. There was a long-term cost to the Bork controversy. Supreme Court appointments became even more bitterly contested, as both conservative and liberal interests realized the importance of mobilizing their forces to maximum effect, and the politics of the nominee loomed larger than his or her judicial record. The affair also served to deepen the venom in regular party politics.

Complementing the loss of the initiative by the Reagan White House on the domestic front were serious economic embarrassments. In January 1987 John Kenneth Galbraith, the authority on the Great Crash of 1929, presciently warned of the possibility of another stock market crash, citing the recent speculation and the feverish corporate buyouts that had sent stock prices to new highs. On Monday October 19 the crisis hit. As the *Washington Post* described it: "The stock market was devastated by the worst one-day collapse in history yesterday in a pandemonium of panic selling that shattered all records and swamped stock exchanges around the country and overseas." The Dow Jones index fell by 22.6 percent on that day, nearly double the drop of October 29, 1929 which had precipitated the Great Depression. The harrowing headlines raised specters of another Great Depression, and the consequent losses in stock markets around the world testified to the electronic and psychological interdependence of the global financial community. "What we've seen essentially is the first global election," said American Stock Exchange Chairman Arthur Levitt Jr., referring to the international turbulence: "By that I mean a very significant massive vote of no confidence in our Congress and in our administration." Over the next several days the market fluctuated greatly. Japanese intervention in securities markets helped to stem the collapse, and the Fed under its new chief Alan Greenspan eased the money supply and brought down interest rates. What helped it to do this was the prevailing low rate of inflation, itself a consequence of the fortuitously large drop in the oil price in 1986. Shares began to inch up again and soon stabilized. The crash underlined the degree to which the American economy was part of a global system, and was in some measure dependent on decisions taken in such financial centers as Frankfurt and Tokyo. Economists pointed to anxieties over the budget and trade deficits and the extent to which they were covered by foreign investors, whose forbearance could not always be counted on. Chrysler Chairman Lee Iaccoca insisted that "we can't keep romping forever on borrowed money." "The budget and trade deficits are the culprits ..." he warned: "The borrowing has to stop."[10]

As the Reagan presidency ended another crisis loomed. As part of its deregulation mission, the administration had lifted controls on the savings and loan (S&L) banks (which provided long-term loans to allow people to buy homes), a measure greeted by the president as the "most important legislation for financial institutions in fifty years." Some easing of these regulations had begun during the Carter administration, but it was the Garn–St. Germain Act of 1982 that permitted these banks to engage in a wide variety of investments, not simply home loans. Perhaps they could thus secure higher returns in a competitive market, and if some of these ventures proved risky, depositors need not worry – the federal government continued to guarantee deposits (up to $100 000 for each individual). In fact the removal of controls unleashed a frenzy of speculative ventures, unsafe loans, and outright frauds in the S&L business. In the 1987 words of the California S&L Commissioner: "The best way to rob a bank is to own one." By the time Reagan left office many of these banks were collapsing. The bill had to be picked up by the taxpayer, and historian William Pemberton estimated the cost as greater than that of the Vietnam War, and "by far the most expensive scandal in world history." The bailout was immense, though proved to be not as high as the early dire predictions; an analysis by the Federal Deposit Insurance Corporation in 2000 was to put the cost to the taxpayer at $124 billion. An immediate legacy of the S&L crisis was a further swelling of the budget deficit, which was to serve as a straitjacket on the incoming Bush administration.[11]

The S&L debacle reinforced the Reagan era's association with financial scandals. The deregulation of finance begun under Carter and continued under Reagan, the giddy performance and the globalization of the stock market, the advent of computer trading, the celebrated "merger mania" of the mid-1980s, and the exploding financial sector created conditions in which the formal and informal safeguards of the past had largely disappeared. "Greed is all right," the celebrated Wall Street financier Ivan Boesky told a campus audience in 1985, a year before he pleaded guilty to insider trading. Another innovative trader was Michael Milken, who made an enormous fortune through high yield or "junk bonds" and dazzling takeover operations. Shortly after Reagan left office Milken was indicted on 98 counts of fraud, racketeering, and illegal trading. For many Americans such spectacular scandals served to contaminate the "Reagan boom," which seemed to benefit the unscrupulous rich rather than the diligent working and middle classes.[12]

Reaganomics had been intended to restore American economic strength, and Reagan regarded the long upswing in the economy after 1982 as his greatest domestic legacy, though there was a threefold irony about his economic policies. They deepened American involvement in the global economy; economic recovery owed more to Keynesian than to supply-side prescriptions; and they did not after all deliver the promised reduction in government.

Saudi Arabian, West German, and Japanese investors bought the Treasury bonds that the administration had to issue to cover its budget deficit. American consumers in significant part spent their tax concessions and their savings on Western European and East Asian products, which furthered the erosion of traditional American industries and increased the trade gap, while foreigners spent their dollar surpluses by buying up American firms, real estate, and corporate and government securities. The declining price of oil abetted this consumer boom, though left the United States even more dependent on this imported and strategic commodity. While the flood of foreign investment and the intensified international competition had roles in driving the restructuring of the American economy, they had in no small part been unleashed by the budget and trade deficits that were not avowed objectives of Reaganomics. "The long-term implication of Reagan's policies was to make the U.S. a genuinely interdependent part of the world," noted a Brookings Institution economist in 1987: "That's the exact opposite of their intentions."[13]

Reaganomics was a far from coherent set of policies, as historian Iwan Morgan has shown, for the administration tacked in different directions in different years, sometimes undoing what had been done before. The economic growth of the 1980s owed less to Reagan's vaunted "supply-side" experiment than to a particular mix of monetary (the responsibility of the Fed) and fiscal policies. Ironically, then, the growth was probably due mainly to a version of Keynesianism, as demand was increased through the tax cut and military spending, for there is little evidence that lower taxes prompted people to work harder and save and invest more and so boost production and government revenue, as supply-side theory had promised. This long boom did owe something to the deregulatory policies that Reagan pursued after their initiation by Jimmy Carter, as it was also assisted by the Fed's blitzkrieg on inflation. The deficits remained as a legacy. They also damaged American prestige. During the Reagan years Japan became the world's leading creditor nation, replacing the United States, which became the largest debtor. Another legacy of Reaganomics, as previously discussed – though exacerbated rather than caused by the administration's policies – was the increasing distance between the richest and the poorest Americans and the stagnancy of wages for many workers. The financial benefits of the boom flowed mainly to the top. The sometime Republican analyst Kevin Phillips reflected that "the two most striking economic groups of 1989" were "billionaires – and the homeless."[14]

Reagan perhaps slowed the long-term growth of government and helped create those conditions that allowed Bill Clinton to say in 1996, "the era of big government is over." But the federal government did not actually diminish, while state and local governments increased their workforces by 20 percent in the decade from 1982. Reagan had been elected promising to abolish the departments of Education and Energy, but they were still there as he left office and had even been joined by a new cabinet department, Veterans Affairs. The budgets and personnel of the federal regulatory agencies, which had been squeezed in Reagan's first term, were growing again during his second, and by the end of Reagan's administration their overall cost had increased by 18 percent in real terms. Murray Weidenbaum, the former chair of Reagan's Council of Economic Advisers, noted in 1989: "The federal government looms larger in the American economy today, any way it is measured: federal spending in real dollars or percent of gross national product, or by the size of government payrolls – all are up since 1980." As Bruce Schulman has noticed in a survey of six industrialized nations, only in the United States did total government outlays increase in the 1980s as a share of GDP.[15]

If Reaganomics did not work as intended, the doctrines associated with it proved beguiling. Reagan's very commitment to lower taxes and curbing the unions endeared him to entrepreneurs around the world, one reason why foreigners were prepared to put money into the American economy. The extended performance of the world's largest economy encouraged other countries more fully to embrace free market doctrines. As early as 1985 Secretary of State Shultz discerned an "intellectual shift" as countries in Asia, Europe, Latin America, and Africa emulated the American success: "we see movement to decentralize, to denationalize, to reduce rigidity and to enlarge the scope for individual producers and consumers to cooperate freely through markets." Free market ideology did indeed grow in these years, though its projection around the world also owed something to the IMF, the World Bank, and the OECD (Organization for Economic Cooperation and Development). It also owed a lot to the recent rapid growth of the East Asian "Gang of Four" (Hong Kong, South Korea, Singapore, and Taiwan), which so impressed development economists. While the American economy achieved a reasonable rate of sustained growth, some other economies were growing faster, sparking fears that American power had already peaked. As financial journalist Robert Kuttner noted, "as the ethic of laissez-faire gained ground, it did so almost in lock-step with the relative decline of its economic sponsor."[16]

Although the degree to which the Reagan era represented a triumph of conservatism has been exaggerated, broadly Reagan did nudge American political culture toward the right. Reagan's personal popularity often exceeded his approval rating, and he could use it to try to bend other branches of government to his will. In his remarkable first year in particular, when his popularity was boosted by his feisty response to an assassination attempt and his flinty reaction to the air traffic controllers' strike, Congress was wary of crossing him. When his influence over Congress weakened, Reagan was prepared to compromise on occasions, and several legislative measures of his presidency, particularly in his second term, were essentially bipartisan, the work of congressional Democrats as well as Republicans.

Yet there were alternatives to legislation. Rather as Reagan came to pursue rapprochement with the Soviet Union at the same time that he was intensifying anti-communist policies in other parts of the world, so he yielded to the Democratic Congress while also doggedly pursuing his conservative agenda through other means. He managed to be both pragmatic and principled, ready to seek half a loaf when he had no alternative without actually abandoning his right-wing beliefs. He developed the so-called "administrative presidency" as a way of bypassing an unhelpful Congress. His priorities were advanced by appointing conservatives to office, not only in the judiciary but also throughout the executive agencies, and his White House aides tended to circumscribe the role that career civil servants played in policy formation. Extensive revision of the rules governing federal programs became an active concern of Reagan's team, serving to reduce the autonomy of executive agencies and enhance control from the White House. Where a strong party system had once helped administrations overcome the constitutional checks and balances laid down by the Founding Fathers, Ronald Reagan relied on his charisma, his power of appointment, and the White House's control over bureaucratic rule making.[17]

Reagan's election in 1980 had owed less to a resurgent conservatism than to a discredited opposition, but sociodemographic and cultural forces, such as suburbanization and the growth of evangelical Protestantism, were working to the Republicans' benefit. During and after Reagan's presidency the conservative right became increasingly influential within the Republican Party. For years hard-line conservatives had tended to be marginalized, but Reagan's endorsement of their values helped to convince many that they could become the mainstream. His approbation opened the way for the advancement of the Christian right into the Republican Party in the late 1980s and 1990s, and others were also drawn into this new right-wing formation. Political scientists Earl and Merle Black have concluded that the realignment of southern white voters in the 1980s was largely attributable to the Reagan presidency, and "made possible the Republicans' congressional breakthrough in the 1990s." When Reagan had introduced his tax-cutting agenda in the early 1980s fiscally conservative Republicans had harbored reservations, but by the early 1990s the party had moved to a strongly anti-tax position. Reagan, then, helped to make right-wing ideas respectable and to put them on the national agenda, and as the Republican Party moved to the right and gained supporters, the hapless Democrats were pulled toward the center.[18]

But while Reagan had some success in pulling American political culture to the right, his success was limited. His remarkable personal popularity did nothing to build a cohesive Republican ascendancy across the political system. The vaunted Reagan Revolution left the party structure largely untouched. Although the number of voters who identified with the Republicans increased during Reagan's two terms, in 1988 the Democrats still led by several points, and there were more Democrats in Congress after the 1988 elections than there had been after the 1980 elections. Reagan may have allowed conservatives to win powerful positions within the Republican Party, but, apart from segments of the media, conservatives controlled little else. Even some New Right organizations, such as the National Conservative Political Action Committee, the Conservative Caucus, and the Moral Majority, weakened or even disappeared by the end of the 1980s. By the end of his presidency Reagan was coming under attack from prominent right-wing figures who thought that he was capitulating to the Soviets and betraying the true conservative cause. Right-wing activist Richard Viguerie complained that Ronald Reagan had "abandoned every last pretense" of standing up against the Washington establishment. "Reagan's not just a lame duck," snorted the Conservative Caucus chair Howard Phillips, "he's a capon." Even business support was not as solid as it had been. Some businessmen had become very unhappy with the size of the government deficit and with the administration's failure to engage adequately with the need to improve American industrial competitiveness, and those obliged to provide health benefits to employees fretted about the White House's apparent indifference to the escalating costs. While the Republicans won the presidential election of 1988, the Democrats narrowly increased their majority in the House and maintained a 10-seat lead in the Senate, and also carried the majority of state governorships and legislatures. And even as the Democratic leadership moved cautiously toward the center under the guidance of the Democratic Leadership Council, outside the party groups less constrained by the need to fashion electoral coalitions continued to fight with some success for progressive causes.[19]

Conservatives may have largely won the economics debate, but in other fields of public policy liberals were still influential. In some areas, such as on education, poverty, and the environment, public opinion polls at the end of the Reagan era indicated majorities supporting greater government action. Much of the opposition to the Bork nomination had rested on the perception that he was unsympathetic to civil rights, and was illustrative of the vigor of liberal lobbies. Over the years, groups like the Leadership Conference on Civil Rights, the NAACP (National Association for the Advancement of Colored People), and the National Urban League had become securely institutionalized, skilled in the arts of lobbying and litigation, and if major new advances proved few in the 1980s, they were at least able to defend their earlier gains. Ronald Reagan publicly blamed Democratic programs for creating "a new kind of bondage" among African Americans, and his administration was disinclined to support the causes of racial and gender equality. It reduced the funding of the Equal

Employment Opportunity Commission, and sought to weaken affirmative action programs. Given this lack of sympathy by the Reagan administration, many civil rights activists turned to the local level, at which they made some headway, such as increasing involvement in the environmental movement. Black youths of the inner cities sent their own messages through hip-hop. But at the national level civil rights leaders had some cause for satisfaction. Affirmative action, like environmental controls, proved to be firmly embedded in the system, and federal rules were not formally changed. Quite apart from civil rights groups, bodies like the National Association of Manufacturers and the Business Roundtable now favored affirmative action mandates, corporations having adapted their procedures accordingly and not caring to offend their minority and female employees. The civil rights lobby also won a symbolic victory with an act making a public holiday of Martin Luther King Jr. Day, passed by Congress with huge majorities in 1983 and signed by a somewhat reluctant Reagan, and a major one in 1986 in securing sanctions against white South Africa, a measure dramatically passed over Reagan's veto. "This is probably the greatest victory we have ever experienced," rejoiced Mickey Leland of the Congressional Black Caucus, celebrating a remarkable reversal of American foreign policy, one which triggered a fall in the South African rand and intensified the accumulating pressures on the apartheid regime.[20]

Liberals could also point to other successes. One was the Family Support Act of 1988, in significant degree shaped by Democratic Senator Patrick Moynihan. Many liberals had become uneasy that the welfare system was encouraging dependency and were sharing with conservatives an interest in work requirements. The final bill's work provision was modest, but it extended federal welfare programs in a number of ways, including new standards for job training and health care, and would increase AFDC (Aid to Families with Dependent Children) costs by about 10 percent. Reagan's conservative aides were appalled, privately calling the bill "abominable," but the president signed it. The Democrats now controlled both houses of Congress, over which a White House weakened by the Iran–Contra and Bork affairs had limited influence anyway, and 1988 was an election year when the electoral impact of presidential vetoes had to be carefully weighed. Other major pieces of legislation, such as the Tax Reform Act and the immigration law of 1986, were also bipartisan measures, as were the clean water and Superfund measures of 1986, and were disliked by many right-wing conservatives.[21]

The *Congressional Quarterly* reported at the end of 1987 that Reagan's success rate in Congress had fallen to the lowest ever recorded since the ratings began in 1953. Liberalism was promoted by an array of well-financed citizen groups that knew how to command press attention, lobby federal bureaucracies and congressional committees, and fight issues through the courts. Environmental, public interest, consumer, feminist, and civil rights groups were prominent in these activities, and some were growing in membership. Even during Reagan's first term, Senator William Proxmire of Wisconsin had called the environmental "the most effective lobby in Washington." "More broadly," Jeffrey Berry has written, "as labor has declined, citizen groups advocating quality-of-life concerns have become the dominant voice of American liberalism." "The power of these organizations now dwarfs that of the conservative social-issue organizations," wrote another analyst in 1992, "lending credence to the charge that liberals rule Washington." Since they were often fiscally conservative, they could coexist with the business lobbies over economic policy. The vigor of such groups, as well as the opposition of the Democrats in Congress and the resilience of entrenched interests, helps to explain Reagan's failure to cut Social Security, to put a right-wing hero on the Supreme Court, and to roll back the gains made by environmental and civil rights campaigners.[22]

In some degree progressive activists were incited by Reagan's rhetorical conservatism, rather as his antipathy to the environment did something to strengthen environmentalism. "Everything falling apart ...," reflected novelist John Updike's protagonist on the 1980s: "eight years under Reagan of nobody minding the store, making money out of nothing, running up debt, trusting in God." If Reagan's focus on a very few goals, such as cutting income taxes and befriending Gorbachev, gave him his triumphs, the limited range of his interests meant that large areas of American life received only fitful attention. His conservative appointments to federal bureaucracies gave a rightward thrust to governance, but their pursuit of a radical agenda and their lack of appropriate expertise sometimes resulted in backlash or political retreat. To Tip O'Neill, "the Reagan years have been one long Christmas party for the Pentagon and the wealthy," and it was apposite that those same years, 1981–1989, also featured the popular television series *Dynasty*, with its preoccupation with the problems of the opulent. But these were also years when homelessness, AIDS, and the use of crack cocaine were also rising fast.[23]

The Reagan administration railed against the drugs culture, but in prosecuting its own "drug war" it replaced addiction experts with conservative political appointees who proved ill prepared to cope with the sudden eruption of "crack" in the mid-1980s. Crack was a smokeable variety of cocaine, and its spread was associated with inner-city crime. In June 1986 the death of basketball star Len Bias from a cocaine overdose attracted wide attention, and in September Dan Rather jangled public nerves with a two-hour CBS Special, "48 Hours on Crack Street." The First Lady, Nancy Reagan, fronted a "Just Say No" campaign, a phrase she had first used in 1982 when a child asked her what to do if offered drugs. She may have had some effect, for in an atmosphere of rising public anxiety the recreational use of drugs declined; according to one calculation the use of marijuana among high-school seniors dropped from 33 percent in 1980 to 12 percent in 1991. Legislation reinforced the message. In October 1986 the Anti-Drug Abuse Act required mandatory minimum sentences for drug offences, and a harsher law specifically directed at crack was passed in 1988. It made the penalty for possessing crack cocaine massively greater than for powder cocaine. It did not go unnoticed that crack was primarily associated with black users and powder with white. The laws of 1986 and 1988 led to a huge increase in the prison population, particularly among young black men. Some scholars saw a racial bias in the drug laws.[24]

The panic over crack roughly coincided with other public alarms. There was a rising number of homeless, partly occasioned by a long-term switch in the care of psychiatric patients from institutions to community care, which intensified in the late 1970s, though community care proved inadequate. But during the Reagan years federal funds for public housing were also cut substantially, and homelessness increased. In May 1986 public attention was arrested by an attempt to form a great human chain right across the continent, "Hands Across America," when some five million or more people held hands in an attempt to raise money for homeless programs. Ronald Reagan joined hands with his staff on the White House lawn. Congress responded with the McKinney–Vento Act in 1987, which allocated funds for shelter programs, though by the end of the decade there were still thought to be 600 000 homeless on any given night, some of them runaway children. It was also in these years that the AIDS epidemic took off, and was soon claiming thousands of victims. But these were initially mainly male homosexuals, and the Reagan White House seemed reluctant to address the issue. It was not until 1985 that Reagan first mentioned AIDS publicly, by which time a number of private groups had been taking their own initiatives. In 1986 the US Surgeon General produced a report on AIDS that included recommendations for public health policies, including sex education in schools, though Reagan distanced himself from it. In 1987 ACT UP (AIDS Coalition to Unleash Power) was founded, and launched a series of demonstrations for an effective national policy to fight the disease, and in 1988 a government educational campaign, "Understanding

AIDS," was finally launched, rather later than in some other countries. By December 1988 over 81 000 cases of AIDS had been diagnosed, and 45 600 people had died. The Reagan White House, with its ideological and political preoccupations, seemed inadequately equipped to respond to such social ills as homelessness, AIDS, and crack.[25]

* * *

Nonetheless, Reagan's firm stands on his central beliefs meant that he was widely seen as a strong president, and his two terms helped to restore faith in the presidency, which had been eroding in the wake of the abdication of Lyndon Johnson, the resignation of Richard Nixon, and the one-term administrations of Gerald Ford and Jimmy Carter. An even greater claim made for Reagan is that he revived the national spirit after the celebrated "malaise" of the late 1970s. His biographer Lou Cannon concluded that Reagan's "greatest service was in restoring the respect of Americans for themselves." Historian Robert Collins has argued that what Reagan termed "the recovery of our morale" may have been his "greatest, or at least the most fundamental" triumph, one which underpinned other successes. Contributing to Reagan's election in 1980 had been fears that the United States was being surpassed in military power by the Soviet Union. Reagan's military build-up and his success in easing the Cold War had at least done something to dispel fears of that kind. But fears about the nation's economic decline were mounting as Reagan left the White House, and these were chipping away at public morale.[26]

Gauging the national mood is an uncertain operation, and while it is the case that many thoughtful observers of the American scene have credited Reagan with restoring American morale, the evidence, such as it is, is hardly conclusive. It is true that as measured by Gallup's surveys of the mood of the country, in which Americans were asked whether they were satisfied "with the way things are going," where 77 percent had expressed themselves as "dissatisfied" in 1979, the number had shriveled dramatically to 47 percent in 1988. Nonetheless, in the latter year the figure for those who were "satisfied" was scarcely any larger at 49 percent, and it was soon plunging again, so that by 1992, by this measure, Americans were about as dispirited as they had been in 1979. Reagan's own appeal was also fading. A poll in May 1988 revealed that most voters wanted the next president to "set the nation on a new direction," not to "keep the country moving in the direction that Ronald Reagan has been taking." He left the presidency with a high approval rating – 66 percent according to an AP poll of late

December 1988 – but by June 1992 Gallup found that it had slumped to 50 percent. By the end of the 1990s, amidst a booming economy, Reagan's approval rating was rising again, and in 2005 an online poll would identify him as the greatest American who had ever lived. Nostalgia was working its wondrous balm, assisted by conservative propagandists eager to turn Reagan into an icon. But in the immediate aftermath of his presidency neither Reagan's personal standing nor the mood of the country was particularly buoyant. If Ronald Reagan had indeed restored American morale, it did not long survive him, as his successor in the White House was unhappily to find.[27]

Chapter 7

Gentleman George, Culture Wars, and the Return of Malaise

The ending of the Cold War and the astonishing collapse of the Soviet empire occasioned not only glee in the United States but also alarm at the unpredictable consequences. As the military threat associated with the Soviet Union diminished, more attention came to be accorded to the economy, which, said many experts, was in a bad way, unable to compete with the new economic giants of West Germany and Japan, which had flourished under American Cold War protection. Further, Ronald Reagan's policies had left enormous budget and trade deficits, severely circumscribing the government's maneuverability in both domestic and foreign policies. The budget deficit in particular was held to be endangering the future economic power of the United States. There were other worries, too. Immigration into the United States was reaching a new peak, a crack cocaine epidemic was despoiling the cities, and the outbreak of "culture wars" threatened social fragmentation. Congress became enmeshed in corruption charges, and before the end of George Bush's term the economy visibly weakened. By 1992 the mood of the nation was as troubled as it had been during the celebrated "malaise" of 1979–1980.

The country battered by these storms was led by a president who considered it his duty to manage the government rather than lead a crusade. George Bush was the president as administrator, competent enough in that respect but lacking the imagination that the times seemed to call for. George Shultz during the 1988 campaign had noted that Bush possessed "a relatively low ideological content compared to the present administration." Contrasting himself with Reagan's crusading vision, Bush was content to offer a "kinder and gentler nation." One analysis of Bush's early days in

Contemporary America: Power, Dependency, and Globalization since 1980,
First Edition. M.J. Heale.
© 2011 M.J. Heale. Published 2011 by Blackwell Publishing Ltd.

the White House observed that he and his team were "masterful in mounting the spectacle of an unspectacular president." As a patrician administrator Bush above all valued stability. When seeking re-election in 1992, asked by friends what he planned for his second term, he simply replied that "he wanted to be there to handle what comes up." Bush would be deeply hurt by the failure of the voters to re-elect him after what he felt was a scrupulous management of the nation's affairs.[1]

Born into an upper middle-class Yankee family and the son of a US Senator, Bush possessed admirable patrician values, believing deeply in his country and noblesse oblige. He betrayed something of himself after he lost an Iowa straw poll in 1987, speculating that his supporters were otherwise occupied at golf courses, air shows, and debutante parties. But he possessed the best manners of any president ever. He regarded it as a privilege to serve in government, an attitude far removed from the populistic distrust of government displayed by his predecessor. "I don't hate government," he told the 1988 Republican convention: "I believe public service is honorable." Instinctively a conservative, he saw government primarily as a device to maintain public order and manage relationships with other powers, and tended to believe that social issues should be addressed through voluntary action rather than public programs. When he took office he issued his appointees with his list of "golden rules," which included such injunctions as "Be frank" and "Work with Congress" – public service values, not policy objectives. Character, not policy, was paramount. During the 1992 campaign it was reported that a disillusioned Ronald Reagan had said of Bush that "he doesn't seem to stand for anything." He did stand for something, but not in terms that the ideological Reagan understood. Bush's sincere commitment to service explains his inconsistency on particular issues. Over the course of his career, as his opponents happily pointed out, he changed his attitude toward such issues as abortion, civil rights, and supply-side theory, compiling an erratic record capped by a fateful volte-face on taxes in 1990. Bush, however, seemed bemused by attacks on his "flip-flops," as if he regarded specific policies as secondary considerations to his primary obligation to offer disinterested management.[2]

*   *   *

George Bush's journey to the presidency had not been unobstructed. He had sought the nomination in 1980, only to be beaten by Ronald Reagan, who chose him as his running mate. The popular Reagan had managed to keep the Republican electoral coalition more-or-less together, but with the approach of his retirement the strains began to show. The religious right, which had become an increasingly important part of the Republican Party, had doubts about the fealty of Bush to their views. Indeed, the celebrated conservative evangelist Pat Robertson made an attempt to win the 1988 Republican nomination himself, as did the mainstream conservative and Senate minority leader Bob Dole, although with Reagan's endorsement Bush secured it.

During the 1988 campaign Bush offered no distinctive policy objectives, preferring to wrap himself in the flag and reproach the opposition. A low-profile vice-president under Ronald Reagan, Bush's managers had worried that he might be seen as a "wimp," and to counter this they launched a ferociously negative campaign directed against the Democratic candidate, the Massachusetts governor, Michael Dukakis. The fastidious Bush seemed to have no problem with allowing his aides to practice the darker political arts. Early in the campaign Dukakis had enjoyed a substantial poll lead, but this eroded as he was depicted as the personification of bleeding-heart liberalism. Ronald Reagan himself denounced Dukakis for appointing "left-wing judges," supporting gun control and being "liberal, liberal, liberal." The celebrated "l-word" deployed against Dukakis was meant to evoke the legendary permissiveness of the 1960s. With the religious right assuming greater influence in the Republican Party, the so-called "culture wars" were impacting on politics. The most notorious tactic was a melo-dramatic television commercial focused on Willie Horton, a black convict allowed a weekend's leave by Dukakis as governor of Massachusetts, who had then raped and murdered a white woman. Dukakis himself had not developed a compelling agenda of his own and he proved a weak cam-paigner. Bush did identify himself strongly with one policy position: "Read my lips. No new taxes." The turnout was the lowest in a presidential election since 1924, and two-thirds of those who did vote regretted that there had not been two different candidates. During the election year, the economy grew quite smartly at 4.2 percent of GDP, and, according to exit polls, Bush owed his victory to his status as the heir of Ronald Reagan. He was elected on Reagan's disappearing coattails.[3]

Over a quarter of Bush voters plumped for Democrats in the congres-sional elections. The Democrats retained their majorities in both houses of Congress, indeed increasing slightly that in the lower chamber, so that Bush took office facing a larger opposition majority than had ever previously confronted an incoming administration. An October 1988 opinion poll had found that 54 percent of respondents thought it "better to have different parties controlling Congress and Presidency." The voters might like a

Republican as president, but it did not follow that they greatly favored his party's policies. The deployment of negative tactics and the reduction of the campaign to sound-bites, together with voters' perception of his "experience," helped the gentlemanly Bush reach the White House. The Democrats had lost yet another presidential election, and the Democratic Leadership Conference resumed its mission to rebrand the party as a centrist or New Democrat organization. A new think tank, the Progressive Policy Institute, was created to help the party develop new ideas.[4]

On taking office, Bush sought to distance himself somewhat from his predecessor. Just three members of Reagan's cabinet were kept in place, and these were men who had been appointed only in 1988 with Bush's approval. Hundreds of other Reagan appointees lost their jobs. Bush, joked Martin Anderson, sacked more Republicans than Dukakis would have done. The new Secretary of State, James Baker, told aides: "Remember, this is *not* a friendly takeover." "Republicans agree that if ideology was the most important quality in the Reagan appointments, the loyalty factor shaped the Bush team," reported the *New York Times*: "Mr Bush has stocked his Administration with old friends from similar affluent Ivy League backgrounds."[5]

George Bush's presidency was dominated by foreign affairs, most notably the disintegration of the Soviet empire and the successful Gulf War of early 1991, and his engagement with such issues was unstinting, but he seemed almost indifferent to the course of domestic affairs. By the autumn of 1991 opinion polls showed dissatisfaction with the president's frequent trips abroad. He tended to react to issues, such as the snowballing crisis in the Savings and Loan industry, and offered little in the way of a legislative program of his own. One unhappy White House aide was to concede that "for four years we had a government that lacked interest in its own domestic policies." Close advisers reportedly conceded that "Bush generally finds domestic issues a bore," and a reporter noticed that on domestic policy Bush seemed "strangely ill at ease and reluctant to act decisively." In any case, as he pointed out in his Inaugural Address, funds were low, there was a deficit to bring down: "We have more will than wallet." "The most visible legacy of the 1980s appears to be the massive debt it has forced on the next generation," observed one analyst.[6]

Bush also inherited a Republican Party in which factional divisions were deepening. Ronald Reagan's affable personality had helped to keep the party just about united during his presidency, although in his later years he was subject to criticism from the right. The ending of the Cold War deprived the party of yet another reason to hang together. What one conservative called "the cement of anticommunism" was dissolving, and right-wing ideologues and evangelicals regarded the Bush leadership with grave misgiving. Whatever Reagan's deviations from the conservative agenda, his rejection of "atheistic communism" and big government seemed rooted in deep conviction, and if some on the right lost faith in him others allowed him the benefit of the doubt. This forbearance was not extended to his successor. "George Bush nibbles around the edges rather than throwing ideological bombs," complained the new Republican House whip Newt Gingrich of the slow incrementalism of Bush's first year. Bush the patrician was never going to provide the rhetorical anti-government conservatism that Reagan had made his hallmark. The Republican right, whose belief in the free enterprise economy seemed vindicated by the ending of the Cold War, was on an ascending trajectory, but one which tended to fracture the party and would eventually depart from rather than meld with public opinion.[7]

It was not only the economic conservatives who were becoming more vocal. It was during Bush's administration that such emotive issues as abortion, gun control, recreational drugs, and gay rights appeared to be so polarizing Americans that the term "culture wars" was coined. The roots of such divisions could be traced to the 1960s, when, according to the conservative critique, a permissiveness had been unleashed that had never been contained, though cultural disagreements also owed something to the heightened awareness of ethnicity triggered by the civil rights movement. The evangelical awakening that had emerged in the late 1970s helped to activate religious conservatives, at much the same time as 1960s liberals were carrying their mostly secular and progressive attitudes into the media, the professions, and the universities. Large-scale immigration furthered the perception of the United States as a multicultural and fragmented society. These cleavages cut across one another: on the one hand essentially tolerant attitudes confronted a traditional moralistic mentality, and on the other the proponents of multiculturalism vied with those who hankered for a common identity. One skirmish in the culture wars was that over the nomination to the Supreme Court in 1987 of Robert Bork (previously discussed), where abortion was a major issue. The various cultural contests also surfaced over such issues as the Official English campaign, school prayer and school textbooks, feminism and gay rights. The increased salience of the culture wars owed something to the tendency of conservatism to fragment as the ending of the Cold War deprived it of a common enemy, so that some on the right came instead to magnify domestic threats. The angst of the traditional moralists also reflected a perception that they were losing the battle. On a range of issues, such as women's rights, racial intermarriage, and homosexuality, public opinion polls by the early 1990s were showing greater tolerance than ever. But the demands of the traditional moralists attracted media attention, and the vigor of the religious right in the Republican Party discomfited the Bush White House.

Social surveys at the outset of the Bush presidency found that strong majorities thought that there was too little public spending on such topics as education, health, and the environment, but Bush had little enthusiasm for extending public programs. Ideally, voluntary service was the answer, and he gave his blessing to what he called "points of light," that is, "the community organizations that are spread like stars throughout the Nation." But such support could only be rhetorical, and Bush offered little, too, in areas where government did have some responsibility. During the 1988 campaign he had promised to be the "education president." Concern about the quality of American education had been heightened by perceptions that the United States was being outpaced by other advanced economies. In 1989 one of Reagan's former economic advisers reported that "the top public policy priority" of American corporate leaders had become improving the educational quality of the workforce so that business could compete in the global market. But the yawning deficit militated against the commitment of funds, and Bush's education policy proved little more than a series of gestures. Health care had also become a major issue, in large part because of its escalating costs and the large number of Americans without health cover, and exacerbated by the terrifying AIDS crisis. But the president gave health little attention. Bush noted in 1991 that the "first rule of economic policy" reminded him of the Hippocratic oath: "Do no harm." A few months later he made the same remark in relation to the government's responsibility for welfare. This attitude seemed to surface in the White House's reaction to the horrendous Los Angeles race riot of 1992, which it attributed to the liberal programs of the 1960s, and the president compounded the appearance of aloofness by being slow to visit the area, which had seen more deaths than in any other such outbreak in American history.[8]

One issue to attract the wavering attention of the Bush administration was drugs, which the president said would be his number-one domestic priority. In May 1988 opinion polls had indicated that the public regarded drugs as the most important single problem, more so than the state of the economy. The use of cocaine was widespread, and even more worrying was the spread of crack, which was associated with street gangs. Lurid media exposés helped to spread alarm; it was not only drug users who appeared to be at risk, but the general public too. Attempts were made to intercept the supply of drugs from Peru and Columbia and to enforce the anti-drug laws with enhanced policing and jail space. The Bush administration doubled the amount spent on combating drug abuse to $12.7 billion. But, like other Bush measures, the drugs strategy remained limited by the budget deficit, which meant that only "smidgens of the needed resources" could be afforded, obliging drug czar William J. Bennett to resort to a high-profile but inexpensive speaking crusade. Some critics argued that the program failed to address the real problem – the growth of an urban "underclass" that seemed beyond the reach of public policies.[9]

Bush failed to make much impact too on the social issues dear to the heart of the New Right. It may have been the patrician in him that led him to sign the Americans with Disabilities Act, which extended civil rights to people with disabilities, including AIDS patients. He did signal his lack of enthusiasm for civil rights in 1990 when he vetoed a bill designed to reverse Supreme Court rulings that had shifted the burden of proof to workers rather than employers in job discrimination cases, but he retreated in 1991 in signing a measure that was little different. Similarly ambiguous was his record over abortion. The White House entered an *amicus curiae* brief in a 1989 case arguing for reversing the *Roe v Wade* decision, but the Court disappointed the religious right in declining to do so, though it did recognize the authority of individual states to place restrictions on abortion in publicly funded clinics. Bush hoped to improve his relations with the right wing by nominating the conservative African American Clarence Thomas to the Supreme Court in 1991, but this too backfired. A major row erupted during the confirmation hearings when a former assistant, Anita Hill, accused Thomas of sexual harassment, and tensions were raised further when male senators attacked her testimony. The ferocity of the row, like that over Robert Bork in 1987, reflected the degree to which the judiciary had become politicized. Bush stood by Thomas, who was narrowly confirmed, but at the cost of some female votes in the 1992 election.

George Bush, a sportsman and hunter, announced himself as the "environmental president," and could claim some success in this area. Public consciousness was raised in 1989 when the oil tanker *Exxon Valdez* ran aground in Alaska, contaminating 6000 square miles of ocean and devastating wildlife. Bush increased funding for the EPA, and appointed a professional conservationist, William Reilly, to head it. He extended wildlife refuges and wetlands, and appropriations for the endangered species program more than trebled. The White House could claim much credit for the important Clean Air Act Amendments of 1990, which tightened controls on the industrial emission of air pollutants and introduced a program for reducing acid rain. But their implementation was weakened by the

White House, which used its authority to revise regulations governing environmental safeguards. With the slowing of the economy in 1991, the White House succeeded in loosening other environmental regulations. If Bush had opened his presidency claiming to be the environmental president, he was ending it as the apologist for American businesses and jobs.

One reason for the growing budget deficit that so plagued the Bush presidency was the peaking of the Savings and Loan debacle, which had its origins in the Reagan administration. Early in his term, finally facing up to the unpleasant truth that many S&Ls had been playing fast and loose with public money, Bush announced a rescue plan, but the bailout costs continued to escalate, and by April 1990 had reached an estimated $325 billion, jolting the public into a greater awareness of the issue. Adding to the president's embarrassment was the revelation that his son was involved in one failing S&L. In the event, the costs were to prove substantially less than the 1990 estimate, but the bailout put a further strain on the federal budget.

By May 1991 the S&L imbroglio had resulted in 550 convictions in major cases, and financial and associated villainy became a leitmotif of Bush's presidential term. The public's appetite for scandal, its magnification by the media, and its ready exploitation by politicians to discredit their opponents showed no sign of abating. When he took office, Bush had made much of his determination to hold his appointees to a high ethical standard, implicitly distancing himself from several unhappy episodes of the Reagan years. But he was tempting fate. He had already nominated John Tower, an old friend and former Republican Senator from Texas, to be Secretary of Defense, but a ferocious resistance developed, focused on Tower's recent lucrative links with defense contractors and his drinking. For the first time since 1959 the Senate rejected a president's cabinet choice. It may be that the Democratic majority in the Senate was still smarting over the venomous treatment of their candidate in the recent presidential campaign. The Republicans were soon responding in kind; "they want to get even," admitted one of them. Grounded in the frustrating persistence of divided government, fed by the passions of the Bork controversy and the 1988 campaign, goaded by the emergence of culture wars and of a 24-hour news cycle, attack politics was on the rise.[10]

In the subsequent months and years Republican legislators passed up no opportunity to expose the improprieties of Democratic politicians, who still controlled both houses of Congress. As right-wing Republicans gained influence in the House, their assault on Democratic figures tended to increase. A major target was the House Speaker, James Wright of Texas. "If you couldn't stomach Tower at the Department of Defense," asked Newt

Gingrich, "how do you feel about Jim Wright being second in line to the president?" Wright was forced to resign in 1989 after charges that included persuading audiences to buy copies of his autobiography, thus enabling him to exceed the limits on outside income. In the following year House Democratic whip Tony Coelho was forced out over a loan from an S&L executive. Other scandals, financial and sexual, erupted with titillating regularity. In 1992 there was the House banking scandal, when it emerged that a majority of members of the House of Representatives had been allowed to run unpenalized overdrafts by the House's own bank, and a number of felonies and improprieties were exposed. To mark his shame as one of its members a Republican congressman made a speech in the chamber with a paper bag over his head. Also beginning to unravel was a scandal focused on embezzlement and money laundering in the Congressional Post Office. Dan Rostenkowski, a prominent Democratic congressman, was eventually indicted on criminal charges. Republican partisans, it seemed, were preparing the way for their party's long-awaited recapture of Congress by discrediting the Democratic leadership, a strategy that was to bear fruit in 1994. The editor of the conservative *National Review* later acknowledged that conservatives in the 1990s used scandal as an "excuse not to engage in frank political and ideological argument." Americans already possessed a generally low regard for their political masters and representatives, and these episodes could only tarnish further the reputation of Washington politicians.[11]

Right-wing Republicans did not confine their criticisms to Democrats. With the ending of the Cold War and the celebration of free market doctrines, political conservatives were on the offensive. The disappearance of the communist enemy meant that they were free once more to resume their attacks on excessive government and permissive values. During the early 1990s the Bush administration came under increasing fire from the political right. The Republican coalition was fragmenting, divided by such issues as free trade, immigration, foreign aid, and abortion. Journalists espied a "conservative crackup" as right-wing groups turned on one another.[12]

Despite Bush's belief in limited government, he was unable to keep down federal expenditures. Federal spending as a proportion of GDP had peaked at 23.5 percent in 1983, as Reagan secured the nation's defenses, but the percentage had eased down to 21.2 percent by 1988. During Bush's term, however, it began rising again, reaching 22.3 percent in 1991. The Gulf War and the S&L bailout accounted for some of the increase. Nonetheless, on this measure the government was growing bigger, and the cost of federal regulations increased. The right-wing Cato Institute was outraged:

"Domestic spending is expanding at a faster clip under Bush than it did under other recent presidents typically labeled as big spenders ... Incredibly, Bush is on the way to being the biggest champion of new domestic spending since Franklin Roosevelt."[13]

But it was the economy which presented the Bush administration with its most problematic domestic challenge. "There ... seems to be a consensus that the United States has lost its economic hegemony," wrote one analyst in 1990, "and to correct new imbalances it must put its fiscal house in order." During the election campaign Bush had promised no new taxes – "read my lips" – but by 1990 the projected budget deficit was again burgeoning alarmingly. Bush made addressing the deficit a priority, harboring hopes for a bipartisan agreement with the Democratic majority in Congress, but his overtures achieved little beyond annoying right-wing Republicans. A sustained economic boom might just have generated the revenues needed, but instead the economy slowed. A Democratic Congress reluctant to cut spending and a president committed to no tax increases were soon locked in a protracted deadlock, and divisions within Congress, where Republican right-wingers were not disposed to help the president out, rendered agreement even more elusive. There were divisions in the administration too, where the influential Budget Director Richard Darman was more determined than his predecessors to do something about the deficit. One aide was told that "nobody at a senior level in the Bush White House cared about supply-side economics because nobody there believed in Reaganomics!"[14]

By the summer of 1990 the president reluctantly recognized that there would have to be tax increases "because the deficit was worse than anyone had envisaged." A conventional response to a looming recession would have been to pour money into the economy, but the level of debt precluded this. The Federal Reserve was refusing to cut interest rates (which might have boosted the economy) until a plausible deficit reduction plan had been agreed. Needing to increase the defense budget for a possible war in the Gulf, the president capitulated to the Democratic majority in Congress, and the "compromise" budget included an increase in the top rate of income tax and higher excise taxes. The federal tax increases, in dollar volume, were the second largest in American history. One outcome was to make congressional Republicans even more reluctant to engage in further budget deals that might violate their deepening belief in the sanctity of tax cuts.[15]

True to his patrician values, Bush's decision on taxes reflected his willingness to put the public interest first, and later, in 1998 when the budget deficit was eventually eliminated, he felt vindicated by analyses citing the 1990 compromise as the first step toward that end. But his responsible presidential stand did him no political good at the time. Conservative Republicans, a growing force in Congress, felt betrayed, not least the true believers in Reaganomics, led by their brash House whip Newt Gingrich. So did the Republican candidates in the imminent mid-term elections of 1990 who had been loyally supporting the president's promise of "no new taxes." The president's approval ratings promptly dropped by 25 points, and his party suffered further losses in both houses of Congress. In December conservative activist Richard Viguerie complained that "Mr. Bush has done more harm to the GOP than any Democrat in a decade."[16]

Perhaps Bush could have sprung back from this humiliating climb-down, particularly as his handling of foreign affairs was widely acclaimed, but the economic slowdown soon deepened into recession, partly because the Gulf crisis was undermining consumer confidence. The great industrial shakeout of the early 1980s was being resumed. Many businesses sought to "flatten" their structures, eliminating whole layers of management. The administration seemed reluctant to intervene, creating a damaging impression that the economy was being allowed to drift. The recession of 1990–1991 in fact was not particularly severe, but the economy was slow to recover. For a generation real wages had been stagnant, and the advent of yet harder times was deeply disturbing. Further, job losses had spread to the white-collar classes, a feature which attracted media attention and thus served to enhance the anxieties of people likely to vote. Never before, as far as records could show, had the proportion of white-collar workers unemployed actually grown during a recession. In the past, laid-off blue-collar workers could often expect to be rehired when the worst was over, but white-collar workers, with their mortgages and college fees, could not see how they could recover from "downsizing." With jobs disappearing, many households also lost their health insurance, elevating health care as a sensitive political issue. Bush's star rating after the Gulf War, in which he had humiliated Iraq's Saddam Hussein, did not survive the winter of 1991–1992. The war, after all, had lasted only a few weeks and for most Americans was a television spectacle demanding no commitment on their part; Iraq, with an economy the size of Kentucky's, was hardly the threat once posed by the Soviet Union. Americans were now looking inward. Unemployment was actually higher in 1992 than it had been in the trough year of 1991. Bumper stickers appeared with the question: "Saddam Has a Job. Do You?" By February 1992 Bush's approval rating had slipped to 38.6 percent, and thereafter it remained low, dropping to a humiliating 29.6 percent in October. When asked why his domestic record did not match his foreign record, Bush snapped: "I didn't have to get permission from some old goat in the United States Congress to kick Saddam Hussein out of Kuwait. That's the reason."[17]

The sluggishness of the economy and the issue of the deficit were part of a larger concern about the state of the nation. Media stories about a rootless urban underclass, high crime rates, and the pervasiveness of illegal drugs offered little comfort. "The only significant difference between most cities in the Third World and many cities in the United States is that the latter are more dangerous and violent," reflected one sardonic analysis. In the intellectual journals and in a large number of best-selling books, the question was being asked whether the United States was in decline. There had been jeremiads warning of disasters throughout American history, but for many the ending of the Cold War was sobering. As Alan Greenspan later put it, "our vast military power suddenly felt irrelevant" and a nation's standing would now be "defined by economic prowess." In the Bush years the debate about "American decline" was peaking.[18]

One trigger was Paul Kennedy's *The Rise and Fall of the Great Powers*, published in 1987, which brought home to many that the United States was mortal after all. While the economy was performing better than it had been in the 1970s, economists and others were not slow to point out that other economies, such as those of West Germany and Japan, were performing even better. The *Day of Reckoning* was at hand, according to Harvard economist Benjamin Friedman in a devastating 1988 analysis of American economic policy. Paul Krugman warned that the good times were over in the *Age of Diminished Expectations* (1990), while another prominent economist, David Calleo, focused on *The Bankrupting of America* (1992). Several authors warned of the threat from Japan, which according to some indices was poised to overtake the United States as the world's greatest economic power. Others detected other threats to American well-being, whether massive immigration, urban blight, or Wall Street scandals. Paralleling the discourse of economic decline was the rumbling of the culture wars, triggering such bestsellers as Arthur Schlesinger's *The Disuniting of America* (1991). With powerful political implications was *The Politics of Rich and Poor* (1990) by Kevin Phillips, a formerly loyal Republican strategist who was now excoriating supply-side economics for greatly intensifying inequality and fostering a decade of greed. These and other prognostications enjoyed ample coverage in such magazines as *Time* and *Newsweek* and on radio and television. The downbeat scenarios served both to reflect and intensify the malaise that was again settling across the country. No less a figure than Alan Greenspan, the Fed chairman, testified before a congressional committee in March 1992: "There is a deep-seated concern out there which I must say to you I haven't seen in my lifetime." Not everyone agreed with the "declinists," as they became known, but the debate informed the 1992 election campaign.[19]

During 1988, Reagan's last year in office, almost as many Americans were dissatisfied with "the way things are going" as were satisfied, the average figures polled by Gallup through the year being 47 and 49 percent respectively. During Bush's first year the "dissatisfieds" pulled clearly ahead of the "satisfieds" at 50 and 45 percent respectively, and widened their margin yet further in 1990. There was some recovery with Bush's success in the Gulf War in 1991, but in 1992 the downward spiral resumed in headlong fashion, the "dissatisfieds" reaching a record 77 percent. Not since the celebrated "malaise" of 1979 had the mood of the country been so unhappy, if it can be measured by such devices. "And right now," wrote journalist Paul Starobin in November 1991, "the national economic mood is surly and sour, gloomy and grim." In a poll of May 1992 some 83 percent believed the country was on the "wrong track." Most resented of all, according to one survey, was the slow growth in personal income. The gloom-and-doom of the naysaying authors was being matched by the public sentiment. Particularly disaffected, according to some analysts, were white middle-class males, as their incomes were squeezed and their jobs threatened and as rights of various sorts seemed to be conferred on everyone but them, a frustration exemplified in the film *Falling Down*, focused on a sacked white-collar worker at the end of his tether, filmed as the Los Angeles riots broke out and released the following year.[20]

Such disaffection had unhappy implications for the established political leadership. One poll of July 1992 found that 82 percent of respondents agreed that both Democratic and Republican parties "are pretty much out of touch with the American people." Many Americans were looking askance at the forays of the United States abroad, particularly in the light of the dissolution of the Soviet Union, when at home joblessness, crime, and drug addiction were increasing and the infrastructure crumbling. A special election for the US Senate in Pennsylvania in November 1991 produced a shock victory for the Democratic candidate, who had begun the campaign 40 points behind but trounced Bush's own Attorney General with the slogan: "It's time to take care of our own." Further, many suspected that things were changing fundamentally and not for the better, sensing perhaps that the United States could not control its own future. Following the long years of income stagnation for many families, the economic downturn of the early 1990s could only intensify dissatisfaction with government and suspicion of impersonal forces. One sign of discontent was the emergence of a number of populist or outsider candidates during the presidential campaign, expressing outrage at Washington and unhappiness with the plight in which the United States found itself.[21]

One was billionaire businessman H. Ross Perot, described by the *Economist* as "a short little man, with a yapping drawl, sticking out ears, and a head like a bottle brush." Perot had made a huge fortune building up Electronic Data Systems before selling it to General Motors. In 1979 he had famously organized a rescue mission when two of his employees were imprisoned in Iran, a story told in Ken Follett's bestseller *On the Wings of Angels*. "There were two major American rescue efforts in Iran," boasted the publicity for the book: "One failed – and made grim headlines. The other succeeded …" Something of a folk hero, in the early 1990s Perot was articulating a deep disaffection toward Washington. Jack Gargan, head of an organization known as Throw the Hypocritical Rascals Out, announced in June 1991 that he was launching a movement to draft Perot, and early in 1992 the businessman agreed to run as a third-party candidate. The Perot boom took off as the polls showed mounting dissatisfaction with the state of the nation. Perot's main theme, apart from the incompetence of Washington politicians, was the economy, especially the horrendous budget deficit. "The debt is like a crazy aunt we keep down in the basement," he said: "All the neighbors know she's there, but nobody wants to talk about her." Perot's extraordinary candidacy attracted a great deal of media attention, especially when at times the polls showed him running ahead of the major party candidates. In the end, partly because at one point Perot took himself out of the campaign before getting back into it, he was unable to sustain his dizzying poll momentum, but the Perot phenomenon underlined the public distrust of Washington.[22]

Perot was not the only populist candidate to emerge. Among the Democrats there was Jerry Brown of California, the former "Governor Moonbeam," who charged the "incumbent party of Republicans and Democrats alike" with forming "an unholy alliance of private greed and corrupt politics." The Republicans experienced their own populist revolt. Right-wing Republicans who felt betrayed by Bush found their candidate in Patrick Buchanan, a former Nixon speech writer and a fierce critic of the president in talk shows and newspaper articles, who voiced the fury of isolationist Republicans at Bush's activist foreign policy. "Foreign aid is an idea whose time has passed," he insisted, as he also blasted the free trade orthodoxy of mainstream conservatives. He said of Bush: "He is a globalist and we are nationalists. He believes in some pax universalis; we believe in the old republic. … We put America first." Buchanan fared relatively well in the Republican primaries, including a remarkable 34 percent of the vote in New Hampshire, and took his campaign all the way to the convention.[23]

Such angry insurgents as Perot and Buchanan had little chance of making it all the way to the White House themselves, but circumstances favored newcomers. When the federal government is held in low esteem, as it was most of the time in the late twentieth century, there is some advantage in not being part of the national establishment. Outsiders to Washington, like Jimmy Carter in 1976 and Ronald Reagan in 1980, could benefit from the populist disaffection. In 1992 it was the turn of another governor. Bill Clinton had been governor of Arkansas since 1978, apart from a two-year break. A rare intellect combined with drive and charm had catapulted him from a modest background to Georgetown University, Oxford, and Yale, and when he turned to politics he had become the youngest governor in the country at the age of 32. Like several other ambitious Democrats of his generation, Clinton could be classified as a "New Democrat," one of those anxious to get away from the "big spending" image of the New Deal–Great Society tradition. This group, often upwardly mobile professionals from the "baby boom" generation, tended to be liberal on social issues like civil and women's rights, and moderate on economic issues, accepting a need to work with business and to show restraint in budgeting. They often maintained friendly relations with lobbyists from the flourishing liberal citizen groups like the National Organization of Women. Some of them, like Clinton himself and Albert Gore of Tennessee, were founder members of the centrist Democratic Leadership Council. With the Democratic Party's labor core eroding, the DLC also cultivated support among business groups, and developed the capacity to raise significant sums of money. Members tended to believe, as Al Gore put it, that the "old labels – liberal and conservative" were of limited relevance to contemporary issues: "There's no need to rely on an outdated ideology as a crutch." By late March 1992, after a series of successful primary campaigns, the Democratic nomination was effectively sewn up by the young Arkansan, insisting that he was "a different kind of Democrat."[24]

By the time of the Republican convention in Houston in August George Bush was in dire straits. With Perot at this point out of the campaign, Clinton was enjoying a huge lead in the polls. "President Bush staggered into … Houston this week as the most unpopular incumbent president to seek re-election in the past five decades," began one journalist's description. To placate the right the Bush camp allowed the Buchanan people largely to write the platform, and at the convention Buchanan himself gave a fire-eating speech identifying the party with the Christian right and denouncing the Democratic ticket as "the most pro-gay and pro-lesbian ticket in history." This was culture war. Buchanan was identifying the Democrats with 1960s-era permissiveness, and Bill Clinton had indeed admitted that as a student he had smoked pot (even if he had not inhaled). Also imparting a strident tone to the Republican convention was the evangelical leader Pat Robertson. In recent years conservative evangelicals, unhappy with the failure of the Reagan and Bush administrations to push their agenda, had been more actively seeking positions of influence in the state Republican parties, particularly through the Christian Coalition that Robertson had been mobilizing since 1989. But while some Republican activists may have thrilled to the declaration of culture war, the issue was not going to win them the election. The disarray in the Republican Party, the enmity of the right wing toward the administration, and the visibility of the zealots, could only help their opponents.[25]

Also hurting Bush was his patrician image, compounded when he tried to shop at a supermarket and it became clear that he did not know what the scanner at the checkout till was, although they had been in use for years. The central thrust of his campaign was the issue of character directed at Clinton. "I think character is important," he insisted. This was a legitimate reflection of his patrician values, but it also exploited the stories about Clinton's womanizing, his draft dodging, and his reputation for evasiveness. Bush insisted that the election was "a choice about the character of the man you want to lead this nation for another four years." Bush confided to his diary: "I'm a better person, better qualified, and a better character to be President, despite some shortcomings that I may have and there are plenty of them." But his emphasis on personal trust did not sit well with his broken "read my lips" pledge. Critics also questioned whether he really was "out of the loop" in the Iran–Contra affair. Bush's gentlemanly persona could only incite the populistic currents of 1992.[26]

Clinton recognized that much of the public disaffection was located in the middle class, allowing him to fashion a populist approach, characterized by his campaign manifesto, *Putting People First*, which assailed government by "the rich and special interests." He accepted the nomination "in the name of all those who do the work and pay the taxes, raise the kids, and play by the rules, in the name of the hardworking Americans who make up our forgotten middle class." Low-income groups no longer turned out to vote in great numbers, and it was middle-income voters who could sway elections. Clinton wooed the middle classes (which under American definitions included much of what in other countries might be designated the respectable working class) with skill, emphasizing the positive, such as investment in the infrastructure and education, and, not least, a middle-class tax cut. Joining him on the campaign trail was his formidable wife Hillary, whose skills were also to be placed at the disposal of the public. "Vote for me and get one free," Clinton sometimes said, although the tactic risked an anti-feminist backlash and meant that opponents then and later felt it legitimate to make Hillary as well as Bill a political target. Clinton's New Democrat agenda was spelled out in his acceptance speech, when he insisted that the primary solution to the country's various problems was "an expanding entrepreneurial economy of high-wage, high-skilled jobs." Clinton was also determined not to be outflanked by the Republicans on "family values." "I want an America where family values live in our actions, not just in our speeches," Clinton said, emphasizing the need for good education, health care, and child support policies. Not for the New Democrats the liberal permissiveness that the Republicans had imputed to Michael Dukakis in 1988.[27]

Turnout in the election was unusually high at 55.2 percent, over a 5-point improvement on 1988, a likely sign of the public discontent. The Republican coalition was under strain, as right-wingers fumed over Bush's reversal on taxes and the continued growth of government, and as small and medium-sized businesses blamed the Bush administration for not providing them with enough protection. Large numbers of "Reagan Democrats" deserted the Republicans during the economic uncertainty. Union households, for example, had given 42 percent of their vote to Bush in 1988, a figure which slumped to 24 percent in 1992, though many voted for Perot. There were pro-Clinton swings among some middle-class groups too, one analysis typifying these voters as "the insecure professional, the engineer or computer programmer affected by the poor state of the economy." These middle- and lower-class defections were fatal to the Bush cause. Voters in exit polls accordingly tended to cite such concerns as jobs, the deficit, and taxes as issues that had influenced their choice. Cultural issues remained marginal. Bill Clinton won the presidential election with a 5-point lead in the popular vote over George Bush, who secured only 38 percent. This result was a stunning rebuff for the Republican Party – their candidate had dropped 16 percentage points since his 1988 outing and 21 points since the high tide of Reaganism in 1984.

The Democratic ticket, with two southerners at its head, allowed the Democrats to regain part of the South and also to make inroads into the suburbs, both of which the Republicans had been seeking to make their own. The prominent role of Buchanan and other social and cultural conservatives at the Republican convention also hurt Bush among traditional Republicans and independents. Though Ross Perot carried no states, he took a remarkable 19 percent of the popular vote, more than any other third-party candidate in the twentieth century, the three-way election of 1912 apart. The Democrats also retained their majorities in both houses of Congress, and so finally the same party commanded both the executive and the legislative branches of government. Nonetheless, Clinton's share of the popular vote was only 43 percent, the least for a presidential winner since 1912. Most voters had cast their ballots for other presidential candidates. Whatever the election of 1992 was, it was not a mandate for the Democratic platform as defined by Bill Clinton. Yet 62 percent of voters wanted someone other than Bush. Enough people wanted change, and Bush's attempt to make character the issue was an irrelevance in an insecure era when the economy seemed to be going awry.

*   *   *

Ronald Reagan's policies had drawn the United States deeper into the global economic system, for good or ill. The relatively hard times of the early 1990s, the stagnancy of incomes and the downsizing of workforces, owed something to international competition and gave credence to those who argued that there was something fundamentally amiss with the American economy. In the absence of a threatening Soviet Union the conservative coalition itself was coming apart, as evangelicals bucked against the rather secular Republican leadership, as businessmen lost faith in Reaganomics but disagreed about solutions among themselves, and as isolationist and protectionist strains surfaced. In 1992 a Gallup poll found that 49 percent of those consulted believed that Reagan's economic policies were a failure, while only 44 percent counted them a success. The gentlemanly Bush might be the right man to conduct foreign policy, with his capacity to engage with fellow political leaders, but foreign policy no longer seemed so important with the Cold War over, while his lack of interest in domestic matters and his patrician diffidence meant that he was not well placed to promote the restructuring and modernization of an economy exposed to a rapidly changing world. The vote against George Bush in 1992 was of landslide proportions, as it was also a rejection of the policies of Ronald Reagan that Bush had promised to uphold. In his last days in office George Bush pardoned Caspar Weinberger, Reagan's Defense Secretary, and five others who had been indicted for their alleged parts in the Iran–Contra affair. The 1980s were drawing belatedly to an end, terminating as they had begun in a public malaise.

Chapter 8

Groping for a New World Order

"We meant to change a nation, and instead, we changed a world," said Ronald Reagan in his Farewell Address in January 1989: "Countries across the globe are returning to free markets and free speech." The world indeed was changing, though the Cold War was not quite over and it would fall to Reagan's successor, George Bush, to try to discern the outlines of a new international order. Ronald Reagan had hoped to restore to the nation some sense of control over its own destiny, and Bush did inherit his formidable arsenal, though when Bush engaged in his greatest military venture, it was in the company of 28 other nations and was largely paid for by others. The United States may have "won" the Cold War and have emerged as the world's only superpower, but there were limits to a superpower's authority in the new world, as the first President George Bush knew (and as the second was eventually to discover).

It was ironic that the man who was president during these transformative years was one who had little interest in guiding the currents of change. Bush talked about a "new world order" but articulated no clear vision of what it might be. For him, the duty of the president was simply to administer the country's affairs honestly and – especially – conduct foreign policy. As president, Bush immersed himself in foreign issues far more than his predecessor had ever done, though his concern was more to preserve international stability than to pursue the Reaganite creed of "freedom." One aide estimated that Bush spent at least 75 percent of his time on foreign policy. When the press commented that he was more comfortable with foreign than domestic affairs, he conceded to his diary "that is absolutely true." During his term he traveled to foreign countries frequently, and spent

Contemporary America: Power, Dependency, and Globalization since 1980,
First Edition. M.J. Heale.
© 2011 M.J. Heale. Published 2011 by Blackwell Publishing Ltd.

much time on the phone talking to other national leaders. Still, there was to be no Bush Doctrine. "Not having confidence that he could mold the future, he concentrated on managing the present and avoiding the mistakes of the past," Bush's Ambassador to the Soviet Union later wrote. As one senior member of the NSC staff expressed it: "This administration is not ideological ... We don't want to reinvent the world. This is not an administration that is hell-bent on change."[1]

Reinforcing Bush's temperamental disinclination to push change was the disconcerting fact that the world around him was already changing fast. The Reagan administration had achieved an unlikely degree of rapprochement with the Soviet Union, and the winding down of the Cold War was rendering obsolete several decades of foreign policy doctrines. Between 1989 and 1991, as George Bush and his National Security Adviser Brent Scowcroft were to recall with some bemusement, "Eastern Europe threw off Soviet domination, Germany united, and the Soviet Union dissolved, all without significant bloodshed." In several African and Latin American countries, and elsewhere too, authoritarian regimes, some of them previously propped up by the Soviets, were replaced by democracies. As command economies gave way to market forces, many American commentators linked the spread of democracy with the spread of free enterprise, a celebration of the American way. "Surely, America ought to wage democracy ...," wrote neoconservative Ben Wattenberg, "... and democracy American-style specifically." This quest, he thought, should supplant anticommunism as the basis of American foreign policy. In July 1989, musing on the epochal changes around him, Bush hoped that countries would "continue to move towards what works, and what works is freedom, democracy, market economies – things of that nature." Yet the ending of the Cold War, together with the retreat of superpower protection, served to increase political instability in some regions and encouraged the release of nationalist and ethnic rivalries. Bush may have been scorned for his lack of what he uncomfortably called the "vision thing," but the United States could have offered worse international leadership than the president's pragmatic caution.[2]

* * *

George Bush seemed almost reluctant to abandon the Cold War that he knew: "Nineteen forty-five provided the common frame of reference, the compass points of the postwar era we've relied upon to understand ourselves." He had been uneasy about the rapid changes in the relationship with the Soviet Union in Reagan's last years, and he was not going to be rushed into a closer embrace, despite the Soviet regime's celebrated attempts to move toward a market economy and political democratization. "Let's take our time now," Bush replied at his first presidential news conference when asked the administration's position on the Soviet Union. Bush's National Security Adviser was of similar mind, believing that the Reagan White House had "rushed to judgment" over Soviet intentions and doubting that "the forty-year confrontation between East and West" was over. "Still, dangers abound," warned the new Defense Secretary, Dick Cheney: "There are those who want to declare the Cold War ended. ... But I believe caution is in order." Mikhail Gorbachev, who over the years had become familiar with the American leadership, advised his Politburo colleagues that the incoming Bush team had been "brought up in the years of the Cold War" and that "big breakthroughs" were unlikely.[3]

An early sign of this caution came in relation to China. If most Eastern European regimes tended to retreat before the erosion of confidence in socialism and the growing demands of their populations, the Chinese authorities determined to stand firm. Following a series of protests by students and intellectuals in the spring of 1989 in Beijing's Tiananmen Square, a ferocious military crackdown left two or three thousand dead. The communist revolution, it was sardonically remarked in the West, was consuming its own young. While the occasional Eastern European dictator betrayed an envious sympathy for the Chinese regime – East Germany's Erich Honecker remarked that "we took power in order to keep it forever" – the massacre evoked horror around the world. Yet Bush's response was muted. The administration did criticize the Chinese actions and applied modest sanctions, but not the more severe ones wanted by Congress. The president was anxious not to send the People's Republic of China back into resentful isolation, and the administration was soon working to further economic and political relations with it. Within a few weeks of the massacre Bush wrote to his "old friend" Chairman Deng: "We must not let this important relationship suffer further." Bush wanted stability in Asia as much as he did in Eastern Europe, stability more than reform. His instinct was to work with the ruling elites, and he vetoed congressional attempts to end the tariff privileges that China enjoyed under its most-favored-nation status. "The administration continues to coddle China, despite its continuous crackdown on democratic reforms, its brutal subjugation of Tibet, its irresponsible exports of nuclear and missiles technology, its support of the homicidal Khmer Rouge in Cambodia and its abusive trade practices," Arkansas Governor Bill Clinton would complain in December 1991.[4]

But it was the Soviet Union that remained the primary preoccupation of a White House uncertain that the Cold War was ending. At the outset of his presidency Bush instituted an internal policy review of the super-power relationship, a lengthy process during which US–Soviet relations were allowed to cool. Deputy National Security Adviser Robert Gates argued that what was needed was a "conscious pause" to reflect on strategy after the urgent ad hocery of the Reagan era. This was what the Soviets called the "pauza," and there were both Soviet and American officials who feared that opportunities were being lost. After a session with the new president, Jack Matlock, the US Ambassador to the Soviet Union, exploded to his staff: "Our marching orders are clear: Don't just do something, *stand there!*" Bush explained to his aides: "I don't want what I do to complicate the lives of Gorbachev and the others. ... I don't want to put a stick in Gorbachev's eye." In May 1989 Bush conceded that it was time to move "beyond containment," though he asked for evidence of Soviet good inten-tions before supporting "the integration of the Soviet Union into the com-munity of nations." But events were moving faster than American policy.[5]

The Russian Revolution of 1917 had been one of the decisive events to shape the twentieth-century world, and the collapse of the Soviet Union in the early 1990s was no less momentous. Mikhail Gorbachev had been pursuing liberalization since the mid-1980s, and the Soviet Union was visibly changing. Having embarked on arms reduction and withdrawal from Afghanistan, Gorbachev also began reducing Soviet troops in the Eastern European satellites. In Poland, the Communist Party unexpectedly failed to win open elections in the summer of 1989 – "arguably the best news to come out of Eastern Europe in half a century," on one account – and reluctantly admitted Solidarity (the independent trade union) to the government. Characteristically, Bush seemed unhappy with the speed of change in Poland, apparently hoping for the survival of the communist leader, General Wojciech Jaruzelski, with whom he was on fairly friendly terms. But within months communist regimes were also crumbling in East Germany, Hungary, Czechoslovakia, Bulgaria, and eventually Romania. Authoritarian governments came to be replaced by more democratic forms, and socialist economies by capitalistic practices. The Soviet leadership, preoccupied with its critical domestic reforms, and anxious to improve relations with the West, concluded that it could no longer bear the political and financial costs of militarily subduing the resentful populations of its satellites. Each country must be responsible for its own affairs, said Gorbachev. The Soviet Union would not intervene: "We assume others will not interfere either."[6]

With the Soviet retreat mass demonstrations swept across East Germany and the hard-line communist government finally collapsed at the end of 1989. Several border crossings through the Berlin Wall were thrown open and celebrating Germans chipped souvenirs off it. For many its destruction symbolized the end of the Cold War. George Bush himself was not so sure, and was anxious to avoid triumphalist rhetoric for fear of a backlash among hard-liners in East Germany and the Soviet Union, though he cautiously pronounced himself "very pleased." Democratic congressman Dick Gephardt tartly observed: "Even as the walls of Jericho come tumbling down, we have a president who is inadequate to the moment."[7]

In December Bush met with Gorbachev in Malta, where the two forged a personal relationship, the president assuring the latter that the United States would not exploit the situation if Gorbachev allowed the Baltic states to break away peacefully from the Soviet Union. Bush decided that the United States must do what it could to support Gorbachev in his various policies. This was one reason why his response to the epochal changes in Eastern Europe was often low-key. He feared that appearing to gloat at Soviet travails would intensify the instability in much of the old Soviet empire. "It was, after all, Ronald Reagan who had stood before the Berlin Wall and exhorted Mikhail Gorbachev to dismantle the barricade," wrote one disillusioned White House aide: "By contrast, it was George Bush who delivered a speech in the Ukraine urging the reformers to cease their efforts and support the continuation of the Soviet Union."[8]

But Bush was capable on occasion of being moved by a bolder vision, as he strikingly displayed over Germany, the unification of which was to be his abiding legacy. The West German chancellor, Helmut Kohl, was publicly championing German reunification by the end of 1989, and in March 1990 the first free elections in East Germany demonstrated strong popular support and the return of a government favorable to the idea. This was a highly sensitive matter, it having been a principle of postwar Soviet policy that Soviet security depended on the neutrality or division of Germany, at whose hands the Soviets had suffered horrendous losses during World War II. German reunification was by no means welcomed throughout the West; in Britain, the Netherlands, and France in particular memories of two world wars died hard. But the Bush administration developed a skillful strategy to further German reunification, which it helped to bring about even as Germany remarkably remained within NATO (North Atlantic Treaty Organization). For the Soviet Union to lose East Germany, its great prize from World War II, wrote George Bush and Brent Scowcroft later, "would mean acknowledging the end of Soviet power in Eastern Europe and the complete erosion of Moscow's security buffer of satellite states, the very core of its security planning." It was almost unthinkable that NATO forces could replace Soviet in the eastern regions of a new Germany, and the Bush administration tried to persuade Moscow that it would be safer with a stable Germany inside NATO than an unpredictable and neutral Germany outside it. Eventually Moscow, following Bush's persistent personal diplomacy, bowed to the inevitable, and in the course of 1990 Germany was reunified as a member of NATO. Moscow's acquiescence was bought in part by the promise of Western aid for the embattled Soviet economy. Kohl and Bush had brought off an extraordinary coup. Scowcroft reflected: "For me, the Cold War ended when the Soviets accepted a united Germany in NATO." Bush could claim that his cautious approach, maintaining quiet dialogue with the Soviets while avoiding grandstanding, had helped bring about German reunification. The relationship he had forged with Gorbachev would also facilitate Soviet cooperation in the crisis that was emerging in the Gulf. With the reunification of Germany and the collapse of communism in other Eastern European states, even American hard-liners could not credibly deny that the Cold War was over. It was not just Germany that was no longer divided but the continent of Europe. Western Europe was no longer threatened by Soviet military power, the ideological basis of the Cold War had dissipated, and the geopolitical balance of power had been reconfigured.[9]

The winding down of the Cold War also provided an opportunity for further arms reductions. Substantial agreement had been reached under Reagan. With the collapse of the Warsaw Pact – dissolved in April 1991 – the Soviet Union had less to defend, and substantial reductions of conventional forces in Europe were agreed. In July 1991 the Soviet Union and the United States signed a Strategic Arms Reduction Talks (START) agreement, reducing strategic nuclear arsenals by 30 percent and establishing equal ceilings on the number of strategic weapons that each could deploy. Shortly thereafter the Soviet Union began to dissolve, and George Bush announced a number of unilateral measures designed to reduce the US nuclear arsenal, hoping that Gorbachev would respond positively, and he in turn announced the proposed elimination of certain weapon categories. Bush maintained dialogue with the new Russian leader, Boris Yeltsin, and in January 1993 the two signed the START II treaty, providing for the further reduction of warheads and the elimination of all MIRVed ICBMs. Ronald Reagan's great dream of a nuclear-free world had moved just a little closer. Seventeen years later President Barack Obama would revisit the dream.

The disintegration of its empire placed immense strains on the Soviet Union. The Soviet Communist Party, through which political power had been wielded, was fast losing authority. In the largest of the Soviet Union's 15 republics, Russia, Boris Yeltsin was elected president in 1990 and demanded the decentralization of the Soviet Union and the autonomy of each republic, and other republics soon made similar claims. A failed coup by the old guard directed at Gorbachev in August 1991 spelled the end of the Soviet system. Statues of Stalin were torn down and the Communist Party disintegrated as an instrument of government. "We have seen our implacable enemy of 40 years vaporize before our eyes," the Chairman of the Joint Chiefs of Staff, General Colin Powell, observed to a Senate committee. In December 1991 the Soviet Union was replaced by the Commonwealth of Independent States, a loose confederation joined by most of the old Soviet republics. Its dominant member would be Russia, which took the Soviet seat on the UN Security Council. In October 1992 Congress offered $410 million to further the democratization of the former Soviet republics. This was hardly commensurate with the problem, but Reagan had left the United States heavily in debt.[10]

Yugoslavia too, which since the early Cold War era had tried to keep its distance from the Soviet Union, also disintegrated in the early 1990s, triggering war in the Balkans in 1991 in a swirl of bitter and seemingly intractable ethnic rivalries. Reports of violence and massacres in what was part of Europe received disturbing attention in the world press, though the Western powers were wary of intervening in what, to them, was a highly confusing conflict for which they could see no resolution. "We're not the world's policemen," Bush rather lamely explained. "We don't have a dog in that fight," said Secretary of State Jim Baker, insisting that the United States was "comfortable" with the Europeans handling the problem. The Europeans for their part tended to look to the UN for guidance. In contrast to the Gulf War, Baker later pointed out, "our vital national interests were not at stake," and public support for US military intervention was unlikely. It would be left to Bush's successor to try to plot a way through the hazardous terrain. By that time, Soviet expert Strobe Talbott observed, "Bosnia had already experienced the worst outbreak of political violence in Europe since World War II."[11]

The United States had arguably "won" the Cold War, although the Soviet collapse was in no small part a consequence of fundamental weaknesses within the Soviet economic and political systems. Whatever the part played by American policies, it could be said that Western ideas at least had triumphed, if more-or-less free elections and especially market economics can be associated with the West. Nonetheless the new global configurations raised the prospect of a rethinking of American foreign policy. Reagan's former UN Ambassador, Jeane Kirkpatrick, suggested that the object of US policy might be to allow the United States to become "A Normal Country in a Normal Time": "With a return to "normal times", we can again become a normal nation – and take care of pressing problems of education, family, industry, and technology."[12]

Perhaps normality literally meant business as usual, that is, commerce. For many commentators, in the post-Cold War world economic power was likely to replace military might as the basis of international relationships. As one wrote: "Geoeconomic competition will contend with, and perhaps surpass, geopolitical competition as the driving force in international relations." In 1992 Bush told the Republican Convention: "The defining challenge of the nineties is to win the economic competition, to win the peace." One logical instrument for promoting a new world order was free trade. In the late 1980s there had been a rash of studies suggesting that the United States was in decline, at least economically, and it was carrying huge budget and external deficits. The Reagan boom had not done much to improve productivity, while such economies as those of West Germany and Japan seemed to be closing the gap with the United States. If the Cold War was over, there was a strong case for putting America's economic house in order.[13]

Bush himself early recognized the need for a more active trade policy. He kept in place Reagan's US Trade Representative, Carla Hills. His goal, he insisted was "to open markets, not close them; to fight protectionism, not to give in to it. We don't want an America that is closed to the world." During his confirmation hearings as Secretary of State, James Baker emphasized international commercial goals, which was one reason why he hoped to resolve conflicts and reduce tensions with countries in such areas as the Middle East and Latin America. In 1990 Bush launched "Enterprise for the Americas," with the hope of reducing trade barriers with the Latin American countries. He looked to international trade to promote economic growth, he explained in 1992, grounded on "an entrepreneurial capitalism that grows from the bottom up, not the top down." The free trade mission was presented as the logical corollary of winning the Cold War, Bush telling the protectionists in Congress: "Our market successes in the 1980s helped inspire people to throw off the shackles of communism and pursue the cause of liberty. It would be ironic if we turned our back on our greatest triumph, and as the Berlin Wall was crumbling, erected our own wall of protectionism."[14]

Bush was a strong supporter of the North American Free Trade Agreement (NAFTA). Economic growth and market expansion in Mexico would create jobs for Americans, the reasoning went, while a revitalized Mexican economy would reduce the amount of illegal immigration to the United States. In February 1991 Bush asked Congress to "fast track" the NAFTA treaty, which would allow the administration to negotiate the treaty in a three-month period, after which Congress would have 90 days to approve it unamended. Since the 1970s presidents had usually been allowed such fast-track authority so that commercial negotiations were not constantly referred back, but with the growth of the trade gap and suffering business interests calling for protection, Congress was less sanguine about foregoing its rights. "Free trade works for everyone involved," Bush insisted: "It gives smaller countries the means and ability to address important concerns within their borders – higher wages, better working conditions, a cleaner environment, healthier food and water supplies, and improved public services." There was fierce opposition to his request, but Bush did secure fast-track status for the treaty. He finally signed it in December 1992, when he had lost the presidential election in part because of the third-party candidacy by Ross Perot, who was passionate in his insistence that the treaty would mean the loss of American jobs.[15]

If the Bush White House moved cautiously with respect to the communist bloc, the ending of the Cold War allowed it greater freedom to act in other parts of the world. No longer needing to calculate with quite so much care the reactions of the Soviets, the United States was in a better position to impose its authority in such troubled regions as Central America and the Middle East. "For the first time in 40 years we can conduct military operations in the Middle East without worrying about triggering World War III," said a State Department official in 1990. It was in these two regions that the Bush administration acted militarily with greatest boldness, and in the Middle East it secured one of its greatest political triumphs.[16]

The winding down of the Cold War meant that such Latin American communists as there were seemed less of a threat to American security; the Soviet Union was also indicating to Third World countries that it could no longer afford them aid. Central American radicals and insurgents were now on their own. The aggressive stance of the Reagan administration no longer seemed appropriate, and Secretary of State Baker used the opportunity to replace Reagan's ideologically driven policies in the region with a more pragmatic approach. A compromise with Congress on Contra aid was quickly achieved, and in 1989 Nicaragua's Sandinista government accepted a peace plan providing for a cease-fire and open elections. In El Salvador too the erosion of Soviet aid hastened the ending of war and revolutionary activity declined. Hostilities also waned in Guatemala. Fidel Castro remained in command of Cuba, but his revolutionary allies in Latin America were disappearing.

Panama was more of a problem, one exacerbated by the ending of the Cold War. The one domestic issue on which Bush placed emphasis in his Inaugural Address was drugs, though it was not solely a domestic matter, for "that first cocaine was smuggled in on a ship," effectively a "deadly virus" eating at "the soul of our country." Bush had been embarrassed by the eruption of the issue during the campaign, since as vice-president he had headed Reagan's narcotics task force, which had seemed powerless to check the spread of cocaine and crack (and thus crime too) on the streets. Much of the cocaine originated in Colombia and Panama, whose leader, General Manuel Noriega, was known to be deeply implicated in the trade. For years the United States had quietly worked with Noriega, who was as hostile to leftist elements as any right-wing dictator, but relations between Washington and his increasingly vicious regime had deteriorated during the late 1980s. As Cold War imperatives eased, the drug menace became a major focus of public worries. "I won't bargain with terrorists, and I won't bargain with drug dealers either, whether they're on U.S. or foreign soil," promised Bush during the presidential campaign. Reagan's attempt to use sanctions to pressure Noriega into giving up office failed, and during Bush's first year as president relations with Panama deteriorated further as Noriega sustained himself in power through fraudulent elections and brutal suppression. A tense atmosphere developed between the Panamanian military and the US forces that remained in Panama to protect the canal, and in December 1989 a US marine was killed and a US naval officer and his wife were physically abused.[17]

George Bush now decided to act, sending in 24 000 troops, albeit without congressional authorization. Noriega was overthrown and extradited to Florida, where he was convicted of drugs offences. Outside the United States this military intervention was widely seen as an example of American imperialism and regarded as of questionable legality, and the UN General Assembly passed a resolution critical of the action by 75 votes to 20, although Gorbachev, preoccupied with his own problems and anxious not to jeopardize his improving relations with the United States, muted Soviet criticism. But the action was popular with the American public, Bush's approval rating in mid-January 1990 shooting up to 76 percent, a figure Ronald Reagan never achieved. The action illustrated something of the new configurations of the post-Cold War era. Nonetheless, the United States had acted unilaterally. James Baker saw this as a virtue, for it demonstrated to the world that the United States was fully prepared to exercise its power alone. Yet Noriega's removal did nothing to stem the flow of cocaine to American city streets.[18]

George Bush's greatest foreign policy success lay in the Middle East, the more remarkable given the hostility in the region toward the United States because of its close relationship with Israel. This venture too reflected the changing geopolitical realities of the world. For a second time the United States struck against a military dictator it had previously been nurturing, and it even managed to do so with the endorsement of the Soviet Union. On this occasion it did not act alone but led an extraordinarily broad coalition with the blessing of the United Nations. It was the Gulf War that allowed Bush to promote his concept of a "new world order," which, he insisted, must be "based upon the rule of law." In the post-Cold War world, aggression would be checked. While Bush apparently preferred to work with international institutions such as the UN to secure this objective, the basic principle of resisting aggression could justify the United States acting alone. Brent Scowcroft later explained that that was "how the new world order concept came up, as a model for dealing with aggressors. The U.S. should behave in a way that others can trust and get UN support." When applied to the Gulf, this principle to cynics looked like cover for protecting US energy supplies.[19]

In August 1990 Iraq's president Saddam Hussein launched an invasion of her oil-rich neighbor Kuwait. This in itself signified the post-Cold War world; the Soviet Union had once been a patron of Iraq, but it was no longer in a position to exercise restraint. Beyond Kuwait lay Saudi Arabia; if Saddam seized that too he would control 40 percent of the world's known oil reserves. During the long Iraq–Iran war of the 1980s the United States had quietly proffered aid to Saddam Hussein, who seemed a lesser evil than the ferociously anti-American Ayatollah Khomeini of Iran. Indeed, one of the final measures of the Reagan administration was to permit the export of military equipment to Saddam Hussein for his personal protection. Although the Iraq–Iran war was over by the time Bush became president, the Iraqi economy was in a parlous state and his administration actually increased the agricultural commodity credits it provided for Iraq. It also resisted congressional calls for the imposition of sanctions on Iraq, prompted by Saddam's notorious brutality and especially his suppression of a Kurdish minority with chemical weapons. The administration wanted to "wean Iraq away" from any dependence on the Soviets. "We were trying to work with Saddam Hussein and trying to bring him along into the family of nations," Bush later explained. But Bush's forbearance proved insufficient to contain Saddam, who decided that the solution to his economic travail lay in the oilfields of Kuwait. George Bush promptly condemned the Iraqi invasion as "naked aggression" and called for "the immediate and unconditional withdrawal of all Iraqi forces." Neither Kuwait nor Saudi Arabia were democracies, and instead of justifying American involvement in terms of defending freedom, Bush characteristically relied on the concepts of "order" and "international law."[20]

Several Arab nations too condemned the invasion, as, remarkably, did a joint declaration issued by the US Secretary of State and the Soviet Foreign Minister, a sign of the new accommodation. For Secretary of State Baker, that declaration marked "The Day the Cold War Ended." The joint declaration isolated Iraq and made it less likely that other Arab states would side with Saddam. Within a few days American troops were on their way to Saudi Arabia, although the president insisted, "The mission of our troops is wholly defensive." The public objective at this stage was the protection of Saudi Arabia. Bush busied himself with what he liked to do best, personal diplomacy with other leaders, quickly fashioning an extensive coalition of nations prepared to present a common front to Saddam. Recalling the mixed international reception of the 1983 invasion of Grenada and the 1989 invasion of Panama, Baker was anxious that American foreign policy should not be seen as governed by a "cowboy mentality." Successive resolutions were passed by the UN Security Council condemning Saddam's action and imposing sanctions against his regime, and eventually in November it adopted a resolution authorizing the use of "all necessary means" to secure the withdrawal of Iraqi forces from Kuwait by January 15, 1991. By that date about half a million American troops were in the region and a formidable international coalition embracing 29 countries had been fashioned. By assembling such might Bush hoped for a quick and decisive victory – this was not to become another Vietnam. Never before had the United States engaged in a full-scale war in the Middle East, and, insofar as it was under UN auspices, it was the biggest UN military undertaking since Korea. A massive air campaign was launched against Iraq on January 16 and ground forces followed in February. Some 75 percent of its tactical aircraft and 40 percent of its tanks were used by the United States against a country which – in GNP terms – was roughly 150 times smaller than itself. By the end of the month the Iraqi forces had been overwhelmed, though the Saddam regime survived. The American military at last was able to show off the new weaponry that Reagan's defense spending spree had provided.[21]

The United States had spectacularly mobilized a huge multinational force, secured the acquiescence of the Soviet leadership, and imposed its will. "By God," said George Bush, "we've kicked the Vietnam syndrome once and for all." Some conservatives took the view that the victory proved that the US military had not been allowed its head in Vietnam; overwhelming military force and political will could still ensure the global dominance of the United States. Some also held that American forces should have driven deep into Iraq and overthrown Saddam, although such regime change was not an avowed war aim and would not have been supported by many of the coalition's participants, particularly the Arab states. The cautious Bush, as ever, was content to restore the status quo ante.[22]

With the successful resolution of the Gulf War George Bush's approval rating, according to one poll, shot up to an astronomic 92 percent. One consequence of this homage was the decision by a number of leading Democrats not to seek their party's nomination for the presidential election of 1992, in which Bush's re-election seemed all but guaranteed. As the president's son observed to a newsman in August 1991: "Do you think the American people are going to turn to a Democrat *now*?" Yet even in the United States the Gulf War had had its critics. The administration's earlier friendliness toward Iraq had not gone unnoticed. When the president built up US forces in the Middle East in the summer and autumn of 1990 he had emphasized their defensive intent – Operation Desert Shield – and he delayed announcing the near doubling of this deployment, with its offensive implications, until after the mid-term congressional elections of November 1990. The public was not being invited to debate a case for war, and the president also seemed reluctant to take Congress fully into his confidence. He considered going to war without congressional authorization (as he had also contemplated going ahead without UN endorsement), but eventually decided that he needed to maximize public and political support. In January 1991 the Senate did authorize the use of military force, though as many as 47 senators – all but two of them Democrats – voted against the resolution, which passed with 52 votes. Without the UN resolution it is doubtful that Bush would have won even this modest endorsement. The House of Representatives gave Bush a larger majority, but even so 183 members opposed the motion. There had not been so much resistance in Congress to authorizing hostilities since the War of 1812. There were anti-war demonstrations in the United States, invoking memories of Vietnam and calling into question the ethics of a war about oil. While much of the criticism came from Democrats and the liberal left, there were conservative Republicans too who disliked the move to war. Among them was

Patrick Buchanan, who, fearful of another quagmire, insisted that the barbarous Saddam was "no threat to us" and questioned whether American "vital interests" were really involved.[23]

Buchanan had asked a legitimate question. Bush himself was troubled by the charge that "oil is the sole reason that we are involved in this enormous commitment. And that is simply not correct." Rather the "main reason we're there is to set back aggression, to see that aggression is unrewarded," though he conceded that "the restoration of the security and stability in the Persian Gulf region clearly relates to the world's economic interest." Bush also connected the stability of the Middle East to the West's interest in oil in a statement explaining the deployment of troops to Saudi Arabia: "The stakes are high. Iraq is already a rich and powerful country that possesses the world's second largest reserves of oil and over a million men under arms. ... Our country now imports nearly half the oil it consumes and could face a major threat to its economic independence."[24]

As the crisis over Iraq deepened Bush seemed increasingly to see Saddam as the personification of evil, another Hitler, whose barbarous acts fully justified the military mobilization against him. It is true that Saddam's gruesome reputation made it difficult for other powers to embrace him as an ally, and his erratic behavior meant that strategists doubted the wisdom of allowing him to become the strongman of the region. Oil alone may not have preoccupied the minds of Bush's advisers, but for them the supply of oil was intimately linked to a peaceful Middle East. Jim Baker observed to a press conference in November 1990: "The economic lifeline of the industrial world runs from the Gulf, and we cannot permit a dictator such as this to sit astride that economic lifeline. And to bring it down to the level of the average American citizen, let me say that means jobs." (In the subsequent furor, this was interpreted as saying the United States was going to war because of oil, obliging Baker to insist that he was trying to point out that allowing Saddam power over oil prices could mean recession in the West.) In December Defense Secretary Cheney cited the domination of global oil supplies as the second reason for the US stance toward Iraq, with the fear of "further aggression" being the first. Ideally the Bush administration would like to have seen Saddam deposed, but having run him out of Kuwait it drew back from the kind of open-ended commitment that would have resulted from an invasion of Iraq itself. Its justification for action had been the resistance of aggression, not regime change. Thereafter there was an attempt to contain Saddam through an economic embargo and UN Security Council resolutions requiring the destruction of his weapons of mass destruction, to be enforced by international inspections, though

Saddam's repeated obstructions of the inspectors were to prove a major headache for Bush's successors.[25]

To some American critics, the Gulf War was a diversion from the country's real economic and political problems. It occurred at a time when the economy was slowing and when economists were seriously worried about the capacity of the United States to compete in the world. It may have enhanced American international prestige, wrote one critic, but "there is a risk that this renewed American sense of confidence and global importance will be used as an avoidance mechanism – a diversion from the compelling need to address deep-seated domestic economic and social problems." Much of the American public shared sentiments of this sort by the time Bush was thinking of re-election. Complaints about Bush's preoccupation with foreign affairs and his frequent trips abroad led him to postpone a tour of the Far East in November 1991.[26]

Still, the Gulf War for the moment established Bush's authority at home and reasserted the United States' primacy in the world. Success in that war consummated a period when many countries were embracing democratic political systems, and the former communist countries were turning to market economics. The triumph of Western ideas was coinciding with an extraordinary American diplomatic coup and military success. Foreign policy pundit Robert Hormats wrote: "At no time in recent memory have more nations been more comfortable with America in the global leadership role." Nonetheless, the Gulf War was not an unproblematic tribute to US power and authority. The United States supplied much of the firepower, but the war was largely paid for by Japan, Germany, and the friendly oil states (what government officials privately referred to as "Project Tin Cup"). Not since the War for Independence had the United States sought outside help in a war. It could almost be said that the United States had been hired by Saudi Arabia and Kuwait, both authoritarian regimes, in an adventure bankrolled by the US's trading partners. The Reagan administration had left an enormous budget deficit, and the autonomy of the United States was severely compromised.[27]

* * *

Yet the world had changed. When the Bush team took office the Soviet Union was still in existence and they were far from sure that the Cold War was over. But after an initial hesitation the administration pursued the negotiations with the Soviets that Ronald Reagan had begun, and played a key role in bringing about the unification of Germany, ending the divide that had defined the separation of East and West for so many decades. With the Soviets in retreat the White House lost the obsession with a communist threat in Central America that had characterized the Reagan years, although the ending of the Cold War was accompanied by serious instability in some parts of the world as superpower protection was withdrawn. Nonetheless it was possible to perceive authoritarian regimes of both the left and the right yielding to some measure of democracy, in Latin America, Eastern Europe, South Africa, and elsewhere. The Middle East remained highly unstable and its regimes autocratic, their global significance immeasurably enhanced by their control of a huge portion of the world's reserves of its most important energy source. Bush's "new world order" may have been a vacuous phrase, but some glimpse of the emerging geopolitical configurations was given by the decision to go to war in the Gulf. The Soviet Union had vanished, and the new threat to American well-being and security had become the instability and passions associated with the Middle East.

Chapter 9

The Era of Globalization

As Americans tried to make sense of the post-Cold War world, a new term was frequently encountered in public discourse. "Globalization" was not coined in the 1990s, and it described a process that arguably had been underway since the age of Christopher Columbus, but it was in these years that American academics, journalists, and politicians gave unprecedented attention to the diverse ways in which the United States was being transformed by forces outside its own borders. There was no single definition of globalization, though it was often used to describe a phenomenon through which different countries and peoples were being drawn into a world system, which is to say into economic, cultural, social, and political networks of interdependence. In the late twentieth century international trade, financial transactions, and investment were growing faster than the world economy as a whole, and international migration was also at an exceptionally high level, which meant that national economies and societies were increasingly intertwined. State sovereignty and cultural autonomy everywhere, it seemed, were being eroded, and countries were vulnerable to distant happenings. When the Group of Seven (G7) held a summit meeting in June 1996, it entitled its communiqué "Making a Success of Globalization for the Benefit of All." "Whatever else they may have been, the 90's were the decade of globalization," wrote economist Paul Krugman in 2000. Not everyone welcomed it.[1]

The intricate threads that were binding the United States with the wider world, of course, had been assembling for decades, indeed for centuries, but in the final years of the twentieth century they seemed to be reaching a kind of critical mass. Such interconnections could take a variety of forms, cultural, political and otherwise, but three phenomena help to illustrate the changes that American society experienced. Most important was economic

Contemporary America: Power, Dependency, and Globalization since 1980,
First Edition. M.J. Heale.
© 2011 M.J. Heale. Published 2011 by Blackwell Publishing Ltd.

– globalization was most often defined in economic terms – and by the mid-1990s some Americans were celebrating the emergence of a "New Economy" which promised everlasting growth in part because of its integration with a global order. American demography was also changing, particularly because immigration was reaching ever higher levels. Significant too was a growing recognition in the United States that both it and the world it inhabited were vulnerable in a new way, that their mutual environment was under threat. As the American economy meshed ever more fully with the global economy, great floods of people were making their way to the United States, and the planet was warming up.

* * *

"The past two decades or so," wrote one scholar in 2001, "have witnessed a fundamental transformation in the global economy." When the postwar attempt to stabilize exchange rates collapsed in the 1970s, controls on the money markets were relaxed and capital moved more readily around the world. The free market doctrines of the Reagan administration in the United States and of the Thatcher government in Britain pointed in the direction of a more globalized world, and major international companies intensified their support of free global trade and investment. The regular "summits" of the finance ministers of the G7 industrialized countries from 1976 became the globalized world's equivalents of the geopolitical "summits" of the Cold War era. By the late 1980s, as one economist has put it, free trade views "had become predominant amongst economists, economic policy-making bureaucrats and corporate boardrooms in most Western countries." Free market ideology was then greatly boosted by the end of the Cold War, symbolized by the tearing down of the Berlin Wall. It was not just the Soviet empire that had collapsed, but the whole seductive idea of socialist economics. A full-page newspaper advertisement placed by Wall Street bankers Merrill Lynch in 1998 celebrated "the global economy" that was "born when the Wall fell in 1989," sparking the "spread of free markets and democracy." As recently as the late 1970s only about a quarter of the globe practiced free enterprise capitalism; by the mid-1990s all but a handful of countries did so. This was a staggering transformation. Journalist Thomas Friedman argued that "globalization has replaced the Cold War as the defining international system." Some doubted whether it was an improvement. Suspiciously viewing the major corporations, think tanks, government bureaucrats, and major party leaders that were championing the emerging new world, critics often characterized globalization as the mission of economic and political elites. To some, demobilization after the Cold War meant that political empires were being displaced by business empires.[2]

Economic policy in the United States in the Cold War years had frequently been subordinated to strategic security considerations. In "almost every instance where there was a clash in priorities between economic policy and national security," wrote one analyst of that era, "the latter prevailed." Louisiana Senator Russell Long in 1976 had complained to Secretary of State Henry Kissinger: "if we trade away American jobs and farmers' incomes for some vague concept of a 'new international order', the American people will demand from their elected representatives a new order of their own." The international institutions founded in the wake of the war – the UN, IMF, World Bank – were designed more to promote world stability than the US economy as such. By the end of the century, however, this situation was changing. The United States had become subject to what economists Jagdish Bhagwati and Douglas Irwan called the "diminished giant syndrome," where it wanted "finally" to "look after its own interest." The economy began to edge out national security as a priority.[3]

For the United States an unsettling feature of the new order was the rise of competing economies. The United States, of course, had abetted this process, most notably in the aid it provided for Western Europe and Japan after World War II. But if by the 1990s the United States was the "only remaining superpower," its relative economic power was not quite what it had been. The United States in 1970 possessed a formidable 54.6 percent of economic capabilities among what were to become the G7 nations; by 1980 this had dropped to 41.1 percent, and by 1995 to 38.2 percent. Together, Japan and Germany almost equaled America's capabilities. There were other measures, too, that offered warnings. International comparisons showed the United States performing relatively poorly in the attainments of pupils in secondary education, especially in mathematics and science. Between 1980 and 2003, the American share of world industrial patents dropped from 60 percent to 52 percent, while that of Japan climbed from 12 to 21 percent. For the United States to retain a leading position in the world, its economy too would have to be competitive, which is one reason why successive administrations placed emphasis on improving education and training in the United States, and why some authorities argued that immigration laws needed to be changed to attract more talent from elsewhere. Neoconservative Francis Fukuyama likened the United States to a star gone supernova, its light still blazing brightly, "but the energy at the core is rapidly extinguishing."[4]

While globalization meant that the United States could never be sole master of its own destiny, the country arguably had more to gain from it than almost any other. Militarily, of course, the United States was by far the most potent country in the world. Its 1995 defense budget represented about 37 percent of the world's military expenditure, over three times what any other country spent. Its armed forces contributed to the security of large parts of the world, and its military and naval bases were scattered widely. The massive size and reach of its "hard power" was matched by that of its "soft power," the influence wielded through its commercial, media, and entertainment global networks. If relatively diminished, the United States unquestionably remained a major economic power. In 2000 its share of world output was 21 percent, much less than it had been in the wake of World War II and below its 1960 figure of about 26 percent, but the share had remained fairly stable during the previous two decades and was still vastly more than that of any other country. The reach of its multinational media and cultural corporations was growing as the century ended, when the United States housed the headquarters of 59 of the largest 100 companies in the world by market value.

Further, the United States was better placed than any other country to influence the politics of globalism. Economist Rudi Dornbusch only lightly exaggerated when he said: "The IMF is a toy of the United States to pursue its economic policy offshore." International organizations like the UN and the IMF for the most part could only effectively operate with US consent. The pervasiveness of American soft power meant that "globalization" was sometimes equated with "Americanization." As Thomas Friedman noted: "What bothers so many people about America today is not that we send our troops everywhere, but that we send our culture, values, economics, technologies and lifestyles everywhere." A Californian trade show in the early 1990s reached a television audience of a billion people in 94 different countries. "The world speaks American, sings American, dances American, dresses American, eats American," said a hyperbolic Peter L. Berger in 1992. Of course, the process was not all one way. Japanese comics, British soccer, and Thai restaurants, among many other phenomena, not to mention Hispanic influences spreading from the Southwest, made their way into the United States, even if they were not usually disseminated by corporate chains. Nonetheless, the expanding reach of the great multinationals arguably contributed to the ignorance of ordinary Americans about the world outside their borders, which was becoming submerged by American culture.[5]

What enormously facilitated the rapid movement across traditional borders of information, capital, commerce, and people were both a thrust toward free trade and advances in technology. The plummeting cost of transmitting information was fundamental to this process. By the beginning of the twenty-first century computer power cost less than one percent of what it had done in the early 1970s – if the cost of new cars had dropped as fast as that of semiconductors, by 2000 it would have been possible to buy one for about $5. The advent of the cheap personal computer and the spread of the internet were mutually reinforcing, connecting people and businesses around the world. Columbia economics professor Jagdish Bhagwati explained in a lecture in 1996: "Firms in different countries can access similar technologies, borrow at similar interest rates, and produce where it pays a little more to do so, in a manner that was still difficult in the mid-1980s." Production was being internationalized, as its ingredients, such as labor, capital, and entrepreneurship, were no longer concentrated together but were often deployed in differing proportions around the globe. The American Barbie doll was assembled in factories in Indonesia, Malaysia, and China, using cotton cloth supplied by China and plastic and hair supplied by Taiwan and Japan, before being shipped to the United States via Hong Kong. "Ford isn't even an American company, strictly speaking," said its head in 1995: "We're global. … Forty percent of our employees already live and work outside the United States, and that's rising. Our managers are multinational. We teach them to think and act globally." Such comments raised the issue of whether such companies owed their first loyalty to the United States or to their global investors. "The United States does not have an automatic call on our resources," warned a vice-president of Colgate-Palmolive: "There is no mindset that puts this country first."[6]

The amount of money swishing around the world at the touch of a computer button increased enormously. This was the "electronic herd," as Thomas Friedman called it, that disciplined the global economy, obliging governments to follow policies that would not jeopardize such investments. In the early 1980s the pool of capital available on the international money markets was about $1.5 trillion; by the early 1990s it was over $5 trillion. The United States might hope to be the dominant power, even one which could serve as a model for the new world that was taking shape, but it could not hope to stand aloof from it.[7]

The same processes that promoted globalization also revitalized the American economy. The declinist jeremiads of the Reagan–Bush years, deploring the uncompetitive nature of the economy, disappeared as the country surged comfortably ahead of its competitors. Whatever contributions the celebrated supply-side policies of Ronald Reagan may have made to economic restructuring, it was during the Clinton presidency that economic health visibly returned. Where the economy was once driven by the motor companies, now it was information technology (IT), which accounted for between a quarter and a third of economic growth. Also having a dynamic impact was the foreign sector. In the mid-1970s exports and imports had constituted 17 percent of the US economy; by the mid-1990s they claimed 25 percent of GDP. The two were connected. With falling tariff barriers and global competition, goods became cheaper, all the more so as they came to be produced by low-wage labor in the developing world. Increasingly too, services were being outsourced, such as by locating call centers in southern Asia. The imports demanded by American consumers nonetheless exceeded exports, but foreigners were happy to pour money into the American economy, as one study put it, "helping to finance" a new "infrastructure network, the Internet." With falling prices, demand increased and world trade boomed, producing profits that could be productively invested. International competition spurred technological innovation, further enhancing efficiency. One mark of confidence in the American economy was the booming stock market, which quadrupled in the decade following the 1987 crash, fired by good growth, low inflation, and thus the prospect for business profits. The New York and NASDAQ stock exchanges alone added over $4 trillion in value between 1994 and 1998, said to be "the largest accumulation of wealth in the history of the United States." The stock market boom and the wider economic boom were mutually reinforcing.[8]

IT had been infiltrating American business for some years. In January 1983 *Time* magazine abandoned its traditional choice of "man of the year" for "machine of the year," as it weighed the implications of the soaring sales of personal computers. Microsoft launched Windows in 1985, and faster and more powerful versions were introduced regularly through the rest of the century. As the creator of the software which activated the tiny silicon chips inside computers, Microsoft's annual revenues exploded from $198 million in 1986 to nearly $2.8 billion in 1992, and made its founder Bill Gates the country's richest man. The proportion of workers using computers jumped from a quarter to nearly half in the nine years after 1984. By the early 1990s desktop computers were being linked together into networks. Tim Berners-Lee, a British scientist working at CERN in Geneva, made possible the creation of the World Wide Web, vastly increasing the access of users to information by connecting documents on the Internet. The Yahoo! domain was created in 1995 and the Google search engine was incorporated as a private company in 1998. The application of IT in American business accelerated; between 1985 and 1998 the information technology sector increased its share of GDP by over two-thirds. In the 1980s the dizzy success of Japanese consumer electronics had helped to undermine American morale; confidence returned in the second half of the 1990s as American information technology conquered the world. The stock market boom of the late 1990s was fronted by what became known as the "dot.com bubble," as investors poured money into companies promising IT miracles. The faster growth of the US economy than those of other countries in these years was attributed to the greater deployment of computer technology. "Knowledge is power" went an ancient slogan, and the knowledge industry was led by the United States at the end of the twentieth century.[9]

The global technological revolution had profound implications for governments and other traditional authorities, for it could empower individuals and groups. Some commentators attributed the collapse of the Soviet Union to globalization: "Indeed, it was the information revolution of the 1980s – global networks of news and marketing driven by computer technology that moved power from centralized government bureaucracies and towards individuals and activist groups – that ultimately nailed the coffin shut on communism." If individuals sometimes felt helpless in a global world, they could also search for information and allies on the web. Information, said one upbeat analysis, "ineluctably democratizes societies." Campaigns could be launched through e-mail and the internet, and could sometimes be turned against those in power. Globalization helped to energize international NGOs (non-governmental organizations or INGOs), which more than quadrupled in the 1990s. Such bodies as Friends of the Earth, Amnesty International, and Médecins sans Frontières established branches in many countries, and gained some influence with governments and the United Nations. "The whole globe is linked together by the networks established by the INGOs," observed Harvard historian Akira Iriye. In 1997, following a campaign by activist groups around the world connected through the internet, 121 governments signed the international landmine treaty, intended to reduce the accidental maiming of children and others in former war zones. Larry Summers, the Secretary of the Treasury in the late 1990s, remarked: "I always felt that it was surely no accident that communism, planning ministries and corporate conglomerates all ran into great difficulties in the same era, because with the PC and the microchip it became much more efficient to empower individuals who could get more information and make more decisions themselves rather than having a single person at the top trying to direct everything."[10]

Most governments were resilient enough, but they tended to find their options limited. Once committed to the free market system – shrinking the state, lowering tariffs, removing restrictions on foreign investment – government had fewer policy choices. Thus in the United States President Bill Clinton could proclaim that the era of big government was over, as he could also complain that his government was the captive of the bond market. "In a highly integrated world economy," noted one journalist as Clinton struggled with his first budget, "U.S. fiscal policy is held hostage to international finance." Governments needed to keep their financial affairs in order to avoid poor credit ratings, which would make borrowing more costly. In 1970 the share of US Treasury securities held by non-citizens was under 9 percent; by 1997 it was 38 percent. When the Japanese prime minister in June 1997 intimated that Japan might sell some of its US Treasury bonds, the Dow Jones stock index promptly fell by 192 points. In the United States, as elsewhere, public policies could not but be conditioned by this global context.[11]

If high IT investment was part of the explanation for the vibrant American economy in the 1990s, another part was its increasing integration with the outside world, abetted by successive administrations. The military alliances of the Cold War era were being supplanted by free trade pacts. "I think protectionism is just 180 degrees wrong," said President George H.W. Bush in 1992: "We're in a global economy. ... We can't live behind these borders." "No country can escape the global economy, and the greatest, largest, most powerful country in the world cannot escape the global economy," agreed President Clinton in 1994. The end of the Cold War, he added, "gives us a responsibility to finally take advantage of the interconnections that exist in the world today."[12]

The Reagan and Bush administrations had rather tentatively tried to unpick the constraints on international commerce; however, the Cold War over, and clearly grasping the need for new strategies, it was President Clinton who became the most energetic champion of free trade. In contrast to the suspicions in much of his own party, he was convinced that aligning the United States with global forces would powerfully boost the US economy. "The truth of our age is this and must be this," he said on one occasion: "Open and competitive commerce will enrich us as a nation. It spurs us to innovate. It forces us to compete. It connects us with new customers." When world leaders met in Denver in June 1997, Clinton seized the opportunity to proselytize, arguing that the American example of welcoming free trade and celebrating the new global economy was a model for the world, indeed "the strategy we want everyone to embrace."[13]

During the Bush administration the American, Canadian, and Mexican governments had entered negotiations for a North American Free Trade

Area, with a view to removing most trade and particularly investment impediments between the three countries. NAFTA was controversial in the United States (see Chapter 11 for the political context), but Henry Kissinger heralded it as "the most creative step toward a new world order taken by any group of countries since the end of the Cold War." A new international architecture was in the making. Bill Clinton pummeled Congress into approving NAFTA, which came into effect in January 1994. Almost all barriers to the movement of goods, services, and capital between the three countries were eliminated over the next decade. Clinton's crowning achievement was the successful conclusion in 1994 of the Uruguay round of the General Agreement on Tariffs and Trade (GATT), the global body monitoring international commerce. The new pact brought dramatic reductions internationally in tariffs and subsidies, so opening more foreign markets to American products. Of particular advantage to the United States was the opening of markets for information and financial services, in which Third World countries could not compete. Also created was GATT's stronger replacement, the World Trade Organization (WTO). The various free trade initiatives helped boost foreign trade, which expanded dramatically in the Clinton years. Companies and trade unions in sectors hurt by foreign competition continued to demand protection, but the powerful corporations engaged in the international economy lobbied energetically against trade barriers, and American consumers benefited from the downward pressure on prices that competition brought. The globalizers usually won. In 1998 almost 60 percent of all US imports entered the country tariff free. "The economic benefits of the tariff reductions we negotiated during the Clinton administration represents the largest tax cut in the history of the world," Treasury Secretary Lawrence Summers boasted. Where Reagan had sought to revitalize the American economy through income tax cuts, Clinton turned to lower tariffs.[14]

Following the creation of the WTO, governments throughout the world removed trade barriers, encouraged foreign investment, and sold off public enterprises. During the Cold War era constraints on trade by Third World countries had often been tolerated if they were otherwise reasonably friendly to Washington, but now they were expected to open their economies and deregulate their financial systems. In 1999 another agreement prepared the way for China to join the WTO, which would allow foreign companies to conduct business there with greater confidence, guaranteed some protection by international law. The restructuring of the international system, however, was not without its critics, who suspected the self-interested power of corporate capitalism. By the late 1990s the WTO's operations were encountering fierce protests in the United States and in many parts of the world. Critics were gathering evidence that seemed to show that the rules of trade primarily favored the rich countries at the expense of the poor.

For the most part the globalization of the 1990s appears to have been good for Americans, or rather most Americans. By many measures, the American economy was flourishing. According to the OECD in 2000, the economy had been "expanding continuously for longer, albeit not more rapidly, than at any time in modern history." After the hesitation of the early 1990s, the American economy had entered one of its boom decades, ushered in by the continued restructuring. By 1998 some 55 percent of the workforce was in a new job. The economy could not match the dynamism of the 1960s, but in the 1990s as a whole an impressive annual growth rate of 3.03 percent in GDP was achieved. Rising consumer spending helped to account for this boom, which was accentuated by the phenomenal rise of the stock market, making many households and businesses richer and therefore more prepared to borrow against their assets and spend. In 1998 e-commerce began to boom as consumers bought online. (This burgeoning American consumption, of course, was also promoting the further industrialization of China and low-wage Third World countries.) Most striking was a marked spurt in productivity. From the beginning of 1993, productivity growth greatly improved on its performance of the previous two decades, and from the fourth quarter of 1995 averaged a very healthy 3 percent a year. Foreigners rushed to pour more capital into American financial assets, bringing down interest rates and adding to stock market exuberance. During the Reagan and Bush years doubts about the economic well-being of the United States had never quite disappeared. By the end of the 1990s the high-tech boom was impacting on American psychology, economic jeremiads were very few, and a new genre had appeared, one which celebrated the arrival of a "new economic paradigm" or a New Economy, which apparently promised everlasting growth.[15]

One apostle of the New Economy was *Business Week*'s Stephen B. Shepard, who identified it with the interaction of two broad trends: "the globalization of business," that is, the spreading of capitalism around the world, and "the revolution in information technology," represented by cell phones, the internet, and, especially, "the digitization of all information." Champions of the New Economy usually attributed it to some combination of technological innovation and globalization breakthrough, which together raised productivity and offered the possibility of ever greater productive capacity as demand increased. In such circumstances, productivity increases need not be negated by inflation; rather, ever higher standards of living could be expected. In the United States at least, by the second half of the 1990s these conditions had apparently been met: economic growth coexisted with both low unemployment and low inflation, a rare combination. There was talk of the US economy having escaped the ancient cycle of "boom and bust." Alan Greenspan spoke of an emerging "virtuous cycle" and the prospect of "extraordinary" profit growth that "extended into the distant future." A new service-based economy based on ideas and information, it was said, had displaced the unwieldy economy of factories and goods, simultaneously creating nicer jobs. Critics derided the idea of a New Economy, *The Economist* magazine dismissing it as "verging on claptrap." To some on the radical left it was a mirage projected to hide an employer and governmental assault on labor and the welfare state, which they thought better explained the new profitability of American business. The President's Council of Economic Advisers, however, found the idea of a New Economy irresistible. In January 2001 it boasted that the New Economy had been made possible by a "combination of mutually reinforcing advances in technologies, business practices, and economic policies," the last including the fostering of globalization. "Indeed," concluded the Council, "it is no coincidence that the New Economy has emerged in the United States at the same time that U.S. participation in the global economy has reached new heights, because globalization and the recent advances in information technology are inextricably linked."[16]

Clinton's economic team could hardly claim sole credit for the good times. Whether there was a New Economy or not, policies and processes underway since at least the Carter presidency had played their part, and the Clinton administration sustained the deregulatory thrust. The Telecommunications Act of 1996 further opened up competition among telephone and cable companies, and the competition spurred yet more innovation. Within about six years the multiplying telecom companies invested a trillion dollars in "wiring the world." In keeping too with its free trade credentials, the administration promoted the further liberalization of capital. Financial deregulation had begun under Jimmy Carter, was further pushed by Ronald Reagan, and continued piecemeal through the 1990s. The most important piece of financial deregulation was the Financial Services Modernization Act of 1999. This completed the dismantling of the 1933 Glass–Steagall Act, which had separated commercial banks from investment banks, so preventing the savings of ordinary depositors being used for highly speculative ventures. Banks and other finance companies insisted that they needed to diversify, and that they were losing out to foreign banks that were not hindered by such restrictions. Progressive financial deregulation, in the United States and elsewhere, let loose the financial markets to seek profits where they could, triggering the proliferation of ever more complex financial devices and forms of speculation. In the 1990s financial sector profits came to account for a larger proportion of total corporate profits than at any time since World War II. The 1999 act, it later appeared, was a significant root of the financial crisis of 2008–2009.

Pressure on American industry was also maintained by the deepening trade deficit, as the flood of imports threatened inefficient firms. American industry had little alternative to continuing the restructuring that had been underway since the late 1970s. Mergers, relocations to low-wage areas, and workforce reduction were as much features of the Clinton years as the Reagan years, and indeed the takeovers of the 1990s dwarfed those of the 1980s. Large firms continued to "downsize," so that job insecurity remained at a fairly high level. Services provided nearly 80 percent of American jobs in the mid-1990s. By 1999, 13 of the country's top 25 corporations were in high technology and communications (it had been just three in 1979). The American multinationals were on a roll. Such vast enterprises as Microsoft, Yahoo!, and Wal-Mart (which overtook General Motors as the largest US employer in 1997) dwarfed the old oil and manufacturing companies which had once been at the center of the economy.

It was VISA that could claim to be "the first truly transnational corporation," with its credit card that made possible consumer payments wherever it was accepted, for it had begun operations in the United States in 1970 with 30 million cards, and by 2000 boasted a billion cards useable in over 130 countries. FedEx began operations in April 1973, when it delivered just 186 packages, all within the United States; by 1998 it was delivering three million shipments daily to 211 countries, with a fleet of 615 aircraft. In 1980 McDonalds had about 1000 restaurants abroad, a figure dwarfed by its 6000 in the United States, but by the end of the century over half its outlets were elsewhere, some 26 462 in 119 countries. The chain opened its first restaurant in Russia near Red Square in Moscow in January 1990 – it was the largest McDonalds on the planet and served 20 000 customers on its first day. When South Africa was preparing for its first free elections, a journalist found black South Africans sitting in "a Kentucky Fried Chicken restaurant, sipping Coca-Cola and listening to a Whitney Houston tape." Some economists related the increasing productivity of the late 1990s to the economies of scale made possible by the mass markets for the goods and services of such companies as Microsoft and Wal-Mart. But, important as they were, the multinationals were not the only kind of business to profit. With the new technology – e-mail, the internet, modern software – individuals and small businesses too found that they could prosper in this world with relatively modest capital outlay. The high-tech boom of the end of the twentieth century enriched many ingenious entrepreneurs, even if many others quickly burned out.[17]

As in the 1980s, this dynamic economy owed something to the forbearance of foreigners. As so often with fast American consumer growth, more imports were sucked in, and the US current account deficit rose sharply in the late 1990s. In the fourth quarter of 1999, that deficit was the greatest since World War II as a proportion of GDP. The dive into the red continued yet more steeply into the twenty-first century. There had been no abating in the voracious appetite of Americans, who by 2004 were consuming not only yet more of their own products but around 10 percent more of *world* output than they had been a dozen years earlier. The United States, in short, was still living well beyond its means. To sustain this lifestyle it resorted to borrowing from abroad.[18]

Yet foreign loans apart, there were downsides for Americans to globalization. Although American multinationals flourished in world markets, the public response to globalization was ambivalent. In one poll of 2002, some 15 percent of Americans favored the United States "trying to reverse" globalization and another 24 percent "trying to slow it down," against 35 percent favoring "allow it to continue" and another 14 percent thinking the US should "actively promote" further globalization. Consolidating those figures suggests a modest but unenthusiastic plurality in favor. In another survey in 2002, some 55 percent thought globalization to be good for US companies, with 30 percent doubting it, while 51 percent thought it bad for the job security of American workers. In a broad survey of 19 countries, 11 displayed a more positive attitude toward globalization than did Americans. There was always an undercurrent of distrust in the United States with policies or phenomena involving greater exposure to the outside world. While the major party leaders, corporate interests, and other elite professionals were strongly committed to trade liberalization, there was less enthusiasm outside Washington. Kevin Phillips wrote that the free trade goal was "obviously beneficial to perhaps 10 to 15 percent of the population, detrimental to some 30 to 50 percent."[19]

Those figures could be questioned, but they point to the strains inevitable with any extensive economic restructuring. The growing immersion in the world economy tended to increase individual insecurity; economic risk was being transferred back to families, much as had been the case before the rise of welfare provision. While the reasons for job losses were complex, those who experienced this fate not unreasonably suspected that government was not protecting them as once it had. The state no longer functioned so well as a buffer against the outside world, and employers too had reduced the amount of protection (such as health care) that they were willing to furnish workers. The postwar years of full employment, increasing living standards, and an expanding welfare state were in the past; the somewhat straitened circumstances of many Americans toward the century's end suggested to them that government must be doing something wrong. During that earlier golden age opinion polls had generally discovered a high trust in government, but in the late twentieth century confidence in government was historically low. Further, in the 1990s in particular, there were elements that reacted very specifically against greater involvement with the outside world.

One impact of globalization was to intensify income stratification, although there has been debate over how much. Some economists have emphasized other causes, most notably technological change, which served to undermine demand for unskilled workers, but such change could not be entirely divorced from the influences associated with a growing immersion in the world economy. In the 20 years before 1997, GM (General Motors), faced with international competition, reduced the number of its hourly jobs from over half a million to less than a quarter-million, often replacing them with machines. As traditional industries were racked by foreign competition, some capital migrated to expanding high-tech sectors in which the United States had an advantage, and even some traditional industries invested in new labor-saving technology to fend off competition. While those with high skills and exceptional talents were able to demand more for their services, low-paid and unskilled workers were squeezed as corporations fought to remain solvent. International competition, it was sometimes said, was promoting a "race to the bottom." "Are your wages set in Beijing?," asked one labor economist; factory wage levels in China were over 30 times lower than those in the United States. Even *Business Week* conceded that "global competition is dragging down pay for lower-skilled workers – widening the gulf between rich and poor." Journalists Michael Lind and John Judis spoke of the "Brazilianization of America," characterized by "the increasing withdrawal of the white overclass into its own barricaded nation-within-a-nation, a world of private neighborhoods, private schools, private police and even private roads, walled off from the spreading squalor beyond." Princeton political scientist Nolan McCarty and his colleagues drew attention to the degree to which the increasing polarization of American politics, as the Republican Party moved quite sharply to the right in the late twentieth century, tracked the rising economic inequality. Social surveys indicated growing dissatisfaction with wage inequality.[20]

Of less immediate concern to Americans was the fact that an increasing stratification of income was also occurring globally. The gap between rich and poor nations was growing wider. So was that between global elites and the mass of the world's population. In the 1990s the top 20 percent of the world's people had combined incomes almost 60 times greater than those of the bottom 20 percent, a ratio that had doubled since 1960.[21]

Globalization certainly made workers feel less secure. Economist Jagdish Bhagwati was skeptical that globalization had much to do with increasing stratification, but he did argue that it served to increase job insecurity, particularly among middle-income earners. There was a marked increase in the volatility of American family incomes in the 1990s, with incomes rising and falling more sharply and unpredictably from year to year. In that decade the average householder in his or her worst year received only about a quarter of the income received in the best year, representing a greater fluctuation than in the recent past and one now impacting on well-educated workers as well as the working poor. While unemployment was low and real incomes generally rising in the mid- and late 1990s, job insecurity remained rife. In a survey of 444 large companies in 1986, only 20 percent of employees had feared being laid off; by 1996 the proportion had jumped to 46 percent, although unemployment was much lower. Alan Greenspan himself, in explaining declining inflationary pressures and the economy's strong performance in 1997, attributed this in part to "a heightened sense of job insecurity and, as a consequence, subdued wages." A job loss, of course, also often meant cancellation of health cover and reduced pension benefits, so simply the prospect of unemployment could be extremely daunting, especially to those already in debt. The years of international competition and new technology, with their accompaniments of corporate downsizing and increasing use of temporary and contract labor, had left their psychological mark.[22]

If globalization threatened the livelihoods of those tied to a particular place, the owners of capital were not so encumbered. "The suspicion is that NAFTA will help the elite," admitted Clinton's Secretary of Labor. A corporation could close its plants in Ohio or Tennessee and open new plants in low-wage Mexico. Unions complained bitterly of corporations using the globe "like their own private sweatshop." One illustration was a strike in October 1995, in which one of the workers' strongest grievances was the export of their jobs. At the Boeing plant in Everett, Washington, the International Association of Machinists and Aerospace Workers took exception to their corporation's global policies, which allowed parts of aircraft to be built in such countries as China and Korea. Local workers were particularly incensed when they discovered their own specialized tools were being shipped to the overseas plants. "On a daily basis I saw my jobs going out of the door," said a shop steward. These workers were hardly alone in doubting the benefits of globalization. And globalization seemed to have other unsavory aspects too. As one scholar noted: "The free flow of drugs and the free circulation of crime have accompanied the formation of a global world economy."[23]

As unease with globalization bubbled through the decade, Congress itself became more wary of international economic entanglements. While it was the Senate's responsibility to ratify treaties, commercial pacts necessarily required considerable negotiation, and Congress had for years allowed the president a free hand, according him "fast-track" authority to conclude deals. But during Bill Clinton's second term Congress finally rebelled, urged on by labor unions, environmental lobbies, and human rights activists. Clinton was obliged in 1997 to abandon a massive lobbying effort to secure "fast-track" authority over new trade negotiations, a setback characterized as "the first major defeat for the proglobalization coalition in the 1990s." "Bill Clinton never sat around a steelworkers' hall and just listened to their concerns ...," complained one Ohio congressman: "He's a bit more interested in pleasing the elites than I would like." By this date the AFL-CIO was one of the strongest anti-globalization forces in the United States. One response of the American labor movement was to engage in its own globalizing activities, developing links and coordinating strategies with labor movements in other countries. Groups interested in such issues as sweatshops, environmental problems, and human rights were also organizing across borders in what one sociologist called the "new internationalism."[24]

Populist suspicions of globalization surfaced on both left and right. With real wages stagnant for a generation and employment insecure, multinational corporations and their allies in the political classes made tempting targets for public anger. Pro-labor Democrats looked askance at policies promoting trade liberalization, and most congressional Democrats voted against NAFTA. Philosopher Richard Rorty tried to rally his fellow academics to the cause, calling on them to revive "a politics centered on the struggle to prevent the rich from ripping off the rest of the country." The AFL-CIO was joined by such critics as consumer champion Ralph Nader, and some environmental groups too charged the multinational corporations with plundering the planet's resources and despoiling large parts of it. In this perspective, globalization was a rapacious force orchestrated by the economic and political elites of the rich countries, determined to preserve their dominance at the expense of others. In 1995 a coalition of environmental, labor, consumer, and community groups was formed as Global Trade Watch, which helped to organize the extensive protests at the WTO Seattle meeting in 1999. Some 50 000 or 60 000 trade unionists, environmentalists, consumer advocates, human rights activists, and student opponents of globalization from many countries, mobilized in large part by NGOs using the internet, effectively brought trade negotiations to a halt. A central charge was that the WTO and other international financial institutions did not function in a democratic and transparent way; ultimately the rich countries called the tune. On the right, latter-day nativists denounced international institutions like the IMF and the UN, sometimes aligning themselves with workers by deploring the export of jobs to the Third World. Pat Buchanan's bid for the Republican nomination in 1992 involved denunciations of NAFTA and immigrants, and he explained that he was running against "the insider game, the establishment game." The third-party campaigns of Ross Perot in the 1992 and 1996 elections also ripped into NAFTA and career politicians, though as a billionaire he did not make a very convincing champion of the ordinary Joe for whom he claimed to speak. Out on the fringes was the militia movement, with its intense distrust of government and foreign influences. More measured criticisms of globalization came from the celebrated financier George Soros who, in *The Crisis of Global Capitalism*, excoriated the consequences of an unquestioning faith in market forces, and from Nobel Prize-winning economist Joseph Stiglitz, who believed that the globalizing policies of the IMF that unintentionally damaged Third World countries in the 1990s were shaped by the "perspectives and ideology of the financial community," in the United States and elsewhere.[25]

A major weakness of globalization became frighteningly evident during the second half of the 1990s, when recurring international financial crises revealed that global structures were less than robust. The very suddenness with which financial abysses opened up in a global system in which capital could bolt at a moment's notice was unnerving. From the mid-1990s currency and banking crises periodically sent shock waves sweeping round the world.

Clinton's free trade crusade almost foundered in 1995. The elaboration of NAFTA had centered attention on Mexico, acclaimed as a model for developing economies, but early in 1995 the Mexican peso was on the verge of collapse. The World Bank and the IMF did not have the capacity to arrange a rescue package of the necessary size, and if Mexico was to be saved the United States would have to act. "Letting Mexico Go" would have serious repercussions for the American economy, possibly costing 700 000 jobs, and could also bring the larger movement toward globalization into question. Other developing countries might be reluctant to adopt the market reforms that Western economists were urging on them. Yet the United States taking the lead in using taxpayers' money to rescue Mexico would hardly be popular. A White House aide worried about the public reaction to what "seems like bailing out people who made dumb investments." A *Los Angeles Times* poll showed that the public opposed a rescue package by the whopping margin of 79 to 18 percent. What would they think a year from now, wondered Clinton, "when we have another million illegal immigrants, we're awash in drugs from Mexico, and lots of people on both sides of the Rio Grande are out of work …?" He decided to face down public opinion and took executive action to provide the loan guarantee Mexico needed, at $20 billion the largest non-military commitment of the US government since the Marshall Plan. The IMF came up with further aid. *New York Times* columnist Thomas Friedman in May 1995 described the rescue as "the least popular, least understood, but most important foreign policy decision of the Clinton presidency." Bill Clinton was sometimes charged with indecision, but on this occasion he acted quickly in defiance of prevailing political pressures. "He didn't hesitate at all," said National Economic Council director Robert Rubin. Clinton was soon vindicated. The Mexican economy quickly recovered and the loan was repaid ahead of schedule, although the so-called "tequila effect" had pushed other Latin American countries into recession.[26]

But other crises followed. The exposure of the American economy to outside forces was brought home by the Asian financial crisis of 1997–1998. To economist Paul Krugman the crisis raised the prospect of "the return of depression economics" of the kind experienced in the 1930s. In the early 1990s, encouraged by the prophets of globalization, several Asian countries had opened up their financial systems, making it easier for their citizens to operate abroad in financial markets and for foreigners to operate in theirs. American and European financiers eager to cash in on the "Asian miracle" set up funds to channel money into the Asian stock exchanges. The Asian financial crisis blew up in the summer of 1997, and its knock-on effects over the next year put the entire global financial system in jeopardy. Declining demand in Asia resulted in a fall in the price of oil, which contributed to the Russian financial crisis of 1998. In August the Russian government defaulted on its debt, one immediate reaction to which was a fall in the Dow Jones index of 357 points. For a moment it looked as if Russia would take down the rest of the global financial system. The Russian crisis in turn led to the collapse of the US corporation Long-Term Capital

Management after it had lost billions of dollars. LTCM, with Nobel Prize winners on its staff, had been described by *Institutional Investor* as possessing the "best finance faculty in the world." Its use of "hedge funds" and "derivatives" introduced these new terms to a wider if uncomprehending audience. Fearing a general panic, the Fed arranged with a group of investors for a rescue of the LTCM hedge fund (though without the use of public funds), and also cut interest rates. LTCM, it seemed, was "too big to be allowed to fail," a refrain that was to be heard again 10 years later. Alan Greenspan was obliged to explain to a congressional committee why "a private firm designed for millionaires" had to be saved by a plan "brokered and supported by a federal government organization." Speculators, it seemed, could be bailed out, while workers could not (even less the workers and peasants in the Third World countries hit by the widening Asian crisis). The US credit system was stabilized, but the US alone could not restore global stability. In September Greenspan warned that the United States could not remain an "oasis of prosperity" in a failing global economy.[27]

But many Americans saw the Asian crisis as a reason for the United States to minimize its involvement with the outside world. Some blamed the earlier bailout of Mexico for encouraging countries to adopt reckless policies. Critics of globalization were reinforced in their skepticism, identifying a crisis of global capitalism. American critics of the IMF grew harsher in their criticisms, questioning why the United States should participate in such international institutions if they were powerless to avert global financial disorder. Joseph Stiglitz argued that it was IMF policies that "brought the world to the verge of a global meltdown." Congress balked at the continued US contribution to the IMF, but eventually allowed funding after promises of reform. The global crisis was contained, through cooperation between the United States, the IMF, the World Bank, and other governments. As in the earlier S&L debacle and the Mexican crisis, the US government had become the ultimate bailout lender, the guarantor of the nation's and the world's credit markets. Proponents of globalization concluded that such cooperation had vindicated itself, and stressed the need for continued engagement between national governments and international financial institutions. Critics drew the lesson that interdependence served to spread contagion. "The world needs to do better next time," wrote the former Under Secretary for Commerce Jeffrey Garten, for "the one certainty is that we have not seen the end of serious global financial turmoil." A decade later it seemed that governments had not sufficiently learned the lessons of the global financial crisis of 1997–1999.[28]

*   *   *

One irony is that while the United States became more fully meshed in the global economy, in certain respects Americans were learning less about the rest of the world. Aspects of foreign culture did invade, not least because the tidal wave of immigration added to the variety of urban lifestyles. Yet as the American news and media industries conquered the world, Americans risked becoming less informed. The proportion of the global film market commanded by Hollywood doubled between 1990 and 1998. But foreign films no longer reached an American audience. In 1960 foreign films had claimed 10 percent of the American film market; by 2000 the proportion was down to a risible 0.75 percent. A similar story can be told about the news industry. CNN, Ted Turner's cable and all-news station, took off in the 1980s, and won renown for its remarkable coverage of the Gulf War in 1991. By the mid-1990s CNN was able to boast that its global network reached over 75 million viewers. Another media mogul was Rupert Murdoch, an Australian who was obliged to take US citizenship in 1986 so that he could own American newspapers and television stations; with the use of satellites he came to command a global empire that embraced major newspapers and television stations. Yet at the same time the American news media grew more parochial. Between 1989 and 2000 the TV networks closed foreign bureaus and reduced their foreign news content by about two-thirds. During 1989 ABC had devoted a total of 3733 minutes to foreign coverage on its nightly news programs, though by 1996 the figure had fallen dramatically to 1838 minutes; at NBC the corresponding figures plummeted from 3351 to 1175 minutes. Of course, interested Americans had unprecedented access to foreign news via the internet and specialized cable and satellite channels, but the mass audience was exposed to little about daily events beyond American borders. Perhaps the global outreach of American corporations militated against Americans learning much about other countries. After all, in the words of a Coca-Cola executive in 1991: "American culture broadly defined – music, film, fashion, and food – has become the culture worldwide." Further, with the ending of the Cold War there was less reason for Americans to fear an outside threat to their security. The image of the United States sitting astride a commercial and media empire reinforced popular perceptions of American supremacy and the insignificance of other peoples. Arguably there was little point in investigating the rest of the world. According to Benjamin Barber: "America is perhaps the most parochial empire that has ever existed, and Americans ... are the least cosmopolitan and traveled of peoples who husband such expansive power."[29]

Chapter 10

Porous Borders and Global Warming

The nation state, some were arguing in the 1990s, was fast becoming an anachronism. President Clinton's deputy US Secretary of State made a bold prophesy: "I'll bet that within the next hundred years, nationhood as we know it will be obsolete: all states will recognize a single, global authority." Global trade and communications were fast eroding national barriers. In other ways, too, Americans were constantly reminded that they were not alone. More people than ever were seeking entry to the United States, in one of the biggest surges in immigration in American history. At the same time Americans were increasingly being invited to see themselves as passengers aboard Spaceship Earth, as members of a species subject to common experiences. The industrialization of the preceding 200 years, intensified by the economic globalization of the end of the twentieth century, was having consequences that demanded international cooperation if humankind was to ensure its own survival. The tidal wave of newcomers and the mounting evidence of global warming, in their different ways, carried the message to Americans that they could not easily barricade themselves off from the outside world.[1]

* * *

It was not only goods and capital that were moving in accelerating speed and quantity across national borders, but people too. Air travel and tourism were booming industries, and great migrations were taking place across the globe. While American multinationals were busily thrusting their services into almost every nook and cranny of the world, huge numbers of people

Contemporary America: Power, Dependency, and Globalization since 1980,
First Edition. M.J. Heale.
© 2011 M.J. Heale. Published 2011 by Blackwell Publishing Ltd.

were heading for the United States. There were about 300 ports of entry to the country, and in any given year around the turn of the century some 475 million people and 125 million vehicles passed through them. The mushrooming international commerce was accompanied by an escalation in business travel, while the decreasing cost of flying encouraged more Americans to take holidays abroad. The number of people taking international flights from US airports jumped dramatically from 24.9 million in 1985 and to 55.5 million in 2000. If more Americans than ever were venturing beyond their own borders, they were also increasingly conscious of the foreigners that were appearing in ever greater numbers in their towns and cities. Immigration became a highly charged issue as the century was ending. As with other features of globalization, the American response was ambivalent. Some insisted that the nation of immigrants should abide by its traditions, and that in any case the immigrants were necessary to the new economy that was emerging. But others recoiled at the sheer volume and some feared that the America they knew would be overwhelmed.

Whatever the American image abroad, and whatever other countries felt about the invasive forms of American capitalism they were experiencing, the United States remained an immensely attractive destination for both regular and illegal immigrants and refugees. The numbers undoubtedly gave cause for concern. As many as 9.1 million newcomers were legally admitted in the 1990s, exceeding even the record of the first decade of the century, if a smaller proportion of the population. These were supplemented not only by large numbers seeking admission as refugees, well over 100 000 a year, but also by unknown numbers of illegal immigrants. There were thought to be 2.2 million illegal residents in the country in 1988 and 7 million in 2000. The streams of migrants from Latin America – especially Mexico – and from Asia continued apace. The top four source countries for legal immigration in 1995 were Mexico, the Philippines, Vietnam, and the Dominican Republic. But the winding down of the Cold War also precipitated new flows of refugees that the United States could hardly refuse. American administrations had long been prodding the Soviet Union to permit Jewish people to emigrate, and in 1987 Mikhail Gorbachev eased exit restrictions, enabling large numbers to leave for the United States and elsewhere. After the Chinese authorities had mown down student demonstrators in Tiananmen Square in 1989, Congress allowed Chinese students stranded in the United States to remain, and provision was subsequently made for certain Chinese categories to win asylum. Muslims from the Middle East were also arriving. By 1995 there were estimated to be over a million immigrants of Iranian origin in the United States, and other Islamic immigrants too, legally, illegally, and as asylum seekers, had also found refuge there.[2]

As these newcomers poured into the United States there were growing calls not merely to control illegal entry and rationalize refugee policies but – rather more emphatically than in the recent past – also to limit all forms of immigration. In 1986 some 49 percent of the public had wanted to reduce immigration, according to polls, a figure that moved dramatically up to 61 percent in 1990. Immigration policy emerged as a more serious issue than for decades. There were also demands to restrict the access of immigrants already in the country to public benefits. The Official English movement had already heightened sensitivities about American identity, and it continued to gain adherents through the 1990s. A so-called "new white nationalism" emerged, as some groups used the logic of multicultur-alism to argue not for racial superiority but for white solidarity. Such attitudes colored the debate over immigration. Towards the end of the century shriller voices demanding the preservation of an Anglo-European culture were added to those worried about the displacement of the native-born poor and to those soberly pointing out that it was questionable whether so many immigrants could be accommodated.[3]

Presidential administrations were wary of initiating major changes in legislation on such a divisive issue, but were broadly sensitive to the need to contain immigration, particularly from Latin America. American border controls were periodically strengthened, though without much visible effect on the numbers. One impulse behind US support for NAFTA was the belief that a prosperous Mexican economy would remove an incentive for migration. In the 1990s both the Bush and Clinton administrations tried to stem an influx from Haiti by instructing the Coastguard to turn back their boats, and in 1994 the Clinton administration orchestrated an attempt to depose the dictatorship of Haiti with a view to promoting reform there and discouraging emigration. The war on drugs also obliged American administrations to address the problem of the porosity of US borders. Stemming the flow of cocaine was one of the rationales for George Bush's action against General Noriega in 1989. President Clinton deter-mined to try to root out the problem of drug smuggling at its source, and in 2000 secured an agreement with the Columbian government to provide it with military aid to crack down on cocaine dealers. The war on drugs served to give a global aspect to the American prison population, which more than quadrupled between 1980 and 2005. Many of those smuggling drugs into the country were foreigners, and in 2004 it was estimated that at least a quarter of federal inmates would be subject to deportation on completion of their sentences.[4]

But while there was broad agreement on the need to bolster border controls, what is striking at the opening of the 1990s was the strength of the forces defying the opinion polls and arguing for the liberalization of immigration policy. There were even calls from civil liberties, business, and Hispanic groups to abolish the employer sanctions of the 1986 act; a General Accounting Office report found that there was "widespread discrimination" against job applicants of "foreign" appearance. With the collapse of the Soviet empire and the student unrest in China, there were those who felt that the United States should demonstrate that it was still a haven for the world's oppressed. One reality being borne in on Congress was the low American fertility rate, so that, without immigration, population would soon decline. "Without newcomers," spelled out the *Washington Post*, "there will be far fewer taxpayers and workers to support the Social Security system in the next century." The powerful free market doctrines of the era reinforced the arguments against restriction. Most important was the pressure from corporations, business schools, and economic journalists for the overhaul of immigration policy to admit more highly trained and skilled workers in order to improve American competitiveness in a globalized economy. *Business Week* in 1992 welcomed the "bonanza of highly educated foreigners."[5]

The focus around 1990, after years of concern about the illegals, had shifted back to legal immigration. Reports of the late 1980s, when there were growing fears about American competitiveness, had emphasized the lack of skills in the nation's workforce, a situation expected to worsen. Further, charged one economist, the quality of immigrants was declining: "What we need is a policy that encourages admission of immigrants from anywhere in the world who have the skills to prosper in a post-industrial economy." The emphasis on family reunification that had prevailed since 1965 had to be replaced by one emphasizing skills: "We will be in sharp competition not only with Japan, but with dynamic technological competitors in a United Europe and the newly industrialized countries on the periphery of Asia." Economist George Borjas presented statistics showing that the skills of immigrants had declined markedly in relation to those of natives in recent decades, a feature he blamed on the family reunification priorities: "The evidence is clear that the American offer is becoming progressively less attractive to the world's most talented people." Canada and Australia, with immigration policies geared to the needs of their economies, were scooping up the skilled immigrants, he claimed.[6]

The act of 1990 reflected these liberalizing pressures. It provided for a substantial increase in the quotas while attempting to place a cap on overall immigration. There would be a limit of 700 000 immigrants annually (675 000 from 1995), and while family reunification still secured nearly three-quarters of the total, the increased number meant that the pool reserved for business-related immigrants was enlarged. What the *Wall Street Journal* called its "most significant features" were a tripling of visas allotted to high-skill professionals such as researchers, engineers, and scientists, including investor-immigrants who ploughed at least $1 million each into the economy. Some 40 000 visas would be assigned each year to "priority workers," those immigrants with "extraordinary ability." "These people are the solid superstars, the prospective Nobel laureates," explained a Department of Labor official. The "economic benefit can only increase as the U.S. enters a period of labor shortage," offered the *Wall Street Journal* in its strong support for the measure: "The Baby Boom generation is aging, the fertility rate is falling, and global competition for human capital will be intense."[7]

But even as the 1990 act was being passed, sentiment against immigration was mounting, particularly with the recession of 1990–1991. If the growing international competition was tending to erode the earnings of unskilled workers, so did the influx of low-skill labor from Mexico, the Philippines, and elsewhere. The recession, when relatively high unemployment lingered after the economy recovered, increased public unease about immigration, and fears for job security remained high. Subsequent analyses suggested that American-born workers do not appear to have been displaced in significant numbers by immigrants, but many believed their livelihoods were threatened. In the mid-1990s some 60 percent of African Americans said they were worried about their economic futures; the figure was 38 percent for whites, who were generally in somewhat more secure jobs.[8]

Cultural insecurities reinforced the economic and were broadcast in a series of angry polemics. Lawrence Auster led off in 1990 with *The Path to National Suicide*. Patrick Buchanan sought the 1992 Republican presidential nomination in part on the grounds that massive immigration was threatening American identity and social cohesion. In that year financial journalist (and British immigrant) Peter Brimelow published a lengthy article in the *National Review*, denouncing the indifference of liberal elites to the problem of uncontrolled immigration and "the drive to transform America from a nation into a charity ward," and urged greater restrictions on migrants from Third World countries. In *Importing Revolution* (1994) William R. Hawkins assailed the Ford Foundation, civil liberties, and Mexican groups for frustrating attempts to restrict immigration. Chilton Williamson Jr.'s *The Immigration Mystique* (1996) blamed the misguided multiculturalism of liberal elites for allowing the nation's Anglo-Saxon core to be threatened by so many of "opposing values." As in the debates over NAFTA and free trade, liberal elites were being assailed for their permissive cosmopolitanism, their willingness to allow foreign influences into American life.[9]

The anti-immigration blasts did not go unanswered. Academic studies appeared assailing the "new nativism" and pointing to the economic and other benefits that immigrants brought to the United States. Some suspected that the sensationalizing of immigration was part of "a larger political strategy targeted at Mexican American, Latino, and other minority civil rights and community activists who have recently begun to exert a significant influence in American politics." High-tech corporations pointed out the degree to which their sector relied on recruiting highly skilled foreigners. In its communications sciences section about 40 percent of researchers at AT&T Bell Laboratories in the early 1990s were foreign-born, as were around a third of the scientists and engineers in California's Silicon Valley. The service sector valued immigrants too; a high proportion of hospital doctors were foreigners; other employers, including big agriculture, valued the ready supply of low-wage laborers.[10]

With national politicians for the most part wary of this political minefield, immigration issues tended to emerge first at state and local levels. Most significant were events in the West, in which some older communities feared being swamped by the Hispanic tide. One analyst noted in 1996 that "one large immigrant stream is flowing into a defined region from a single cultural, linguistic, religious, and national source: Mexico." A former mayor of San Antonio was alarmed: "These population dynamics will result in the browning of America, the Hispanicization of America." Chicano activists did little to allay such concerns. "California is going to be a Hispanic state," insisted one: "Anyone who doesn't like it should leave." Spokesmen on both sides tended to exaggerate the imminence of the takeover, for if California, for example, was to be Hispanic it would take time for its politics to reflect its demography. Many Mexican settlers were not registered to vote, and those that were did not always use it. By the early twenty-first century, the non-Hispanic white population had indeed fallen to less than half of California's population, but this minority of whites still accounted for at least two-thirds of those who regularly went to the polls.[11]

The recession of the early 1990s deepened the backlash against immigrants at state level. Several Sunbelt states were hit the harder because of the post-Cold War contractions of defense and aerospace industries.

Southwestern politicians called for higher fences and armed troops on the border, while El Paso and other frontier towns tried to erect their own blockades. Florida in 1994 sued the federal government for the educational, welfare, and other costs occasioned by illegal immigrants, in a suit soon joined by other states. In California, where the economy was slow to recover from the 1991 slowdown, a movement gathered force to deny them benefits. Promoted by a group called Save Our State, initially it was not expected to succeed, but it touched a popular nerve, and in August 1993 the Republican Governor Pete Wilson, facing an uphill struggle for re-election, enlisted in the cause. His poll ratings improved sharply, and illegal immigration became a major campaign issue. Anti-immigrant activists, with some help from the state's Republicans, gathered enough signatures to put Proposition 187 on the ballot. The measure, which barred state benefits for illegal immigrants – that is, schools, medical and other public services – passed in 1994 with 59 percent of the votes cast. Florida, Illinois, New York, and Texas were soon considering similar measures, and in Congress House Republicans proposed that legal immigrants be subjected to cuts in disability payments for the elderly, student loans, and school lunches. The courts later negated California's Proposition 187, but not before Wilson himself was handsomely re-elected. His campaign, in the words of one authority, "was built on a simple, powerful, and effective message: illegal immigrants committed crime, took jobs, and exacerbated the effects of the recession through their use of public services."[12]

The success of Wilson and Proposition 187 in California was not lost on other Republicans, although while some were excited by it others were alarmed, not wanting to deter Latino voters unnecessarily. When the Republicans won a resounding victory in the 1994 election, increasing the number of conservatives in Congress with nativist suspicions, the prospects for new restrictionist legislation sharply increased.

Encouraged by the California example, exultant conservative Republicans discussed ways of limiting citizenship and reducing immigrant quotas. For many, immigration had become a welfare issue, with the public having to bear the cost of the importation of poverty. "My ancestors … came to this country not with their hands out for welfare checks," complained Texas Republican Congressman Bill Archer in 1995, evidently unaware of the high proportion of immigrants on welfare rolls in the early twentieth century: "They came here for the opportunity for freedom and the opportunity to work." Such Republicans saw immigrants "as a population that, once legalized, would be able to claim legitimate title to government aid while petitioning to bring in even more of their relatives." As the Republicans were testing their influence in Congress in 1995, the US Commission on Immigration Reform issued a report recommending new crackdowns on illegal immigration, reducing legal immigration by a whopping 40 percent, shifting priorities toward those with skills, and ending family chains by limiting preferences for relatives. President Clinton endorsed the proposals, but business reaction was sharply hostile to the proposed reduction in business visas. "Recommending a reduction in the number of foreign workers U.S. companies can hire shows an ignorance of how business operates in today's global market," expostulated the National Association of Manufacturers vice-president.[13]

But by the mid-1990s, as the numbers remorselessly mounted, there were growing doubts over assimilability. "Recent migrants appear to have less incentive to make a decisive break from their home countries," wrote one scholar: "Fax machines, direct-dial telephones, next-day videos of home country entertainment and news, abundant foreign-language TV stations, cheap jet travel – all those nurture and reinforce an enclave mentality." Leading political scientist Samuel Huntington argued that not only relatively easy contact with their homelands but also their tendency to concentrate in large numbers and create their own Spanish-speaking enclaves meant that Hispanics had less reason than earlier immigrant groups to assimilate. "In Miami there is no pressure to be American," said a Cuban-born sociologist. Globalization in this perspective promoted a kind of parochialism on the part of the newcomers. Restrictionists in Congress determined to try to cut immigration drastically, and a House task force appointed by Republican Speaker Newt Gingrich proposed a raft of harsh proposals, including abolishing the Constitution's automatic extension of citizenship to the US-born children of illegal immigrants. The skillful lobbying of business, civil rights, and ethnic groups rebuffed this attack, and the ensuing 1996 act did little more than authorize the strengthening of border controls. The Border Patrol became the largest federal domestic uniformed service.[14]

Conservative anti-immigrant sentiments spilled over into other legislation. The Personal Responsibility and Work Opportunity Reconciliation Act of the same year, which recast the nation's welfare system, bowed to public opinion in curbing the eligibility even of legal aliens for federal benefits, such as Social Security. Distinctions were being drawn between native-born citizens and other legal residents. But in 1997, after the Republicans had lost seats in the House as well as the presidential election of 1996, Congress agreed to restore many of the welfare benefits. At state level, too, there were further attempts to reduce the services available to immigrants. In 1998 California voters passed Proposition 227 by a large margin, limiting bilingual language programs to one year for each pupil, to encourage pupils to adapt themselves quickly to English.

It was the Republican Party that was the most disrupted by the populist temper. California's Pete Wilson found that an anti-immigrant stance worked to his electoral advantage, but other conservatives, aware of Hispanics becoming US citizens and registering to vote, feared the reverse effect. Governor George W. Bush of Texas and Mayor Rudy Guiliani of New York, each representing favorite immigrant destinations, distanced themselves from the nativism of Proposition 187. Two former Republican cabinet members, Jack Kemp and William Bennett, warned that such measures would push Latinos and Asians more firmly into the Democratic Party. Whatever the short-term gains, there were dangers in turning the Republicans "inward to a protectionist and isolationist and more xenophobic party." Bush had been elected governor of Texas in 1994 with significant Latino support, and won re-election in 1998 with half the Latino vote. Other Republicans began to get the message that the anti-immigrant agenda was not necessarily an electoral asset.[15]

By the turn of the century anti-immigrant sentiment had eased somewhat, soothed by the booming economy. A 1999 poll found that only 44 percent of Americans wanted to reduce immigration levels, down over 20 points since 1995. By this date globalization was demonstrating its virtues, as the growth in foreign trade was accompanied by the creation of new jobs and unemployment was at its lowest for decades. In the late 1990s Congress agreed to more generous provisions for skilled immigrants, and in 2000 the American Competitiveness in the Twenty-first Century Act raised their quota further to 195 000 a year for the subsequent three years. High-tech companies had intensively lobbied for more skilled workers as the economy boomed, amplifying their message with generous campaign contributions to congressional candidates. "We need to recruit as many of the great brains of the world to work and become American as we can," said House Majority Leader Trent Lott. Two candidates for the 2000 Republican presidential nomination, George W. Bush and John McCain, promised to increase the numbers of skilled immigrants. In 2000 the AFL-CIO, which had traditionally been hostile toward illegal immigrants, declared in favor of an amnesty program to legitimize the presence of millions of them. Law-and-order conservatives still wanted more restrictive immigration laws, but business conservatives tended to prevail. In 2001 the US Chamber of Commerce president told the Senate Judiciary committee that immigrants are "our best hope to curb chronic American labor shortages."[16]

To remain competitive, it seemed that America's vaunted New Economy needed both large numbers of workers willing to take low-pay jobs (for which American-born citizens, it was widely suspected, had little appetite) and educated immigrants with either capital or advanced skills or both. The "utility of the immigrant groups," said the dean of a business school, "is that they bring their fearless spirit of competing globally." Immigration would remain a highly contested issue, but in a globalized world it was becoming increasingly recognized that the United States could no more afford to close its borders to people than to trade and investment.[17]

* * *

By the 1990s Americans were becoming increasingly conscious that it was not only goods, capital, and people that were crossing American borders. The "war on drugs," for example, was largely conceived in terms of combating an imported menace, as exemplified in George Bush's inaugural address of January 1989. Disease, too, could reach Americans from abroad, as the AIDS epidemic tragically demonstrated, and there were other examples, such as the first outbreak in the United States in 1999 of the West Nile virus, thought to have entered through an infected bird or mosquito. The recognition that disease could spread from abroad, of course, was not a new one, but the rapid increase in international trade and the movement of people in the late twentieth century served to increase the risk. When a deadly bird flu appeared in Asia in the early twenty-first century, the United States engaged with other countries and committed hundreds of millions of dollars to combating it.

Toward the end of the twentieth century Americans became increasingly aware also of environmental threats to their well-being, and national boundaries no longer offered much protection. Discharges of nuclear radiation could drift across continents; border controls were of little help against air and water pollution; the depletion of the ozone layer in the atmosphere exposed all human beings to the dangerous risk of the sun's ultraviolet light; global warming threatened the earth's fragile ecology. Environmentalists pointed out that Americans could not afford to stand aloof from developments in distant parts of the globe: the destruction of tropical rain forests diminished the production of atmospheric oxygen; desertification of agricultural areas in Africa and elsewhere threatened the earth's food supply; a soaring population threatened to outstrip the planet's ability to support it.

The modern environmental movement in the United States may be traced to the late 1960s, but by the 1980s and 1990s its leaders were emphasizing the transnational nature of many environmental problems. Environmental activism was stronger in the United States than in any other country, and by the late 1980s its principal organizations had an international as well as a national presence. Their expertise was called on to assist movements abroad, and they increasingly adopted a global orientation. Apart from mainstream bodies like the Sierra Club, American scientists were prominent in international organizations like the International Union for the Conservation of Nature and Natural Resources. If American governments sometimes seemed slow to address global environmental problems, non-governmental organizations in the United States were in the forefront of international environmental activity. International NGOs were to be influential in persuading governments to accept guidelines for protecting the environment.

American environmentalism expanded greatly in the 1980s, in part in outraged response to the indifference of the Reagan administration to their cause. The membership of the 11 major environmental groups almost doubled between 1979 and 1990. By the latter date several groups, such as the National Wildlife Federation and Greenpeace USA, claimed memberships of over half a million. Between 1969 and 1990 the number of registered environmental lobbyists in Washington grew from just two to nearly a hundred. The global dimension of environmentalism was receiving unprecedented publicity. In October 1988 *U.S. News & World Report* carried a cover story on "Planet Earth," though it offered a relatively optimistic take on the capacity of scientists to answer, "how the Earth's machinery will react to the monkey wrenches that humans have thrown into the works." *Time* magazine in January 1989 named "Endangered Earth" as "Planet of the Year," in place of the customary "Man of the Year." In September *Scientific American* offered a special issue on "Managing Planet Earth." On April 22, 1990 many Americans and others around the world celebrated Earth Day, on the twentieth anniversary of the first Earth Day in 1970. Newspapers, television, and radio accorded extensive coverage to the parades, teach-ins, and demonstrations that marked the 1990 occasion. Time Warner produced "The Earth Day Special" for ABC, a spectacular TV documentary featuring Bette Midler as Mother Earth, supported by a huge cast of celebrities. In a 1981 opinion poll only 45 percent had supported measures to improve environmental protection "regardless of cost"; in 1990 the figure reached 74 percent.[18]

While the Reagan administration's indifference incensed environmentalists, more important in raising awareness of the global dimension of environmental problems was a series of disasters in the 1980s. In 1984 in Bhopal in India over 2000 people died and many others were maimed by the accidental release of poison gas by a plant jointly owned by the US company Union Carbide. A huge spillage of toxic chemicals into the Rhine river in 1986 from a Swiss plant of Sandoz, a multinational headquartered in Germany, threatened lives in four European countries. Commanding enormous publicity in 1986 was the Chernobyl disaster. Explosions at a nuclear reactor in the Ukraine sent a massive radioactive cloud into the atmosphere, where it drifted across Russia, Europe, and eastern North America. In the Soviet Union 336 000 people had to be evacuated. Western Europeans and Americans, it seemed, were in danger of radioactive poisoning, perhaps from eating the meat of animals that grazed on contaminated grass in their own country. In 1988–1989 a severe drought in the United States triggered public anxieties about climate change – according to one calculation, its losses in agriculture, energy, water, and other sectors of the economy made it "the most expensive natural disaster ever to affect the nation." Also close to home was the *Exxon Valdez* incident, when a giant tanker ran aground, spilling nearly 11 million gallons of oil into Prince William Sound, Alaska, in March 1989, with devastating consequences for the wildlife. These various disasters received extensive media coverage, television in particular conveying graphic images into almost every household, and governments were obliged to respond to public anxiety. Following Chernobyl, two multinational treaties for prompt notification and emergency assistance in case of nuclear accidents were quickly agreed. The *Exxon Valdez* spill precipitated passage of the 1990 Oil Pollution Act.[19]

Yet while these emergencies served to raise public awareness of the environment, they were not as serious threats to the future of the globe as were other issues that were troubling scientists, such as the depletion of the ozone layer and global warming. On the ozone layer the United States had quite a good record, though when the problem was identified in the mid-1970s the country had been producing nearly half of the world's CFCs (chlorofluorocarbons, widely used in aerosol sprays and responsible for thinning the layer). Nonetheless the producers were relatively few and it was possible to find alternatives to CFCs, which were prohibited in aerosol sprays in the United States from 1978. The Reagan administration, along with environmental activists, worked to secure an international ban. The discovery of the ozone hole in the Antarctic in 1985, and with it greater public awareness, added to the urgency, and a major agreement was secured with the Montreal Protocol of 1987, which established a schedule for the phasing out of CFCs. At a meeting in London in 1990 international agreement was reached to ban CFCs by the year 2000. It was hoped that the ozone layer was on the road to recovery. Twenty years after the signing of the Montreal Protocol there was evidence that ozone-depleting substances in the atmosphere were indeed declining, and Kofi Annan, recently retired as Secretary General of the UN, called the Protocol: "Perhaps the single most successful international agreement to date."[20]

By the date of the Montreal Protocol climate change was eclipsing the ozone layer at the top of environmentalists' agenda. Even governments were beginning to get worried. A report published in 1987 by an international commission chaired by Prime Minister Brundtland of Norway posited the goal of "sustainable development": fostering economic growth in such a way as to respect the environment and, critically, ensuring that the needs of the present generation did not compromise those of future generations. At the July 1989 Paris summit meeting of G7 countries, the environment was a major issue. When the G7 leaders met again in Houston in 1990, the major environmental organizations held a counter-summit in the city, calling on the industrial nations to develop policies to reduce the greenhouse effect.

Terms like "global warming" and the "greenhouse effect" were appearing regularly in the popular media. Magazine stories and television programs explained that gases in the earth's atmosphere trapped heat rising from the earth's surface, a natural and indeed necessary phenomenon which kept the earth warm enough for life to flourish – the greenhouse effect. But over the last hundred years earth's surface temperature had been rising – the result, many scientists believed, of the build-up of carbon dioxide and other gases in the atmosphere as a result of human activity, such as burning coal and oil, as well as deforestation. If the rise continued the consequences could be catastrophic; as polar icecaps melted, low-lying areas would become flooded, and changing weather patterns would cause chaos and threaten the world's food supply. Time was running out if global warming was to be contained.

Scientists had long known about the greenhouse effect, but by the late 1970s had begun to recognize that global warming could represent a major threat to the planet. In the 1980s some concerned scientists and environmental groups were attempting to secure the attention of the wider public and of government. An August 1981 article on global warming did reach the front page of the *New York Times*, and other newspapers gave the issue occasional attention. Congress showed somewhat more interest than the

White House, as Senator Al Gore of Tennessee and others held hearings from the early 1980s on climate change and invited scientific testimony. Scientist James Hansen made outspoken statements to a congressional committee in 1986 and 1987, but what greatly aided him in getting his message across were the heat waves and drought of 1988, reportedly the worst since the dustbowls of the 1930s. In June, during torrid heat outside the chamber, Hansen testified "with 99 percent confidence" that global warming was underway, and that frequent storms, floods, and horrendous heat waves should be expected over the next 50 years. His testimony made headlines, not least because as the fearsome summer wore on elderly people died in the heat, water rationing was introduced in many areas, and the water level of the Mississippi fell to such a low that barge traffic came to a stop. Hurricane Gilbert and the worst forest fires of the century added to the sense of crisis. In Washington itself the summer of 1988 was the hottest on record. On one count, the number of newspaper articles in 1988 on global warming was 10 times that of 1987. Over 30 bills dealing with the climate were introduced into Congress, and such notions as a "carbon tax" on CO_2 emissions began to be debated.[21]

Environmental groups such as the Environmental Defense Fund and the Sierra Club made reducing greenhouse gases a top priority. In the research institutes and universities research into climate topics burgeoned. In 1988, under the auspices of the World Meteorological Organization and the UN Environment Programme, scientists and government bureaucrats formed an Intergovernmental Panel on Climate Change (IPCC); its first report in 1990 unequivocally confirmed that the world had been warming and warned that this was likely to continue. There were far-reaching implications ultimately for the fate of the earth and more immediately for the industrial world. Around 80 percent of CO_2 emissions arose from fossil fuel energy (coal, oil, gas), that is, from the core industries in economic development, which constituted powerful interests in the United States and other countries.

The environment for once had been something of an issue in the 1988 presidential campaign, in which George Bush promised to be the "Environment President." "Those who think we're powerless to do anything about the greenhouse effect are forgetting about the White House effect," he said in a glib line that came back to haunt him. The public and congressional interest in the environment helped him secure passage of the Clean Air Act Amendments. In 1990 some 700 members of the American National Academy of Sciences, including 49 Nobel Prize winners, wrote to the president urging him to take action to combat global warming. But if environmentalists were mobilizing, so were their opponents. In 1989 oil, coal, auto, and other companies formed the Global Climate Coalition, which lobbied to resist immediate action on reducing greenhouse gases. Bush's enthusiasm for the environment waned with the slowing of the economy, and there were prominent scientists saying that more research was needed before government could adopt a focused program. Bush's inveterate moderateness prevailed, and influential figures in his administration, such as John Sununu and Richard Darman, were deeply suspicious of the environmentalist cause. "Americans did not fight and win the wars of the twentieth century to keep the world safe for green vegetables," sniffed Darman.[22]

Climate change was to be high on the agenda of the Earth Summit held in Rio de Janeiro in 1992. The first Earth Summit, convened by the UN Conference on the Environment and Development, had been held 20 years earlier in Stockholm, when just two heads of state or government had attended. The Rio Conference attracted over a hundred national leaders; never before had so many heads of state met together. Crowding into the city too were thousands of journalists, NGOs, and government delegates. Broadly, the more highly industrialized countries, attuned to such issues as environmental pollution and species preservation, were arrayed against the developing countries, which were suspicious of the effects that regulation might have on their own economic development.

For several months it was unclear whether President Bush would dignify Rio by attending. In the event he did so. "I am the one that is burdened with the responsibility to find a balance between sound environmental practices on the one hand and jobs for American families on the other ...," he said: "If they don't understand it in Rio, too bad." Rio was coinciding with his re-election campaign. The administration, not without reason, feared that environmental activists would make the United States the villain at Rio. One of Bush's advisers muttered about double standards: "Japan's out there killing whales and running driftnets, for God's sake, while we've got the world's toughest environmental laws and we're twisting ourselves into knots over how many jobs to abolish to save a species of an owl." (The northern spotted owl had become a symbol, as attempts to preserve its old habitat in the Pacific Northwest had impacted on the timber industry.)[23]

Before the summit were two major propositions. One was the Biodiversity Convention, an international treaty aimed at preserving the earth's genetic diversity. There had been growing concern over the rapid increase in the rate of species extinction as a consequence of economic development. The United States upset many by revealing beforehand that it would not sign such a convention, the only advanced country not to do so. The treaty was held to cut across existing American programs; it also had implications for companies dependent on genetic resources and for intellectual property rights. Bush said that it threatened American jobs: "We cannot permit the extreme in the environmental movement to shut down the United States." Also adopted at Rio was the UN Framework Convention on Climate Change, designed to stabilize greenhouse gas concentrations in the atmosphere, primarily through the industrialized countries trying to reduce their greenhouse gas emissions to their 1990 levels by the year 2000. Despite the Bush administration's reluctance to agree specified targets for CO_2 stabilization, the United States did sign this Convention, whose target provisions, largely at US insistence, were non-binding. More scientific research was needed, insisted the Bush team, before targets were made obligatory. A legacy of Rio was a recognition that "sustainable development" had to be the objective of international economic and environmental agreements.[24]

One critic of the American role at Rio was Senator Al Gore, who was present and who had long developed a high profile on environmental issues, as illustrated by his 1992 book, *Earth in the Balance*. "This has been a disgraceful performance," he said: "It is the single worst failure of political leadership that I have seen in my lifetime." Bush in turn contemptuously referred to Gore as Ozone Man. "You know why I call him Ozone Man?" he asked at one election rally: "This guy is so far off in the environment extreme, we'll be up to our necks in owls and out of work for every American. ... He is way out, far out. Far out, man!" Environmental groups contributed about $1.3 million to congressional candidates in the 1992 campaign, though the energy and other corporations contributed many times more.[25]

The election of Bill Clinton as president, with Gore as vice-president, brought into power an administration that was receptive to environmental issues, at least in principle. Clinton promised to make his government "the greenest in history." He rejected the assumption of his Republican predecessors that there was a necessary conflict between economic and environmental goals, that the alternatives were either "jobs" or the "environment," and embraced the concept of sustainable development that the UN and other international bodies were promoting. He quickly established the blue-ribbon President's Council on Sustainable Development: "America must lead the way in promoting economic growth and environmental preservation at home and abroad." Bruce Babbitt, a former Arizona governor and president of the League of Conservation Voters, became Secretary of the Interior.[26]

In June 1993 the administration, having persuaded the major pharma-ceutical and biotechnology firms that their interests were not threatened, promised to sign the Biodiversity Convention, which was duly referred to the Senate for approval. The Senate, however, left it in limbo. The admin-istration also committed itself to the Rio objective of reducing CO_2 emis-sions to 1990 levels by 2000 and announced a range of other environmental goals. Environmental justice, said Clinton, meant "calling a halt to the poisoning and the pollution of our poorest communities." To broaden support for NAFTA, and a mark of the strength of the environmental lobbies, Clinton secured the North American Agreement on Environmental Cooperation with Mexico and Canada, providing for the monitoring of each country's environmental enforcement and the clean-up of the toxic strip along the US–Mexican border, making NAFTA, however modestly, "the 'greenest' trade agreement ever negotiated." There was also novel if limited attention to environmental concerns in the Uruguay Round trade negotiations. But environmentalists were disappointed with the progress made during the early Clinton years. Congressional opposition frustrated an attempt to raise the Environmental Protection Agency (EPA) to cabinet status, spurning the practice of most advanced countries.[27]

When the Republicans won their mighty congressional victory in the mid-term elections of 1994, the Clinton White House found itself fighting off their attempts to tear up environmental regulations. For most of the period since the Nixon administration, there had been substantial agree-ment between congressional Democrats and Republicans on necessary environmental legislation, but from the early 1990s small businessmen in particular were complaining vociferously of the mounting costs of compli-ance, while in an era of "downsizing" large companies were also questioning the necessity of every EPA edict. The ascending right-wing Republicans took up their cause, many happy to be returning to the agenda of the early Reagan White House. Every environmental law was targeted by the party for revision or repeal. The Republican Whip, Tom DeLay, said of govern-ment regulations that "I can't think of one" he would keep, and famously compared the EPA to the Gestapo. The new Republican Speaker, Newt Gingrich, insisted that the policies of the previous 20 years had been "absurdly expensive, created far more resistance than was necessary and misallocated resources on emotional and public relations grounds without regard to either scientific, engineering, or economic rationality." Bill Clinton campaigned around the country to resist the Republican assault: "The environment is still not able to protect itself." In August he publicly lamented that 25 years of bipartisanship on the environment were over.[28]

The Republicans' attack on green legislation, however, for the most part failed. The environmental lobbies were now influential forces. By 1995 there were reckoned to be 10000 environmental groups with an aggregate membership of over 40 million. Between 1987 and 1996 the donations received by environmental bodies rose by 91 percent, much more than those for other charities. The major groups employed large staffs, commanded considerable technical expertise, and generally had public opinion behind them, while their visibility and trustworthiness gave them heightened coverage in the media. The Sierra Club spent $7 million on voter education and support for candidates in the 1996 elections. Aided in the Clinton years by threats of presidential vetoes, the environmentalists were usually able to see off the business lobbyists. Jeffrey Berry, in reviewing the 12 most significant bills involving environmental policy in 1995–1996, found that the environmentalists won on 10 occasions, lost on one and drew on one. As he concluded, "the environmental lobbies, congressional Democrats, and, occasionally, moderate Republicans, consistently defeated the efforts to weaken environmental protection statutes." When the Republicans dropped an attempt to ease the meat inspection regulations, journalist Anthony Lewis commented that their "constituents did not like the idea of dying from infected meat."[29]

If the environmental lobbies and public opinion helped Bill Clinton preserve environmental safeguards, equally he could not secure new environmental legislation. "Great shield, no sword," commented an environmental spokesman of Clinton's first term performance. While the Clinton administration showed some interest in reforming the country's environmental policies, such as by promoting clean technology or introducing incentives to encourage energy-saving behavior, the deadlock in Congress frustrated major change. Clinton did make some administrative revisions in ways favored by environmentalists, as when the EPA introduced tighter standards for tailpipe emissions for cars, buses, and trucks. "In the next decade, every person in this country will breathe cleaner air," its head confidently predicted. Clinton himself discovered that under the terms of the Antiquities Act of 1906 he had the authority to designate large wilderness areas as national monuments without congressional approval, and managed to bring nearly six million acres under protection, the greatest of any twentieth-century president. His Republican opponents, furious at the lack of consultation, called his first such designation "the biggest land grab since the invasion of Poland." Clinton finished his term in reasonably good odor with environmentalists. Carl Pope, head of the Sierra Club, said that Clinton would be remembered as "one of the great defenders of the environment."[30]

But however gratified the president may have been by comparisons to Theodore Roosevelt on his conservation record, the most critical issue to the scientific and environmental communities remained global warming. This the administration took seriously, and Vice President Gore was sent to lead the American delegation at the international conference held at Kyoto, Japan, under UN auspices, to try to agree an international treaty to control greenhouse gases. This was meant to put in place the binding emissions targets left voluntary at Rio in 1992. Many corporations, economists, and politicians in the United States were distinctly unhappy about the thrust of the Kyoto talks, which retained the understanding reached at Rio that it would be up to the advanced economies to limit their CO_2 and other emissions while other countries would be excused. The major oil companies and their industrial associates mobilized to resist Kyoto, particularly through the Global Climate Coalition, which mounted a $13 million campaign. In July 1997, before the Kyoto Protocol was finalized, the US Senate passed by a stunning 95–0 vote a resolution stating that the United States should not be a signatory to any protocol that did not include binding targets and timetables for both developing and industrialized nations or involved "serious harm to the economy of the United States." A protocol was nonetheless agreed, under which developed countries undertook to reduce greenhouses gases to the 1990 levels by the year 2012. Developing nations, including China, were exempted. In December 1997 Clinton hailed the accord as "environmentally strong."[31]

Though Clinton signed the protocol, the administration conceded that it would not be submitted to the Senate for ratification until key developing nations participated. Public opinion polls found that "an overwhelming majority ... embraces the idea that global warming is a real problem that requires action" and that "a strong majority of Americans favors Senate ratification of the Kyoto Treaty." But conservative think tanks had also emerged as influential contributors to the climate change debate; the Republicans who commanded Congress after 1994 ensured that scientists skeptical of climate change testified before congressional committees and received media coverage. As with immigration, public opinion seemed to be on one side and Congress, with its interest group pressures, on the other. In 1998 Clinton did secure a large increase in spending on climate change research, and some corporations acknowledged the reality of global warming and began to adopt strategies looking to a post-fossil-fuels world. To most environmentalists the accord was only a first step toward combating the climate threat that the planet faced. Eventually, in 2005, the protocol did go into effect after Russia had approved it, but the United States and Australia still remained aloof.[32]

Environmentalists had been engaging in electoral politics since the Reagan era, harrying candidates for office, but in the 1990s some decided to enter politics directly. Green parties began to form at state level, and through the decade ran candidates for local and state offices. In 2001 there were thought to be 91 elected Green officials scattered across 21 states. While novel, this was a tiny number, and some hankered for the publicity of a presidential campaign. In 1996 the Green Party of California persuaded the prominent consumer activist Ralph Nader to stand as its candidate for president, though on this occasion he ran a strictly limited campaign. A more serious effort followed in the 2000 election, when Nader reached 44 state ballots. The protesters at Seattle in 1999 had included environmentalists, some denouncing globalization as "a conspiracy against the environment," and the strength of those demonstrations raised hopes that there could be a green insurgency in 2000. But just how "green" Nader's candidacy was, however, was open to question. What spurred Nader himself was not so much the environment as his conviction forged by decades of campaigning that public interest groups were denied effective access to Washington. His objective, he said, was "to build a major political progressive force in America." The two major parties were "Tweedledum and Tweedledee," equally dominated by business corporations. A few celebrities joined his campaign, but he was subjected to fierce Democratic attacks accusing him of dividing the anti-Republican vote, and in the final weeks of the campaign his support dwindled. The fear that a vote for Nader was a vote for the Republican Party discouraged some environmental and other progressive lobbies from backing him, the Sierra Club and the League of Conservation Voters running ads that implied that a vote for him could be unhelpful to the cause. Nader did enjoy significant media attention on this occasion, and several state Green parties increased their memberships. But he secured only 2.7 percent of the popular vote, well short of the targeted 5 percent needed to secure federal funding for 2004. This outcome was hardly an adequate index of environmental sentiment. A campaign that was more anti-corporate, anti-Washington, and anti-global than explicitly environmental had been unable to summon the populist sentiments that had been in evidence a few years earlier.[33]

* * *

As with other features of globalization, both the immigration of the 1990s and the environmentalist campaign over global warming had their American critics. Pat Buchanan was again railing at liberal elites in 2002 in

The Death of the West, pointing out that large majorities in opinion polls wanted immigration reduced and English to be the official language: "The people want action. The elites disagree and do nothing." Some corporations funded studies that cast doubts on the science emphasizing the dangers of the greenhouse effect, and unilateralist conservatives were wary of the United States becoming entangled in international conventions. Oklahoma Senator Jim Inhofe, who described the Kyoto Treaty in 1997 as "scientifically dubious, economically disastrous and militarily stupid," was soon arguing that catastrophic climate change was a hoax. Both immigration and global environmentalism seemed to touch a lingering isolationist nerve. According to President Clinton's pollster, a core of almost 40 percent of Americans was "really isolationist, opposed to having much of a foreign policy at all." Such impulses seemed quixotic in the global era. As the millennium approached, anti-immigrant sentiments were faced down and quotas were again changed to admit yet more skilled immigrants, held to be necessary for American economic survival in a globalized world. The hostility to the Kyoto Treaty in Congress could not be overcome, though when in 1999 a chunk of ice the size of Rhode Island broke off Antarctica, Bill Clinton promptly headed there to publicize the danger of global warming. On these and other matters, outcomes were determined by the complex interaction of interest groups, partisan posturing, executive-legislative rivalry, and public opinion, though interest groups were displaying their potency. The prosperity of those last years of the twentieth century did help to ease the discontents that had emerged early in the decade, but these issues would have to be confronted again in the new millennium.[34]

Chapter 11

The New Age of Bill Clinton

The age of Bill Clinton was also the age of Steve Jobs of Apple and Bill Gates of Microsoft, of the Hubble Space Telescope and of Dolly the Sheep, whose cloning in Scotland triggered fierce debate in the United States. Marvelous new pharmaceutical products were launched, among them Viagra, which by the end of the decade was said to be reaching annual sales of $1 billion. Some 130 million people in the world had internet access in 1998, and nearly half of them were Americans. DVDs appeared on the market, and the sales of video games, laptop computers, and mobile or cell phones soared. In March 1999 the Dow Jones Industrial Index closed above $10 000 for the first time – it had reached $5000 only in November 1995.

"Change is the key to your security," Bill Clinton told audiences during the 1992 campaign. In one respect this was a curious claim because Clinton was no radical, but such rhetoric was intended to align him with the mood of the 1990s, with the high-tech revolution and with globalizing processes. "Now the sights and sounds of this ceremony are broadcast instantaneously to billions around the world," said the president at his inauguration: "Communications and commerce are global. Investment is mobile, technology is almost magical, and ambition for a better life is now universal." Some of Clinton's aides were uneasy that he was identifying himself too much with the forces of technological and global change. "Too yippity about productivity," was how Larry Summers characterized Clinton's enthusiasm. But Clinton was determined to convey the message that the United States had to work with the processes that were transforming the globe and the American place within it. "There is no longer a clear division between what is foreign and what is domestic," he added: "The world

Contemporary America: Power, Dependency, and Globalization since 1980,
First Edition. M.J. Heale.
© 2011 M.J. Heale. Published 2011 by Blackwell Publishing Ltd.

economy, the world environment, the world AIDS crisis, the world arms race – they affect us all."[1]

Bill Clinton was the poor boy from Hope, Arkansas, who had stood up against an alcoholic stepfather to protect his mother, whose intellectual prowess had taken him as a Rhodes Scholar to Oxford, and who at 32 had become the "boy governor" of Arkansas. A man with a zest for life, large appetites, and an unrivaled reputation for schmoozing the electorate, Clinton was fascinated by public life and public issues, often confounding experts by his knowledge of their subjects. His intellectual grasp was matched by the empathy that he was able to display for others. "I feel your pain," he told an AIDS activist during the 1992 campaign, a phrase that would later be immortalized on T-shirts. Open to ideas, Clinton's ebullient personality and tactical dexterity made him "a natural" as a politician, earning him the title "Slick Willy," known for his capacity to stage impressive "comebacks" after political reverses.

Clinton personified the new age. His opponent in the 1992 campaign, George Bush, had served bravely in World War II and been a determined Cold Warrior, but the war was now a distant memory and even the Cold War had stuttered stunningly to an end. Bill Clinton, by contrast, had been born after World War II and had no identification with the Cold War establishment. As a student he had even demonstrated against the Vietnam War, as his political enemies liked to remind the public, reinforcing the image that he was of a new generation. Further, more than Bush, he seemed to have an understanding that the changes in the world went beyond the epochal disintegration of Cold War patterns. He was the baby-boomer, a child of the Sixties, a bridge from the old industrial order to a new postindustrial world. This image was reinforced by his vice-president, Al Gore, another young and energetic figure, one of those earlier known as Atari Democrats, a group who had seen "investment and high technology as the contemporary answer to the New Deal," and who had moved on to environmental causes. Gore had played a role in the development of the internet, and his 1992 book, *Earth in the Balance*, reached the *New York Times* bestseller list. Clinton and Gore were offering leadership for an age of electronic information and international interdependence. But only a minority of those who went to the polls in 1992 had voted for them.[2]

The identification with the high-tech revolution was no nerdish obsession. Rather it arose from the fears that the United States was confronting decline, particularly in relation to its economic competitors, as so many pundits and the Clinton campaign had insisted. Silicon Valley and what it represented could be the answer. In September 1992 over 30 Silicon Valley CEOs, many of them former Republicans or Independents, had endorsed Clinton, since, unlike the Bush White House, he had seemed to grasp their concerns. After "20 years of declining relative productivity," argued Clinton a month into his presidency, the best investment was "in the education, the skills, the reasoning capacity, and the creativity of our own people" for the purpose of "competing and winning in the global economy." He assured his fellow Americans: "We are wired for real time." In 1995 he would enthusiastically urge on a C-SPAN audience Benjamin R. Barber's *Jihad vs. McWorld*, with its penetrating critique of the perils of globalization, which to Clinton constituted a "challenge" to be confronted.[3]

Yet in the networked globe of Clinton's vision, governments did less and individuals more; it was a world in which international credit could flee at the touch of a button. Clinton had to reconcile his commitment to change with a relatively conservative economic philosophy. As chair of the DLC (Democratic Leadership Council) he had identified with the New Democrat agenda, with its recognition of the need to work with business and exercise restraint in government spending without abandoning liberal values on such social issues as civil and women's rights. For the 1992 campaign Clinton had developed his theme of a New Covenant, one crafted for the postmodern age. On the one hand it emphasized "opportunity," invoking the enterprise culture of the Reagan years. Government should provide the conditions for "opportunity," and it was up to citizens to seize it, though in return they had to accept "responsibility." As Clinton expressed it before a largely black audience in Memphis: "If you can go to work, you ought to go to work," a sentiment for which he was warmly applauded. The New Covenant theme offered a vital role for government, though an enabling one, not the government largesse of New Deal days.[4]

The New Covenant was an attempt to convey the message that neither conservative Republicanism nor the Democratic liberalism of the New Deal tradition offered appropriate models of governance for the modern age. The New Democrats were seeking to transcend the old categories of left-wing and right-wing politics and identify a new dynamic synthesis, one which might draw on elements of both traditions but would not simply be a compromise between them. "We reject both the do-nothing government of the last twelve years and the big government theory that says we can hamstring business and tax and spend our way to prosperity," said the 1992 Democratic platform: "Instead we offer a third way." It was not until Clinton's second term that the "third way" became a staple of political rhetoric, as centrist politicians on both sides of the Atlantic sought to distance themselves from older prescriptions, but it was already being anticipated. Cutting the United States off from the global economy, it was argued, would mean stagnation and deepening decline. Market forces had to be embraced. A freer market was an insecure one, so instead security had to be provided by ensuring that people had the skills and resources to succeed in the new economy, through such means as education and retraining, portable pensions and affordable health care. The state would be "leaner but not meaner," steering the economically displaced to new jobs rather than to welfare. At the same time, the New Democrats insisted, the family should be helped to perform its traditional child-rearing roles through effective child support and medical facilities. Economic growth rather than income redistribution was the key, and the task of government was to help all able-bodied adults participate in the economy. The message was that entrepreneurial capitalism was to be embraced but housetrained. As the DLC later explained: "The Third Way philosophy seeks to adapt enduring progressive values to the new challenges of the information age." It was Bill Clinton's role to lead the United States into this bright technological future.[5]

* * *

In his Inaugural Address Clinton evinced a Reaganesque optimism: "There is nothing wrong with America that cannot be cured by what is right about America." Like Reagan too, Clinton was clear that his first priority was the economy, on which he wanted to focus "like a laser." That Clinton was no economic radical became evident in his appointments to his economic team, which reflected a Wall Street and corporate bias at odds with the populism of his election campaign. Lloyd Bentsen, former chair of the Senate Finance Committee, respected in the business world for his sound fiscal views, became Secretary of the Treasury, arguably a fitting role for someone whose Senate career had earned him the nickname "Loophole Lloyd." Even better known on Wall Street, where he had made a fortune, was Robert Rubin, who became director of the National Economic Council, created to coordinate economic policy. Also declaring himself a "deficit hawk" was the new Budget Director, Leon Panetta, a former California congressman. In the background was Alan Greenspan, the inherited and conservative head of the Federal Reserve Board, independent of the administration but influential because of his power to set interest rates. "Greenspan has the most important grip in town," said one cabinet member: "Bill's balls, in the palm of his hand."[6]

Selecting these reassuring figures, reflected Greenspan, made Clinton "seem about as far from the classic tax-and-spend liberal as you could get and still be a Democrat." Several other cabinet-level appointments also went to successful baby-boomers and well-heeled lawyers. "He ran as a populist, and now has surrounded himself with the intellectual elite of his party," complained one supporter. A member of that elite was Robert Reich, an old friend of Clinton from student days, who became Secretary of Labor. More liberal than the others on the economic team, Reich was a Harvard professor whose latest book, *The Work of Nations*, was a bestseller which had explicitly addressed the issue of how an advanced nation could prosper in a globalized world. Where once the United States had created an industrial giant through the exploitation of its natural resources, it argued, in the new era it was human capital that was critical. Clinton had devoured the book, which had emphasized developing those few resources that were under the control of a national economy, that is, education, the training of the workforce, and investment in the infrastructure. Mid-career training would enable displaced workers to find opportunities in the high-tech economy. "Free markets *and* human capital investment may be the only combination that can lead to enduring prosperity," Reich said in 1993.[7]

In the event, Reich's proposals for an ambitious investment program were to take second place to other considerations. By the early 1990s the deficit was touching a public nerve, perhaps because Americans were beginning to suspect that it might have something to do with the distressing times they had been experiencing. Economic commentators and the serious newspapers were almost obsessed with it. In 1980 the deficit had been about $1 trillion; by the end of the Reagan–Bush era it was about $4 trillion, and the national debt had been growing faster than the economy. In Greenspan's words, "the hard truth was that Reagan had borrowed from Clinton, and Clinton was having to pay it back." The interest that had to be paid on the debt had become the third largest cost in the federal budget. Ross Perot had made the deficit the centerpiece of his presidential campaign, and his stunning 19 percent of the popular vote thrust it high on the Clinton camp's agenda. "My God …," said New York Senator Pat Moynihan as the Democrats took over the government: "Now it's *our* deficit." Reich believed the deficit had become a symbol of a government that seemed out of control, just as people felt they were losing control of their own lives: "The government's failure to balance *its* checkbook seems particularly galling to an American public having trouble balancing its own family checkbook." Driving past a large crowd soon after his inauguration Clinton noticed someone holding up a sign: "Just do something."[8]

During the transition period the implications of the ascent of the financial sector in the economy during the 1980s were driven home to a writhing Clinton. As the vice-chair of Goldman Sachs International put it, "the global bond market can be a very tough disciplinarian. Bond buyers have a very conservative bias." Not only bankers, rich foreigners, and institutional investors but also pensioners and Americans of all kinds had been putting their money into mutual funds as Wall Street boomed, and the bond market did not care for uncontrolled deficits and inflation. In a meeting with his aides in January 1993 Clinton expostulated: "You mean to tell me that the success of my program and my re-election hinges on the Federal Reserve and a bunch of fucking bond traders?" Clinton's great task thus came to be to save the country from Reaganomics, or at least from big budget deficits.[9]

It was during the transition, as his aides poured over the implacable figures, that Clinton capitulated and concluded that even more urgent than measures to boost the economy was a reduction of the deficit; without that a sustained economic expansion – which would fund new policies – would not be possible. Reduce the deficit, the theory went, then interest rates would go down, and there would be more money for investment in the private sector, ultimately driving up productivity and fostering growth. During brainstorming sessions Clinton came to recognize the deficit as the "threshold" issue. "I know it won't be easy," he said: "But I was elected to deal with the economy and this was what we need to do to get the economy back on track." But reducing the deficit implied constraining expenditure, which would disappoint many Democrats hoping that their electoral success would mean policies to help struggling families. "We're Eisenhower Republicans here and we're fighting the Reagan Republicans," Clinton privately complained: "we stand for lower deficits, free trade, and the bond market. Isn't that great?" He was right – he was offering a sophisticated variant of supply-side economics, in that the aim was to boost investment and production, rather than (as Keynesian orthodoxy suggested) boosting demand. Alan Greenspan was impressed that Clinton did not fudge the issue; his early commitment to deficit reduction rather than to traditional Democratic priorities was "an act of political courage."[10]

Ronald Reagan, assuming the presidency in a similar period of economic uncertainty in 1981, had laid out his economic plan within a month of taking office, on February 18; Clinton made a point by publishing his on February 17. It was, said one journalistic analysis, "a program for the most dramatic shift in U.S. fiscal policy since Ronald Reagan took power 12 years ago." It had a twofold aim, to move toward a balanced budget and to stimulate the economy. The first priority was to reduce the ballooning deficit, through higher taxes on corporations, the rich, and on energy (a broad-based tax on the use of thermal units or BTUs), and through spending cuts, not least on defense. The middle-class tax cut promised during the campaign had disappeared. The proposed economic stimulus was more modest than once anticipated, though it reflected Reich's recipe of "investment" in the infrastructure like transport and in "human capital" like education and skills, especially in worker retraining. "Absolutely," said a Clinton adviser when asked whether the intention was to undo the economics of the 1980s: "We think we're reversing some unacceptable trends." The Republicans, convinced that they had lost the election because of Bush's volte-face on taxes, immediately assailed the tax hikes, even though they would only begin to take effect on households with taxable incomes of at least $140 000. To many of them it had been Reagan's tax cut that had unleashed the 1980s boom, and Clinton was offering the reverse. Prominent Republican congressman Dick Armey called the plan "a disaster for the performance of the economy," and Republican Senator Phil Gramm called it "a one-way ticket to a recession." A new breed of ideological conservative was jostling for control of the Republican Party.[11]

By dint of compromise Clinton maneuvered his package through a suspicious Congress. On the deficit Clinton essentially got what he wanted, a hefty cut of about $500 billion over five years. Some social programs were trimmed, and defense spending was reduced. The energy tax was abandoned, to the dismay of environmentalists, but there was a tax increase on the top 1.2 percent of taxpayers, thus shifting the tax burden back to those who had gained from Reaganomics. But congressional opposition further eroded the investment proposals. "I won't have a goddam Democratic budget until 1996!" fulminated Clinton: "Education, job training – none of the things I campaigned on," though he salvaged about half the investment package. Clinton also engineered some liberal measures into the budget. If spending programs were largely ruled out, Clinton, as a New Democrat looking for new means to further a progressive agenda, recognized the potential of the tax system. He massively expanded the Earned Income Tax Credit, a program modestly introduced in 1975 to provide tax relief to the working poor. Clinton consummated EITC's conversion into a major social policy, using it to deliver something to the low paid. Thus, in keeping with New Covenant philosophy, more Americans should stay in work rather than go on welfare. "This is the most important thing we can do in welfare reform," explained Clinton, "– to make a simple statement that if you have kids and you work 40 hours a week, you will not be in poverty." The bill also established AmeriCorps, a national service program giving participants a year's work in education, health, and the environment, which would soon attract far more participants than the Peace Corps. A defining feature of Clinton's presidency, AmeriCorps exemplified the New Covenant, "a new service approach focusing on civic responsibility and real government/civil society partnerships." However, Clinton's accompanying stimulus program was torpedoed by a filibustering Republican minority in the Senate. Still, with the dramatic casting vote of Vice President Gore, the economic plan was finally approved by the Senate in August 1993. "It sends a clear signal to the markets that interest rates should stay down," said a jubilant president. "I've seen lots of presidents and lots of victories," exclaimed Lloyd Bentsen, "but this is the sweetest."[12]

With the budget bill, as with his free trade policies, Clinton was looking to the relatively long term. There was no immediate political pay-off, and he had strained relations with Democratic liberals. It took time for the measures to have an impact, but within a couple of years the economy was recovering strongly, much as Robert Rubin had predicted. With the restoration of fiscal discipline interest rates did come down, business confidence increased and with it investment, so that new jobs were being created and productivity was rising. The inherited budget deficit, as a percentage of GDP, fell markedly by 1994, an improvement that reflected the tax increases and spending cuts, as well as renewed economic growth. In that year productivity in non-farm businesses posted its second largest gain in 10 years.[13]

Parallel to the budget was Clinton's "Reinventing Government" initiative. Citing the public's disturbingly high distrust of government, the president reasoned that the only way to restore trust was "by giving people better value for their government." Like business downsizing, he was "trying to downsize the Federal Government." Deregulation was part of the larger process, and Vice President Gore was charged with reducing regulations and making government more efficient. Each agency was asked to halve its regulations; many regional offices were closed, and some functions were privatized, such as passing government printing to private firms. Clinton later boasted of reducing the federal workforce by 300 000 and reducing government to its 1960 size.[14]

Clinton's determination to reinvigorate the economy did not depend on the budget alone. Equally important was persuading Americans of the need to interact positively with the rest of the world. Clinton's prioritizing of the deficit in his economic plan had been something of a gamble – sort out the deficit and the money markets will allow the economy to rebound. His thrust toward free trade was a greater gamble, since it meant bucking the mainstream in his own party. Many congressional Democrats feared for the jobs of their constituents if trade barriers were reduced, and unions too, usually party allies, were deeply suspicious of policies that threatened to increase international competition. As Alex Waddan has noted, "the free trade project within the party was a top down one from the White House." Further, the disaffection or public malaise that had helped elect Clinton was in significant part connected to the widespread insecurity generated by the rapid economic restructuring of the United States and its immersion in the wider world. But Clinton decided to face protectionist pressures head on. There was a downside to globalization, he acknowledged, so individual security in such an economy meant "access to education and training, permanent non-job based health care, transferable pensions – and all with an international accent."[15]

The greatest confrontation erupted over NAFTA. After the Cold War the United States had to decide whether to extend its influence around the world or to retreat into an aloof Fortress America, and NAFTA came to symbolize the American future. Wrapped up in the NAFTA debate, as a *New York Times* columnist observed, were the great changes coursing through American life: "increased competition from abroad, ever fewer blue-collar jobs, declining military industries, greater opportunities for workers with education, skills and knowledge of new technology." To Clinton, the choice was between "the politics of hope" and the "politics of fear," that is, new jobs in a new economy or economic decline. Robert Reich thought NAFTA would benefit American wage earners, but recognized that further measures were needed to help workers remain productively employed. "With or without NAFTA, if this society is to join the new global economy, we have to create pathways for all people to get good jobs," he said: "Otherwise people will try to preserve the past." The risk of that was great. The United States had become a great industrial power with the help of a well-paid blue-collar class, but did such a class now have a future? Real wages had been eroding for years, and workers could hardly be expected to welcome further marginalization. "There's a palpable fear," said a Democratic congressman from Kentucky, "that NAFTA signifies the beginning … of a profound change – that it'll never, never be like it was before." To suspicious opponents of NAFTA, the choice was between "the people" and the "cultural elite," or between protecting American jobs on the one hand and bowing to the imperatives of the liberal ruling class and multinational corporations on the other.[16]

During the 1992 campaign Clinton had stalled on the issue, but he eventually endorsed the treaty that the Bush administration had agreed, while promising that there would be tough side agreements over workers' rights and the environment. With the election over Clinton put his energy behind NAFTA, believing that economic growth in Mexico would promote regional stability and that freer markets would mean more American jobs being created than lost. He did secure some modest side agreements, though ratification of the NAFTA treaty provoked a storm. AFL-CIO leader Lane Kirkland fulminated: "We worked our *asses* off to elect Bill Clinton. I'll be goddamned if my members are going to lose their fucking jobs on some vague promise by Mexico to improve their labor standards." A Democratic president seemed to be abandoning the core allies his party had depended on since the 1930s. Labor and environmental groups and many liberal Democrats remained unhappy with the treaty and Ross Perot continued his campaign against it. Protectionist sentiment among Democrats in Congress had been growing since the mid-1980s as foreign competitors ate into American industries, and there was considerable unease about NAFTA among the president's own party lieutenants. The Democratic whip in the House of Representatives, David Bonior, charged that NAFTA "profits basically the elites of both countries." On the other side, American multinationals, such as General Electric and American Express, spent huge sums in lobbying for the treaty. Senior politicians, economists, and major newspapers came out for the treaty, so the dispute seemed to poise the economic and political elites against the trade unionists, environmentalists, and the "ordinary Americans" that Perot claimed to speak for. Clinton and Al Gore personally lobbied some 200 members of Congress, wheeling and dealing in the tradition of Lyndon Johnson. "It's obscene, this horse trading of votes," muttered one Democratic congressman. Gore met Perot in a televised debate and decisively bettered him, exposing him "as a bossy old billionaire bully who blows his cool when confronted in a fair fight." The majority of Democrats in the House of Representatives voted against NAFTA, but with Republican support the treaty was approved in November 1993. The president had stood firm and the White House at least had won a major political victory, even if it divided the party. When he took office, Clinton claimed, NAFTA was "dead in the water" and he had rescued it.[17]

By early 1994 Clinton could claim considerable political success. His economic plan had been approved. He had signed the Family and Medical Leave Act (first proposed in the mid-1980s and previously vetoed by George Bush), which allowed family members to take unpaid leave to care for newborn children and sick relatives, and he took satisfaction in signing the National Child Protection Act, providing for a national database so that child-care centers could check the background of job applicants. New Democrats like Clinton were keen to advertise their commitment to a version of "family values." He signed the Brady Bill, which required a seven-day waiting period before handguns could be purchased, so that mental health and criminal records might be checked, thus earning the abiding hostility of the powerful National Rifle Association. He also issued executive orders revoking bans on stem-cell research and on funds for clinics counseling women on abortion. On the foreign front too, despite harrowing bloodshed in Bosnia, Clinton had successes, such as extending the moratorium on nuclear testing. He had also presided over a White House ceremony in which Israel's Yitzhak Rabin and Palestine's Yasser Arafat had signed the West Bank accord, a part of the Middle East peace process, described by one aide as the "most inspiring day of his presidency." By some measures Clinton was thriving, as was the economy by 1994. In November 1993 the *Congressional Quarterly* reported Clinton's extraordinarily high success rate with Congress, winning 88 percent of floor votes, the same as Lyndon Johnson at his 1964 high point, a record he would repeat in his second year. Yet his public support was ebbing.[18]

Clinton of course had been elected with only 43 percent of the popular vote, and the Senate Republican leader, Bob Dole, had immediately insisted that he would represent the other 57 percent: "It's not all going to be milk and honey for the Democrats." Clinton did manage a 59 percent approval rating from Gallup after his first five – honeymoon – weeks in office. But by the middle of 1993 his public support was slipping badly, with a low of 37 percent approval rating in June. Thereafter there was some temporary improvement, but in mid-August 1994 his approval rating was at 39 percent, with 52 percent disapproving.[19]

Whatever credit the Clinton administration might claim for its economic plan, on other fronts it had got off to a spectacularly bad start, particularly in terms of public perception. Clinton had advertised his empathy with the people by promising to appoint a cabinet that looked "more like America than previous administrations," and he duly recruited four women, four African Americans, and two Hispanics, more in each category than any of his predecessors, though arguably reminiscent of 1960s values. Undermining the New Democrat image too, thought some strategists, were liberal White House appointments. James Carville, the 1992 campaign manager, apparently told pollster Dick Morris that "liberals are like fucking water damage; they just seep in all the time." One of Clinton's eye-catching nominations, Zoe Baird as the first female Attorney General, turned out to have hired illegal immigrants as home help, and a hostile public reaction forced Clinton to withdraw her nomination on his third day in office. A few months later he had similarly to abandon his friend Lani Guinier as civil rights chief, after her record revealed support for "proportional representation" in local elections, so that conservatives assailed her as a "quota queen." The most harmful furor was over Clinton's promised support for equal treatment of homosexuals in the military, against which the military chiefs revolted. Clinton, whose own avoidance of military service left him in a weak position to confront them, vacillated and eventually announced a compromise recruitment policy based on the principle "don't ask, don't tell." Sighed a White House aide: "It was unfortunate that gays in the military was the President's first major issue. The danger is that people around the country are saying to themselves: 'Oh, My God. So this is why this guy sought office.'" Also leaving an unhappy mark was the administration's handling of a siege at Waco, Texas, where an apocalyptic sect had fortified themselves inside their compound and shot at government agents. In April 1993, after a 51-day standoff, the FBI attacked the compound, which was consumed by a ferocious fire, leaving 86 dead, some of them children. While public opinion broadly conceded the benefit of the doubt to the administration, it was Attorney General Janet Reno who fronted to newsmen while the president kept a low profile. On the foreign front, the president seemed unable to develop an effective policy with respect to Bosnia, the site of bloody ethnic warfare in the aftermath of the disintegration of Yugoslavia.[20]

The president's legislative and foreign policy successes left less of an impact on the public mind than the unremitting headlines focused on White House embarrassments and vacillation. The *Doonesbury* comic strip depicted Clinton as a waffle. A focus group in May 1994 used such terms as "over his head," "indecisive," and "immature" to characterize Clinton's performance. But even worse was to come. With his public standing already eroding, Clinton was in a weak position to withstand the blows of 1994. By the end of the year Clinton's administration seemed in almost terminal decline, and there were mutterings among the Democrats about finding a new presidential candidate for 1996.[21]

In part the damage was done by Whitewater. This was an issue that surfaced in the 1992 campaign but re-emerged more ominously in late 1993. Among the institutions taken down by the S&L collapse was an Arkansas bank headed by James McDougal, known as Madison Guarantee Savings and Loan, and in 1993 investigators recommended its prosecution. Madison had had dealings with the Clintons, and at one point they and McDougal had invested together in a resort development along the White

River in Arkansas. As the media probed McDougal's murky career (he had been acquitted of fraud in 1990) and pointed to the public money consumed in bailing out Madison, demands for a fuller investigation mounted, including into the Clintons' part in the Whitewater venture, although they had actually lost money in it. No previous president had ever been subjected to an official investigation for alleged corruption during his pre-presidential career, and the Clintons at first indignantly refused to hand over their private papers for scrutiny, only fueling suspicions of a cover-up. "I haven't heard anything yet that says this is all that big a deal," dismissively said former Republican presidential candidate Barry Goldwater, but his fellow Republicans were not so restrained. To many conservatives Clinton and his wife were interlopers. The right-wingers assuming leadership positions in Congress were already practiced in using investigation as a political weapon. Eventually, in January 1994, under unrelenting public pressure, and because he was confident nothing serious against him could be found, Clinton made the fateful decision to ask the Attorney General to appoint a special counsel to investigate the matters surrounding Whitewater. The first family's private affairs were being probed amidst excited press speculation. For the next few years both Bill and Hillary Clinton were to be harried relentlessly by the right-wing media over "Whitewater," which became an all-purpose vehicle for allegations of wrongdoing directed at them. In agreeing to a special counsel Clinton set off a chain of events that would eventually lead to his impeachment.[22]

As Whitewater took its toll, Clinton was trying to advance other items of the New Democrat agenda. He did succeed in securing a rather draconian crime bill, which featured a ban on certain kinds of assault weapons, prison expansion, and the principle of "three strikes and you're out" for federal crimes. He also attempted to make good on his promise of welfare reform, but with liberal Democrats disliking the package and Republicans unenthusiastic about the cost, the bill was stillborn. On another issue Clinton suffered a really stunning defeat.

For some years health care had been a growing political issue and it had figured prominently in the 1992 campaign. The United States had the highest health care costs among industrial countries, yet nearly 40 million Americans were without health insurance. The federal government had spent 9 percent of its revenue on health care in 1971; by 1991, thanks to the accelerating cost of Medicare and Medicaid, it was up to 21 percent. How was it, asked Clinton, that the United States was the only advanced country that had not "figured out … how to give health care security to everybody"? Sorting out health care was a focus for his greatest political ambitions. Adviser George Stephanopoulos wrote that Clinton wanted "to forge another New Deal, to succeed where FDR, Truman, Kennedy, Johnson, and Carter had all failed, to be remembered as the president who made health care, like a secure retirement, the birthright of every American." Perhaps universal health insurance, like the New Deal reforms, could help build a grand alliance of working and middle class, black, ethnic, and white voters for the Democratic Party. The idea also connected with Clinton's globalizing agenda. Freer trade increased job insecurity, and had to be balanced by programs such as retraining and non-job-based health care.[23]

Soon after taking office Clinton named his wife Hillary as the head of a task force to prepare a plan for the kind of universal health insurance found in other developed nations. This decision identified the proposal even more strongly with the Clintons; an alternative would have been to allow a senior member of Congress to take charge of the bill. Meeting behind closed doors, the task force's plan was ready in September 1993. (The difficult reform of the Social Security system in 1983 had been worked out in secret meetings.) Opinion polls at this time showed that Hillary had a higher approval rating than her husband, and the plan enjoyed an initially favorable public response. Contributions would be collected from both employers and employees, but the poor and small businesses would be subsidized, and "sin" taxes (notably on tobacco) would help pay for the program. The ambitious package ran to over 1300 bemusing pages, and even Robert Reich, the cerebral Secretary of Labor, admitted privately that he had a "hard time" understanding it. The Republicans in Congress decided to block the bill in what was an election year, and it soon ran afoul of a range of business, medical, and conservative lobbies. Small businesses and the smaller insurance companies were particularly active in mobilizing opposition, and interest groups spent $60 million on a captious television advertising campaign. The amount donated by medical and insurance companies to members of Congress in 1993–1994 was double what it had been in 1989–1990. Public opinion turned against the plan, some 55 percent expressing disapproval by July 1994, apparently persuaded that it represented an extension of government. Unhelpful too was the continued storm over Whitewater. When radio shock jock Rush Limbaugh told his 20 million audience that "Whitewater is about health care," Hillary Clinton sardonically agreed. G. Gordon Liddy, a former Watergate defendant turned radio show host, suggested using cardboard cut-outs of Bill and Hillary for target practice, and when Hillary took a bus tour (on one occasion wearing a bullet-proof vest) to publicize her plan she was met with such placards as "Bill and Hillary are immoral homosexual communists." The administration finally conceded defeat in September 1994 in the face of Republican obstructionism in the Senate. Having set so much store by health care reform, its defeat was a major humiliation for both Bill and Hillary Clinton.[24]

The White House, it seemed, could not even get a Democratic Congress to endorse its program, despite its first-year successes. It had failed fully to recognize the stresses within the congressional Democratic Party. Some New Democrats disliked the perceived departure from their agenda in the health care imbroglio, and the traditional labor wing was unhappy with the free trade initiatives. Widespread disaffection and an anti-government mood had helped to elect Clinton in 1992; two years later his administration was the target of the same animus. The economic insecurity of the early 1990s had not eased as restructuring continued apace and as Clinton trumpeted his global agenda. The proportion of people who believed that government could be trusted "to do what was right" either "just about always" or "most of the time" had slumped to 22 percent, a historic low. With the Democrats controlling both the White House and Congress, there was little doubt which party was most at risk.[25]

"People are surly, resentful, anxious," reflected Robert Reich on his travels around the country: "The economic stresses that have been building for years are taking their toll, and anyone with power and visibility in our society is a potential target of resentment." The confusing health plan suggested that the Democrats had not after all repented their big government ways. The earlier fuss over gays in the military had associated Clinton with 1960s permissiveness, as did continued allegations about extramarital affairs, issues that affronted the resurgent Christian right and hardly reassured the New Democrats wanting to recover the support of socially conservative whites. Exacerbating public disaffection were the charges of impropriety associated with Whitewater. One press analysis discovered that there had been over 31 000 stories on Whitewater compared to 2400 on the health care proposal since the latter had been introduced.[26]

It was in this lacerated condition that the White House faced the 1994 mid-term elections. The Democrats hardly expected to do well, but they were not prepared for the astonishing Republican offensive, the opening round in an audacious attempt to wrest American government from the control of the party that had won the presidential election. The Republican leader in Congress, Newt Gingrich of Georgia, had long been directing attacks on the Democratic leadership in the House, alleging financial and other improprieties, and had already claimed a number of scalps.

Gingrich had been developing his strategy since at least 1989, when he told his associates of his desire to bring about change, "as a consequence of which we will win control of the House and the country." He now insisted that the elections should be a referendum on the "Great Society, counterculture, McGovernik" heritage of the 1960s. For the House election he and other Republican leaders had drawn up a "Contract with America," which proposed several major initiatives to reverse the thrust of Democratic government and would together ensure "the end of government that is too big, too intrusive, and too easy with the public's money." Its preamble was instructive, being largely directed at Congress itself, which it promised to clean up and render more accountable. The implication was that decades of Democratic control had left Congress hopelessly corrupt and out of touch with the American people. In this they echoed Ross Perot, as they did also over the deficit. To tighten the screw, the Republicans now committed themselves to a balanced budget, to be enforced by a constitutional amendment. The Contract itself promised 10 major bills, including a bill to set term limits "to replace career politicians with citizen legislators"; also on offer were an anti-crime package, welfare reform to deny aid to teenage mothers, the restriction of US forces in UN peacekeeping operations, and that conservative favorite, a capital gains tax cut. Missing were such charged issues as abortion reform and school prayer that might have frightened moderate Republicans; the emphasis was on shriveling government and balancing the budget. For the first time ever a party's candidates for Congress were united behind a specific program that they were committed to enact.[27]

One group that was recruited to the campaign was the growing religious right, which was able to put keen activists on the ground, especially in the South. The Christian Coalition reckoned that 75 000 of its members participated in the campaign. Where the Republicans had won 66 percent of the votes of white "born again" Christians in the 1992 presidential election, in 1994 the figure jumped to a remarkable 76 percent. These efforts were supplemented by the many "talk programs" that had been emerging on television and especially radio, perhaps 70 percent hosted by conservatives. The number of news-talk stations shot from about 250 to over 1000 in the 10 years to 1994. The Federal Communications Commission had once required that broadcasters treat controversial issues in a balanced way, but in 1987 it had abandoned this "fairness doctrine," making possible the flourishing of such right-wing commentators as Rush Limbaugh, who unabashedly pilloried liberals in extravagant terms. The advent of the 24-hour news cycle encouraged the rise of attack politics. "I represent middle America's growing rejection of the elites," said Limbaugh in 1994. Gingrich had figured that one answer to divided government and a fragmented society was a disciplined political party, driving forward its ideological goals even at the cost of greater political polarization.[28]

Exit polls suggested that the Democrats had lost many of the "Reagan Democrats" that Clinton had reclaimed in 1992. A high proportion of Independent voters also switched to the Republicans, as did two-thirds of those who had voted for Perot in 1992. With white men voting Republican in large numbers, journalists speculated on how far the outcome of the election could be attributed to "angry white males," though analyses showed white women switching to the Republicans too, if not as heavily as their menfolk. Once, perhaps, the fears of many of these voters might have been directed at the Soviet Union; now the federal government became their enemy. One Republican elected to Congress explained that "big government" was the target of populist anger: "It was too big and wouldn't listen. I'd go do an event and ask, What do you think we should do about Congress? The answers: take a sledgehammer to it ... And that washed a number of us right in here." The Republicans made their greatest gains in the South, which was continuing to grow fast, for the first time winning more seats in the region than the Democrats. The party made a net gain of 52 seats in the House and eight in the Senate, winning firm control of both houses. These Sunbelt and southern conservatives were viscerally hostile to liberal Democratic policies and the ethos of secular humanism, as well as fiercely laissez-faire on the economy. They had been selected as candidates in primary elections, in which relatively small numbers of strongly motivated activists could wield disproportionate influence. In some degree, the Republican turn to the right on economic issues reflected the increasing income inequality of recent decades; wealthier voters tended to have disproportionate influence.[29]

Not since 1952 had the Republicans won control of both houses, and their routing of the apparently permanent Democratic majority in the lower house, including the defeat of Speaker Tom Foley, suggested that something profound was happening to the electorate. This conclusion was powerfully reinforced by the races at state level. The Republicans won another 15 state legislative chambers and made a net gain of 11 governorships. Some Democratic chieftains went under, most prominently New York's Governor Mario Cuomo, and the redoubtable Democratic governor of Texas, Ann Richards, was ousted by George W. Bush. But while the Republicans clearly benefited from the potent anti-Washington and anti-incumbency animus, their victories in elections in which turnout was low also reflected the energies of local conservative activists. The party still held only a minority of seats in the state legislatures. The 1994 elections may have represented "a rebellion against the Democratic party and Bill Clinton," but the new Republican Congress was to find that it was not truly representative of the public at large. The parties in Congress were further apart than ever, though polls showed that polarization in the public at large on most issues, abortion apart, had been declining.[30]

No one in the White House had predicted such disaster and morale slumped to a new low. Support for Clinton in the Democratic Party at large faltered, and there was renewed talk of finding another Democratic presidential candidate for 1996. About two-thirds of Democratic respondents in a poll wanted to see such a challenge. Some congressional Democrats threatened to switch parties, and during 1995 five of them in the lower house, all southerners, actually did so. The Clinton era seemed to be over. As Clinton ruefully observed of both the 1992 and 1994 elections, "we didn't hear America singing, we heard America shouting." In his State of the Union Address in January 1995 he still insisted that the "most important job of our government in this new era is to empower the American people to succeed in the global economy," but he seemed to bow to the public verdict when he acknowledged that "Our job is to get rid of yesterday's government" in favor of "a government that's smaller, smarter and wiser."[31]

*　*　*

Clinton's ambitious plans to project his country toward a shining, efficient, and humane twenty-first century were crumbling almost before they had gotten underway. It was ironic that this champion of a high-tech world and an enabling government was pilloried as a dangerous liberal. That image was a false one, as his career in the DLC testified, and largely arose from his Sixties student days and Hillary's feminist identity. The flap over gays in the military together with the selection of a cabinet that "looked like America" reinforced the impression of 1960s-style liberalism, while the health fiasco strengthened the idea that Clinton was an unreconstructed Democrat. These features exposed him to ferocious conservative assault, despite his emphasis on deficit reduction and NAFTA and his general embrace of neoliberal economic policies. His closest associates suspected a "conspiracy" of a far right that simply could not forgive Clinton his Sixties past and his effrontery in winning the 1992 election. To some right-wing conservatives, he was an illegitimate president, arguably a sufficient justification for attempts to remove him by any means available. After the mid-term elections of 1994 they hoped that the governing initiative would rest with them.

Chapter 12

Democracy for the World

Like Ronald Reagan before him, fixing the economy was the new president's
first priority. Bill Clinton's overriding passion was for domestic affairs and
he initially seemed to regard the outside world as a tiresome distraction.
There were even doubts as to how interested he was in overseas' matters.
Of the top foreign issues, he reportedly said that he did not "see a winner
in the whole lot," and his foreign policy advisers were told: "Keep the president informed, but don't take too much of his time." Clinton himself
complained soon after becoming president that "foreign policy is not what
I came here to do." During the campaign he had criticized Bush for an
over-preoccupation with the outside world, and if that preoccupation had
contributed to Bush's defeat, the new administration had no wish to repeat
the mistake.[1]

Clinton's attitude was at least in tune with that of the general public,
which showed little appetite for foreign policy adventures. "The public is
motivated by a pervasive sense that domestic problems warrant the bulk
of America's energies," was a commonplace observation among political
commentators. In 1991 a survey had shown that the saving of American
jobs should be the first foreign policy goal, followed by protecting the
interests of Americans working abroad and securing adequate supplies of
energy, a lesson pointed up by the Gulf War. In 1995 only 2 percent cited
a foreign policy issue in a Gallup poll asking what was the most important
problem facing the country, way down on what had been the norm for the
Cold War era. A public opinion wary of overseas commitments was to be
a constraint during Clinton's presidency. Congress too, with the Cold War
in the past, could not be counted on to support presidential foreign initia-

Contemporary America: Power, Dependency, and Globalization since 1980,
First Edition. M.J. Heale.
© 2011 M.J. Heale. Published 2011 by Blackwell Publishing Ltd.

tives, even less when the Republicans took command of it after 1994. But, like some of his predecessors, Clinton became increasingly preoccupied with his world role as time moved on, and by the end of his administration he had visited more countries than any of them.[2]

*   *   *

Yet Clinton had no intention of abdicating his country's international leadership. "Today, as an old order passes, the new world is more free but less stable. Communism's collapse has called forth old animosities and new dangers," he said in his Inaugural Address: "Clearly, America must continue to lead the world we did so much to make." Isolation was not an option. The task would be a challenging one, he emphasized, because of the globalization of economic and environmental issues. Yet there were opportunities too for the diffusion of American ideals in this age of instant global communication: "Our hopes ... are with those on every continent who are building democracy and freedom. Their cause is America's cause." And if Clinton wrenched his attention to foreign affairs a little reluctantly, by 1994 he had come to see foreign and domestic policy as indivisible. A July policy document argued that "the line between our domestic and foreign policies has increasingly disappeared – that we must revitalize our economy if we are to sustain our military forces, foreign initiatives and global influence, and that we must engage actively abroad if we are to open foreign markets and create jobs for our people."[3]

During the 1992 campaign, Clinton had said that he wanted the United States to lead "a global alliance for democracy as united and steadfast as the global alliance that defeated Communism." In September 1993 National Security Adviser Anthony Lake, in a major foreign policy address, explained that "the successor to a doctrine of containment must be a strategy of enlargement, the enlargement of the world's free community of market democracies." Where the "containment" of communism had provided the operative framework for the Cold War generation, Clinton's team searched for a new formulation, uneasily conscious both of the widespread perceptions that the United States was in decline and of the danger of a resurgence of isolationism. "Democratic enlargement" was the answer to both. It became the philosophical theme of Clinton's foreign policy, much as the New Covenant underpinned his domestic policy, though critics did not perceive much intellectual depth in either. (Yale's foreign policy luminary Gaddis Smith described the former as "banality on stilts.") Democracy and free market economies were intertwined in the world of the 1990s. Rather as it bought into the idea of a New Economy, the Clinton White House also bought into the idea of the beneficence of democracy. Clinton himself explained that "the habits of democracy are the habits of peace": "Democracy is rooted in compromise, not conquest. It rewards tolerance, not hatred. Democracies rarely wage war on one another. They make more reliable partners in trade, in diplomacy, and in the stewardship of our global environment."[4]

What became known as "democratic peace theory," though it was hardly novel, was gaining a following among some intellectuals, holding that democracies were inherently peaceful and cooperative; it was sometimes added that openness promoted economic growth and the fostering of a consumerist middle class interested in peace and prosperity. It was America's "overriding purpose," said Clinton in September 1993, "to expand and strengthen the world's community of market-based democracies." It was not only in the former Soviet Union that democratic governments were emerging; the economic hard times experienced by several Latin American countries in the 1980s had led to revolts against their dictatorial governments, and democratic regimes had also appeared in such places as South Korea and Thailand, followed by Taiwan in the 1990s. South Africa too was embarking on the same course with the release of Nelson Mandela in 1990. According to one count, there had been 44 democracies in 1972; by 1993 there were 107. Supporting democracy, explained Deputy Secretary of State Strobe Talbott, did not necessarily displace other objectives, but rather was "a strong thread to be woven into the complex tapestry of American foreign policy." And it served US interests: "Only in an increasingly democratic world will American people feel themselves truly secure."[5]

Pursuing democratic enlargement, thought the administration, required a multilateral strategy, ideally using the United Nations. With the ending of the Cold War, perhaps, the United Nations would come into its own, and its role in the Gulf War modestly improved its reputation in the United States. Madeleine Albright, the new Ambassador to the UN, coined the phrase "assertive multilateralism," and spoke of a "new beginning" for the UN at her confirmation hearings. In the event the early enthusiasm for working through the UN waned somewhat as the organization's limitations were exposed by successive crises, and multilateralism also incited the suspicions of congressional right-wingers. With the disappearance of the need to contain a Soviet threat, conservatives were freer to air their distrust of such bodies as the UN and the IMF. In 1995 the House Speaker Newt Gingrich would accuse the administration of wanting to "subordinate the

United States to the United Nations," although by then its multilateralist agenda had been severely qualified.[6]

While the promotion of democracy provided a defensible public objective for the United States in the post-Cold War world, at the heart of the new administration's foreign policy was an economic vision. Clinton formulated his foreign policy to serve his ambition of domestic renewal. Free commerce and instant information, he believed, would define the post-Cold War world, and the United States must press home its advantages. "We have put our economic competitiveness at the heart of our foreign policy," he said in 1994. Many foreign policy pundits agreed that, as phrased in a Carnegie Foundation report, "America's first foreign policy priority is to strengthen our domestic economic performance." Jeffrey Garten found the Commerce Department to be a "sexy place" to work during Clinton's first term: "We used Washington's official muscle to help firms crack overseas markets. The culture was electric: we set up an economic 'war room' and built a 'trading floor' that tracked the world's largest commercial projects." *Business Week* commented that American ambassadors had become "unabashed peddlers in pinstripes, vigorously lobbying local officials on behalf of Corporate America."[7]

The primary aim was revitalizing what was seen as a dysfunctional American economy. For Clinton, political scientist Henry Nau has observed, trade policy would promote the "domestic economic reforms that create high-wage jobs and accelerate changes in technology, education, and public infrastructure." The American share of global production had been fairly static for years, but the United States had become the world's largest trader, and it could use this advantage to recharge its own economy by prying open foreign markets. Further, in the realm of information technology, for which international demand was growing fast, it was the world leader. As with Clinton's deficit-reducing measures, the ultimate objective was economic growth. In a series of remarkable initiatives, Clinton pursued free trade agreements with the countries of the Pacific Rim, with the rest of the Americas, and with Europe. It made some sense to take advantage of the collapse of communism by trying to rewrite the rules of the world market in such a way as to favor American business. What facilitated this energetic commercial strategy, with its basis in neoliberal economics, was its general acceptance by congressional Republicans, who on many other issues were only too ready to obstruct Clinton's policies. Between 1993 and 1996 over 200 market-opening agreements were reached, helping to create 1.6 million American jobs, according to Secretary of State Warren Christopher. Nonetheless, Clinton's free trade doctrines were hardly all-conquering;

Congress proved less cooperative after 1997 and some of the regional initiatives did not deliver much.[8]

If Clinton's foreign initiatives were guided by the objective of domestic renewal, he nonetheless believed that globalization would help to reduce Third World poverty and that free markets would tend to promote democracy. (Some critics disagreed, viewing globalization as a more-or-less witting attempt by economic and political elites to exploit Third World countries.) Democracy and markets became almost interchangeable terms for the Clinton team. "In the Cold War the concept was containment," explained a Commerce Department official: "now it's to enlarge the scope of democracy. It's all about widening market access." The aid that the United States supplied to the former Soviet empire was distinctly modest, in view of the budget deficit and a suspicious Congress, but during his re-election campaign Clinton was not averse to claiming credit: "With our help, the forces of reform in Europe's newly free nations have laid the foundations of democracy. We've helped them to develop successful market economies, and now are moving from aid to trade and investment." Democracies, it was believed by many theorists at the time, did not fight one another. The economic counterpoint was expressed by the noted columnist Thomas Friedman, who coined the aphorism: "No two countries that both have a McDonald's have ever fought a war against each other." (On a different level, economic philosopher Amartya Sen argued that famines never occurred in democratic countries.) The more the world was knit together by trade, the argument went, the safer it would be, as would be the United States. As technological and commercial change was creating "an increasingly interdependent world," said Strobe Talbott, international cooperation was vital to withstand such dangers as drugs, criminals, and terrorists, and cooperation was best achieved through democracies.[9]

Not infrequently though, market access abroad seemed to take precedence over enlarging democracy. "If the Cold War enemy was communism," wrote one analyst of Clintonian foreign policy, "the post-Cold War villain was protectionism." Clinton conspicuously committed himself to the pursuit of a liberal global economic order early in his term, toward the end of 1993 securing congressional endorsement of NAFTA, attending the Asian–Pacific Economic Summit, and displaying a keen interest in the Uruguay round discussions of GATT. At the same time, too, the administration was incorporating environmental considerations into its foreign policy, and a new under secretary for global affairs was created to take charge of this dimension. But not everyone was convinced of the wonders of international commerce. "A foreign economic policy is not a foreign policy and it is not a national security strategy," sniffed international affairs expert Leslie Gelb.[10]

The American pursuit of free trade agreements during the 1990s has been discussed earlier, and can be seen as part of the strategy of democratic enlargement. But the strategy did not provide much of a guide for action outside the commercial sphere. "For the first time since the early 1930s," as Madeleine Albright put it, "we face no single powerful enemy to concentrate the mind." The absence of such an enemy was pointed up by the emergence of what the administration came to call "borderless threats," such as terrorism and environmental degradation. Among the greatest was the tendency of a world rather suddenly freed from Cold War constraints to disintegrate into fractious parts. Absent Clinton's vision of a liberal globalization, the White House struggled with what British Prime Minister Harold Macmillan had once called "events, dear boy, events"; or, in the American phrase, "stuff happens." Much of the stuff that happened suggested that the one remaining superpower would not necessarily prevail in the "new world order." The Cold War over, what was to be the role of the United States when local wars, coups, famines, or other emergencies threatened global stability? Before his first year was out Clinton was being accused of "Band-Aid diplomacy" as he resorted fitfully to crisis management. A Pentagon official tagged the policy "muddling through."[11]

Arguably the Cold War had imposed a kind of stability on the world, albeit one achieved through a balance of terror (although outside the superpower framework there had been many bloody conflicts). But with the ending of the East–West standoff there was a tendency for parts of the world to fragment. Nationalism and tribalism erupted as superpower rivalry evaporated. Sometimes the dissolution was peaceful; for example, Czechoslovakia separated into the Czech Republic and Slovakia. Often it was not. Over a hundred nationalities had lived in the old Soviet Union alone, and some took to arms to secure their self-determination. The Muslim province of Chechnya sought its independence from Russia, which used military force to try to subdue these determined insurgents. Secretary of State Warren Christopher worried in 1993 that "We'll have 50 000 countries rather than the hundred plus we now have."[12]

The post-Cold War unrest was felt well beyond Eastern Europe and the Soviet Union. Third World crises in particular served to underline the limitations of US power. Anarchy engulfed parts of Africa. In Somalia, for example, there had been civil war and famine after the ending of the aid provided by the superpowers during their Cold War rivalry, and in December 1992 George Bush had sent in marines as part of a UN peacekeeping force. American public support for this operation rapidly waned, however, after a US action in October 1993 went badly awry, culminating in fighting in which 18 American soldiers were killed, as well as hundreds of Somalis (the encounter was the focus of the 2001 film *Black Hawk Down*). The American TV audience was appalled by footage of a dead American soldier being dragged through the streets of Mogadishu. The administration's rhetoric about "democratic enlargement" seemed to have little purchase on reality. "Boy, do I ever miss the cold war!," muttered Bill Clinton to an aide. The unhappy Clinton White House saw little alternative to retreat, and by April 1994 all US troops had been withdrawn. This may have been wise, but it was hardly testimony to the country's capacity to impose its will on other parts of the world. The image of the UN in the United States was further damaged, as Somalia became a symbol of its incompetence. Less was heard from the administration about "assertive multilateralism." Presidential Directive 25, issued in May 1994, created a "vital national interests test" that limited US participation in UN peacekeeping operations, and the tragedy significantly contributed to the White House's hesitation about getting involved militarily elsewhere.[13]

One such area was Rwanda, where the United States and other Western countries proved unable to end massive massacres; no American "vital national interest" was involved. In a brief three months in 1994 perhaps a million died in what one author characterized as "the most efficient killing since the atomic bombing of Hiroshima and Nagasaki." Horrifying images were beamed around the world by CNN, an illustration of the new global role of communications. Huge numbers of refugees fled, and conflict in other parts of Central Africa precipitated further migrations, overwhelming the relief agencies. Yet this fearful humanitarian crisis apparently stemmed from intense tribal rivalries rather than international politics, and neither the United States nor any other major power had strategic interests in the region, which, in any case, was relatively inaccessible to them. Somalia was a recent unhappy memory in the White House. The UN Secretary General called for international action, but little was forthcoming, and that mostly too late. It would be "folly" for an ill-prepared UN force to venture quickly into the "maelstrom" of Central Africa, said Madeleine Albright. As she later sadly recorded, during the months in which American, African, European, UN, and other officials agonized over what to do about the crisis, "no country offered to send troops to Rwanda for the purpose of actually fighting."[14]

Clinton also stumbled on another foreign front, when, having criticized George Bush for refusing entry to Haitian refugees fleeing their country by boat, he was forced even before his inauguration to abandon his commitment to grant temporary shelter when it seemed that 100 000 or more were preparing to make the hazardous journey. But breaking his promise did not resolve the issue. In 1991 the government of the democratically elected Father Jean-Bertrand Aristide had been overthrown and Haiti returned to military dictatorship. When Clinton's aides failed to come up with a convincing solution to the Haiti problem, Clinton exploded: "I want to give the people down there some hope that they really will see democracy, not just a lot of words and empty promises." Finally, recoiling before the human tidal wave, distressed by stories of the terrors inflicted by the military regime on its citizens, pressured by the Congressional Black Caucus, and sanctified by a UN Security Council resolution, in 1994 the Clinton administration orchestrated an attempt by a group of American countries to depose the dictatorship of Haiti. As Strobe Talbott noted, "for the first time the United Nations had called for international action to restore a democratically elected leader." Despite opinion polls indicating strong public opposition to the use of force, American troops were dispatched to restore Aristide, and the military junta quickly capitulated. In the following year a new president succeeded Aristide in a free election. Democracy, perhaps, had been enlarged.[15]

With many Americans according low priority to foreign policy, the setbacks of Clinton's early years served to amplify the charges of his critics. Russia was one problem, with the White House wondering how far it could offer support to its embattled president, Boris Yeltsin, whose position had become precarious as the economy plummeted following the "shock therapy" administered by Western proponents of the "Washington Consensus." Particularly corrosive was the chaos and relentless bloodshed in the Balkans, about which the Clinton White House seemed no more prepared to offer decisive leadership than the Bush administration. By September 1994 approval rating for Clinton's foreign policy had fallen to 34 percent. Clinton was nettled in 1995 when the French president remarked that "the position of leader of the free world is vacant." (The timing was unfortunate – with Gingrich's Republicans dominating American domestic politics an irritated Clinton in April had been forced to insist: "The president is relevant.") Clinton's early reputation for indecision and vacillation on foreign policy matters was to prove difficult to shake off. Several years later a British journalist still held the view that "Mr Clinton's foreign policy had the spine of a raspberry pavlova."[16]

Yet if Clinton's foreign policy troubles mirrored his unhappy domestic policy experience in 1994–1995, he was soon displaying an unanticipated resilience. This was all the more remarkable because the political calculus had moved against him. When the Republicans stormed to their majorities in both houses of Congress in November 1994, there seemed a risk that the president's globalizing agenda would be undone by a new isolationism. The isolationist strain in American political culture had been contained for years by the Soviet threat, but in the 1990s there were fears that it would burst forth again. Isolationist pressures had surfaced in the 1992 presidential campaign, not only in the protectionist rhetoric of Ross Perot but also more explicitly in the "America First" platform of Pat Buchanan, who would reprise his offensive in the 1996 campaign. A nativist temper animated many of the Republicans elected in 1994. It was said that two-thirds of them did not have passports, and one who did, the new House Majority Leader Richard Armey, disavowed any interest in visiting Europe since he had "already been there once." The chair of the Senate Foreign Affairs Committee was assumed by Jesse Helms, a highly conservative North Carolinian celebrated for his hostility to foreign aid and the UN. The new Congress was soon cutting budget appropriations for foreign affairs. The Republicans resisted returning to an old-fashioned isolationism, and as free traders (many of them) they could be persuaded by some of Clinton's commercial initiatives, but they generally exerted pressures for unilateralist foreign policies and increased defense spending. In the words of Arthur Schlesinger Jr., "The isolationist impulse has risen from the grave, and it has taken the new form of unilateralism."[17]

Congressional opposition meant that Clinton met defeat on some of his foreign policy measures after 1995, such as when he was denied "fast track" authority on trade negotiations, but he also had his successes and public approval of his performance rose. With many of his domestic objectives obstructed, he gave increasing attention to foreign affairs. The dramatic revival of the American economy by the mid-1990s was dispelling notions that American power was in decline and encouraged Clinton to assume a higher profile in the world.

The turnaround came in 1995 in Europe, notably over what had been Yugoslavia, where since 1991 nearly 300 000 people had been killed. The ending of the Cold War had meant chaos in the Balkans. In 1991 Yugoslavia split up, as Slovenia and Croatia declared their independence, heralding years of turmoil. Focused on Bosnia, this was rooted in animosities between the Serbs, who were Eastern Orthodox in religion and generally dominant in Belgrade and the federal government, the Catholic Slovenes and Croats, and the Bosnians, who were Muslim. In the early 1990s the Serbs in Bosnia, supported by the Belgrade government under Slobodan Milosevic, engaged in "ethnic cleansing" to drive out the Muslims. Western governments, appalled by the slaughter, found it difficult to construct a coherent policy, particularly since Russia was opposed to any Western interference in the region. Imposing peace in that mountainous area would require a massive military force, placed there perhaps indefinitely, for which there was little stomach in the West. In the United States, opinion polls tended to show some 60 or 70 percent opposed to US involvement. Many regarded Serbia's aggression in Bosnia as the responsibility of the European powers; the Balkans, after all, were part of Europe.

During the 1992 campaign, Clinton had criticized the Bush administration for doing little in response to Serbian aggression, but once in office he tended to follow the same rather minimal line. Bosnia, said Secretary of State Warren Christopher, was "the problem from hell." The UN's emissary, Cyrus Vance, and the former British Foreign Secretary David Owen, did come up with a plan in 1993 to partition Bosnia, with Western troops to keep the peace, but the lack of US support for it contributed to its failure. Owen later complained that the administration "had decided that the price of putting US troops on the ground in order to reverse ethnic cleansing was too high." The Clinton team continued to argue that Bosnia was primarily the responsibility of the European powers, while the Europeans doubted that any lasting settlement could be secured without serious input from the United States. An arms embargo and economic sanctions were deployed, UN peacekeepers were used to try to protect Muslim enclaves and ensure a supply of food and medicine, and NATO conducted limited air strikes against the Serbs. But the crisis dragged on, with the Serbs continuing to kill and drive out the Muslims in Bosnia while Russia gave some cover to Slobodan Milosevic's murderous regime. By late 1994 Bosnia had become an emblem of the failure of Clinton's foreign policy, and he determined on a new initiative to settle the war.[18]

What helped to turn opinion were the massacres of thousands of Bosnian Muslims in July 1995 by Serb forces in Srebrenica, supposedly a "safe haven" protected by UN peacekeepers. Opinion around the world was outraged. Finally prepared to use more force, the president agreed to the intensification of NATO bombing in the summer of 1995, eroding the Serbs' strength and pushing them toward negotiation. The use of US ground forces remained out of the question. Eventually the combination of economic sanctions and NATO airstrikes brought the Serbs to the negotiating table. The leaders of the principal factions met under American auspices at Dayton, Ohio, and the Dayton Accords were thrashed out in November 1995. These provided for a cease-fire, the deployment of 60 000 NATO troops (including a US contingent) in 1996 to keep the peace, and the incorporation of elected representatives of the Bosnian Serbs, Croats, and Muslims into the Bosnian government. The US negotiator, Richard Holbrooke, noted that after suffering repeated criticism for his uncertain policy through most of his first term, Clinton was finally being praised, not least in Europe, and in the United States too he was getting a better press. A September 1996 NYT/CBS poll gave a foreign policy approval rating of 53 percent, and two months later, of course, the electorate endorsed Clinton by re-electing him.[19]

"The fact is America remains the indispensable nation," said Clinton in 1996, in a phrase also used by Madeleine Albright: "... There are times when America, and only America, can make a difference between war and peace, between freedom and repression, between hope and fear." Bosnia had pointed up the limitations of American power, but the actions of 1995 also showed that as the world's one remaining superpower only the United States had the authority – sometimes – to resolve international crises. For the rest of his administration Clinton tended to act on this premise. The Clinton White House sometimes chose to act unilaterally and sometimes multilaterally, but act it did where it seemed the United States could make a difference. Clinton urged the need for international measures to combat terrorism, global warming, and the spread of AIDS. Democratic enlargement remained a central preoccupation, and he continued to pin his faith in globalizing processes: "Democracy and free markets are taking root on every continent." "The world clearly is coming together," he added in 1999, and it was the "solemn responsibility" of the United States "to shape a more peaceful, prosperous, democratic world."[20]

During Clinton's second term a major preoccupation was the enlargement of NATO (North Atlantic Treaty Organization). With the strategy of containment rendered obsolete, what purpose had the Atlantic alliance? There was little interest in dissolving it, but it could be recast in new form. This was borne in on Clinton in his first years as president, when some of the newly independent Eastern European countries, uneasy about breaking away from a highly militarized Russia, sought NATO membership. "We are all afraid of Russia," explained Poland's Lech Walesa in 1993. But to Clinton the issue became not so much the containment of Russia, which he cultivated assiduously, as the promotion of democratic politics across Europe, and in any case he felt that the wishes of the new democracies could not be disregarded. As National Security Adviser Sandy Berger later explained, what "drove" NATO enlargement on "was the President's sense of the transformation of Europe and the integration of Central Europe into the West

– his vision of the opportunity to create for the first time in history a Europe that was free, democratic and secure." By 1996 both Democrats and Republicans broadly agreed on NATO growth, partly because of the lobbying energies of Eastern European ethnic groups in the United States, although many members of the old foreign policy establishment were strongly against it. At a NATO summit in July 1997 it was formally agreed to admit Poland, Hungary, and the Czech Republic, a significant act in that it meant "the largest increase in the American commitment to Europe in decades." In a sense, NATO expansion was a version of "democratic enlargement." One anticipation was that expansion of the European Union would follow NATO enlargement, so that Clinton would be "the president who united Europe." In 1997–1998 the Clinton administration engaged in a determined effort to secure Senate approval, which came after intensive lobbying.[21]

To Russia, NATO enlargement was a hostile act. From the beginning the Clinton White House had worked hard to find a modus operandi with the Russians. This meant trying to support the reform elements there; the provision of economic aid could be justified in terms of both stability and democracy promotion, it being hoped that Russia too would move toward a more open system. Clinton repeatedly insisted that an enlarged, democratic, and stable NATO would actually be in Russia's interests, and tried to overcome Yeltsin's resistance by working to bring Russia into the G-7 (which would become the G-8) and into the World Trade Organization (WTO), another illustration of his faith in the civilizing effects of commerce.

A similar attitude was adopted toward the world's largest surviving communist power, whose expansive economy meant that it could rival the United States as a center of power in the twenty-first century. Both Russia and China, Clinton insisted, must be brought "into the international system as open, prosperous, stable nations." He had criticized Bush for "coddling" China in the 1992 campaign, but in office he changed tack, concluding that promoting trade with China might eventually nurture democracy there. In 1994 he renewed China's "most favored nation" trading status, and by his second term was championing China's cause strongly, a particular goal being to bring it into the WTO. One Republican congressional critic compared Clinton's China policy to Britain's appeasement of Hitler in the 1930s, but the president prevailed in 1999, when an understanding was reached that China would open its market to American companies and the United States would reciprocate by supporting China's entry to the WTO, which was formally effected in 2001. An "undisputed" aspect of Clinton's legacy, reflected the *Washington Post*, was "an aggressive commitment to prying open foreign markets, even with distasteful regimes, in the hope that democracy will one day flow from prosperity."[22]

If the United States was the "indispensable nation," it was incumbent on it to respond to other issues left unresolved by the ending of the Cold War. One was the control of nuclear and other weapons of mass destruction (WMDs). The disintegration of the Soviet empire left three nuclear powers in Ukraine, Kazakhstan, and Belarus, and Clinton had some success in persuading them to scrap their missiles. A Chemical Weapons Convention, prohibiting the development, stockpiling, and use of chemical weapons, had been signed late in the Bush administration, but conservatives in Congress obstructed its ratification until Clinton prevailed in 1997, and Russia then followed suit, undertaking to destroy its large chemical weapons arsenal. Clinton also championed the Comprehensive Test Ban Treaty (CTBT), designed to discourage the further development and spread of nuclear weapons and encourage reductions in their stockpiles, though India soon dashed hopes by refusing to sign it, and in 1998 both India and Pakistan exploded nuclear devices. Jesse Helms said that India's action "clearly constitutes an emerging nuclear threat to the territory of the United States," and the Senate refused to ratify the CTBT, although opinion polls showed strong support for it. The Republicans preferred to rely on America's own nuclear weapons rather than on some system of collective security to deter aggressors, a stance in keeping with their reluctance to pay UN dues or to increase foreign aid. The public may have been against nuclear testing, but in the aftermath of the Cold War foreign issues did not concern it very much and congressional neo-isolationists could sometimes get their way.[23]

The United States was also the only country that might be able to impose some authority in the Balkans, which remained a powder keg, despite the Dayton Accords. The Serbian leader, Slobodan Milosevic, turned his attention to Kosovo, a province of Serbia in the old Yugoslavia settled mainly by Albanian Muslims. By 1997 the Kosovo Liberation Army was fighting for Kosovo's independence from the Serb republic and the Serbs were striking back. The Western powers were again reluctant to intervene and by 1998, with the Clinton White House embroiled in the scandal over the president's relationship with Monica Lewinsky, the violence in Kosovo was intensifying. The NATO powers hoped to contain Milosevic with the threat of bombing, but he remained intransigent, knowing that he could expect some support from Russia, which, as before, was resentful of Western intervention in a country regarded as within its sphere of interest. Finally, with Clinton acquitted of impeachment charges in February 1999, he was ready to take action, and without explicit UN sanction. Russia for its part, exasperated by Milosevic's behavior, moderated its obstructionist tactics to NATO intervention. To placate Congress the president disavowed the intention of using ground troops, but in March, as the Serbians were attempting to drive the Albanians from Kosovo, an intensive bombing campaign began. As Trevor McCrisken has commented: "It appeared that the use of air power rather than ground troops to resolve conflicts was becoming an established strategy." For once, air power seemed to work, though adding to the pressure was the credible threat to send ground troops. Early in June Milosevic capitulated and accepted NATO's terms, unable to withstand high-tech airpower and the defection of his erstwhile Russian ally. Later in the year he fell from power. In the meantime a UN force had arrived in Kosovo to assist it toward self-government. But it was American power that had driven Milosevic from Kosovo.[24]

Another symptom of the instability of the post-Cold War world was the growth of international terrorism. "The impact of globalization means that terrorist acts will be easier to plan and conduct, weapons will be easier to acquire and transport, and the enemy will be easier to reach than in the past," wrote a leading authority on terrorism. "Terrorism is the enemy of our generation," warned Clinton in a 1996 public address – nothing was more urgent than "the struggle against terrorism," which he described as "an equal opportunity destroyer, with no respect for borders." The roots of terrorism were complex, though some authors pointed to the effects of globalization in intensifying the unequal distribution of income in parts of the Third World and in the stringent neoliberal economic and fiscal policies imposed on governments seeking aid from the IMF. Relevant too was the Mujahidin's war against the Soviets in Afghanistan in the 1980s, which served to generate numbers of ardent Muslim radicals bent on purifying the whole Islamic world, a major affront to them being the US military presence in the Saudi Arabian holy land. Insurgent movements often saw the West, and particularly the United States, as the enemy. Movements such as this, lacking governmental power of their own, were sometimes tempted to use terrorism to present their case. One example was the bombing of the World Trade Center in Manhattan in February 1993; focused on the underground garage, this did not do as much damage as intended, but six people died. The United States was targeted in attacks on American barracks in Saudi Arabia in June 1996, on US embassies in Kenya and Tanzania in August 1998 (when most of those who died were Africans), and on an American destroyer, the USS *Cole*, in Yemen in October 2000.

The assault on the two embassies, in which over 200 people died, was credited to Osama bin Laden's al Qaeda guerrilla organization, and Clinton responded with cruise missiles on a suspect factory in Sudan and a training camp in Afghanistan. In a major foreign policy address in February 1999, Clinton emphasized that "the most likely threat to our existence is not a strategic nuclear strike from Russia or China, but the use of weapons of mass destruction by an outlaw nation or a terrorist group." The Clinton administration took the threat of terrorist attacks on Americans at home or abroad seriously, enhancing the intelligence agencies and securing anti-terrorist legislation, though did not give it the highest priority. When it handed over responsibility to the incoming Bush administration in 2000–2001, it appears "genuinely to have conveyed the seriousness of the threat."[25]

What Clinton did do toward the end of his administration, like Jimmy Carter two decades earlier, was to increase American defense expenditures. Partly this was an accommodation to the pressure of congressional Republicans, though increasing public unease over international terrorism also legitimated greater attention to national security. Clinton had initially reduced the priority of what remained of Reagan's celebrated Star Wars program, but he was eventually persuaded to investigate the prospects of an Anti-Ballistic Missiles (ABM) shield, and expensive research resumed. The new ABM system, he said, should there be an eventual decision to deploy it, could be used "against emerging ballistic threats from rogue nations." Clinton also agreed to Pentagon demands for more conventional weaponry.[26]

The tensions in the Middle East also continued to challenge the White House. The Gulf War of 1991 had left Saddam Hussein in command of Iraq, but to avoid UN sanctions he was required to dismantle all chemical and biological weapons and be subjected to scrutiny by UN inspectors. Soon after the war had ended protests by Shia Muslims and Kurdish Iraqis against Saddam's regime were violently repressed. The United States, with the United Kingdom and France, claiming authority under a UN Security Council resolution, established the Iraqi no-fly zones to protect Kurdish and Shi'ite populations from attacks by the Iraqi regime's aircraft. Saddam, however, repeatedly obstructed the weapons inspectors, and Iraq was subject to frequent American and British air attacks during the Clinton administration, as well as import sanctions that were blamed for hundreds of thousands of civilian deaths owing to the shortage of food and medicines. By the late 1990s containment of Saddam was giving way to a semi-covert effort to overthrow him; it was subsequently reported that the CIA had spent $120 million in abortive moves to this end. Clinton also made an energetic if somewhat belated attempt to further the Middle East peace process. During his first year in office he had orchestrated a celebrated handshake between Israel's Yitzhak Rabin and Palestine's Yasser Arafat, consummating the Oslo Accord, although his own contribution to that had been minimal. During his second term Clinton gave the peace process more serious attention, hosting talks at Camp David between Ehud Barak and Arafat in 2000. The two did reach agreement on a number of issues, but ultimately the talks ended in failure.

As the leader of "the indispensable nation," one keen to promote international commerce and democracy, Bill Clinton in his second term also lent his services to other causes. He took a keen personal interest in the troubles in Northern Ireland, sometimes aggravating British governments by his interventions in a matter they regarded as an internal responsibility. The Good Friday Agreement of 1998, bringing a fragile peace to the province, was the product of a range of forces, but among them was Clinton's active diplomacy. As John Dumbrell has commented, this "fitted into the general peace-promotion/democracy-promotion agenda" of the Clinton White House.[27]

* * *

Toward the end of the Clinton years Madeleine Albright observed: "Today, for the first time in history, electoral democracy is the world's predominant form of government." Some months later, Clinton himself pointed out that "for the first time in history, more than half the world's people elect their own leaders." The United States could claim to have played a part in this, although not too much, since Congress remained hostile to spending much on foreign aid. In relative terms, the official development assistance of the US was the smallest of all OECD countries, save Turkey and South Korea. Nonetheless, some help was given, as Albright explained: "From Asia to Africa to the Andes, U.S. agencies and nongovernmental organizations are training judges, ... teaching the rules of parliamentary procedure, supporting efforts to protect children and empower women, fostering the development of independent media, and otherwise helping friends to assemble the nuts and bolts of freedom." Freedom House, an international nongovernmental organization located in Washington (formally independent though reliant on US governmental sources for much of its income), confirmed that by its measures the level of freedom worldwide had expanded significantly during Clinton's presidency; the number of states where human rights and civil liberties were respected was held to have reached its highest level ever.[28]

How far Bill Clinton could claim credit for this is open to question. But he had set democratic enlargement and the growth of market economies as his foreign policy goals, and after an uncertain start had used American power and influence to further peace processes in the Balkans, the Middle East, Ireland, and elsewhere. At the time of Clinton's election Americans had been fretting at the prospect of losing their commercial predominance to Japan and the Asian tigers. But the president had pursued his commercial and political objectives through securing approval of NAFTA and the WTO, and the 1990s had witnessed both a massive expansion in global trade and soaring American exports. Clinton had eventually taken charge of security in Europe, and had shown that the United States indeed was the "indispensable nation." Domestic economic renewal was an early objective of his foreign policy, and as the economy took off (in significant part because of expanding foreign trade), Clinton's global role grew somewhat bolder. He sought to persuade his fellow citizens that a prosperous and peaceful world was in America's self-interest, justifying limited US action abroad, and that international cooperation was necessary if the United States itself was to remain safe. Whether he had done enough to protect his country from international terrorism and drug smuggling, to counter the workplace insecurity that globalization intensified, or to convince Americans and other countries of the dangers of global warming is debatable, but he had sounded the alarm and he had insisted that the United States could not isolate itself from the rest of the world.

But global problems required global solutions, and like many presidents before him Clinton never found a way of reconciling the need for international action on a range of issues with the resistance of the American public to an energetic foreign policy. Further, while he recognized intellectually that democratic advance and business enterprise could work against rather than for one another, he relied more on rhetoric than on substantive policies to accommodate the two. Toward the end of his administration the *Foreign Policy* journal concluded that "Bill Clinton understood sooner, better, and more profoundly than many other leaders that globalization was not simply a trendy buzzword, noting that: 'Everything from the strength of our economy, to the safety of our cities, to the health of our people depends on events not only within our border but half a world away.'" He understood, and he tried to educate his fellow Americans in his understanding, an important duty for a president, but acting proved more difficult than teaching.[29]

Chapter 13

The Comeback Kid v. the Gringrich Who Stole Christmas

At the end of 1994 Bill Clinton's transforming vision for America seemed no more. One aide described the atmosphere of the White House as "bunker-like." Like Reagan during the depths of the Iran–Contra agony, after the disastrous mid-term elections the president sank to a psychological low, his energy for a time replaced by a demoralized passivity. Despite the considerable intellectual and political talent with which he had surrounded himself, Clinton had been unable to convince the country that he was successfully "reinventing" government, and the Republicans had swept the Democrats out of both houses of Congress and out of many state capitols.[1]

At the beginning of 1995 the press was giving less than its customary attention to the White House. The political initiative had passed elsewhere, particularly to the House of Representatives, triumphantly seized by the Republicans for the first time since 1953 and led by the flamboyant Newt Gingrich. It would be Gingrich and his allies, concluded many political journalists, they would have to watch over the next two years. The crippled administration of Bill Clinton would become a footnote in history. When a reporter asked Clinton about his reduced press coverage in April 1995, he blustered: "The president is relevant. The Constitution gives me relevance." Yet the 1994 elections were more a rebuff of the Democratic incumbents than an endorsement of the radical brand of conservatism espoused by many of the newly elected Republicans, and as his energies returned Bill Clinton was to demonstrate that his centrist policies as well as his own formidable persona still had an appeal to the American public. As one aide early noticed about Clinton, he might make mistakes but he "figures out

Contemporary America: Power, Dependency, and Globalization since 1980,
First Edition. M.J. Heale.
© 2011 M.J. Heale. Published 2011 by Blackwell Publishing Ltd.

what went wrong and he fixes it." Clinton was eventually to leave office with some of the highest approval ratings ever recorded for a departing president.[2]

* * *

The jubilant Republicans elected Newt Gingrich Speaker of the House of Representatives, and he promptly delivered a 43-minute speech, after the manner of a president's Inaugural Address. His task now, he told a journalist, was that of "creating a new order." He quickly embarked on fashioning an alternative government, promising to introduce the measures listed in the Contract with America within "the first hundred days," a phrase associated with new presidential administrations. At the conclusion of the hundred days he addressed the nation on prime-time television, another first for a Speaker. "Gingrich seems to think of himself as a kind of Prime Minister, chosen by the House of Representatives," former US Senator Eugene McCarthy observed, "ready to act as a kind of 'counter government.'"[3]

A southerner like the president, and from the same postwar political generation, Gingrich shared with Clinton an enthusiasm for new technology, which he hoped would further his vision of returning power from Washington to local communities and replacing bureaucracy with voluntarism. One offhand suggestion was to give the poor a tax break so they could buy laptop computers, which he quickly recognized as "dumb," though the point remained, he insisted, that "somehow there has to be a missionary spirit in America that says to the poorest child in America, 'Internet's for you. The information age is for you.'" Both men believed that government had to be "reinvented" for the new age.[4]

With the White House humiliated by the electorate, Gingrich calculated that his disciplined troops would provide the rule that Clinton could not. He began by appointing energetic Republican loyalists as committee chairs, rather than distributing offices by seniority. These Republicans aimed to be even more conservative than Reagan. As one put it: "In the 1980s, Republicans believed in government. Now they don't," later adding: "The twenty-first century is about the power of the individual, not the power of the bureaucracy." The new Republican chair of one House committee, Thomas Bliley of Virginia, agreed: "The American people sent us a message in November, loud and clear: Tame this regulatory beast! Our constituents want us to break the Feds' stranglehold on our economy and to get them out of decisions that are best left to the individual." A bemused Michigan

Republican explained: "When you have a group of individuals frustrated for 40 years, and they're suddenly given the keys to do it, going overboard is natural." Not one of the Republicans now in the House had ever experienced being in the majority before.[5]

Inexperienced in government they may have been, but they quickly set about implementing the Contract with America, with its objective of tearing down government. Central to the Republican offensive was the balanced budget, ideally to be mandated by a constitutional amendment. "I regard getting to the balanced budget as the fulcrum to move the whole system …," reflected Gingrich: "It's the only thing that gives you the moral imperative to change the whole structure of the welfare state." Trent Lott, the Republicans' majority whip in the Senate, told pollster Dick Morris on the latter's account: "It's not balancing the budget, it's not cutting taxes that we're all about. It's cutting government spending," adding: "It's not really the spending either. It's the entitlements. We've got to cut the entitlements." The biggest growth in government spending, debt interest apart, had indeed come in the entitlement programs, especially Medicaid and Medicare. Less was said about the hidden state subsidies which had also been increasing, such as the deductions for private pension contributions. When Reagan had secured his 1981 tax cut, critics had accused him of trying to defund the welfare state. Right-wing Republicans had now grasped that the budget could be used to roll back the social spending they believed was crippling the economy. Nonetheless, much of "entitlement" spending, 43 percent on one calculation, including many Social Security payments and tax breaks for household mortgages, actually went to middle-income Americans, and an assault on this edifice carried political dangers.[6]

One of the great political battles of the 1990s was now joined. The cause of a constitutional amendment to balance the budget was a popular one – up to a point. One opinion poll showed 80 percent support, though the figure dropped dramatically to 30 percent if the result was to cut Social Security. The amendment failed by a single vote to secure the necessary two-thirds vote in the Senate. The real confrontation between the White House and Gingrich's troops, however, was over the annual budget. As Clinton understood, the strategy of balancing the budget to enforce spending cuts left the Republicans politically vulnerable if popular programs like Medicare or environmental protection were reduced while the well-to-do benefited. Some Senate Republicans were cool toward the determination of their House colleagues to lay waste to government. John Chafee, the chair of the Senate Environment and Public Works Committee, was one: "It has great appeal, but it's terrible legislation," he said of the House Republicans' mission, adding: "When all the artichoke leaves are peeled away, they are out for the Clean Air Act, the Clean Water Act, the Endangered Species Act; that's what they're gunning for." What also worried some observers was that the Republicans appeared to be allowing interest groups to write much of their legislation.[7]

The White House took its stand on Medicare, a significant target of the Republican plan. Medicare was the program, introduced by Lyndon Johnson, providing health insurance for the over-65s, much appreciated by the extensive middle class. "Medicare cuts are your single biggest weapon against the Republicans," pollster Dick Morris told Clinton: "They are hated by the public, old and young." Opinion polls confirmed that most voters would tolerate imbalanced budgets and forego tax cuts as long as Medicare and Social Security remained untouched. Also playing into the White House's hands was a Republican proposal that seemed to threaten the school-lunch program. "We ought not to be stepping on children," said Chief of Staff (and former Budget Director) Leon Panetta on television, "to move forward with tax cuts to the wealthiest in this country." A fateful impasse developed over the budget that had to be agreed between White House and Congress in 1995. Fruitless negotiations dragged on for month after month, with the president insisting that he would protect "Medicare, Medicaid, education, and the environment." The Democratic Party and labor groups mounted an advertising blitz in the districts of Republican incumbents, sending the message that the proposed $270 billion reduction in Medicare funding was to be used to pay for a $245 billion "tax cut for the wealthy." The relative closeness of these figures was not lost on the public. But Gingrich showed little interest in compromising over what had become a Republican totem, and Clinton, who had long been committed to deficit reduction, finally agreed to the goal of a balanced budget, to be achieved in 10 years though eventually he accepted seven. He came to see it as a precondition for progressive reform. "If I'm going to get heard on anything else, I first have to show a balanced budget," he reasoned: "Once I do that, I can talk about progressive programs."[8]

Yet Gingrich clung to his budget proposals, with lower taxes for the well-to-do and cuts in Medicare. Eventually, in November, with no new monies being approved, Clinton actually shut down the government. Nearly 800 000 federal employees were sent home, and federal offices across the country, other than emergency services, locked their doors. Clinton publicly berated the "deeply irresponsible" Republican leaders for cutting Medicare "as a condition of keeping government open." Opinion polls soon showed the public siding with him and blaming the congressional

Republicans for the shutdown by about 2 to 1. Gingrich did succeed in getting the Republican version of the budget through Congress, but Clinton vetoed it in December 1995. Again a partial government shutdown occurred, stretching into January for an unprecedented three weeks. The House Speaker was scorned as "the Gringrich who stole Christmas." As journalist Robert Samuelson commented, Clinton had "constantly made the Republicans look mean, petty and silly." Eventually the budget passed in April 1996, several months into the fiscal year it funded. Republican obduracy had weakened as the Gingrich Republicans were seen as both the enemies of Medicare and other valued programs and obstructive of the governing process. On other fronts too Gingrich found himself frustrated. His strident rhetoric tended to alienate rather than attract support, and he himself eventually became the subject of ethics investigations. Early in 1997 the House Ethics Committee would find Gingrich guilty of various violations of House rules and fine him $300 000. His approval rating dropped to under 30 percent.[9]

At the end of the first year of the Republicans' majority only three minor Contract items had been enacted. The excesses of the Gingrich Republicans had helped to rally the Democratic Party behind the president, and the AFL-CIO mobilized its troops against the Contract. But it is a moot point who won the Gingrich–Clinton confrontation. Clinton after all was now committed to a balanced budget, as he had not been at the beginning of 1995, and in his State of the Union Message of January 1996 he famously conceded that "the era of big government is over." But he had fended off the Republican attacks on social spending and environmental regulation.

As the battle of the budget waged through 1995, Clinton had also moved to blunt the Republicans' offensive by appropriating some of their issues, a strategy encouraged by Dick Morris, who reminded the president of the need to radiate Reaganite sunniness: he "should be telling the public that things are wonderful." Clinton did not need much encouragement to assume a centrist stance, for he had been doing that since his DLC days. In the year following the Republican triumph Clinton worked hard to dispel any notion that he was a feckless child of the Sixties. "In this White House," noticed one visitor, "men trembled at the thought of being antimarket or critical of business." On such issues as welfare and crime Clinton left the Republicans with little space, calling for more police officers on the street and policies designed to reduce teenage pregnancies. In July 1995 he addressed the sensitive issue of affirmative action, which congressional Republicans were planning to abolish, its political salience having been raised by the stagnation of middle-class incomes and business downsizing.

Distressed whites could look askance at the rights accorded to minorities. The Supreme Court in June had insisted that strict standards should be applied to affirmative action programs, and Clinton managed to uphold the Court's ruling against quotas and reverse discrimination while insisting: "Let me be clear, affirmative action has been good for America." His theme of "mend but don't end" managed both to satisfy civil rights groups and give pause to the conservative campaign to end affirmative action.[10]

A fearful tragedy also redounded to the president's benefit. In April 1995 a bomb exploded at a federal building in Oklahoma City, leaving 168 people dead, including 19 children. Speculation that Islamic terrorists might be involved was soon dispelled with the arrest of Timothy McVeigh, a right-wing army veteran, who seemed a personification of the growing militia movement, with its loathing of the federal government. At a prayer service in Oklahoma City Clinton urged Americans to take a stand against "the forces of fear" and the "talk of hatred … talk of violence." The tragedy did something to discredit the militia movement and check the extremist rhetoric of the talk radio hosts. Clinton's speedy and empathic response gave him a temporary boost in the polls, and from the autumn he was regularly pulling ahead in approval ratings.[11]

The president's New Democrat philosophy was further demonstrated in the congressional battle over welfare reform. Welfare entitlements had been burgeoning since the 1960s and for the most part middle Americans had no particular affection for them, suspecting them of being subsidies for the feckless. In 1970 the average monthly number of families receiving Aid for Families with Dependent Children (AFDC) had been just over 1.9 million; by 1994 the figure had jumped to 5 million. The proportion thinking it was "the responsibility of the government to take care of people who can't take care of themselves" had slumped from 74 percent in 1988 to 57 percent in 1994. The malaise of the early 1990s, perhaps, had taken its toll on the public's compassion. During the 1980s unmarried mothers had become the most numerous recipients of welfare, and the continued rise in their numbers troubled many, with Gingrich and others trying to make illegitimacy a central issue in the welfare debate. Ronald Reagan had notoriously made rhetorical attacks on "welfare queens" and some suspected a racist subtext in such campaigns, as in Gingrich's despairing plea: "It is impossible to maintain civilization with 12-year-olds having babies, 15-year-olds killing each other, 17-year-olds dying of AIDS, and 18-year-olds getting diplomas they can't read."[12]

The Democrats had been harried over welfare for decades, and Clinton himself believed in the need for change, hoping, among other things, that its reform would reduce the incidence of racism in American politics. In 1992 he had promised to "end welfare as we know it." With their new majorities in Congress the Republicans mounted a powerful assault on the "welfare mess," eager to put an end to the handout culture they believed New Deal Democrats had left them. The Personal Responsibility and Work Opportunity Reconciliation Act of 1996 transferred the major welfare programs to the states, something Reagan had been unable to effect, and provided for a cut-off point at which a person's payments would cease. States were required to ensure that at least half of their welfare recipients had jobs or were enrolled in training programs. Access to food stamps was also greatly curtailed. The measure represented a fundamental overhaul of the welfare structure, one in tune with conservative doctrine in its emphasis on "workfare" and its threat to end payments to substantial categories of people, including single mothers with young children. Liberals fiercely denounced the bill as regressive, the AFL-CIO president calling it "anti-poor, anti-immigrants, anti-women and anti-children." The act was more severe than the reform Clinton had wanted and he detested some of its provisions. "This is a decent welfare bill wrapped in a sack of shit," he told his aides, but in the summer of 1996, as the presidential election loomed, he signed it into law. He had after all promised to end the old system, and had apparently concluded that the unpopular system had to be abandoned before a new one could be devised.[13]

Clinton's gamble seemed vindicated by the experience of his second term, when, with assistance from the flourishing economy, welfare rolls dropped by nearly half, the proportion of the poorest women taking jobs rose markedly, and the number of children living with single parents declined. He could also claim a longer-term political benefit: Republicans were no longer able to use the welfare issue against the Democrats. It was EITC (Earned Income Tax Credit), providing tax credits for the working poor rather than handouts, that characterized Clinton's approach to welfare.

By the date of the passage of the welfare bill, with the presidential campaign rolling, Clinton was riding relatively high in the polls. On both the balanced budget and the social issues he was outflanking the Republicans. Further, more than previously he was seizing family values from them. "Our first challenge is to cherish our children and strengthen America's families," he had said in his 1996 State of the Union Message: "Family is the foundation of American life." With the deficit fast declining Clinton was even able to please his labor constituency by securing an increase in the minimum wage, the Republicans not risking further public displeasure by obstructing it. He also helped to see off the Republicans' assault on environmental protection laws, as discussed in Chapter 10. Clinton could claim credit for wise economic management, while the Republicans had been damaged by public perceptions of their inflexibility over the budget negotiations and responsibility for the government shutdown. Democratic television commercials in 1996 hammered the Republicans for not working with the president to solve budgetary problems. The Clinton campaign, together with the Democratic National Committee, spent over $85 million on TV advertising, an unprecedented amount and over twice the 1992 figure. Clinton carefully monitored and refined the TV spots himself.[14]

The front-runner for the Republican nomination was Bob Dole, the Senate Majority Leader. A respected political operator, he was not comfortable with the brash political offensive conducted from the lower house by Newt Gingrich, but the two attempted to maintain an accord. Patrick Buchanan made another bid for the Republican nomination, and improved on his 1992 performance by carrying the New Hampshire and three other state primaries. He railed against the Washington establishment and promised that the "peasants are coming with pitchforks." His denunciation of NAFTA, which he claimed was responsible for 300 000 job losses, in particular caused a stir. A stung Robert Dole admitted: "I didn't realize that jobs and trade and what makes America work would become a big issue." But the party regulars delivered the nomination to Dole, though at 73 his age and dour manner counted against him. The centerpiece of his campaign was a large 15 percent tax cut proposal, which reflected the tax-cutting agenda of the Republican right but was unconvincing coming from someone who had previously prioritized controlling the budget deficit. Dole also aligned himself with the rising anti-immigrant sentiment and avowed his support for California's Proposition 187. The Clinton team happily cast Dole as "a creature of Washington," seeking to turn the anti-establishment animus against him.[15]

The Democrats for their part courted cultural conservatives by presenting themselves as the party of the family, focusing on children and work. Clinton emphasized such issues as the Family and Medical Leave Act and tough enforcement of the child support laws. The 1992 refrain of "people first" was replaced by "family first." Clinton reprised his New Covenant theme. Government, he insisted, "is not your enemy; it is your servant, your partner." Yet he was able to combine his advocacy of traditional values with a contemporary perspective, emphasizing, as he had done so frequently, that the country was moving from an industrial economy to a high-tech economy, and that it was up to government to lead this process and protect those who might suffer from it.[16]

Electioneering was in Clinton's blood, and he easily outperformed his rival. "We are better off than we were four years ago," he said confidently in the first presidential debate, with its echo of Reagan's mocking taunt in 1980. Also competing for the presidency again was Ross Perot, but he evoked much less public interest than in 1992. The populist anger of 1994 seemed to have abated. Indeed, the 1996 election campaign generally failed to ignite much public enthusiasm. Campaign coverage on the television networks' nightly news fell by 40 percent from 1992, and turnout was the lowest since 1924. Perhaps this apathy helped the incumbent; with the economy in good shape voters were not disposed to unseat him. Clinton coasted home with a lead of over 8 million votes, though – at 49 percent to Dole's 41 percent – he was disappointed not to win 50 percent of the popular vote; Ross Perot's share slipped to 8 percent, and the Republicans retained control of both houses of Congress. Still, not since Franklin Roosevelt had a Democratic president been re-elected.[17]

The election returns confirmed that income levels if anything were becoming more important in explaining voting behavior; in recent elections, and most markedly in 1996, the tendency for those with low incomes to vote Democrat and those with high incomes to vote Republican was more pronounced than it had been in the mid-twentieth century. A related feature was the marked tendency for working and single women to back the Democratic Party, with its greater sympathy for protective measures for women and abortion rights. The religious right's emphasis on traditional values seemed to be limiting the appeal of the Republican Party to women.[18]

By 1996 the issues associated with Whitewater and Clinton's reputation for womanizing were not doing him serious damage. In a poll in which voters were asked, "Which was the more important in your vote – issues or character?" 58 percent said issues, and of these 70 percent voted for Clinton. Yet exit polls found that over 60 percent thought he had lied about aspects of Whitewater. The tolerant ambiguity of the public was caught in a cartoon that showed a Democratic housewife telling a canvasser: "I'm for the scumbag." Perhaps the Republicans should have taken more note of these public attitudes, but during Clinton's second term they made character the central issue of American politics.[19]

The great budget battles of Clinton's first term paid off in his second, when the economy finally achieved the kind of buoyancy it had last experienced in the mid-1960s. Having lost to the president on the issues of the tax hike in 1993 and curtailing social spending in 1995, the Republicans proved somewhat more amenable, though they did secure reduced estate and capital gains taxes in the balanced budget act of 1997. Their dire predictions in 1993 that increased taxes would produce a recession were shown to be spectacularly wrong, while the budget and environmental fights of 1995–1996, as well as the 1996 elections, had suggested that the country was not as anti-government as the radical Republicans had assumed. Some among their number began to grope their own way toward the center. Historian Steven Gillon has unearthed evidence that in 1997 Bill Clinton and Newt Gingrich were engaged in secret negotiations to form a political alliance aimed at the long-term reform of Social Security and perhaps of Medicare too, which would rank as their major legacies. In the event the eruption of the Monica Lewinsky scandal destroyed whatever accord might have been possible between them.[20]

Each year during his second term Clinton advanced a progressive agenda a little, though just a little. In 1997 he proclaimed a Presidential Initiative on Race, which characteristically he linked to his globalizing agenda, with American minorities in business engaging with their counterparts in Africa and Asia, thus "enhancing our economic power in the twenty-first century." There was money for a health insurance scheme for poor children, and it was made easier for people changing jobs to take their health insurance with them. Legal immigrants were again given access to welfare, something they had been denied in the 1996 act, and funding was found for more elementary school teachers. Higher education won significant gains. There were more college scholarships and new tax credits, to the relief of millions of middle-class parents. In 1999 some 59 percent of students were recipients of federal grants and loans, up from 43 percent in 1992. Several of these measures did involve more money, but, New Democrat that he was, rather than major boosts on the spending side, where possible Clinton used tax credits for low-wage workers and other tax contrivances to expand health insurance, retirement savings, and to help meet the expense of college education. Through such devices, the market more than government was being relied on to produce the benefits.[21]

This was the so-called "Third Way," and in his 1998 State of the Union Address Clinton congratulated himself on its success: "We have moved past the sterile debate between those who say government is the enemy and those who say government is the answer. My fellow Americans, we have found a third way. We have the smallest government in 35 years, but a more progressive one." Indeed: "We have shaped a new kind of government for the Information Age." The DLC described the approach as "pay-as-you-go progressivism."[22]

A new confrontation between White House and Congress loomed as the federal deficit disappeared, an event marked by the *New York Times* in 1998 as the "the fiscal equivalent of the Berlin Wall." The administration actually achieved budget surpluses in the three financial years 1998 to 2000, something not experienced since the late 1940s. The background to this remarkable turnaround was the roaring economy, which, together with the 1993 tax increases, boosted tax revenues and made possible a proportionate decline in federal spending. By 2000 federal expenditure represented 18.12 percent of GDP, down from 21.87 percent in 1992. Defense costs, as a proportion of GDP, had fallen most significantly, though by the same measure spending on education and science, transportation, and poverty were down too.

The sudden eruption of a surplus changed the dynamic between the White House and the congressional Republicans. The Republicans insisted that the right response was to give their own money "back to the people," that is, a tax cut. Such an argument was more moralistic than economic, unlike the supply-side doctrine of Reagan's day. "We see the surplus as the best opportunity to bring some fairness to the tax code," said the House Speaker, suggesting that the rich were expected to give up too much of their income. "Because of record-high taxation," joked a Republican congressman, "the surplus is raging out of control." But Clinton was not going to jeopardize social spending, and in his State of the Union Address of January 1998, as his opponents were ferociously assaulting him over an alleged sexual relationship with a White House intern, Clinton coolly argued that ensuring the solvency of Social Security had to come before tax cuts – as he defiantly put it, "Save Social Security First." The Republicans' dream of a Reagan-like tax cut would have to await the administration of George W. Bush.[23]

"Mr. President," Newt Gingrich had once told Clinton, "we are going to run you out of town." If the House Republicans had been rebuffed on the budget, they were now convinced they had another means of bringing Clinton down. Despite his stringent fiscal orthodoxy and his toughness on crime and welfare, Clinton could never free himself from the taint of the 1960s and the suspicion of scandal. The charges over Whitewater had refused to go away, now zealously pursued by Kenneth Starr, who had taken over as independent counsel. Independent Starr may nominally have been, though he was a conservative Republican closely associated with some of the president's more intemperate enemies. He seemed determined to expand his brief and drive it to a successful conclusion, no less than the impeachment and conviction of a president. The emergence of yet another sex scandal allowed him his opportunity. Early in 1998 a charge emerged that Clinton could not shake off. The partial government shutdowns had meant that the White House had to rely more than usual on young interns rather than the regular messenger service, one of whom the president had befriended. This was Monica Lewinsky, who told a friend of sexual encounters in the Oval Office. As denials followed the allegations, congressional committees and federal officials unleashed investigations of any improprieties or criminal cover-ups, and the whole sorry episode escalated into an issue that virtually monopolized the headlines and the attention of Congress and White House. "I did not have sexual relations with that woman, Miss Lewinsky," the president insisted on television: "I never told anybody to lie, not a single time." But the investigation pressed on remorselessly and the humiliated president was obliged to testify before a grand jury under oath and to provide a blood sample. In August 1998 Clinton finally admitted to the prosecutors and later in a televised statement to the public that he had indeed had "inappropriate intimate contact" with Monica Lewinsky.[24]

The Republicans now had Clinton in their sights, presenting him as the detestable personification of the counterculture that had breached so many traditional values. Robert Bork, once the victim of progressive political currents, believed that impeachment would "kill off the lax moral spirit of the Sixties." The immediate objective of the Republicans, it seemed to the White House, was to overturn the result of the 1996 election. Hillary Clinton was not alone in believing that "the prosecutors were undermining the office of the Presidency by using and abusing their authority in an effort to win back the political power they had lost at the ballot box." In his more fanciful moments, Gingrich even seemed to think that successful impeachment proceedings could be advanced against Vice President Gore as well as Clinton, leaving him as Speaker next in line for the presidency! Kenneth Starr presented a lengthy report to Congress, producing evidence of what he considered to be the president's "abundant and calculating lies" under oath. Little was said about Whitewater, the ostensible subject of the investigation, though Clinton's alleged sexual adventures received abundant coverage. Actually public opinion polls showed some sympathy for the president, and after a videotape of Clinton's grand jury testimony was broadcast, one poll showed his approval rating jumping nine points. But congressional Republicans were undeterred and launched impeachment proceedings as the mid-term elections approached.[25]

Despite the polls during the autumn of 1998 indicating public distaste for the Starr Report and the impeachment proceedings, Gingrich seemed to have convinced himself that the Republicans would win another decisive electoral victory, calculating perhaps that the Christian right would turn out to vote in large numbers while demoralized Democrats would stay at home, as in 1994. He was badly mistaken, since the Democrats actually gained five seats in the House, bucking the tradition that the president's party lost seats in mid-terms. The outcome of the elections was a huge rebuff for Gingrich in particular. The strategy that he had developed over several years to discredit the administration and to build the Republican Party through the exploitation of scandal was being undone by the voters. Gingrich promptly announced his resignation as Speaker and his departure from the House.

Yet the Republicans stuck to their course, driven by moral outrage over a president lying under oath and spurred on by constituency activists and right-wing radio shock jocks. The Republican House whip, Tom DeLay, later told a church group of his "biblical worldview" and that he had pushed for impeachment because Clinton held "the wrong worldview." (DeLay would leave Congress in 2006 after he had been indicted on criminal charges relating to possible violations of campaign finance laws.) The president was duly tried before the Senate on two counts of perjury and one of obstruction of justice. Eventually, in February 1999, he was acquitted because his prosecutors could not secure the two-thirds majority necessary to convict. At the end of that month Gallup reported that the president had a 60 percent approval rating. It seemed that whatever the fury of Republican zealots and the religious right, the bulk of the American people had little enthusiasm for destroying a president for his private peccadilloes, and the partisanship of his Republican accusers seemed no more admirable than Clinton's economy with the truth. This latest battle in the culture wars had again illustrated the fervor of the moral conservatives, as it also exposed their minority status. Surveys indicated that the public was more liberal on such issues as sexual morality, abortion, and gay rights than it had been a generation earlier, notwithstanding the zeal of the Christian right, and the Lewinsky affair would have little electoral impact.[26]

The Republicans had spent millions of public money in pursuing investigations against the Clintons and other members of the administration. The politics of scandal certainly distracted officials from their public duties, but the Republicans won few scalps in the process. There was not a single conviction of a top Clinton official for a crime involving public conduct in office, although a Secretary of Housing and Urban Development did plead guilty to a misdemeanor. After the Iran–Contra and other scandals of the Reagan administration, some 32 government officials had been convicted of crimes.

Clinton had bounced back once again, though his remaining achievements on the domestic front were fairly modest. There were still Republican majorities in both houses of Congress, and the *Wall Street Journal*, for example, was able to report of the 1999 legislative session that "Congress Leaves Business Lobbies Almost All Smiles." In 1999, on the *Congressional Quarterly* score, Clinton won only 38 percent of roll call votes in Congress, the lowest since the tabulation began in 1953, except for his own even lower score of 36 percent in 1995 when Gingrich's Republicans were in full cry. One reason for this trough was that partisanship had become so intense that neither side showed much interest in shaping compromise legislation. Clinton was able to secure some progressive advances through executive action, adding, for example, to the western land he was able to protect from developers by designating large areas as national monuments (see Chapter 10).[27]

Yet the economy was booming, for which polls gave Clinton much credit, and as his administration came to an end the world was more-or-less peaceful. The fumbling foreign policy episodes of his early years had been succeeded by more impressive accomplishments since 1994. Clinton, like Reagan before him, had survived a major scandal and left the presidency on a high. As Joe Klein has observed, "he would leave office with the highest sustained job approval ratings of any President since John F. Kennedy."

But Clinton's capacity to engage with the public could not rub off onto his successor as Democratic presidential candidate, Vice President Al Gore. The populist currents which had been agitating American politics in the early 1990s seem largely to have evaporated in the wake of the prosperity of the end of the decade, when both major parties selected wealthy presidential candidates from the political establishment. The Republicans nominated the Texas governor and son of George Bush, George W. Bush. Gore and Bush were the early front-runners in their respective parties, and neither was seriously confronted by popular insurgencies. Bush, in a contrast to the sharp-edged rhetoric of the Gingrich Republicans, portrayed himself as a "caring conservative," as he also promised a "humbler America." Gore had the difficult task of distancing himself from the more tawdry aspects of the Clinton presidency. His team celebrated the arrival of the "New Economy," with its characteristics of increasing productivity, low inflation, and impressive economic growth. The good times were illustrated by the successive budget surpluses. Al Gore wanted the surpluses to be used for the staged paying off of the national debt; George Bush wanted to return the people's money to them via hefty tax cuts. Gore's strategy was supported by the opinion polls; tax cutting no longer generated quite the excitement it once had.

A populist note was sounded in the campaign by Ralph Nader, who ran as the Green Party's presidential candidate. His central thrust was an anti-corporate one, as he assailed the two major parties for being funded and controlled by big business. The only difference between Gore and Bush, he said, "was the velocity with which their knees hit the floor when corporations knock on the door." Nader's candidacy did prompt Gore into a few populist flourishes of his own, but for the most part the Democrats charged that Nader was enhancing the possibility of a Republican victory by dividing the liberal vote. In the event Nader secured a disappointing 2.7 percent of the popular vote, though enough to be blamed by Democratic leaders for costing them the election. But the populist moment had passed.[28]

The campaign concluded with a protracted election that once more illustrated the divided state of the American polity. Al Gore won the popular vote with a lead of over 500 000, but he was to be denied the prize. Election night produced no clear winner of the electoral vote, and attention focused on the uncertain outcome in Florida, of which Bush's brother was governor. Confusing ballot designs, malfunctioning voting machines, partial recounts, and court challenges characterized a prolonged constitutional crisis. Eventually, on December 12, the US Supreme Court itself, most of its members appointed by Republican presidents, had to resolve the impasse, which it did so in a 5-to-4 decision that declared George W. Bush to be elected president. The politicization of the judiciary had reached its consummation. The congressional elections were also suggestive of an irresolute electorate. The Republicans' narrow command in the lower house was trimmed slightly, while they lost their majority in the Senate, which divided evenly between 50 Democrats and 50 Republicans. Democratic rule had ended, but the Republicans had hardly been given a mandate to govern.

*   *   *

Bill Clinton, like Ronald Reagan, had taken office in a time of malaise, when public confidence in the condition of the country was low. Reagan has been frequently credited with restoring American morale, though, if measured by opinion polls, it was under Clinton that the public mood experienced its most sustained experience of "satisfaction." Where the "dissatisfieds" had outnumbered the "satisfieds" in each year of the George H.W. Bush presidency in Gallup's Mood of the Country polls, the former touching an astronomic 77 percent in 1992, the "satisfieds" began to edge up during Clinton's first term and regained the lead in 1997. They kept it through

2002, averaging around 60 percent in the last three years of the Clinton presidency, a level that had been reached under Reagan only in 1986. The highest satisfaction levels were recorded in the first two months of 1999, when Clinton was being tried before the Senate, a period when he was also securing high approval ratings for his conduct as president. Clinton too, it seems, had helped to restore American morale.

Clinton, like Reagan, had primarily been elected to put the economy back on course, and he could claim to have done it. The Clinton administration naturally took credit for the impressive economic performance of the second term, but in a globalized economy external factors mattered too, particularly the fall in import prices which helped to keep down inflation. After spiking in the early 1990s with the Gulf War, for example, the international price of oil in real terms remained low through the rest of the decade. The Fed played a part in adopting a looser monetary policy, its lowering of interest rates made possible by the attack on the deficit in Clinton's 1993 budget, while a property boom allowed families and businesses to borrow and spend more. The prosperity of these years was owed to a combination of public saving, as the budget moved into surplus, and private debt, as Americans borrowed to consume and to invest in the stock market.

There were many good stories to be found in the economic statistics of Clinton's second term: an unemployment rate in 2000 that was the lowest in decades; more jobs for women, partly attributable to the 1996 welfare reform and the expanded EITC; falling welfare caseloads and unemployment rates for minorities at historic lows; rising real household incomes, with the rise for blacks faster than that for American families generally. The Clinton presidency also coincided with a marked drop in the crime rate, the disturbing upward trend that had obtained since the 1960s finally going into reverse. Perhaps even more striking, the remorseless increase in income inequality, which had characterized the economy since the late 1970s, ground to a halt in the second half of the 1990s. Rich and poor, it seemed, were no longer growing further apart (though the process was to resume after the turn of the century). Contributing to this outcome was Clinton's success in making the tax code somewhat more progressive, with his tax increases on the rich and the expansion of credits for the working poor. Nonetheless, the official poverty rate in 2000, at 11.3 percent of all individuals, though significantly lower than in Clinton's first year, was actually higher than it had been in 1972–1973. In 1998 Deputy Treasury Secretary Larry Summers conceded that "a child born today in New York is less likely to live to the age of five than a child born in Shanghai."[29]

Clinton's cherished New Economy had other limitations too. Job insecurity remained rife, with surveys showing higher numbers fearful of losing their jobs than had been the case during the Reagan boom. In the wider world there was evidence of the instability of the global financial system, disturbingly illustrated by the Asian Crisis of 1997. Although some economists called for increased regulation, a 1999 act, a bipartisan measure agreed after years of attempting to rewrite the financial services laws, increased the flexibility of operations in the American banking and financial sectors, arguably leaving the system vulnerable to the kind of crisis that would devastate it in 2008–2009.

But Bill Clinton, like Ronald Reagan, had demonstrated that the president mattered, something that seemed open to question when Newt Gingrich had tried to take over the government. On a range of public policies, economic, social, and environmental, Bill Clinton had turned aside the assaults of a resurgent radical right. The dispatching of the budget deficit had removed an issue that had dominated the domestic agenda for two decades. More than that, whether by good policy or good luck, he had delivered on his promises of a high-tech and globalized economy, a diminished but enabling government, and a foreign policy which emphasized engagement with the outside world, served American interests, but mostly kept American troops at home.

Yet the prudent means that Clinton used to advance his agenda, as well as the doctrinaire opposition of his political enemies and the damaging recklessness of his personal life, meant that the progressive goals that he so craved were only modestly advanced. As Robert Reich noted in 1999, the great weakness of the "third way" was that it had "no preexisting constituencies … no grass roots." A highly polarized political system was not conducive to constructive outcomes. Other than on its free trade initiatives, the reigning Republicans in Congress had little interest in cooperating with Clinton's agenda, and the liberal and labor elements in his own party feared that minimizing government would mean less protection for the weaker members of society. Further, few public policies survived running the gauntlet of well-financed interest groups unscathed. "The problem with the third way," wrote Robert Kuttner, "is that you begin by meeting the conservatives halfway. When that doesn't quite succeed, you meet them halfway again. And again." By the end of his second term, Clinton had achieved his celebrated budget surplus, but, as well as acceding to some tax reductions for the rich, he was proposing to use it to pay off the national debt rather than develop more fully the ambitious educational, worker retraining and health care programs that had been part of his vision in 1993. His early talk of building workers' rights and environmental protections into trade agreements seemed to be largely forgotten. "Clinton in the trade area fulfilled the explicit vision of Reagan and Bush – a global economy that protects investors but not workers and the environment," said Jeff Faux of the Economic Policy Institute. Clinton's near virtuoso performance in the White House after 1994 had given him commanding personal prestige and had kept alive the New Democratic dream of a style of politics in which rather conservative economic policies could be fused with liberal policies to enhance the quality of life for all Americans. But the precise content of this so-called third way, which had promised a creative synthesis between a market economy and activist government, remained opaque as Clinton left the presidency.[30]

Chapter 14

Since 2001: Decade of Crises

If the 1990s could be characterized as the "era of globalization," the following 10 years could be called a "decade of crisis." Scarcely had the twenty-first century begun when the deadliest ever foreign assault on US soil was perpetrated. On September 11, 2001, two planes turned by hijackers into flying bombs destroyed the monumental towers of the World Trade Center in New York, another was flown into the Pentagon, and a fourth crashed before it hit its target. Nearly 3000 people died. This shocking event profoundly shaped the decade, though before it was over the country's major banking institutions began collapsing, and the financial turmoil of 2008–2009 threatened an economic depression of the scale last experienced in the 1930s. These crises framed the administration of George W. Bush, which was also punctuated by Hurricane Katrina, which devastated the historic city of New Orleans in 2005. The United States may have entered the new century as the only remaining superpower, but the vulnerability of its citizens had been brutally exposed by foreign terrorists, by the murky complexities of the vaunted New Economy, and by nature itself.

These were global events. The fearful tragedy of 9/11, as it quickly became known, had been plotted by Islamic fundamentalists deeply resentful of the role of the United States in the world, in part using the electronic communication systems that were supposedly creating the "global village." In the World Trade Center the citizens of over 90 countries lost their lives, and the offices of major international corporations were annihilated. To a significant degree the financial crisis of 2008–2009 did have its roots in the United States, but its repercussions could not be confined to American borders. American banks and finance houses were intimately connected

Contemporary America: Power, Dependency, and Globalization since 1980,
First Edition. M.J. Heale.
© 2011 M.J. Heale. Published 2011 by Blackwell Publishing Ltd.

with one another and with others throughout the world, and the economies of several countries faced havoc. Hurricane Katrina may or may not have had anything to do with climate change, but the savagery of its impact did help to raise the issue in public consciousness, in the United States and elsewhere.

It is sometimes argued that 9/11 "changed everything." It changed a lot. It set the administration on its fateful War on Terror, with its immense human, political, and economic costs, for Americans and for others. But 9/11 did not change everything. American political leaders may have quickly agreed that national security was an imperative priority, but the intense partisanship of the 1990s soon reappeared and, if anything, American politics became yet more polarized. After a brief dip the American stock exchange index resumed its upward course and the economy expanded steadily, fueled by a consumer boom and military spending, much as in the Reagan years. Americans remained as insatiably attached to debt as ever, the budget deficit adamantly returning and the trade deficit assuming ever more heroic proportions. As before, huge sums had to be borrowed from abroad. In other fundamental respects, too, patterns that had emerged in the late twentieth century continued to assert themselves. Immigrants, both legal and illegal, still poured into the United States in huge numbers, precipitating much the same divided political responses as earlier. On environmental issues, most notably climate change, there was also gridlock, although the ineffective sympathy of the Clinton administration was replaced by the skepticism of the George W. Bush White House. The huge wealth gap between rich and poor Americans, which had briefly stabilized in the late 1990s, recommenced its widening advance, and the sharp fluctuations in income experienced by many remained a major source of insecurity.

After the fearful deeds of 9/11 the new American administration moved determinedly to use its superpower status to reorder the world. Scholars debated the phenomenon of an "American empire." As the decade ended, the question was being raised whether America's imperial moment was over. Humpty Dumpty, some said, had fallen off the wall and was irretrievably broken.

*   *   *

The new decade did not get off to a propitious start. The celebrated "dot. com bubble" had burst in March 2000, when the NASDAQ Index, tracker of the internet firms, began its steep downward spiral, and many communications companies went out of business. But the Dow Jones index largely rode out the high tech collapse and the wider economy did not go into recession until March 2001. By the end of the year, despite the alarm triggered by 9/11, the recession was over, helped by successive interest rate cuts by the Fed, still chaired by Alan Greenspan, the "Maestro" whose reputation was reaching mythic proportions. The Fed kept interest rates low for years, and Americans, some of whose fingers had been burned by the dot.com collapse, used cheap loans to plunge into the housing market instead, producing a price bubble which was to have fateful consequences later in the decade. But other economic uncertainties emerged too. In December 2001 the giant energy company Enron went into a spectacular bankruptcy, the victim of the greed and arrogance of its executives, several of whom were to receive long prison sentences. Extensive fraud was uncovered too in the case of WorldCom, a major telecommunications company, which filed for bankruptcy in July 2002, the largest thus far in American history. The pricking of the dot.com bubble had exposed the pretensions of the New Economy, while the accounting scandals called into question the deregulatory mission of the late twentieth century.

However, any doubts about the economy were driven from the public mind by the terrible experience of 9/11. The commercial airliners used in the attacks had been hijacked from American airports by 19 men associated with al Qaeda, a fellowship engaged in a global holy war on behalf of Islam under its leader, the wealthy Saudi Osama bin Laden. At its 1998 founding, al Qaeda had enjoined on all Muslims a duty "to kill the Americans and their allies." When news of this crime against humanity broke, televised images showed a stunned-looking President Bush reading a book to children at a Florida school, but within a few days he was standing defiantly amidst the rubble of the World Trade Center, promising that "the people who knocked these buildings down" would hear from the United States "soon." His Gallup approval rating, which had stood at a modest 51 percent, quickly soared to 90 percent. The experience was a shattering one for Americans, most of whom had not anticipated that the kind of major atrocities sometimes perpetrated in other countries could be visited on their own. The president himself voiced disbelief at the "vitriolic hatred for America in some Islamic countries": "Like most Americans, I just cannot believe it because I know how good we are."[1]

The administration declared a "War on Terror." The centrality of al Qaeda to the attacks was quickly established, and since bin Laden and his lieutenants were holed up in Afghanistan, under the protection of its fundamentalist Taliban government, the administration demanded their rendering to American justice, but in vain. In October 2001, American and coalition forces launched Operation Enduring Freedom, which, together with the Afghan opposition forces of the Northern Alliance, quickly over- threw the Taliban regime. The objective of capturing bin Laden, however, was frustrated.

But the War on Terror could not easily be contained, and it came to dominate the United States in the new millennium. The elusiveness of the al Qaeda leaders meant that foreign troops continued to occupy Afghanistan, to the increasing resistance of elements of the local population. One con- sequence of 9/11 was the strengthening of the so-called neoconservative forces in the Bush administration. This label was now being applied not so much to the former liberals who had moved right in the 1970s as to those who believed that the United States could exercise a kind of "benevolent hegemony" in the world. To authors Stefan Halper and Jonathan Clarke the neoconservatives were "like a coiled spring before 9/11 and simply needed the right moment to translate the attacks into their frame of reference." Vice President Dick Cheney and Defense Secretary Donald Rumsfeld were, by most definitions, traditional Republican conservatives, but they now somewhat misleadingly came to personify the newly aggressive neocon- servative faith, along with such figures as Deputy Defense Secretary Paul Wolfowitz, who had better claims to the title.[2]

In the wake of the Cold War, at much the same time as the discourse of economic decline was capturing attention, conservative intellectuals had been searching for a new basis for American foreign policy, confident of American supremacy in the post-Cold War world. Two of them, William Kristol and Robert Kagan, in a 1996 article, had argued for an American "benevolent hegemony," which would involve the country "supporting its friends, advancing its interests, and standing up for its principles around the world," that is, promoting "democracy, free markets, respect for liberty." Another envisaged a "unipolar moment," with the United States "unasham- edly laying down the rules of world order and being prepared to enforce them." Extending the area of democracy aligned such neoconservatives with the Clinton administration, though they seemed less interested in the commercial growth that was central to Clinton's vision. Rather, they evinced a defiant unilateralism and an eagerness to take the fight to the enemy.[3]

The War on Terror allowed the moderate members of Bush's team, such as Secretary of State Colin Powell, to be marginalized, while the neocon- servatives and their nationalistic conservative allies increasingly secured the ear of the president, whose inveterate optimism made him a ready listener. For them, the issue was not simply to destroy al Qaeda but also to secure a new balance of power in the Middle East, one which would serve to promote democracy in the region, the dangerous instability of which was personified by Iraq's Saddam Hussein. The message was that by removing Saddam the world would be safe and the Middle East free, though to cynics the subtext was that the Middle East with its oil reserves would be brought under American control. Action in Afghanistan was inevitable, but the supporters of terrorism were hardly confined there. Within days of 9/11 Wolfowitz in particular was arguing that there was a chance that Saddam Hussein was somehow implicated in the attacks. The president himself told his war council: "I believe Iraq was involved." That al Qaeda might try to follow up its attack by securing weapons of mass destruction had to be regarded as a possibility, and given Saddam's hostility to the United States it seemed to the White House that he might make his weapons available to the likes of bin Laden. In his State of the Union Address of January 2002 Bush spoke of an "axis of evil," the "rogue" states of North Korea, Iraq, and Iran, that could acquire such weapons and "provide these arms to terrorists." Bush ratcheted up the threat to the United States and the world: "Our war on terror is well begun, but it is only begun."[4]

In its pursuit he was evolving a relatively novel rationale. "After September the 11th, the doctrine of containment just doesn't hold water, as far as I'm concerned," said Bush in January 2003. The administration had earlier published its *National Security Strategy*, in which the doctrine of pre-emption, soon known as the Bush Doctrine, was unveiled. The Cold War had ended, the president said, with victory over totalitarianism and "a single sustainable model for national success: freedom, democracy, and free enterprise." But new "shadowy" enemies were now openly seeking weapons of mass destruction: "America will act against such emerging threats before they are fully formed." The United States had taken pre-emptive action before, but a president had never fully embraced it as a major principle. Many in the old foreign policy establishment were unhappy with the Bush Doctrine, with its apparent justification for preventive war, Brent Scowcroft for one fearing that its public avowal would tend "to add to the world's perception that we are arrogant and unilateral."[5]

Through the autumn of 2002 Bush regularly made speeches in which he recalled the attacks of September 11 and stressed the danger represented by Saddam Hussein. In January 2003 he revealed that intelligence sources had established that "Saddam Hussein aids and protects terrorists, including members of al Qaeda," and could help them acquire deadly weapons. "Fuck Saddam, we're taking him out," Bush privately told a group of senators in March. Pre-emption was becoming "regime change." The problem remained the legitimacy of the action, and while some members of the administration were prepared for the United States to act alone, criticism from some conservative Republicans and international comment persuaded the White House to seek UN endorsement, specifically a resolution demanding that Iraq give up all its weapons of mass destruction (WMD). These had been prohibited under the terms ending the 1991 war, since when Iraq had been subject to monitoring by UN weapons inspectors, although their surveillance had often been obstructed by Saddam. A resolution was adopted, though it warily stopped short of explicitly threatening war, and an attempt to secure a stronger version from the UN Security Council failed. The United States would have to go it alone, or at least with such allies as were prepared to stand by it. But it would be a "cakewalk."[6]

On March 19, 2003, the United States launched its war against the Saddam regime. Within three weeks of "shock and awe," in Rumsfeld's phrase, Saddam had fallen. On May 1 Bush landed on the USS *Abraham Lincoln* in battle dress and declared Mission Accomplished, associating "the images of celebrating Iraqis" with "the ageless appeal of human freedom." As in Afghanistan, the American military had quickly demonstrated its dazzling power. The initial celebrations in Baghdad and elsewhere, however, were soon followed by disenchantment among Iraqis who watched their country descend into anarchy. The relatively small American and British forces were enough to topple Saddam but not enough to maintain security in the aftermath. More US troops were soon on their way to Iraq, and they would remain there unhappily for years. Unhappily for the White House too, the weapons of mass destruction that had provided the rationale for the allied invasion could not be found, and it increasingly appeared that Saddam had previously abandoned their development. Further, no evidence of links between the Saddam regime and al Qaeda was uncovered – experts had regularly testified to the mutual hostility between the two – though as Iraq degenerated into chaos al Qaeda sympathizers established a presence there.[7]

Domestically the War on Terror had its repercussions too. It allowed the administration to advance claims for extending executive power, and often to act on the assumption that the president held ultimate authority in the polity. Just six weeks after 9/11 the Patriot Act enhanced the power of federal agencies to search telephone and e-mail communications, financial and other records, and made immigrants more readily subject to detention and deportation. A major restructuring of American government followed, with the creation of the Department of Homeland Security (DHS), designed "to secure the United States from terrorist threats or attacks" and to respond to national disasters; it became the third largest cabinet department.

The War on Terror, with its consequent wars in Afghanistan and Iraq, became the defining mission of the Bush administration, and, together with the exalted expectations of the Bush Doctrine, provoked huge controversy. One escalating cottage industry was a debate among academics and political commentators about the nature of American power in a world in which the Soviet Union had disappeared and Japan and the European community were not the economic powerhouses once promised. As one author rhetorically asked, "what word other than empire better described this extensive system that was the American international order with its host of dependent allies, its vast intelligence networks, its five global military commands, its more than 1 million men- and women-at-arms on five continents, its carrier battle groups on watch in every ocean, and its 30 percent control of the world's economic product?" Whether "empire" was the appropriate term may be debated, but it caught something of the grandiose ambitions of the Bush White House, which put little reliance on social engineering policies at home but which apparently expected to deliver democracy and free enterprise elsewhere. Could the other "rogue" states be in line for similar attention as Iraq? As one senior Bush adviser reportedly put it, arguing that the administration was no longer part of "the reality-based community": "We're an empire now, and when we act we create our own reality. And while you're studying that reality ... we'll act again, creating other new realities, ... and that's how things will sort out." Spreading democratic government across the globe, if necessary with military means, it seemed, would end the terrorist threat and make possible a peaceful world order. As political scientist Tony Smith has commented, the neoconservative vision owed something to the liberal intellectuals of the 1990s who had promoted the "enlargement of market democracies."[8]

The domestic policies of the Bush White House also bore a distinctly right-wing imprint. The circumstances of George W. Bush's election to the presidency had hardly given him a mandate, and political correspondents had speculated that he would be obliged to govern from the center. But congressional leaders like Tom DeLay saw things differently: "We have the House, we have the Senate, we have the White House, which means we have the agenda" (command of the Senate depended on the casting vote of the vice president). That agenda largely prevailed. While the appointment of such moderate Republicans as Paul O'Neill at the Treasury and Christine Todd Whitman at the Environmental Protection Agency suggested some willingness to accommodate, it soon became clear that primary influence lay with figures like Vice President Cheney, Defense Secretary Rumsfeld, and Karl Rove, the President's Senior Adviser and right-wing political strategist, later dubbed "Bush's Brain." Within days of taking office Bush signed an order banning federal funds to international planning groups that supported abortion, and he subsequently prohibited the use of federal funds for human stem cell research. Like Reagan, he appointed right-wingers to the federal bureaucracy, and in due course would nominate judicial conservatives to the Supreme Court. Not exactly an ideologue himself, having previously pitched to the political center with "compassionate conservatism," Bush's instincts seemed close to those of the right-wing conservatives who had despised the patrician leadership of his father. The doctrinaire thrust of the administration was such that after four months Senator Jim Jeffords of Vermont, a moderate Republican, quit the party to become an independent.[9]

Bush's political talent lay in his capacity to appeal both to the religious right and to the economic conservatives who had long constituted the Republican Party backbone. In broad terms, Republican politicians had been moving to the right in recent decades, intensifying a political polarization that paralleled the growing distance between rich and poor. A massive tax cut had become the ruling passion of congressional Republicans, and on the very first day of the new Congress Bush asked for just that. Opinion polls during the 2000 campaign had shown that using the recently emerged budget surplus to bolster Social Security and Medicare attracted about twice as much support as using it to reduce taxes, and an internal memo in the Bush White House itself recognized that the "public prefers spending on things like health care and education" to tax cuts. But within months Bush had secured the largest tax cut in postwar history.[10]

One element was a rebate to taxpayers, but the greater part of the 2001 act focused on income tax reductions, mostly in the form of rate cuts that would progressively be phased in. An analysis by Citizens for Tax Justice (CTJ) found that 63 percent of the cuts would go to the richest 20 percent of Americans. "Congress has given the President what he truly cared about – gigantic tax cuts for the rich," said CTJ director Robert S. McIntyre. There was one element of caution, inserted largely at the instance of Secretary Treasury Paul O'Neill, who had old-fashioned hankerings for a balanced budget, and this was a proviso that the tax cuts would lapse after 10 years. But the White House was not finished yet. The coming years would see further cuts, attempts to make them permanent, and the sacking of unhelpful Secretary O'Neill. Although the budget deficit had returned with a vengeance, a 2003 measure was the third largest tax cut in American history.

Even then the Republicans were not satisfied. "This ain't the end of it," warned House Majority Leader Tom DeLay, "– we're coming back for more." And more there was, in tax bills of 2004 and 2005, despite the expensive wars in Afghanistan and Iraq. "It's class warfare, my class is winning, but they shouldn't be," said billionaire Warren Buffet. To its critics, the Bush administration seemed more interested in pleasing its business contributors and ideological activists than in serving the national interest, and the public had reservations too. An opinion poll in November 2004 found that reducing the deficit was rated as a higher priority than tax cuts by a two-to-one margin. Inheriting a handsome budget surplus of $124.5 billion, as early as 2004 Bush was carrying a deficit of $374.7 billion. A generation before, mainstream Republicans would have been aghast at such apparent fiscal recklessness.[11]

"Reagan proved deficits don't matter," Vice President Cheney once remarked to Paul O'Neill. Such insouciance may explain why a conservative administration was so prepared to spend money that commentators began to speak of "Big Government Republicanism." As during his father's term, federal spending was on the rise during George W. Bush's presidency, not all of it war-related. During the 2000 campaign Bush had presented himself as a "compassionate conservative," partly to distance himself from the abrasive Gingrich model, and in that mode had committed the party, which not long since had proposed to abolish the Department of Education, "to bold reforms in education – to make every school a place of learning and achievement for every child." American higher education was arguably the best in the world, but for decades the elementary and secondary school system had been a source of grave concern, and conservatives as well as liberals acknowledged its importance in the creation of a civilized society, not to mention a productive economy in a competitive world. Three days after taking office Bush submitted his plan to Congress, and with inputs from such liberals as Senator Edward Kennedy, it passed in December by large majorities in both houses. Based on the principle of setting high standards for schooling, No Child Left Behind obliged states to assess the basic skills of their pupils in order to secure federal funding. The Department of Education's budget increased by a third in four years. Not all educators appreciated the program. "The federal Department of Education is obsessed with regulations," complained an Indiana school superintendent in 2004 as she waded through the directives from Washington. "They are trying to micromanage us – and it is driving us crazy." This was hardly "getting government off the backs of the people," as Reagan had once promised.[12]

Also pushing out the boundaries of federal responsibility was a major new health measure enacted in 2003, designed to subsidize prescription drugs for senior citizens, said to be "the most expensive new federal program since the 1960s." Conservatives worried about the costs and liberals were critical of the design, which contained an element of privatization as private firms were used instead of traditional Medicare. The program required people to sign up with plans offered by insurance companies, and in turn, it was alleged, drug companies would be able to charge premium prices. Economist Paul Krugman dismissed it as a "drug bill written by and for lobbyists," but it went into effect in 2006 amid concern about the potential costs to a federal government already running a large deficit.[13]

In other areas too, such as in banking and utility regulation, authority was tending to shift from state to federal level, partly because with the growth of national and international markets some businessmen considered national standards preferable to a patchwork of state rules, and that Republican regulation would be less onerous than anything devised by a Democratic administration. At the same time the administration continued the process of "hollowing out," outsourcing many government functions to private companies. The Clinton administration had begun to use the private sector for federal information technology, but the practice intensified after 9/11 and by 2004 the US government was outsourcing 83 percent of its IT work. The defense giant Lockheed, for example, through its massive computer expertise, acquired roles in producing Social Security checks, counting the census, and tracking child support. In Iraq, companies like Blackwater and Halliburton were contracted to carry out functions that would previously have been the responsibility of the military. The number of federal contractors jumped from an estimated 4.4 million in 1999 to 7.5 million in 2005. The Republican version of "big government," at once expanded but hollowed out, often seemed to critics to consist of handing over responsibility and public money to private firms.[14]

Social conservatives too had their own reasons for encouraging big government. George Bush pleased his religious right by giving his support to a constitutional ban on gay marriage. Evangelicals had not turned out markedly for him in 2000, but they did so in 2004. Early in 2005 the case of Terri Schiavo flared into national consciousness, centered on a brain-damaged patient, judged by doctors to be in a permanent vegetative state, whose husband had wanted her feeding tube removed. Schiavo's parents and right-to-life groups vigorously contested this, and when the Florida courts failed to rule in their favor congressional Republicans rushed through a bill attempting to make the case a federal responsibility, duly signed by Bush. In the event, the US Supreme Court allowed the state decision to stand and Schiavo died as her husband wished. Public opinion was with him, an ABC Poll finding that 60 percent opposed the new law while 70 percent thought it inappropriate for Congress to get involved.[15]

There was no real chance of a constitutional amendment to ban gay marriage, and in the Schiavo case too the administration was rebuffed. After 2002 the Republicans had majorities in both houses of Congress, but governing became no easier. On some of the major issues of the day gridlock remained the norm, the product of party polarization in national politics and the paralyzing impact of competing interest groups.

On the environment the Bush White House was able to wave its Reaganite credentials, though it also soon encountered an impasse. Bush had committed himself to boosting domestic oil and gas production and opening the Arctic National Wildlife Refuge (ANWR) to oil exploration. Although he appointed Christine Todd Whitman, a moderately environmentally inclined governor of New Jersey, as EPA administrator, the general thrust of his policy, abetted by the conservative Republicans in Congress, was to narrow the kind of protective policies pursued by the Clinton administration. Like O'Neill, Whitman did not last long and was replaced in 2003, and conservatives suspicious of green causes were placed in other environmental positions.

Just two months into his presidency Bush rejected the Kyoto Protocol. Bush, who had rarely traveled abroad before he became president, later confessed to being "surprised" when lectured on global warming at his first meeting with European Union leaders. The White House held that the Kyoto accord imposed unreasonable costs on the American economy and should not have excused developing countries from measures to contain their own emissions. It also questioned the science of global warming, though in 2002 seemed to concede the reality of climate change while insisting that it was "a long-term problem," to which the answer was new technology rather than Kyoto-style reduction programs. "We want no part of that," said an administration spokesman of the Kyoto discussions that were to resume in 2005. A brouhaha erupted in 2004 when leading scientists complained that the Bush administration cherry-picked science to suit its policy agenda. News leaked of a report commissioned by the Pentagon and apparently suppressed by the White House that warned of the catastrophic consequences of global warming, which "should be elevated beyond a scientific debate to a US national security concern." On climate change, as on some other issues, administration policy seemed more closely aligned with conservative activists than with public opinion.[16]

Instead, climate change was subordinated to energy policy, and one of the president's first decisions was to create a task force, headed by Vice President Cheney, to produce a national energy plan. After consultation with representatives of the oil and other fossil fuel companies, the Cheney group quickly issued a report putting its faith in increasing the supply of fossil fuels; little was said about measures to reduce demand for fuel and nothing about global warming. It met a cool reception, deepened by suspicions of the role of oil companies in framing it and by a proposal to open ANWR to drilling. That bill stalled, though an energy act was eventually passed in 2005, by which time the ANWR and other controversial proposals had been dropped. It authorized a range of subsidies for "clean coal technology," new nuclear power plants, and hybrid vehicles, though did not tighten motor vehicle efficiency standards and failed to require reductions in greenhouse gases. Democratic Congressman Edward Markey called the act a "moral and political failure because it's what's not in this bill that was important." Overall, on the legislative front, as in the 1990s, gridlock tended to obtain, with neither the environmentalists nor the business lobbies securing major victories but each often managing to frustrate the ambitions of the other.[17]

With the federal government slow to respond to environmental concerns, several states accepted responsibility. Among the leaders was California, even before Governor Arnold Schwarzenegger began to take an interest. In the United States as a whole, per capita electricity use increased by nearly 50 percent in the 30 years from 1975; in California it remained roughly constant. In 2001 the six New England states joined with a number of eastern Canadian provinces in an agreement to reduce their regional greenhouse gas emissions to 1990 levels by 2010. In 2002 California enacted the first carbon dioxide emissions standards for motor vehicles in North America and 10 other states followed suit. By 2006 over half of the states had enacted climate legislation or issued executive orders setting formal requirements for reducing greenhouse gases. Nonetheless, action at this level was variable, and several states adopted laws blocking action on climate change.[18]

The formulation of a coherent policy on immigration also proved impossible. In most years of the 2000s over a million newcomers arrived, an annual volume that had been exceeded only twice in the 1990s. Mexico, as usual, supplied much the greatest number, though a sign of the times was the large number from Asia. In 2008, for example, second and third place went to China and India respectively, reflecting not only their large populations but also the intensifying connections between them and the

United States in a globalized age. And, despite the Iraq war, Muslim immigration rose after the hiatus occasioned by 9/11. In 2005 nearly 96 000 people from Muslim countries were admitted, from Indonesia, Egypt, Pakistan, and elsewhere, more than in any year in the previous two decades. The number of undocumented aliens also continued to grow, and again became the source of public discord. As they spread into regions of the South and Midwest that had not previously encountered them on a large scale, and partly because 9/11 heightened worries about just who might be crossing American borders, the issue of immigration was being more fully thrust from a regional to a national concern.

The legislation of 2000, with its emphasis on the need for highly skilled immigrants, had not been welcomed by those wanting a stricter policy, though the 9/11 attacks strengthened their hand by thrusting national security up the political agenda. Controls at the nation's airports and land borders were tightened, though not enough to satisfy everyone. The 2001 Patriot Act, despite civil libertarian criticisms that it demonized some kinds of immigrants, did not even result in greater numbers of aliens being deported.

The immigrant flood deepened divisions in both the major political parties, but most destructively among Republicans. George Bush, consistent with his earlier strategy of trying to build some support for his party among Hispanics, favored giving legal status to undocumented farm workers, and others advanced variations on what were known as guest worker proposals, which often allowed such workers in due course access to permanent residency and even citizenship. The US Chamber of Commerce, the Catholic Church, and some labor groups, as well as free market conservatives, supported the guest worker idea, which would at least address the reality that millions of undocumented workers were already entrenched in the workforce. Conservative Republicans in the House of Representatives, however, fiercely resisted any proposals that looked like affording amnesty to illegal immigrants, and, in the atmosphere of heightened concern about border security, they demanded much more stringent legislation, including making illegal residency a criminal rather than a civil offence. In 2006 a bill containing a felony provision triggered large street rallies, including a huge protest in Los Angeles variously estimated at between 500 000 and one million people. Bush went on television in May 2006 for the first time on a domestic issue to call for a temporary worker program and a path to citizenship, while also promising much stricter border controls. His proposals were not well received by Republican conservatives, and fractious congressional debates continued through the year. With liberals and conservatives deadlocked in Congress over comprehensive reform, all that was secured was a law strengthening the policing of the US–Mexican border, more or less a repeat outcome to that which had resolved a similar impasse a decade earlier. In 2007 another reform bill succumbed to the opposition of two-thirds of the Senate Republicans. Amidst the infighting of interest groups and the differing calculations of elected politicians, consensus on immigration policy was as elusive as ever. The immigrant was still stereotyped as needy and problematic, though a report in 2010 found that in 14 of the country's 25 largest metropolitan areas, more immigrants were employed in white-collar occupations such as lawyers, executives, and administrators than in low-pay jobs like cleaners and laborers.[19]

But on his flagship domestic policy, tax cuts, George Bush was repeatedly successful, and in 2004, when he was seeking re-election, his War on Terror still commanded patriotic support. After 9/11 Bush had discovered his calling as a war leader, a mantle he confidently donned for the campaign, when he insisted that American security was still at stake and contrasted his decisiveness with his opponent's "flip-flops." His opponent was Senator John Kerry of Massachusetts, who had voted in favor of the Iraq war, though subsequently, when no WMDs were found, had criticized Bush for misleading the country: "When the president of the United States looks at you and tells you something, there should be some trust." Bush was re-elected with 50.7 percent of the popular vote, against 48.3 percent for Kerry, the narrowest incumbent victory of modern times.[20]

Bush voters, according to an exit poll, cited the issues of "terrorism" and "moral values" as their most important considerations, and when asked which quality in the president mattered to them most, 91 percent cited his "strong religious faith." Some pundits predicted that cultural values on such issues as abortion and gay rights would now become the dominant theme of American politics. In recent elections, strongly religious Americans, Catholic as well as Protestant, had tended to vote Republican, while the more secular-minded on balance preferred the Democrats, who seem to have picked up some votes from those reacting against the religious right. But culture wars did not dominate the rest of the decade, quickly returning to their customary place on the political margins. The primarily economic structuring of American politics, with the higher-income groups tending to vote Republican and the lower-income groups the converse, remained intact.[21]

Bush himself had ambitions for his second term: "I earned capital in the campaign, political capital, and now, I intend to spend it." One ambition was the reform of Social Security through partial privatization, an idea conservatives had nurtured for decades. Employees would be able to set aside part of their payroll taxes in individual accounts that could be invested in the private sector, which, Bush claimed, would give them better returns than the public program. Critics feared the proposal was a first step toward the dismantling of Social Security, suspicions that were not allayed by the "town meetings" that the White House called to promote the plan, at one of which conservative students chanted "Hey hey, ho ho, Social Security has got to go." Labor and liberal groups and the big pensioners' organization, the American Association of Retired Persons, mobilized extensive opposition, and many congressional Republicans too proved wary. Congress dragged its feet on the idea in 2005–2006, and Democratic success in the mid-term elections doomed it.[22]

By this date the Bush administration had been seriously weakened by its response to Hurricane Katrina, which hit New Orleans and neighboring areas in August 2005. "Tonight," reported CNN on August 29, "more than a million people … are without power, roads flooded, trees down, houses waterlogged, lives changed forever." Worse was to come, as the rising waters crashed through the levee system of New Orleans, flooding 80 percent of the city. Over 1800 people lost their lives in what the Louisiana governor called "the single largest natural disaster in the history of the United States" (though this was not true in terms of lives lost). Before the storm arrived a mandatory evacuation order had been issued for New Orleans, but most public transport had stopped and many simply could not escape, some 26 000 eventually taking shelter in the Superdome. Over a million people from the Gulf area did seek refuge elsewhere, and for days television pictures vividly conveyed scenes of the homeless and stranded, often in desperate need of food and medicine, waiting pathetically as the authorities struggled with the disaster. Troops sporting guns rather than provisions seemed to be first on the scene. Bush addressed the nation on August 31, in what the *New York Times* described as "one of the worst speeches of his life," compounded the impression of an uncomprehending Washington by failing to hasten to the region, and was then filmed bemusedly looking down on it from the safety of a plane. In the months that followed immense criticism was directed at the authorities both for failing to ensure that New Orleans was adequately protected in the first place and then for the inadequacy and slowness of the response – slower, it was charged, than for some Third World disasters. Cynics connected the apparent lethargy of the authorities with the fact that the city's residents were mostly poor and black. Six months after the hurricane the population of New Orleans was less than half what it had been, and three years later was still down by over a quarter. This was hardly the finest hour of Bush's vaunted DHS, and particularly of its Federal Emergency Management Agency, whose head resigned in September. The fragility of civilized society had been unnervingly exposed. A century earlier, when Galveston was devastated by a flood, charitable relief was rushed to the area and great expectation was not placed on the federal authorities, but, despite the Reaganite turn against government, responsibility was now assumed to lie with Washington. The Bush administration never shook itself free of the pall left by Katrina.[23]

The kind of catastrophe represented by Hurricane Katrina had been predicted by some environmentalists, and the event both sparked popular speculation and intensified scientific research about the relationship with climate change. The 2005 hurricane season was the busiest on record. "Is Global Warming Fueling Katrina?," asked a *Time* magazine article just after the hurricane hit. The debate carried on inconclusively for years, although some scientific evidence suggested that the world faced fewer but stronger hurricanes.[24]

In mid-October 2005 the mood of the country was at its lowest ebb since early 1996, only 31 percent saying they were "satisfied" with "the way things were going" in Gallup's regular poll, with 66 percent dissatisfied. The public mood remained sour for the rest of Bush's term, the "dissatisfieds" reaching 72 percent in May 2006. Bush's presidential approval ratings, which had shot up in the aftermath of 9/11, had generally been on a declining trajectory since 2002, and in October 2006, as the mid-term elections loomed, they were down to 37 percent. Most Democrats had supported the war in Iraq in the patriotic temper of 2003, but by 2006 opinion polls showed that where three-quarters of Republicans still supported it, about the same proportion of Democrats did not. In an unusually high turnout for mid-term elections, the Democrats wrested control of the House of Representatives, and with the help of two Independents also won control of the Senate, as well as a majority of state governorships and legislatures. The neoconservative aspiration to world hegemony had effectively been rejected by the electorate. Donald Rumsfeld resigned as Secretary of Defense. After the election, when American respondents were asked "to name a famous person to be the biggest villain of the year," Bush headed the poll with 25 percent of returns, well ahead of Osama bin Laden in second place. (Bush was also "the biggest hero of the year" with 13 percent.)[25]

Damaging the administration party in addition to the war news was a series of political scandals in which leading Republicans were implicated.

Most serious was the affair surrounding Jack Abramoff, a top lobbyist, who was charged with major fraud and with trading expensive gifts in exchange for political favors, and the investigations not only led to his conviction but also to the implication of White House and congressional aides and a congressman. Earlier the House Majority Leader, Tom DeLay, had been obliged to step down after being charged with violating campaign finance laws. The Democrats charged that there was a "culture of corruption" in Washington, centered on the lobbyists with their offices in K Street and their links with mainly Republican members of Congress and their aides.[26]

The wars in Afghanistan and Iraq, where it had proved easier to overthrow the existing regimes than to create stable governments, were not going well. The Americans and their allies had become "invaders" rather than "liberators." The White House had laughed off warnings that the invasion of Iraq could result in a Vietnam-style quagmire, but three years on sectarian violence was intensifying and the number of insurgent attacks on coalition forces was reaching record levels. In December 2006 the Iraq Study Group, composed of leading figures from both major parties, reported that American forces in Iraq "seem to be caught in a mission that has no foreseeable end." Afghanistan too remained in turmoil, while terrorist attacks associated with al Qaeda or other radical Islamic groups were being experienced by other countries, including the bombing of a Manila ferry and Madrid commuter trains in 2004, the London underground in 2005, and Mumbai trains in 2006. The War on Terror, critics charged, was actually provoking greater terror. The august defense think tank the Rand Corporation testified before Congress in 2008 that while the US military might assist in state building, it "should generally resist being drawn into combat operations in Muslim countries where its presence is likely to increase terrorist recruitment."[27]

Further corroding the administration's position were reports of the physical and sexual abuse of Iraqi prisoners by US personnel, allegations that torture was being used against terror suspects, and questions about the treatment of prisoners at Guantánamo Bay, the US military base on Cuba. The Guantánamo inmates, decided the US Supreme Court in 2006, were protected by the Geneva Conventions and could not be detained permanently without trial. Some members of the administration implied that the War on Terror could not be fought with kid gloves, an attitude that seemed to be manifest in *24*, a popular TV show that ran through the decade, in which agent Jack Bauer was periodically seen brutally extracting information from the bad guys, so much so that in 2006 uneasy West Point officials asked the producers to tone down this aspect.

The performance of the economy was also less than reassuring. There had been good if unspectacular growth since 2003, which Bush was happy to attribute to his successive tax cuts, and certainly the budget deficit, which is to say federal spending, contributed to it. There was significant productivity growth too. One mark of the expansive times was the phenomenal increase in the number of millionaires, from 1 800 000 in 1997 to 7 500 000 in 2005. But the benefits from the productivity gains were not distributed downward. Job growth had remained very weak, too weak to improve the living standards of most workers. Further, the proportion of men in "good jobs," that is, those paying at least the median wage and offering health insurance and a retirement plan, fell fairly sharply from 31.6 percent in 2000 to 27.2 percent in 2006. If income inequality had stabilized in the late Clinton years, it resumed its widening course during the Bush presidency. The greater the distance between the income classes, it seemed, the greater the difficulty of climbing them. Studies in 2006 found that there was less upward mobility in the United States than in seven European countries. The poverty rate was increasing again, and as usual it was the poorly educated, the low-paid, and Hispanics and African Americans who were most at risk. The low levels of health insurance among such groups contributed, for example, to the high US mortality rate among women giving birth, which had doubled since 1987 and was higher than in 40 other countries in 2006. The erosion in the economic security of middle- and low-income Americans and vulnerable ethnic groups was seen by some as continuing evidence of the impact of competition from low-wage countries and other global forces. Americans were still "growing apart." The trade figures did tell a worrying story. The trade deficit was hitting a new record, reaching over 6.0 percent of GDP in 2005–2007, much higher than under Reagan. With a gargantuan budget deficit too, as in the Reagan years the twin deficits were largely financed by foreigners. By early 2005, it was estimated, it was Asian central banks in particular, led by the People's Bank of China, that were financing at least 75 percent of the American current account (or balance of payments). Historian Niall Ferguson remarked that "the People's Republic of China has become banker to the United States of America." Former Treasury Secretary Larry Summers referred to the US relationship with East Asia as "the balance of financial terror."[28]

In the event it was not a push from abroad but an internal crisis that exposed the vulnerability of the American economy. In Bush's last year as president the financial system of the United States, indeed of the world, faced meltdown. The trigger was the collapse of the subprime mortgage market in August 2007. As financial regulation had loosened in the late twentieth century, and with interest rates low, a housing boom had taken off, in turn sustaining a boom in consumption as people borrowed against the value of their homes. It was further accelerated by the selling of risky mortgages, often unscrupulously, to people with low incomes, toward which the authorities took a relaxed attitude. Checks on borrowers were often minimal, and such "subprime" mortgages as a proportion of all mortgages jumped from 10 percent in 2001 to 29 percent in 2006. Home ownership by ethnic and racial minorities increased by over 3 million between 2002 and 2007, in significant part financed by subprimes; in 2006, for example, close to half the loans given to African Americans and Hispanics were subprime, over twice the rate for whites. When interest rates rose again many new homeowners could not meet their obligations. But in the meantime, with housing and the economy booming, investment bankers had bought up these mortgages and repackaged them together into financial products that could be sold on the world market as securities – securities that were as "safe as houses." Such "securitization," many believed, meant that risk was spread. By 2007 over half of the US mortgage market had been securitized. The great Wall Street firms made huge profits from these deals, and they sought to capitalize on the good times by running up much more debt. Yet these firms and others were now intimately interconnected. When mortgage holders began defaulting, the banks rather suddenly found themselves holding near-worthless securities and quickly reined in their own lending. The "credit crunch," as businesses and individuals were unable to secure loans, in turn impacted on the equity markets, and stock prices fell. By the end of 2007 the United States was entering a recession, one that was to prove longer than any since the Great Depression. "The wheelings and dealings of the mortgage industry in the United States will be remembered as the great scam of the early twenty-first century," said Nobel Prize-winning economist Joseph Stiglitz.[29]

Major financial institutions began to fail, a critical matter when the financial sector had reached a chunky 20 percent of GDP (it had been 13 percent in 1970). In September 2008 the almost unthinkable happened, when the venerable investment bank, Lehman Brothers, which had been extensively drawn into subprime territory, went bankrupt, the largest bankruptcy in American history. The Dow Jones index dropped by over 500 points on that day. Another investment bank, Merrill Lynch, was rescued by a takeover by the Bank of America, and other financial institutions too had to scramble to survive. The Bush administration in principle was committed to the doctrine of free markets, but the financial hurricane cowed it, and the US Treasury acted to avert further slaughter. It nationalized

Freddie Mae and Fannie Mae, mortgage giants that it had long effectively guaranteed. In early October 2008 the White House secured enactment of the Troubled Assets Recovery Program, through which the Treasury would take over up to $700 billion of mortgage-related assets, though a little later diverted up to $250 billion directly into bank equity. This was what Stiglitz called the "Great American Robbery," which had its critics on both the right and the left, the former because it contravened free market doctrines, the latter because it protected corporations rather than individuals.[30]

While these measures averted total financial meltdown, they could not of themselves secure economic recovery, which seemed to become ever more remote as banks remained reluctant to lend. Between September 2008 and June 2009 unemployment jumped from 6.2 to 9.5 percent, the equivalent of five million jobs. The US Treasury had adopted the reverse of policies it had urged on developing countries when they had confronted crises. "Struggling to contain the crisis," one analyst has written, "it had stumbled into the most sweeping extension of state intervention in the economy since the 1930s." The free market model was not self-correcting after all. "I found a flaw," admitted a humbled Alan Greenspan of the philosophy he had long personified.[31]

As was inevitable in a globalized economy, the collapse that began in the United States spread to other countries. By 2010 some 170 million people around the world were estimated to have lost their jobs, and governments were busily shifting the burden to their taxpayers in the form of higher taxes and poorer public services, the victims, it could be said, of the greed that had driven the money markets to their excesses.

It was thus the economy that dominated the 2008 presidential election. The Democratic Party, in a remarkable choice, nominated a young African American as their candidate, the first-term Senator from Illinois, Barack Obama, a graduate of Harvard Law School, law professor and civil rights lawyer who had embarked on a political career in the mid-1990s. In securing the nomination he had defeated the formidable Hillary Clinton, transformed from First Lady to Senator from New York, who aspired to be the first woman president. Literate, reflective, and highly articulate, Obama was no radical and clearly found the savagely partisan character of American politics highly distasteful; "let us reason together" was his philosophy. His Republican opponent was John McCain, an Arizona senator since 1986, once a naval hero and prisoner of war in Vietnam. Now rather elderly, he was generally associated with conservative positions, though he liked to see himself as a maverick. Another "maverick" was his running mate, Governor Sarah Palin of Alaska, a sassy "hockey mom" and social conservative if unreliable campaigner. With Obama personifying "change" and McCain emphasizing "experience," the dominant issue at first was the increasingly unpopular Iraq war, which Obama had opposed and which McCain supported. For much of the campaign the polls were relatively close, some of them putting Obama and McCain neck-and-neck, but as the economy plummeted that fall the advantage shifted decisively to the Democrat. Obama won with 53 percent of the popular vote, against 46 percent for McCain; even the southern states of Virginia, North Carolina, and Florida voted for the parvenu black Yankee.

For many people, both in the United States and abroad, the overriding historic significance of the election was that it showed that an African American could be president. Few men, however, had become president at a more fearful moment in the nation's history, with war in Afghanistan and Iraq and a collapsing economy. It remained to be seen whether President Obama could lead a country which, with its host of powerful and competing interest groups, intensely partisan politics and frustrating institutional constraints, seemed to some political commentators to be all but ungovernable.

* * *

The mood of the country was low at the end of the decade. In March 2010 Gallup reported that 79 percent of Americans were "dissatisfied with the way things are going," with only 19 percent pronouncing themselves "satisfied," figures very similar to those found during the episodes of malaise at the end of the 1970s and in the early 1990s. The Pew Research Center reported that trust in government was "among the lowest measures in half a century." Long since gone were the optimism and confidence reported in the early 1960s. There was no single reason for this declining public faith, though in the past such episodes as Watergate and Iran–Contra had helped undermine trust in politicians, and more recently the unhappy course of the war in Iraq and the unnerving banking crisis had both soured the public mood and increased frustration with Washington. The broader experiences of the United States since about 1980 had also left their mark. Americans had long been raised to be wary of government, but the limitations of government were more fully exposed in a globalized world. Washington struggled to provide opportunity and security for the members of society most vulnerable to the impact of international competition, and it was no closer to "regaining control of American borders" than it had been three decades earlier. Governments around the world did urgently confer as crises confronted the globe, but as of early 2010 had been unable to reach agreement on the regulation of international finance and on combating global warming. Individual governments protected their own national interests first, while the American system of politics, with its combative style heightened by the 24-hour news cycle, seemed more adept at magnifying problems than in finding solutions.[32]

Ronald Reagan in 1980 had wanted to restore American authority by revitalizing the nation's economy and rebuilding its military. His free market prescriptions and his political success had been seductive enough to persuade his Democratic rivals to adopt aspects of his neoliberal policies, but they had not taken government "off the backs of the people." In 2008 federal outlays represented 20.7 percent of GDP, hardly a dramatic improvement on the 21.7 percent of 1980, and the figure would rise as the financial crisis deepened. Of course, the United States was a military colossus, even if its venture into global hegemony had gone badly awry, and its economy was the world's largest. Its technology was awesome, its top universities were the world's best, and its remarkable capacity to innovate was a legendary resource. The country's future could not be safely foretold. Yet the United States was not autonomous, the globalizing processes of the previous decades having moved it a long way from the relative self-sufficiency of the mid-twentieth-century "golden age." "We are running up obligations to the rest of the world, and they are buying our assets at the rate of almost $2 billion a day," warned Warren Buffet in 2005: "And that will have consequences." A poll taken in November 2009 found that 44 percent of Americans regarded China as the world's top economic power, with only 27 percent placing their own country first. Power tends to follow money. A near bankrupt and dependent country is unlikely to provide a model for others, some pundits argued, whether in its economy, its culture, its folkways, its whole "way of life." The capacity to lead seeps away when the wealth goes. But whether the United States really is facing "the end of influence" remains to be seen.[33]

Notes

The notes are used mainly to identify the sources of quotations and of relatively inaccessible statistical and other data. The Select Bibliography that follows indicates the main sources from which background material was gleaned. The Public Papers of the Presidents can be consulted online by accessing the American Presidency Project or individual presidential libraries. Much official statistical data can also be consulted online, such as through the Bureau of Economic Analysis of the US Department of Commerce, and the annual *Economic Report of the President*; much poll material can be similarly accessed, e.g. at Gallup Brain. Many newspapers and journals are also available online, and the major think tanks provide material on their own websites.

Abbreviations

NYT   *New York Times*
PP   *Public Papers of the Presidents*
WP   *Washington Post*
WSJ   *Wall Street Journal*
CQWR   *Congressional Quarterly Weekly Report*

Chapter 1   Losing Control: The United States in 1980

1   G.H. Gallup, *The Gallup Poll, 1979* (Wilmington, 1980), 1, 100, 220; *Business Week*, March 12, 1979, 36–42; R.M. Collins, *Transforming America* (New York, 2007), 14; J.R Greene, *The Presidency of George Bush* (Lawrence, 2000), 3.
2   J. Updike, *Rabbit Is Rich* (London, 2006), 1.
3   G. Lundestad, "'Empire by Invitation' in the American Century," *Diplomatic History*, 23 (Spring 1999), 194.

Contemporary America: Power, Dependency, and Globalization since 1980,
First Edition. M.J. Heale.
© 2011 M.J. Heale. Published 2011 by Blackwell Publishing Ltd.

4   J.K. Galbraith, *The Affluent Society* (Boston, 1958); D.M. Potter, *People of Plenty* (Chicago, 1954); D. Riesman, *The Lonely Crowd* (New Haven, 1950); G. Hodgson, *America in Our Time* (Garden City NY, 1976).

5   M.D. Lassiter, *The Silent Majority* (Princeton, 2006), 3; J. Garreau, *Edge City* (New York, 1991), 5, 8; G. Hodgson, *The World Turned Right Side Up* (Boston, 1996), 58.

6   L. Cohen, *A Consumers' Republic* (New York, 2003), 202.

7   M.B. Katz, *Improving the Poor* (Princeton, 1995), 64.

8   A.M. Schlesinger, *The Disuniting of America* (New York, 1992), 41.

9   T.H. White, *America in Search of Itself* (London, 1983), 154; J. Dumbrell, *The Carter Presidency* (Manchester, 1993), 3; A. Greenspan, *The Age of Turbulence* (London, 2008), 84; T.B. Edsall, "The Battle of the Budget," *The Nation*, May 10, 1980, 551.

10   J. Hogan, "Back to the 1970s," in Hogan, ed., *The Reagan Years* (Manchester, 1990), 14.

11   S.M. Lipset, *American Exceptionalism* (New York, 1996), 282.

12   M. Fiorina, *Congress*, 2nd edn (New Haven, 1989), 164–165.

13   "Congressional Democrats Beware," *National Journal*, August 9, 1980, 1304–1308; T.B. Clark, "After a Decade of Doing Battle, Public Interest Groups Show Their Age," *National Journal*, July 12, 1980, 1136–1141; J.M. Berry, *The New Liberalism* (Washington, 1999), 20.

14   S.R. Diamond, *Roads to Dominion* (New York, 1995), 205; S. Blumenthal, *The Rise of the Counter-Establishment* (New York, 1986), xiii; D.P. Moynihan, *Came the Revolution* (San Diego, 1988), 17.

15   J.B. Judis, "Beyond McPopulism," *American Prospect*, June 23, 1993.

16   C.O. Jones, *The Trusteeship Presidency: Jimmy Carter and the United States Congress* (Baton Rouge, 1988), 10, 16; M. Schaller, *Right Turn: American Life in the Reagan–Bush Era, 1980–1992* (New York, 2007), 24.

17   Jones, *Trusteeship Presidency*, 151.

18   Hodgson, *World Turned Right Side Up*, 229.

19   Hodgson, *World Turned Right Side Up*, 217; P. Jenkins, *Decade of Nightmares* (New York, 2006), 155.

20   J.A. Califano, Jr., *Governing America: An Insider's Report from the White House and the Cabinet* (New York, 1981), 124.

21   M.P. Leffler, *For the Soul of Mankind* (New York, 2007), 301; M. McAlister, *Epic Encounters* (Berkeley, 2001), 202.

22   Leffler, *For the Soul of Mankind*, 332, 335.

23   H. Jordan, *Crisis: The Last Year of the Carter Presidency* (London, 1982), 64, 362.

24   Jordan, *Crisis*, 60, 313.

25   "Now We Begin," *The Nation*, June 14, 1980, 707.

26   P.A. Klinkner with R.M. Smith, *The Unsteady March* (Chicago, 1999), 300; R.J. Walton, "Now Is the Time," *The Nation*, May 10, 1980, 556.

27   M. Foley, "Presidential Leadership and the Presidency," in Hogan, ed., *The Reagan Years*, 33; N.R. Peirce and J. Hagstrom, "The Voters Send Carter a Message," *National Journal*, November 8, 1980, 1878; E.C. Ladd, "The Brittle Mandate," *Political Science Quarterly*, 96 (Spring 1981), 19; A. Clymer, "The Collapse of a Coalition," *NYT*, November 5, 1980, A1, A18.

28   Peirce and Hagstrom, "The Voters Send Carter a Message," 1878; R. Lingeman, "The Hollow Man," *The Nation*, November 15, 1980, 501.

Chapter 2 Borrowing as a Way of Life: A Dependent Economy and a Fragmenting Society

1 *Economic Report of the President, 1995*, 3, 19.
2 J. Medoff and A. Harless, *The Indebted Society* (Boston, 1996), 213.
3 D.P. Moynihan, *Came the Revolution* (San Diego, 1988), 318; J.E. Garten, "Gunboat Economics," *Foreign Affairs: America and the World 1984*, 546, 548; J.A. Frieden, *Global Capitalism* (New York, 2006), 374.
4 Frieden, *Global Capitalism*, 379; B.M. Friedman, *Day of Reckoning* (London, 1989), 4; R. Brenner, *The Economics of Global Turbulence* (London, 2006), 212; P. Blustein, "Dollar Looms Bigger in the Fed's Decisions," *WSJ*, May 19, 1987, 1; D.K.H. Walters and W.C. Rempel, "Trade War Victim," *Los Angeles Times*, December 1, 1987, 1-1.
5 Medoff and Harless, *Indebted Society*, 13, 14, 29, 33, 143; F. Bergsten, *America in the World Economy* (Washington, 1988), 50; Friedman, *Day of Reckoning*, 29.
6 F. Bergsten, "Economic Imbalances and World Politics," *Foreign Affairs*, 65 (Spring 1987), 770; *Economic Report of the President, 1995*, 299 (trade figures 1987 dollars); S.J. Tolchin, *The Angry American*, 2nd edn (Boulder, 1999), 76.
7 R. Lekachman, "The Crash of 1980," *The Nation*, July 5, 1980, 16; B.R. Barber, *Jihad vs. McWorld* (London, 2003), 36–37.
8 R. Brenner, *The Boom and the Bubble* (London, 2002), 81; R. Reagan, *An American Life* (New York, 1990), 357.
9 M.L. Dertouzos, R.K. Lester, and R.M. Solow, *Made in America* (Cambridge, MA, 1989), 7, 9–10.
10 E.M. Graham and P.R. Krugman, *Foreign Direct Investment in the United States*, 2nd edn (Washington, 1991), 52–53; "For Sale: America," *Time*, September 14, 1987, 30–37; Friedman, *Day of Reckoning*, 67.
11 J. Burgess, "One Town's Foreign Policy," *WP*, June 11, 1989, H1; Graham and Krugman, *Foreign Direct Investment*, 32.
12 R.B. Reich, *The Work of Nations* (New York, 1991), 71; Carter, State of the Union Address, January 23, 1979; Frieden, *Global Capitalism*, 399; J. Ehrman, *The Eighties* (New Haven, 2005), 94–95.
13 S. Strange, *The Casino Society* (London, 1984); A. Bianco, "Playing With Fire," *International Business Week*, September 16, 1985, 54–66.
14 B. Harrison and B. Bluestone, *The Great U-Turn* (New York, 1988), 27; A. Bernstein, "The Global Economy," *International Business Week*, August 10, 1992, 31.
15 M. Elbaum, *Revolution in the Air* (London, 2002), 249.
16 E. Boris and N. Lichtenstein, eds, *Major Problems in the History of American Workers* (Lexington, MA, 1991), 593–594, 598; J. Mazur, "Labor's New Internationalism," *Foreign Affairs*, 79 (January/February 2000), 85.
17 Dertouzos, Lester, and Solow, *Made in America*, 6–7, 11–12, 15–16, 30; A. Glyn, *Capitalism Unleashed* (Oxford, 2007), 81.
18 J.S. Hacker, *The Great Risk Shift* (New York, 2006), 2, 23–24; E.B. Kapstein, "Workers and the World Economy," *Foreign Affairs*, 75 (May/June 1996), 26.
19 L. Mishel, J. Bernstein, and H. Shierholz, *The State of Working America, 2008/2009* (Ithaca, 2009), 149, 233; R. Valletta, "Rising Wage Inequality in the U.S.," Federal Reserve Bank of San Francisco, Economic Letter, 97-25, September 5, 1997; J.

Madrick, *The Case for Big Government* (Princeton, 2009), 90–91, 103, 105–106.

20 Reich, *Work of Nations*, 206; J. Cotton, "Opening the Gap," *Social Science Quarterly*, 70 (December 1989), 803–819; Mishel, Bernstein, and Shierholz, *State of Working America, 2008/2009*, 50, 250; R. Wilkinson and K. Pickett, *The Spirit Level* (London, 2009), 80.

21 *Statistical Abstract of the United States, 1999*, 474; M.W. Horrigan and S.E. Haugen, "The Declining Middle-Class Thesis," *Monthly Labor Review* (May 1988), 3–13; M.C. Daly, "The 'Shrinking' Middle Class?" Federal Reserve Bank of San Francisco, Economic Letter, 97-07, March 7, 1997.

22 L. Mishel, J. Bernstein, and J. Schmitt, *The State of Working America, 1998–99* (Ithaca, 1999), 259; C. Lasch, *The Revolt of the Elites and the Betrayal of Democracy* (New York, 1995), 35, 176; M. Lind, *The Next American Nation* (New York, 1996), 137.

23 K. Phillips, *Boiling Point* (New York, 1993), 48–49, 62; Ehrman, *Eighties*, 120; Mishel, Bernstein, and Shierholz, *State of Working America, 2008/2009*, 220–222; G. Hytrek and K.M. Zentgraf, *American Transformed* (New York, 2008), 83; N. McCarty, K.T. Poole, and H. Rosenthal, *Polarized America* (Cambridge, MA, 2006).

24 Mishel, Bernstein, and Shierholz, *State of Working America, 2008/2009*, 101, 103, 105–106; Wilkinson and Pickett, *Spirit Level*, 160, 162; H.R. Clinton, *Living History* (London, 2004), 98–99.

25 M.P. Leffler, *For the Soul of Mankind* (New York, 2007), 461.

26 S. Ishihara, *The Japan That Can Say No* (New York, 1991), 21; M. Weidenbaum, "Facing Reality in the George Bush Era," *Society*, 26 (March/April 1989), 28; R.D. Hershey, Jr., "Why Economists Fear the Deficit," *NYT*, May 26, 1992, D1; P.G. Peterson, "The Morning After," *Atlantic Monthly* (October 1987).

Chapter 3   Strangers in the Land: Open Borders and American Identity

1   E. Hobsbawm, *Age of Extremes* (London, 1994), 259, 345; P. Kennedy, *Preparing for the Twenty-First Century* (London, 1993), 65–66; S. Castles and M.J. Miller, *The Age of Migration*, 2nd edn (Basingstoke, 1998), 4.

2   *Yearbook of Immigration Statistics: 2004*, 5.

3   P. Loeb, D. Friedman, and M.C. Lord, "To Make a Nation," *U.S. News & World Report*, October 4, 1993, 51.

4   R. Reinhold, "Flow of 3d World Immigrants Alters Weave of U.S. Society," *NYT*, June 30, 1986, A1; P. Loeb, "A Caribbean Community Grows in Brooklyn," *U.S. News & World Report*, October 4, 1993, 53; W. Broyles, "Promise of America," *U.S. News & World Report*, July 7, 1986, 26; L.R. Chavez, *Covering Immigration* (Berkeley, 2001), 139.

5   Reinhold, "Flow of 3d World Immigrants," A1; M. Lind, *The Next American Nation* (New York, 1996), 134; G. Hodgson, *More Equal Than Others* (Princeton, 2004), 117.

6   M.J. Mandel and C. Farrell, "The Immigrants," *International Business Week*, July 13, 1992, 76, 79; G.J. Borjas, *Heaven's Door* (Princeton, 1999), 8, 13; J.P. Smith and Barry Edmonston, eds, *The New American* (Washington, 1997), 4–8, and chs 4 and 5; E. Martinez, *De Colores Means All of Us* (Cambridge, 1998), 9.

7   B.O. Hing, *Defining America Through Immigration Policy* (Philadelphia, 2004), 95; T.H. White, *America in Search of Itself* (London, 1983), 363; C. Shanks, *Immigration and the Politics of American Sovereignty, 1890–1990* (Ann Arbor, 2001), 200.

8   R. Alba and V. Nee, *Remaking the American Mainstream* (Cambridge, MA, 2003), 177; V.M. Briggs, *Mass Immigration and the National Interest*, 2nd edn (Armonk, NY, 1996), 157.

9   D.M. Reimers, *Unwelcome Strangers* (New York, 1998), 80; J. Gibbs, "The Cuban Adjustment Act and Immigration from Cuba," in P. Davies and I. Morgan, eds, *America's Americans* (London, 2007), 295; D. Brinkley, ed., *The Reagan Diaries* (New York, 2007), 20.

10 P.G. Min, ed., *Mass Migration to the United States* (Walnut Creek, CA, 2002), 4; S.P. Huntington, *The Clash of Civilizations and the Remaking of World Order* (London, 2002), 202.

11 R. Daniels, *Coming to America* (New York, 1990), 389; J.G. Gimpel and J.R. Edwards, *The Congressional Politics of Immigration Reform* (Needham Heights, MA, 1999), 135; P.H. Schuck, *Citizens, Strangers, and In-Betweens* (Boulder, CO, 1998), 103.

12 Shanks, *Immigration and the Politics of American Sovereignty*, 209–210; D.G. Gutiérrez, *Walls and Mirrors* (Berkeley, 1995), 210; Reimers, *Unwelcome Strangers*, 37; Center for Immigration Studies website: www.cis.org/.

13 Daniels, *Coming to America*, 381; Shanks, *Immigration and the Politics of American Sovereignty*, 197.

14 Shanks, *Immigration and the Politics of American Sovereignty*, 216.

15 R. Pear, "The Immigration Bill," *NYT*, October 21, 1986, B6; Daniels, *Coming to America*, 391; Gimpel and Edwards, *Congressional Politics*, 137; Susanna McBee, "Foreign Roots on Native Soil," *U.S. News & World Report*, July 7, 1986, 31.

16 Hing, *Defining America*, 104.

17 R.D. Lamm and G. Imhoff, *The Immigrant Time Bomb* (New York, 1985), 49; R. Daniels and O.L. Graham, *Debating American Immigration* (Lanham, MD, 2001), 51, 174; J. Stefancic and R. Delgado, *No Mercy* (Philadelphia, 1996), 11.

18 Lamm and Imhoff, *Immigrant Time Bomb*, 1–2.

19 R. Reinhold, "Reaction to Immigration Bill Is Sharply Split," *NYT*, October 16, 1986, B15; N. Cohodas, "Congress Clears Overhaul of Immigration Law," *CQWR*, October 18, 1986, 2596; Brinkley, ed., *Reagan Diaries*, 445.

20 R. Pear, "The Immigration Bill," B6; N. Cohodas, "Congress Clears Overhaul of Immigration Law," *CQWR*, October 18, 1986, 2595–2598; Gimpel and Edwards, *Congressional Politics*, 176–177, 179; Schuck, *Citizens, Strangers, and In-Betweens*, 110.

21 "Speaking for English as the Official Language", 1983, in W.C. Fischer *et al.*, eds, *Identity, Community, and Pluralism in American Life* (New York, 1997), 246–249; Lamm and Imhoff, *Immigrant Time Bomb*, 100.

22 R. Lindsey, "Debates Growing on Use of English," *NYT*, July 21, 1986, A1; J. Crawford, ed., *Language Loyalties* (Chicago, 1992), 2.

23 Stefancic and Delgado, *No Mercy*, 17; Crawford, ed., *Language Loyalties*, 2, 90–94; D. Baron, *The English-Only Question* (New Haven, 1990), 20; R. Schmidt, *Language Policy and Identity Politics in the United States* (Philadelphia, 2000), 31.

24 Schmidt, *Language Policy*, 32–34; Baron, *English-Only Question*, 19, 21; E.S. Cohen, *The Politics of Globalization in the United States* (Washington, 2001), 155; Crawford, ed., *Language Loyalties*, 93.

Chapter 4   Glad Morning Again: A Reagan Revolution?

1   F. FitzGerald, *Way Out There in the Blue* (New York, 2001), 191; Reagan, "Farewell Address to the Nation," January 11, 1989, PP; R. Brookhiser, "Where's the Rest of Him?" *National Review*, February 22, 1980, 218; R. Reagan, *An American Life* (New York, 1990), 27.

2   G. Wills, *Reagan's America* (New York, 2000), ix; P.D. Erickson, *Reagan Speaks* (New York, 1985), 2.

3   L. Speakes, *Speaking Out: The Reagan Presidency from Inside the White House* (New York, 1988), 116.

4   W.E. Pemberton, *Exit with Honor: The Life and Presidency of Ronald Reagan* (Armonk, NY, 1997), 86.

5   K.K. Skinner, A. Anderson, and M. Anderson, eds, *Reagan, In His Own Hand* (New York, 2001), 13, 15.

6   Pemberton, *Exit with Honor*, 86; P. Light, *Artful Work* (New York, 1985), 118.

7   M.K. Deaver, *Behind the Scenes* (New York, 1987), 41; S. Blumenthal, *The Rise of the Counter-Establishment* (New York, 1986), 314.

8   D.T. Regan, *For the Record* (New York, 1989), 159, 161.

9   T. O'Neill with W. Novak, *Man of the House: The Life and Political Memoirs of Speaker Tip O'Neill* (London, 1987), 342, 345.

10   L. Cannon, *President Reagan* (New York, 2000), 56, 84; Reagan, First Inaugural Address, January 20, 1981; D. Stockman, "How to Avoid an Economic Dunkirk," *Challenge*, 24 (March/April 1981), 20.

11   "Address Before a Joint Session of the Congress on the Program for Economic Recovery," February 18, 1981, PP.

12   Cannon, *President Reagan*, 114; H. Johnson, *Sleepwalking Through History* (New York, 1991), 162–163.

13   E. Cowan, "Jack Kemp's Economics," *NYT*, November 30, 1980, F8; P.C. Roberts, *The Supply-Side Revolution* (Cambridge, MA, 1984), 28–29.

14   M. Feldstein, "American Economic Policy in the 1980s," in Feldstein, ed., *American Economic Policy in the 1980s* (Chicago, 1994), 21n; M. Anderson, *Revolution*, expanded edn (Stanford, 1990), 151; Roberts, *Supply-Side Revolution*, chs 6 and 7; D.A. Stockman, *The Triumph of Politics* (London, 1986), 10; W.T.M. Riches, *The Civil Rights Movement*, 2nd edn (Basingstoke, 2004), 122.

15   Anderson, *Revolution*, 245; Stockman, *Triumph*, 94, 142.

16   Stockman, "How to Avoid an Economic Dunkirk," 18; W. Greider, "The Education of David Stockman," *Atlantic Monthly* (December 1981); T. Kornheiser, "Tip O'Neill's Toughest Inning," *WP*, May 31, 1981, F1.

17   Greider, "Education of David Stockman"; Reagan, *American Life*, 235.

18   Stockman, *Triumph*, 9; Reagan, "Address to the Nation on the Economy," February 5, 1981, PP; J.A. Frieden, *Global Capitalism* (New York, 2006), 380; S. Moore, "The Profligate President," Policy Analysis no. 147, February 4, 1991, Cato Institute.

19   Roberts, *Supply-Side Revolution*, 229; D.P. Moynihan, "Reagan's Bankrupt Budget," *New Republic*, December 31, 1983, 19–20; D. Stockman, "Budget Policy," in Feldstein, ed., *American Economic Policy*, 270.

20 Reagan, "Remarks and a Question-and-Answer Session with Reporters on the Air Traffic Controllers Strike," August 3, 1981, PP; D.S. Broder, "Don't Mess With This Guy," WP, August 9, 1981, E7; E. Morris, *Dutch* (New York, 1999), 448; R. Brenner, *The Economics of Global Turbulence* (London, 2006), 196n; Johnson, *Sleepwalking*, 154.

21 Light, *Artful Work*, 121; M. Derthick and S.M. Teles, "Riding the Third Rail," in W.E. Brownlee and H.D. Graham, eds, *The Reagan Presidency* (Lawrence, 2003), 184; L.I. Barrett, *Gambling With History* (New York, 1983), 158; K. Phillips, *Boiling Point* (New York, 1993), 73.

22 Anderson, *Revolution*, 249–250; M. Mussa, "Monetary Policy," in Feldstein, ed., *American Economic Policy*, 112; L. Galambos, "The U.S. Corporate Economy in the Twentieth Century," in S.L. Engerman and R.E. Gallman, eds, *The Cambridge Economic History of the United States* (Cambridge, 2000), vol. 3, 960.

23 P. Noonan, *What I Saw At the Revolution* (New York, 1990), 56, 101–103, 108; T.H. Bell, *The Thirteenth Man* (New York, 1988), 52–55; L.E. Lynn, Jr., "The Reagan Administration and the Renitent Bureaucracy," in L.M. Salamon and M.S. Lund, eds, *The Reagan Presidency and the Governing of America* (Washington, 1984), 340.

24 M. Tolchin and S.J. Tolchin, "The Rush to Deregulate," *NYT*, August 21, 1983, Magazine, 34; C.A. Newland, "Executive Office Policy Apparatus," in Salamon and Lund, *Reagan Presidency*, 163.

25 J.K. Stine, "Natural Resources and Environmental Policy," in Brownlee and Graham, *Reagan Presidency*, 236; S.P. Hays, *Beauty, Health, and Permanence* (Cambridge, 1987), 495; Tolchin and Tolchin, "Rush to Deregulate," 34.

26 P. Shabecoff, "Reagan and Environment," *NYT*, January 2, 1989, 1, 12.

27 J. Kraft, "It's Been a Reagan Year," *WP*, December 29, 1983, A17.

28 R.M. Collins, *More* (New York, 2000), 196–197; Reagan, "Remarks at a Reagan–Bush Rally in Fairfield, Connecticut," October 26, 1984, PP; G.M. Pomper, "The Presidential Election," in Pomper et al., *The Election of 1984* (Chatham, NJ, 1985), 70; Stockman, *Triumph*, 402.

29 Cannon, *President Reagan*, 437; M. Shields, "Where's His Mandate?" *WP*, November 2, 1984, A23.

30 J.R. Dickenson, "Democrats Seek Identity After Loss," *WP*, December 17, 1984, A6; O'Neill, *Man of the House*, 357.

31 Reagan, "Address Before a Joint Session of the Congress Reporting on the State of the Union," January 25, 1983, PP; D.S. Broder, "The Words Do Mean Something," *WP*, January 30, 1983, C7.

Chapter 5 Reviving and Winning the Cold War

1 R.W. Tucker, "The Purposes of American Power," *Foreign Affairs*, 59 (1980–1981), 243.

2 Reagan, "To Restore America," March 31, 1976: http://reagan2020.us/speeches/To_Restore_America.asp; "Reagan Rampant," *The Nation*, February 9, 1980, 129.

3 "Remarks and a Question-and-Answer Session at the University of Virginia in Charlottesville," December 16, 1988, PP; W.G. Hyland, *Clinton's World* (Westport, CT, 1999), 5.

4 "The President's News Conference," January 29, 1981, PP; M. Schaller, *Reckoning with Reagan* (New York, 1992), 123.

5   K.K. Skinner *et al.*, eds, *Reagan In His Own Hand* (New York, 2001), 31; R.M. Gates, *From the Shadows* (New York, 1996), 174; B.A. Fischer, *The Reagan Reversal* (Columbia, MO, 1997), 19–20; E. Meese, *With Reagan* (Washington, 1992), 164.

6   Reagan, "Question-and-Answer Session with Reporters," August 13, 1981, PP.

7   A. Clymer, *Edward M. Kennedy* (New York, 1999), 331; "Proposed Catholic Bishops' Letter Opposes First Use of Nuclear Arms," *NYT*, October 26, 1982, A22; "A Pastoral Letter on War and Peace by the National Conference of Catholic Bishops, May 3, 1983": www.usccb.org/sdwp/international/TheChallengeofPeace.pdf.

8   J.F. Matlock, *Reagan and Gorbachev* (New York, 2004), 3; Larry Speakes, *Speaking Out* (New York, 1988), 95.

9   R. Jeffreys-Jones, *The CIA & American Democracy* (New Haven, 1989), 235; Schaller, "Reagan and the Cold War," in K. Longley *et al.*, *Deconstructing Reagan* (Armonk, NY, 2007), 21.

10 A.M. Haig, *Caveat* (London, 1984), 29; Fischer, *Reagan Reversal*, 17; Reagan, *An American Life* (New York, 1990), 306.

11 "Address Before a Joint Session of the Congress Reporting on the State of the Union," January 26, 1982, PP; C. Bernstein, "The Holy Alliance," *Time*, February 24, 1992.

12 Schaller, *Reckoning with Reagan*, 142.

13 Haig, *Caveat*, 129; S.S. Rosenfeld, "Testing the Hard Line," *Foreign Affairs: America and the World 1982*, 496; "The President's News Conference," March 6, 1981, PP.

14 B. Woodward, *Veil: The Secret Wars of the CIA, 1981–1987* (New York, 1987), 289; O.A. Westad, *The Global Cold War* (Cambridge, 2006), 345.

15 J.P. Diggins, *Ronald Reagan* (New York, 2007), 252; Schaller, *Reckoning with Reagan*, 149; R.A. Goldberg, *Barry Goldwater* (New Haven, 1995), 321.

16 Matlock, *Reagan and Gorbachev*, xi.

17 "Address Before a Joint Session of the Congress Reporting on the State of the Union," January 25, 1983, PP; D. Oberdorfer, "Dramatic Shift in Foreign Policy Rhetoric," *WP*, January 26, 1983, A15; Rosenfeld, "Testing the Hard Line," 495; J.R. Block, "We Have to Sell Grain to the Soviets," *WP*, May 5, 1982, A13; T. Smith, *America's Mission* (Princeton, 1994), 272.

18 M. Anderson, *Revolution*, expanded edn (Stanford, 1990), 72; L. Cannon, "President Hails Japan as Partner," *WP*, November 11, 1983, A1.

19 Reagan, "Address … Reporting on the State of the Union," January 25, 1984; Diggins, *Ronald Reagan*, 354; F. Ninkovich, *The Wilsonian Century* (Chicago, 1999), 261.

20 G.P. Shultz, "New Realities and New Ways of Thinking," *Foreign Affairs*, 63 (Spring 1985), 721; J.E. Garten, "Gunboat Economics," *Foreign Affairs: America and the World 1984*, 541–542, 550–553; R.N.L. Andrews, *Managing the Environment, Managing Ourselves*, 2nd edn (New Haven, 2006), 330; G.B. Ostrower, *The United Nations and the United States* (New York, 1998), 177.

21 "What President Reagan Has Said About the Marines' Role in Lebanon," *NYT*, February 9, 1984, A12.

22 J.L. Pasley and A.P. Weisman, "He's Back!" *New Republic*, January 19, 1987, 13–15.

23 J. Schlesinger, "Reykjavik and Revelations," *Foreign Affairs: America and the World 1986*, 439, 441.

24 Schlesinger, "Reykjavik and Revelations," 443; D. Ignatius, "The Contrapreneurs," *WP*, December 7, 1986, D1.

25   A. Pertman and S. Kurkjian, "White House Starts Battle for Its Agenda," *Boston Globe*, January 29, 1987, 21; P. Geyelin, "A Rancid Rerun of the Contra Debate?" *WP*, January 29, 1987, A25.

26   J.E. Persico, *Casey* (New York, 1990), 226; D.T. Critchlow, *The Conservative Ascendancy* (Cambridge, MA, 2007), 195.

27   J.F. Matlock, *Autopsy on an Empire* (New York, 1995), 85; Matlock, *Reagan and Gorbachev*, 237.

28   Matlock, *Autopsy on an Empire*, 271; Ninkovich, *Wilsonian Century*, 273.

29   Matlock, *Reagan and Gorbachev*, 271, 307, 312; Matlock, "Ronald Reagan and the End of the Cold War," in C. Hudson and G. Davies, eds, *Ronald Reagan and the 1980s* (New York, 2008), 73; Meese, *With Reagan*, 173.

30   M. Mandelbaum, "The Luck of the President," *Foreign Affairs: America and the World 1985*, 396; Matlock, *Autopsy on an Empire*, 77.

31   O.A. Westad, "The New International History of the Cold War," *Diplomatic History*, 24 (Fall 2000), 558, 560; G.P. Shultz, *Turmoil and Triumph* (New York, 1993), 714.

Chapter 6   The Morning After: The Limitations of Conservatism

1   J.R. Dickenson, "Democrats Seek Identity After Loss," *WP*, December 17, 1984, A6–7; K.S. Baer, *Reinventing Democrats* (Lawrence, 2000), 81–82; A. Clymer, *Edward M. Kennedy* (New York, 1999), 372.

2   J.B. Judis, "The Pressure Elite," *American Prospect*, March 21, 1992.

3   M.J. Penn and D.E. Schoen, "Reagan's Revolution Hasn't Ended," *NYT*, November 9, 1986, E23.

4   D.T. Regan, *For the Record* (New York, 1989), 412.

5   Reagan, Second Inaugural Address, January 21, 1985; W.E. Brownlee and C.E. Steuerle, "Taxation," in W.E. Brownlee and H.D. Graham, eds, *The Reagan Presidency* (Lawrence, 2003), 172; R. Reeves, *President Reagan* (New York, 2005), 257; J.A. Baker, "*Work Hard, Study … And Keep Out of Politics!*" (New York, 2006), 217.

6   Brownlee and Steuerle, "Taxation," 181, n.64; Reagan, *An American Life* (New York, 1990), 335; Baker, "*Work Hard, Study*," 233.

7   S. Blumenthal, *The Rise of the Counter-Establishment* (New York, 1986), 316; D.K. Williams, "Reagan's Religious Right," in C. Hudson and G. Davies, eds, *Ronald Reagan and the 1980s* (New York, 2008), 135.

8   D. Whitman, "Are Reagan's New Judges Really Closet Moderates?" *WP*, August 9, 1987, C1; E.M. Yoder, "The Real Robert Bork," *WP*, July 12, 1987, C7.

9   H. Johnson, "Out of Touch on the Right," *WP*, October 9, 1987, A2; D. Collin, "Lobbyists Turn Up Heat on Senators over Bork," *Chicago Tribune*, September 23, 1987, 1; E. Bronner, *Battle for Justice* (New York, 1989), 251.

10   "Galbraith's Warning," *San Francisco Chronicle*, January 2, 1987, 32; P. Behr and D.A. Vise, "Stock Market Suffers Largest Loss in History," *WP*, October 20, 1987, A1; H. Johnson, "Wall Street's Message of Blame," *WP*, November 1, 1987, A1; J. Burgess, "Confusion, Warnings Follow Day's Turmoil," *WP*, October 20, 1987, C1.

11   M. Schaller, *Reckoning with Reagan* (New York, 1992), 109–110; H.N. Pontell and K. Calavita, "White-Collar Crime in the Savings and Loan Scandal," *Annals of the American Academy of Political and Social Science*, 525 (January 1993), 37; W.E. Pemberton, *Exit with Honor: The Life and Presidency of Ronald Reagan* (Armonk, NY, 1997), 130; T. Curry and L. Shibut, "The Cost of the Savings and Loan Crisis," *FDIC Banking Review*, 13 (December 2000).

12   H. Johnson, *Sleepwalking Through History* (New York, 1991), 215, 432.

13   A. Murray and E. Hume, "Mixed Report," *WSJ*, November 17, 1987, 1, 32.

14   I. Morgan, "Reaganomics and Its Legacy," in Hudson and Davies, *Ronald Reagan and the 1980s*, 101–118, and *The Age of Deficits* (Lawrence, 2009), ch. 4; K. Phillips, *The Politics of Rich and Poor* (New York, 1991), 3.

15   M. Weidenbaum, "Facing Reality in the George Bush Era," *Society*, 26 (March/April 1989), 25; B.J. Schulman, "The Reagan Revolution in International Perspective," in R.S. Conley, ed., *Reassessing the Reagan Presidency* (Lanham, MD, 2003), 98.

16   G.P. Shultz, "New Realities and New Ways of Thinking," *Foreign Affairs*, 63 (Spring 1985), 715; R. Kuttner, *The End of Laissez-Faire* (New York, 1991), 17.

17   On Reagan as a "pragmatic conservative," see G. Davies, "The Welfare State," in Brownlee and Graham, *Reagan Presidency*, 222–225.

18   E. and M. Black, *The Rise of Southern Republicans* (Cambridge, MA, 2002), 205.

19   H. Sidey, "The Establishment Steps In," *Time*, March 23, 1987; J. Mayer and D. McManus, *Landslide* (Boston, 1988), 387.

20   W.T.M. Riches, *The Civil Rights Movement*, 2nd edn (Basingstoke, 2004), 121; S. Tuck, *We Ain't What We Ought To Be* (Cambridge, MA, 2010), 372–379, 381.

21   Davies, "The Welfare State," 222–223.

22   General Social Surveys, National Opinion Research Center: www.norc.org/GSS; M. Dowie, *Losing Ground* (Cambridge, MA, 1995), 192; J.M. Berry, "The Rise of Citizen Groups," in T. Skocpol and M.P. Fiorina, eds, *Civic Engagement in American Democracy* (Washington, 1999), 370; Judis, "The Pressure Elite."

23   J. Updike, *Rabbit at Rest* (London, 2006), 6; T. O'Neill with W. Novak, *Man of the House* (London, 1987), 340.

24   P.G. Bourne, "'Just Say No,'" in Hudson and Davies, *Ronald Reagan and the 1980s*, 41–56; Interview with Dr Herbert Kleber, 2000, PBS archive; K.B. Nunn, "Race, Crime and the Pool of Surplus Criminality," *Journal of Gender, Race & Justice*, 6 (2002).

25   B. Wolf, "Great Shakes," ABC News, May 23, 2006; P. Dreier, "Urban Suffering Grew Under Reagan," Common Dreams.org, August 5, 2010; M. Donohue, "Homelessness in the United States," *Medscape Ob/Gyn & Women's Health*, July 7, 2004; Centers for Disease Control, HIV/AIDS Surveillance, January 1989.

26   L. Cannon, *President Reagan* (New York, 2000), 746; R.M. Collins, *Transforming America* (New York, 2007), 237.

27   Gallup Brain: http://brain.gallup.com/ (the percentages are averages for each year); Mayer and McManus, *Landslide*, 387; *Associated Press*, December 27, 1988.

Chapter 7   Gentleman George, Culture Wars, and the Return of Malaise

1   D.M. Hill and P. Williams, "Introduction: The Bush Administration," in Hill and Williams, eds, *The Bush Presidency* (Basingstoke, 1994), 9; D. Oberdorfer, *From the Cold*

War to a New Era, updated edn (Baltimore, 1998), 329; A. Devroy, "The Reluctant Activist," *WP*, August 17, 1992, A1.

2   M. Foley, "The President and Congress," in Hill and Williams, *Bush Presidency*, 44; C. Kolb, *White House Daze: The Unmaking of Domestic Policy in the Bush Years* (New York, 1994), 6.

3   S.B. Greenberg, *Middle Class Dreams*, rev. edn (New Haven, 1996), 49; W.E. Pemberton, *Exit with Honor: The Life and Presidency of Ronald Reagan* (Armonk, NY, 1997), 198.

4   G.M. Pomper *et al.*, *The Election of 1988* (Chatham, NJ, 1989), 134, 152.

5   A. Greenspan, *The Age of Turbulence* (London, 2008), 112; M.R. Beschloss and S. Talbott, *At the Highest Levels* (London, 1993), 26; M. Dowd, "Bush's Fierce Loyalty Raises Debate," *NYT*, March 10, 1989, B6.

6   Kolb, *White House Daze*, 336; K.T. Walsh, "Bush's Split Personality," *U.S. News & World Report*, September 17, 1990, 26–27; R.D. Hormats, "The Roots of American Power," *Foreign Affairs*, 70 (Summer 1991), 136.

7   O. Harries, "Introduction," in Harries, ed., *America's Purpose* (San Francisco, 1991), 3; M. Oreskes, "Approval of Bush … Soars in Poll," *NYT*, January 19, 1990.

8   General Social Surveys, National Opinion Research Center: www.norc.org/GSS; Bush, Inaugural Address, January 20, 1989; M. Weidenbaum, "Facing Reality in the George Bush Era," *Society*, 26 (March/April 1989), 28; J. Kentleton, *President and Nation* (Basingstoke, 2002), 262.

9   B. Solomon, "It Takes More Than a Bully Pulpit," *National Journal*, January 13, 1990, 82.

10   T. Kenworthy, "House Democrats Worry Fallout from Tower Fight Will Hurt Wright," *WP*, March 5, 1989, A6.

11   Kenworthy, "House Democrats Worry," A6; R. Lowry, *Legacy* (Washington, 2003), 124.

12   N. Podhoretz, "Buchanan and the Conservative Crackup," *Commentary*, 93 (May 1992), 30–34.

13   S. Moore, "The Profligate President", Policy Analysis no. 147, February 4, 1991, Cato Institute.

14   W.G. Hyland, "America's New Course," *Foreign Affairs*, 69 (Spring 1990), 8; Kolb, *White House Daze*, 87.

15   S. Woolcock, "The Economic Policies of the Bush Administration," in Hill and Williams, *Bush Presidency*, 114; I. Morgan, *The Age of Deficits* (Lawrence, 2009), 142–146.

16   S.R. Diamond, *Roads to Dominion* (New York, 1995), 278.

17   W.C. McWilliams, "The Meaning of the Election," in G.M. Pomper *et al.*, *The Election of 1992* (Chatham, NJ, 1993), 194; L. Fisher, *Presidential War Power*, 2nd edn (Lawrence, 2004), 172.

18   A. King and G. Aston, "Good Government and the Politics of High Exposure," in Colin Campbell and Bert A. Rockman, eds, *The Bush Presidency* (Chatham, NJ, 1991), 280; Greenspan, *Age of Turbulence*, 183.

19   S. Rosenberg, *American Economic Development Since 1945* (Basingstoke, 2003), 257. An early riposte to the "declinists" was S.P. Huntington, "The U.S. – Decline or Renewal?" *Foreign Affairs*, 67 (Winter 1988/89), 76–96; see also J.S. Nye, *Bound to Lead* (New York, 1991).

20   Gallup Brain: http://brain.gallup.com/; P. Starobin, "Confusing Signals," *National Journal*, November 30, 1991, 2907–2908.

21   R. Morin and E.J. Dionne, "Majority of Voters Say Parties Have Lost Touch," *WP*, July 8, 1992, A1; P. Gray *et al.*, "Lies, Lies, Lies," *Time*, October 5, 1992, 32; I.M. Destler,

"Foreign Policy Making with the Economy at Center Stage," in D. Yankelovich and I.M. Destler, eds, *Beyond the Beltway* (New York, 1994), 27.

22   H.S. Parmet, *George Bush* (New Brunswick, 2001), 320; M. McAlister, *Epic Encounters* (Berkeley, 2001), 224; R.M. Collins, *More* (New York, 2000), 216.

23   J.W. Germond and J. Witcover, *Mad As Hell* (New York, 1993), 110, 134–135; P. Buchanan, "America First – and Second, and Third," in Harries, *America's Purpose*, 32, 34.

24   J.F. Hale, "The Making of the New Democrats," *Political Science Quarterly*, 110 (Summer 1995), 223; A.P. Lamis, *The Two-Party South*, 2nd edn (New York, 1990), 259.

25   W.D. Burnham, "The Legacy of George Bush," in Pomper *et al.*, *Election of 1992*, 30; J.R. Greene, *The Presidency of George Bush* (Lawrence, 2000), 171.

26   Bush, "Remarks at a Rally in Ridgewood, New Jersey", October 22, 1992, PP; Germond and Witcover, *Mad As Hell*, 426; Diary entry, September 3, 1992, in George Bush, *All the Best, G. Bush: My Life in Letters and Other Writings* (New York, 1999), 566.

27   J.F. Harris, *The Survivor* (New York, 2006), 20; Clinton, Acceptance Speech to 1992 Democratic Convention, July 16, 1992; E. Drew, *Showdown* (New York, 1996), 20.

Chapter 8   Groping for a New World Order

1   G. Bush, *All the Best, G. Bush: My Life in Letters and Other Writings* (New York, 1999), 480; J.F. Matlock, *Autopsy on an Empire* (New York, 1995), 591; D. Hoffman, "On Panama, Bush Characteristically Cautious," *WP*, October 15, 1989, A1, A16.

2   G. Bush and B. Scowcroft, *A World Transformed* (New York, 1998), xiii; B.J. Wattenberg, "Neo-Manifest Destinarianism," in O. Harries, ed., *America's Purpose* (San Francisco, 1991), 108; "The President's News Conference in Paris," July 16, 1989, PP.

3   Bush, State of the Union Address, January 31, 1990, PP; M.R. Beschloss and S. Talbott, *At the Highest Levels* (London, 1993), 19; Bush and Scowcroft, *World Transformed*, 12; Bush, "Remarks at the Swearing-in Ceremony for Richard B. Cheney as Secretary of Defense," March 21, 1989, PP; J.F. Matlock, *Reagan and Gorbachev* (New York, 2004), 310.

4   M.P. Leffler, *For the Soul of Mankind* (New York, 2007), 430; Bush to Chairman Deng, June 20, 1989, in Bush, *All the Best*, 428–431; W.G. Hyland, *Clinton's World* (Westport, CT, 1999), 110.

5   Beschloss and Talbott, *At the Highest Levels*, 25, 28, 34, 86; J. Dumbrell, *American Foreign Policy* (London, 1997), 139.

6   Beschloss and Talbott, *At the Highest Levels*, 84; Dumbrell, *American Foreign Policy*, 141.

7   J.R. Greene, *The Presidency of George Bush* (Lawrence, 2000), 98.

8   C. Kolb, *White House Daze* (New York, 1994), 20.

9   Bush and Scowcroft, *World Transformed*, 186, 299.

10   R.J. Smith, "Initiative Affects Least Useful Weapons," *WP*, September 28, 1991, A1, A22.

11   G.B. Ostrower, *The United Nations and the United States* (New York, 1998), 205; D. Halberstam, *War in a Time of Peace* (London, 2002), 46; J.A. Baker, *The Politics of Diplomacy* (New York, 1995), 636, 651; S. Talbott, *The Russia Hand* (New York, 2002), 73.

12   J.J. Kirkpatrick, "A Normal Country in a Normal Time," in Harries, *America's Purpose*, 163.

13 R.D. Hormats, "The Roots of American Power," *Foreign Affairs*, 70 (Summer 1991), 133; Bush, Acceptance Speech, Republican Presidential Convention, August 20, 1992.

14 Bush, "Remarks at the Swearing-in Ceremony for Carla A. Hills," PP, February 6, 1989; Bush, "Remarks and a Question-and-Answer Session," PP, September 10, 1992; Bush, "'Fast Track' Really Means 'Good Faith'," *Roll Call*, April 22, 1991.

15 Bush, "'Fast Track' Really Means 'Good Faith.'"

16 G. Kolko, *The Age of War* (Boulder, CO, 2006), 61–62.

17 Bush, Inaugural Address, January 20, 1989; H.S. Parmet, *George Bush* (New Brunswick, 2001), 332.

18 M. Oreskes, "Approval of Bush ... Soars in Poll," *NYT*, January 19, 1990.

19 E.A. Miller and S.A. Yetiv, "The New World Order in Theory and Practice," *Presidential Studies Quarterly*, 31 (March 2001), 61, 63.

20 B.W. Jentleson, *With Friends Like These* (New York, 1994), 98; Parmet, *George Bush*, 446; D. Mervin, *George Bush and the Guardianship Presidency* (Basingstoke, 1998), 177.

21 Baker, *Politics of Diplomacy*, 1; Mervin, *George Bush*, 178; L. Fisher, *Presidential War Power*, 2nd edn (Lawrence, 2004), 169.

22 Dumbrell, *American Foreign Policy*, 154.

23 Beschloss and Talbott, *At the Highest Levels*, 434; P. Buchanan, "Have the Neocons Thought This Through?" August 1990, in M.L. Sifry and C. Cerf, *The Gulf War Reader* (New York, 1991), 213–215.

24 Bush, "The President's Press Conference on the Persian Gulf Crisis," PP, November 11, 1990; "Address ... Announcing the Deployment of United States Armed Forces to Saudi Arabia," PP, August 8, 1990.

25 Baker, *Politics of Diplomacy*, 336; Miller and Yetiv, "The New World Order," 59.

26 Hormats, "Roots of American Power," 134.

27 Hormats, "Roots of American Power," 137; M.T. Jacobs, *Short-Term America* (Boston, 1991), 2.

Chapter 9   The Era of Globalization

1 P. Krugman, "Reckonings," *NYT*, January 2, 2000.

2 T.W. Zeiler, "Just Do It!" *Diplomatic History*, 25 (Fall 2001), 534; G. Dunkley, *The Free Trade Adventure* (London, 1997), 45; T.L. Friedman, *The Lexus and the Olive Tree* (London, 2000), xvi, 7.

3 W.G. Hyland, "America's New Course," *Foreign Affairs*, 69 (Spring 1990), 7–8; A.E. Eckes, *Opening America's Market* (Chapel Hill, 1995), 283; J. Bhagwati, *A Stream of Windows* (Cambridge, MA, 1998), 309 and *Protectionism* (Cambridge, MA, 1988), 62, 65–71.

4 J. Kirton, "Deepening Integration and Global Governance," in T.L. Brewer and G. Boyd, eds, *Globalizing America* (Cheltenham, UK, 2000), 43; T.L. Friedman, *The World Is Flat*, updated edn (London, 2006), 363; "Is America on the Way Down?" *Commentary*, 93 (May 1992), 20.

5 R. Pollin, *Contours of Descent* (London, 2003), 7; Friedman, *Lexus and the Olive Tree*, 385; "Is America on the Way Down?" 19.

6   J.S. Nye, *The Paradox of American Power* (Oxford, 2002), 42; Bhagwati, *Stream of Windows*, 39; J.A. Frieden, *Global Capitalism Century* (New York, 2006), 417; R.B. Reich, *Locked in the Cabinet* (New York, 1998), 282; M. Lind, *The Next American Nation* (New York, 1996), 206.

7   Friedman, *Lexus and the Olive Tree*, 112; Frieden, *Global Capitalism*, 381.

8   B. Eichengreen, "U.S. Foreign Financial Relations in the Twentieth Century," in S.L. Engerman and R.E. Gallman, eds, *The Cambridge Economic History of the United States* (Cambridge, 2000), vol. 3, 501; M.B. Zuckerman, "A Second American Century," *Foreign Affairs*, 77 (May/June 1998), 18.

9   A.E. Eckes and T.W. Zeiler, *Globalization and the American Century* (Cambridge, 2003), 210; *OECD Economic Surveys, 1999–2000* (Paris, 2000), 32–33.

10 Eckes and Zeiler, *Globalization*, 218; J.S. Nye and W.A. Owens, "America's Information Edge," *Foreign Affairs*, 75 (March/April 1996), 35; A. Iriye, "A Century of NGOs," *Diplomatic History*, 23 (Summer 1999), 434; Friedman, *Lexus and the Olive Tree*, 85.

11 J.B. Judis, "Beyond McPopulism," *American Prospect*, June 23, 1993; Brewer and Boyd, *Globalizing America*, 15–16.

12 Bush, "Question-and-Answer Session in Secaucus," PP, October 22, 1992; Clinton, "Remarks on Signing the Uruguay Round Agreements Act," PP, December 8, 1994.

13 Clinton, "Remarks at the American University Centennial Celebration," PP, February 26, 1993; J.F. Harris and P. Baker, "Clinton Neglected to Sell 'Fast Track' to U.S. Public," *WP*, November 12, 1997, A4.

14 H. Kissinger, "NAFTA: Clinton's Defining Task," *WP*, July 20, 1993, A17; *OECD Economic Surveys, 1999–2000: United States* (Paris, 2000), 108–109; J. Klein, *The Natural* (New York, 2002), 79.

15 *OECD Economic Surveys, 1999–2000: United States*, 9, 89; M.B. Zuckerman, "A Second American Century," *Foreign Affairs*, 77 (May/June 1998), 19; *Economic Report of the President, 2001*, 20, 277.

16 S.B. Shepard, "The New Economy," *Business Week*, November 17, 199; Testimony of Chairman Greenspan before Committee on Banking, Housing, and Urban Affairs, US Senate July 21, 1998; S. Lilley, "New Economy R.I.P." *Monthly Review* (April 2004); *Economic Report of the President, 2001*, 23, 50–51.

17 Eckes and Zeiler, *Globalization*, 214–216; F.W. Smith, "Defining the Global Economy," *Vital Speeches of the Day*, 65, December 1, 1998, 126; B. Keller, "American Culture (and Goods) Thrive in South Africa," *NYT*, September 25, 1993, 5.

18 *OECD Economic Surveys, 1999–2000: United States*, 10; H. McRae, "Oil and the US Consumer," *Independent* (London), February 24, 2005, 47.

19 B.E. Moon, "The United States and Globalization," in R. Stubbs and G.R.D. Underhill, eds, *Political Economy and the Changing Global Order*, 3rd edn (Oxford, 2005); K. Phillips, *Arrogant Capital* (Boston, 1994), 71.

20 R.B. Freeman, "Are Your Wages Set in Beijing?" *Journal of Economic Perspectives*, 9 (Summer 1995), 15–32; Eckes, *Opening America's Market*, 78; J.B. Judis and M. Lind, "For a New Nationalism," *New Republic*, March 27, 1995, 19; N. McCarty, K.T. Poole, and H. Rosenthal, *Polarized America* (Cambridge, MA, 2006); K.S. Newman and E.S. Jacobs, *Who Cares?* (Princeton, 2010), 125–129.

21 R.N.L. Andrews, *Managing the Environment, Managing Ourselves*, 2nd edn (New Haven, 2006), 334.

22   Bhagwati, *Stream of Windows*, 16, 21–22; J.S. Hacker, *The Great Risk Shift* (New York, 2006), 23–24, 27–28; S. Rosenberg, *American Economic Development Since 1945* (Basingstoke, 2003), 297; Pollin, *Contours of Descent*, 53.

23   W. Raspberry, "Working-Class Vanishing Act," *WP*, November 17, 1993, A23; Frieden, *Global Capitalism*, 468; S.J. Tolchin, *The Angry American*, 2nd edn (Boulder, 1999), 69–73; S. Hoffman, "The Crisis of Liberal Internationalism," *Foreign Policy*, 98 (Spring 1995), 159–177.

24   E.S. Cohen, *The Politics of Globalization in the United States* (Washington, 2001), 10; J.E. Yang and T.M. Neal, "'Fast Track' Defeat Illustrates Division," *WP*, November 16, 1997, A1; G. Hytrek and K.M. Zentgraf, *America Transformed* (New York, 2008), 66.

25   M. Kazin, *The Populist Persuasion*, rev. edn (Ithaca, 1998), 282; H. Allen, "The Iron Fist of Pat Buchanan," *WP*, February 17, 1992, D1, D10; G. Soros, *The Crisis of Global Capitalism* (London, 1998); J. Stiglitz, *Globalization and Its Discontents* (London, 2002), 207.

26   A. Greenspan, *The Age of Turbulence* (London, 2008), 158–159; R.E. Rubin, *In An Uncertain World* (New York, 2004), 24, 34; B. Clinton, *My Life* (London, 2004), 644.

27   P. Krugman, *The Return of Depression Economics and the Crisis of 2008* (London, 2008), 4; A. Glyn, *Capitalism Unleashed* (Oxford, 2007), 50, 71; Greenspan, *Age of Turbulence*, 194; Rubin, *In An Uncertain World*, 281.

28   Stiglitz, *Globalization and Its Discontents*, 9; Jeffrey Garten, "Lessons for the Next Financial Crisis," *Foreign Affairs*, 78 (March/April 1999), 89, 92.

29   T. Miller *et al.*, *Global Hollywood* (London, 2001), 4; I.R. Tyrrell, *Transnational Nation* (Basingstoke, 2007), 48; Nye, *Paradox of American Power*, ix; G. Utley, "The Shrinking of Foreign News," *Foreign Affairs*, 76 (March/April 1997), 2; B.R. Barber, *Jihad vs. McWorld* (London, 2003), xxv, 62.

Chapter 10   Porous Borders and Global Warming

1   A.E. Eckes and T.W. Zeiler, *Globalization and the American Century* (Cambridge, 2003), 5.

2   *Yearbook of Immigration Statistics: 2004*, 5, 45.

3   S.P. Huntington, T*he Clash of Civilizations and the Remaking of World Order* (London, 2002), 202; C.M. Swain, *The New White Nationalism in America* (Cambridge, 2002).

4   V. Miller, "Race, Class, Age, and Punitive Segregation," in P. Davies and I. Morgan, eds, *America's Americans* (London, 2007), 246, 248.

5   P.M. Barrett, "Immigration Law Found to Promote Bias by Employers," *WSJ*, March 30, 1990, C9; "Needed: More Immigrants," *WP*, April l 7, 1990, A18; M.J. Mandel and C. Farrell, "The Immigrants," *International Business Week*, July 13, 1992, 76.

6   B.R. Chiswick, "A Troubling Drop in Immigration 'Quality'," *NYT*, December 21, 1986, F3, and "Opening the Golden Door," *WP*, October 7, 1990, D3; G.J. Borjas, "The U.S. Takes the Wrong Immigrants," *WSJ*, April 5, 1990, A18.

7   D. Solis and P. Yoshihashi, "Immigration Bill Would Expand Access to U.S.," *WSJ*, November 15, 1990, A20; "Democrats for Vitality," *WSJ*, October 1, 1990, A14.

8   M.C. Dawson, "Globalization, the Racial Divide, and a New Citizenship," in S.B. Greenberg and T. Skocpol, eds, *The New Majority* (New Haven, 1997), 266.

9   L. Auster, *The Path to National Suicide* (Monterey, VA, 1990); P. Brimelow, "Time To Rethink Immigration?" *National Review*, June 22, 1992, 30–46, and *Alien Nation* (New York, 1995); W.R. Hawkins, *Importing Revolution* (Monterey, VA, 1994); C. Williamson, *The Immigration Mystique* (New York, 1996).

10 D.G. Gutiérrez, *Walls and Mirrors: Mexican Americans, Mexican Immigrants, and the Politics of Ethnicity* (Berkeley, 1995), 213; Mandel and Farrell, "The Immigrants," 79.

11 D.M. Kennedy, "Can We Still Afford to Be a Nation of Immigrants?" *Atlantic Monthly*, November 1996; R. Daniels and O.L. Graham, *Debating American Immigration* (Lanham, MD, 2001), 171; D. Myers, "California and the Third Great Demographic Transition," in Davies and Morgan, *America's Americans*, 346–347, 360–361.

12 J. Goldsborough, "Out-Of-Control Immigration," *Foreign Affairs*, 79 (September/ October 2000), 94; P. Loeb *et al.*, "To Make a Nation," *U.S. News & World Report*, October 4, 1993, 51; J.G. Gimpel and J.R. Edwards, *The Congressional Politics of Immigration Reform* (Needham Heights, MA, 1999), 202; A. Wroe, *The Republican Party and Immigration Politics* (New York, 2008), 48.

13 F. Rose, "Muddled Masses," *WSJ*, April 26, 1995, A1; Gimpel and Edwards, *Congressional Politics*, 204; J. Davidson, "Panel's Proposals to Slash Immigration," *WSJ*, June 9, 1995, A5.

14 J.C. Clad, "Slowing the Wave," *Foreign Policy*, 95 (Summer 1994); S.P. Huntington, "The Hispanic Challenge," *Foreign Policy*, 141 (March/April 2004), 43; "Task Force Proposals Seek to End Benefits to Illegal Immigrants," *WSJ*, June 30, 1995.

15 A. Wroe, "The Shifting Politics of Immigration Reform," in Davies and Morgan, *America's Americans*, 270–271.

16 Wroe, *Republican Party and Immigration Politics*, 177, 180; E.A. Palmer, "Well-Timed Push on H-1B Bill Gives Businesses All They Asked," *CQWR*, 58 (October 7, 2000), 2331–2333; S. Murray, "Conservatives Split in Debate on Curbing Illegal Immigration," *WSJ*, March 25, 2005, A02.

17 Mandel and Farrell, "The Immigrants," 78.

18 *U.S. News & World Report*, October 31, 1988, 58; L.K. Caldwell, "Globalizing Environmentalism," in R.E. Dunlap and A.G. Mertig, eds, *American Environmentalism: The U.S. Environmental Movement, 1970–1990* (New York, 1992), 74; S. Hopgood, *American Environmental Policy and the Power of the State* (Oxford, 1998), 118.

19 J. Lancaster, "Offshore Oil Developers Find Opposition Is Deep," *WP*, May 7, 1990, A1; "Understanding Your Risk and Impacts": www.drought.unl.edu/risk/us/compare.htm

20 "Achieving International Success," *EnviroZine* 75 (2007): http://www.ec.gc.ca/EnviroZine/

21 W. Sullivan, "Study Finds Warming Trend That Could Raise Sea Levels," *NYT*, August 22, 1981, 1, 13; M. Paterson, *Global Warming and Global Politics* (London, 1996), 32; S. Weart, "The Public and Climate Change": www.aip.org/history/climate/Public.htm

22 Paterson, *Global Warming*, 35; Hopgood, *American Environmental Policy*, 193; Mark Dowie, *Losing Ground* (Cambridge, MA, 1995), 83.

23 Hopgood, *American Environmental Policy*, 192–193.

24 G.B. Ostrower, *The United Nations and the United States* (New York, 1998), 223.

25 Hopgood, *American Environmental Policy*, 199; J.W. Germond and J. Witcover, *Mad As Hell* (New York, 1993), 495; Dowie, *Losing Ground*, 193.

26 B. Daynes, "Bill Clinton: Environmental President," in D.L. Soden, ed., *The Environmental Presidency* (Albany, 1999), 259; Clinton, "Remarks on the President's Council on Sustainable Development," PP, June 14, 1993.

27 Clinton, ibid.; D. Vogel, "Trade and the Environment in the Global Economy," in N.J. Vig and M.G. Faure, eds, *Green Giants?* (Cambridge, MA, 2004), 235.

28 A. Freedman, "The 104th and the Environment," *CQWR*, October 12, 1996, 2919; J.H. Cushman, "Congressional Republicans Take Aim at an Extensive List of Environmental Statutes," *NYT*, February 22, 1995, A14; N.J. Vig, "Presidential Leadership and the Environment," in N.J. Vig and M.E. Kraft, eds, *Environmental Policy*, 6th edn (Washington, 2006), 100.

29 J.M. Berry, *The New Liberalism* (Washington, 1999), 112; A. Lewis, "Republican Radicals Would Leave Dismal Future For Our Children," *Seattle Post-Intelligencer*, August 1, 1995, A6.

30 C.M. Klyza and D. Sousa, *American Environmental Policy, 1990–2006* (Cambridge, MA, 2008), 25, 117; D. Jehl, "How an Interior Secretary Helped to Encourage a Presidential 'Legacy,'" *NYT*, January 19, 2001, A31.

31 P. Newell and M. Paterson, "A Climate for Business," *Review of International Political Economy*, 5 (Winter 1998), 679–703; M.A. Schreurs, "The Climate Change Divide," in Vig and Faure, eds, *Green Giants?* 214; "Clinton Hails Global Warming Pact," AllPolitics, December 11, 1997, online.

32 A.M. McCright and R.E. Dunlap, "Defeating Kyoto," *Social Problems*, 50 (August 2003), 348–373.

33 J. Dao, "History Could Be Green Party's Toughest Opponent," *NYT*, November 2, 2000, A29; M.L. Sifry, *Spoiling for a Fight* (New York, 2003), 205.

34 Patrick J. Buchanan, *The Death of the West* (New York, 2002), 127; John M. Broder, "Clinton Adamant on 3d World Role in Climate Accord," *NYT*, December 12, 1997, A1; Dick Morris, *Behind the Oval Office* (New York, 1997), 247.

Chapter 11   The New Age of Bill Clinton

1 Clinton, First Inaugural Address, January 20, 1993; Alan Greenspan, *The Age of Turbulence* (London, 2008), 160.

2 E.J. Dionne, "Greening of Democrats," *NYT*, June 14, 1989.

3 J.B. Judis, *The Paradox of American Democracy* (New York, 2000), 185; Clinton, "Remarks at the American University Centennial Celebration," PP, February 26, 1993; B.R. Barber, *The Truth of Power: Intellectual Affairs in the Clinton White House* (New York, 2001), 240, 247–248.

4 G. Stephanopoulos, *All Too Human* (Boston, 1999), 40.

5 Democratic Party platform, 1992; "About the Third Way," June 1, 1998: DLC online: www.dlc.org

6 Clinton, First Inaugural Address; R.B. Reich, *Locked in the Cabinet* (New York, 1998), 66.

7 Greenspan, *Age of Turbulence*, 145; M. Kelly, "White House Memo," *NYT*, February 2, 1993, A1; W. Raspberry, "Working-Class Vanishing Act," *WP*, November 17, 1993, A23.

8 Greenspan, *Age of Turbulence*, 147; W.C. Berman, *From the Center to the Edge: The Politics and Policies of the Clinton Presidency* (Lanham, MD, 2001), 17; Reich, *Locked in*

the Cabinet, 31; Clinton, "Remarks to the Business Community in Atlanta," March 19, 1993, PP.

9   D.R. Sease, "The Vigilantes," *WSJ*, November 6, 1992, A1; J.F. Harris, *The Survivor: Bill Clinton in the White House* (New York, 2006), 5.

10 R.E. Rubin, *In An Uncertain World* (New York, 2004), 119; B. Woodward, *The Agenda* (New York, 1994), 161; Greenspan, *Age of Turbulence*, 147.

11 David Hage *et al.*, "The Bill of Particulars," *U.S. News & World Report*, March 1, 1993, 20, 22; Rubin, *In An Uncertain World*, 125.

12 M.S. Weatherford and L.M. McDonnell, "Clinton and the Economy," *Political Science Quarterly*, 111 (Autumn 1996), 423; Clinton, "Remarks by the President to the … Democratic Leadership Council," December 3, 1993, PP; Barber, *Truth of Power*, 161; Woodward, *Agenda*, 318.

13 *OECD Economic Surveys, 1994–1995: United States* (Paris, 1995), 17.

14 Clinton, "Remarks by the President to the … Democratic Leadership Council," December 3, 1993; Clinton, "Remarks to the Business Community in Atlanta," PP, March 19, 1993; B. Clinton, *My Life* (London, 2004), 488, 513, 647–648.

15 A. Waddan, *Clinton's Legacy?* (Basingstoke, 2002), 155; Barber, *Truth of Power*, 155–156.

16 D.E. Rosenbaum, "Beyond a Trade Pact," *NYT*, November 11, 1993, A22; W. Safire, "Gore Flattens Perot," *NYT*, November 11, 1993, A27; Raspberry, "Working-Class Vanishing Act," A23.

17 Reich, *Locked in the Cabinet*, 68; J. Dillin, "Trade-Pact Foes Sound Job Loss, Populist Alarms," *Christian Science Monitor*, May 19, 1993, The U.S., 1; Safire, "Gore Flattens Perot," A27; G. Ifill, "Both Sides Assert Gain After Debate," *NYT*, November 11, 1993, A1, A22.

18 Stephanopoulos, *All Too Human*, 189; J. Hook, "Clinton's Months of Missteps Give Way to Winning Streak," *CQWR*, 51 (November 27, 1993), 3244.

19 K.S. Baer, *Reinventing Democrats* (Lawrence, 2000), 224; Gallup Brain: http://brain.gallup.com

20 D. Morris, *Behind the Oval Office* (New York, 1997), 192; M. Kelly, "White House Memo," *NYT*, February 2, 1993, A1.

21 Harris, *Survivor*, 149.

22 S. Blumenthal, *The Clinton Wars* (New York, 2003), 81.

23 Clinton, "Remarks … [to] Democratic Leadership Council"; Stephanopoulos, *All Too Human*, 198.

24 Reich, *Locked in the Cabinet*, 107; H.R. Clinton, *Living History* (London, 2004), 245; Stephanopoulos, *All Too Human*, 298.

25 E.C. Ladd, "The 1994 Congressional Elections," *Political Science Quarterly*, 110 (Spring 1995), 13.

26 Reich, *Locked in the Cabinet*, 170; M. Walker, *The President We Deserve* (New York, 1996), 212.

27 K.Q. Seelye, "Files Show How Gingrich Laid a Grand G.O.P Plan," *NYT*, December 3, 1995, 1, 26; Republican Contract with America: www.house.gov/house/Contract/CONTRACT.html.

28 H. Kurtz, "Radio Daze," *WP*, October 24, 1994, B1; A.J. Lichtman, *White Protestant Nation* (New York, 2008), 389.

29   E. Drew, *Showdown* (New York, 1996), 125; N. McCarty, K.T. Poole, and H. Rosenthal, *Polarized America* (Cambridge, MA, 2006).

30   A.J. Tuchfarber *et al.*, "The Republican Tidal Wave of 1994," *PS: Political Science and Politics*, 28 (December 1995), 690.

31   Clinton, State of the Union Address, January 24, 1995, PP.

Chapter 12   Democracy for the World

1   T. Mathews, "Clinton's Growing Pains," *Newsweek*, May 3, 1993; S.E. Ambrose and D.G. Brinkley, *Rise to Globalism*, 8th edn (New York, 1997), 399.

2   R.N. Haass, "Paradigm Lost," *Foreign Affairs*, 74 (January/February 1995), 43.

3   Clinton, First Inaugural Address, January 20, 1993; D. Brinkley, "Democratic Enlargement: The Clinton Doctrine," *Foreign Policy*, 106 (Spring 1997), 110–127.

4   T.L. Friedman, "Turning His Sights Overseas," *NYT*, April 2, 1992, A20; Haass, "Paradigm Lost," 44; "Clinton's Foreign Policy," *Foreign Policy*, 121 (November/December 2000), 18; Clinton, "Address … to the 48th Session of the United Nations General Assembly," September 27, 1993, PP.

5   Clinton, ibid.; S. Talbott, "Democracy and the National Interest," *Foreign Affairs*, 75 (November/December 1996), 52, 63.

6   A. Schlesinger, "Back to the Womb?" *Foreign Affairs*, 74 (July/August 1995), 6.

7   Brinkley, "Democratic Enlargement," 110–127; I.M. Destler, "Foreign Policy Making with the Economy at Center Stage," in D. Yankelovich and I.M. Destler, eds, *Beyond the Beltway* (New York, 1994), 33; J.E. Garten, "The Root of the Problem," *Newsweek*, March 31, 1997; W.C. Berman, *From the Center to the Edge: The Politics and Policies of the Clinton Presidency* (Lanham, 2001), 30.

8   Ambrose and Brinkley, *Rise to Globalism*, 408.

9   Brinkley, "Democratic Enlargement," 110–127; T.L. Friedman, "Big Mac I," *NYT*, December 8, 1996, sect. 4, 15, and "Big Mac II," *NYT*, December 11, 1996, A27; A. Sen, "Democracy as a Universal Value," *Journal of Democracy*, 10 (1999), 7–8; Talbott, "Democracy and the National Interest," 48.

10   Brinkley, "Democratic Enlargement," 110–127.

11   M.K. Albright, "The Testing of American Foreign Policy," *Foreign Affairs*, 77 (November/December 1998), 50; J.F. Harris, *The Survivor: Bill Clinton in the White House* (New York, 2006), 51.

12   D. Binder and B. Crossette, "In Baring Old Hatreds," *NYT*, February 7, 1993, 1.

13   S. Talbott, *The Russia Hand* (New York, 2002), 91; Presidential Decision Directive 25, PP.

14   D. Halberstam, *War in a Time of Peace* (London, 2002), 273; D. Jehl, "U.S. Is Showing a New Caution," *NYT*, May 18, 1994, A1; M. Albright, *Madam Secretary* (London, 2004), 154.

15   P. Constable, "Dateline Haiti," *Foreign Policy*, 89 (Winter 1992–1993), 182; Mathews, "Clinton's Growing Pains"; Talbott, "Democracy and the National Interest," 58.

16   Halberstam, *War*, 305; J. Dumbrell, *Evaluating the Foreign Policy of President Bill Clinton* (London, 2005), 3.

17   S.M. Walt, "Two Cheers for Clinton's Foreign Policy," *Foreign Affairs*, 79 (March/April 2000), 65; Schlesinger, "Back to the Womb?" 5.

18   R.D. Asmus, *Opening NATO's Door* (New York, 2002), 21; D. Owen, *Balkan Odyssey* (London, 1995), 184.

19   R. Holbrooke, *To End a War*, rev. edn (New York, 1999), 361.

20   Clinton, "Remarks by the President on American Security," August 5, 1996, PP; Clinton, "Remarks by the President on Foreign Policy," February 26, 1999, PP.

21   Asmus, *Opening NATO's Door*, xxiii, 27, 254; Brinkley, "Democratic Enlargement," 110–127.

22   Clinton, "Remarks by the President on Foreign Policy," February 6, 1999; "Clinton's Foreign Policy," 20; G. Kessler, "Score One for the Legacy," *WP*, September 20, 2000, E1.

23   W.G. Hyland, *Clinton's World* (Westport, CT, 1999), 192.

24   T.B. McCrisken, *American Exceptionalism and the Legacy of Vietnam* (Basingstoke, 2003), 177.

25   L. Richardson, *What Terrorists Want* (New York, 2006), 232; Clinton, "Remarks … on American Security," August 5, 1996; Clinton, "Remarks … on Foreign Policy," February 26, 1999; Dumbrell, *Evaluating the Foreign Policy of President Bill Clinton*, 15.

26   Clinton, "Remarks … on Foreign Policy," February 26, 1999.

27   Dumbrell, *Evaluating the Foreign Policy of President Bill Clinton*, 14.

28   Albright, "Testing of American Foreign Policy," 63; Clinton, "Remarks … on Foreign Policy," February 26, 1999; Walt, "Two Cheers," 75.

29   "Clinton's Foreign Policy," 19.

Chapter 13   The Comeback Kid v. the Gringrich Who Stole Christmas

1   E. Drew, *Showdown* (New York, 1996), 19.

2   J.F. Harris, *The Survivor: Bill Clinton in the White House* (New York, 2006), 178; T. Mathews, "Clinton's Growing Pains," *Newsweek*, May 3, 1993.

3   Drew, *Showdown*, 15; D.S. Cloud, "Speaker Wants His Platform to Rival the Presidency," *CQWR*, February 4, 1995, 331.

4   Cloud, "Speaker Wants His Platform," 332.

5   K.S. Baer, *Reinventing Democrats* (Lawrence, 2000), 236; Drew, *Showdown*, 210; B. Benenson, "GOP sets the 104th Congress on New Regulatory Course," *CQWR*, June 17, 1995, 1693; B. Daynes, "Bill Clinton: Environmental President," in D.L. Soden, ed., *The Environmental Presidency* (Albany, 1999), 299.

6   N.C. Rae, *Conservative Reformers: The Republican Freshmen and the Lessons of the 104th Congress* (Armonk, NY, 1998), 103; D. Morris, *Behind the Oval Office* (New York, 1997), 172–173; P.G. Peterson, "Facing Up," *Atlantic Monthly* (October 1993).

7   Drew, *Showdown*, 106.

8   Morris, *Behind the Oval Office*, 93; Drew, *Showdown*, 136; Harris, *Survivor*, 215; Rae, *Conservative Reformers*, 110.

9   G. Stephanopoulos, *All Too Human* (Boston, 1999), 404, 406; R.J. Samuelson, "Budget Charade," *WP*, December 27, 1995, A19.

10   R.B. Reich, *Locked in the Cabinet* (New York, 1998), 283, 285; B.R. Barber, *The Truth of Power* (New York, 2001), 149.

11   S. Blumenthal, *The Clinton Wars* (New York, 2003), 132.

12   Cloud, "Speaker Wants His Platform," 331.

13   W.E. Leuchtenburg, "The Clintons and the Roosevelts," in R. Garson and S. Kidd, eds, *The Roosevelt Years* (Edinburgh, 1999), 196; Harris, *Survivor*, 238.

14   Clinton, State of the Union Address, January 23, 1996, PP.

15   S.J. Tolchin, *The Angry American*, 2nd edn (Boulder, 1999), 67–68; B. Woodward, *The Choice* (New York, 1996), 418.

16   R.E. Denton, Jr., ed., *The 1996 Presidential Campaign* (Westport, CT, 1998), 131.

17   R.V. Friedenberg, "The 1996 Presidential Debates," in Denton, *The 1996 Presidential Campaign*, 105.

18   M.P. Fiorina, *Culture War?* (New York, 2005), 103–106; N. McCarty, K.T. Poole, and H. Rosenthal, *Polarized America* (Cambridge, MA, 2006), ch. 3.

19   H.C. Kenski *et al.*, "Explaining the Vote," in Denton, *The 1996 Presidential Campaign*, 281; Harris, *Survivor*, 241.

20   S.M. Gillon, *The Pact: Bill Clinton, Newt Gingrich, and the Rivalry That Defined a Generation* (New York, 2008), esp. chs 12 and 13.

21   P.A. Klinkner with R.M. Smith, *The Unsteady March* (Chicago, 1999), 314–315.

22   Clinton, State of the Union Address, January 27, 1998, PP; "State of the Union Address: The Third Way," DLC Update, January 30, 1998: www.dlc.org/

23   J. Chait, "Clinton's Bequest," *American Prospect*, 11 (December 6, 1999); A. Greenspan, *The Age of Turbulence* (London, 2008), 185.

24   Harris, *Survivor*, 334; J. Kentleton, *President and Nation* (Basingstoke, 2002), 268.

25   J.B. Judis, *The Paradox of American Democracy* (New York, 2000), 235; H.R. Clinton, *Living History* (London, 2004), 443; A. Cockburn, "The People Are Angry," *San Jose Mercury News*, September 24, 1998, 10.

26   Blumenthal, *Clinton Wars*, 501; P. DiMaggio *et al.*, "Have Americans' Social Attitudes Become More Polarized?" *American Journal of Sociology*, 102 (November 1996), 715; M.J. Rozell and C. Wilcox, eds, *God at the Grassroots, 1996* (Lanham, 1997), 267.

27   D.E. Rosenbaum, "Congress Leaves Business Lobbies Almost All Smiles," *WSJ*, November 26, 1999, A1; "Clinton Comes Up Short," *Congressional Quarterly Almanac*, 55 (1999), B3.

28   M.L. Sifry, *Spoiling for a Fight* (New York, 2003), 216.

29   *OECD Economic Surveys, 1999–2000: United States* (Paris, 2000); R. Brenner, *The Economics of Global Turbulence* (London, 2006), 3.

30   R.B. Reich, "We Are All Third Wayers Now," *American Prospect*, 10 (March 1, 1999); E.J. Dionne and R. Kuttner, "Did Clinton Succeed or Fail?" *American Prospect*, 11 (August 2000); G. Kessler, "Score One for the Legacy," *WP*, September 20, 2000, E1.

Chapter 14   Since 2001: Decade of Crises

1   S. Wilentz, *The Age of Reagan* (New York, 2008), 434; R. Crockatt, *America Embattled* (London, 2003), 44, 68.

2   S. Halper and J. Clarke, *America Alone* (New York, 2005), 183.

3   W. Kristol and R. Kagan, "Toward a Neo-Reaganite Foreign Policy," *Foreign Affairs*, 75 (1996), 20, 27; C. Krauthammer, "The Unipolar Moment," *Foreign Affairs: America and the World 1990/91*, 70 (1991), 33.

4   Halper and Clarke, *America Alone*, 204; I.H. Daalder and J.M. Lindsay, *America Unbound* (Washington, 2003), 130.

5   Daalder and Lindsay, *America Unbound*, 125; "The National Security Strategy of the United States of America," September 2002, online; M.R. Gordon, "Serving Notice of a New U.S.," *NYT*, January 27, 2003, A12.

6   M. Elliott and J. Carney, "First Stop, Iraq," *Time*, March 31, 2003.

7   G.W. Bush, *"We Will Prevail": President George W. Bush on War, Terrorism, and Freedom* (New York, 2003), 260.

8   M. Cox, "Empire?" in D. Held and M. Koenig-Archibugi, eds, *American Power in the Twenty-First Century* (Cambridge, 2004), 23; R. Suskind, "Faith, Certainty and the Presidency of George W. Bush," *NYT*, October 17, 2003, Magazine; T. Smith, *A Pact with the Devil* (New York, 2007).

9   AJ. Lichtman, *White Protestant Nation* (New York, 2008), 439.

10 N. McCarty, K.T. Poole, and H. Rosenthal, *Polarized America* (Cambridge, MA, 2006); J.S. Hacker and P. Pierson, "Tax Politics and the Struggle over Activist Government," in P. Pierson and T. Skocpol, eds, *The Transformation of American Politics* (Princeton, 2007), 266.

11 Citizens for Tax Justice, May 26, 2001: www.ctj.org/html/gwbfinal.htm; I. Morgan, *The Age of Deficits* (Lawrence, 2009), 228, 276, 279 (deficits in FY2000 figures); L. Dobbs, "Buffet", CNN, June 19, 2005: CNN.com.

12 R. Suskind, *The Price of Loyalty* (London, 2004), 291; G. Davies, *See Government Grow* (2007), 286; US Department of Education, FY2009 Budget Summary; M. Dobbs, "'No Child' Law Leaves Schools' Old Ways Behind," *WP*, April 22, 2004, A1.

13 D. Cauchon, "Medicare Drug Program Snips $6B from Year's Tab," *USA Today*, October 31, 2008, 1A; P. Krugman, "The K Street Prescription," *NYT*, January 20, 2006.

14 J.D. McKinnon, "Big Government's Changing Face," *WSJ*, April 4, 2005, A4; T. Weiner, "Lockheed and the Future of Warfare," *NYT*, November 28, 2004, Sec.3, 1; P.C. Light, "The Real Crisis in Government," *WP*, January 12, 2010, A17.

15 G. Langer, "Poll: No Role for Government in Schiavo Case," ABC News, March 21, 2005.

16 F. Barnes, "The End of the Line," WeeklyStandard.com, January 4, 2009, online; P. Brown, "US Dashes Hopes for Climate Deal," *The Guardian*, May 14, 2002, 11; M. Townsend and P. Harris, "Now the Pentagon Tells Bush," *The Observer*, February 22, 2004.

17 C.M. Klyza and D. Sousa, *American Environmental Policy, 1990–2006* (Cambridge, MA, 2008), 86.

18 B.G. Rabe, "Power to the States," in N.J. Vig and M.E. Kraft, eds, *Environmental Policy*, 6th edn (Washington, 2006), 41–42; Klyza and Sousa, *American Environmental Policy*, 284.

19 J. Preston, "Work Force Fuelled by Highly Skilled Immigrants," *NYT*, April 16, 2010.

20 "Bush Defends Iraq War in Face of WMD Findings," January 28, 2004, CNN.com.

21 MSNBC, Exit Poll, Election 2004, online; McCarty, Poole, and Rosenthal, *Polarized America*, 196–199.

22   R. Watson, "Ambition Marks Bush's Second Term," *BBC News*, January 20, 2005, online; J. Chait, "Blocking Move," *New Republic*, March 21, 2000.

23   "Hurricane Katrina Pummels Three States," August 29, 2005, CNN.com, online; "Governor Kathleen Babineaux Blanco's Letter to President," States News Service, September 12, 2005, online; "Waiting for a Leader," *NYT*, September 1, 2005; G. Stone *et al.*, "Rapid Population Estimate Project," January 28–29, 2006, online.

24   *Time*, August 29, 2005; "Global Warming Strengthens Hurricanes," eCanadaNow, February 22, 2010, online.

25   "President Bush Top Villain Of 2006," Water Cooler, December 28, 2006, online.

26   J. Weisman and J.H. Birnbaum, "Scandals Alone Could Cost Republicans Their House Majority," *WP*, November 2, 2006.

27   S.G. Jones, "Testimony: Defeating Terrorist Groups," September 7, 2008, Rand Corporation, online.

28   G. Hytrek and K.M. Zentgraf, *America Transformed* (New York, 2008), 99; L. Mishel, J. Bernstein, and H. Shierholz, *The State of Working America, 2008/2009* (Ithaca, 2009), 110, 233; S. Boseley, "US Death Rate of Women Giving Birth 'Scandalous,'" *The Guardian*, March 13, 2010; N. Ferguson, *The Ascent of Money* (London, 2008), 334; I. Morgan, "The Indebted Empire," *International Politics*, 45 (2008), 99.

29   Ferguson, *Ascent of Money*, 260, 266; Mishel, Bernstein, and Shierholz, *State of Working America, 2008/2009*, 294; S. O'Grady, "The Market Isn't Rational," *Independent* (London), Life, February 9, 2010, 4.

30   O'Grady, "The Market Isn't Rational," 4.

31   J. Cassidy, *How Markets Fail* (London, 2009), 4–5.

32   "Distrust, Discontent, Anger and Partisan Rancor," Pew Research Center, April 18, 2010, online.

33   L. Dobbs, "Buffet," CNN, June 19, 2005: CNN.com; H. Meyerson, "America's Decade of Dread," *WP*, December 16, 2009; S.S. Cohen and J.B. DeLong, *The End of Influence: What Happens When Other Countries Have the Money* (New York, 2010).

Select Bibliography

Among the many studies covering the themes of this book, the following are particularly helpful. The editions cited are those used by the author; some are UK editions, though in almost all cases the same books have also been published in the United States, most often in New York.

A. Introduction

For general studies see James T. Patterson, *Restless Giant: The United States from Watergate to Bush v. Gore* (New York, 2005), Sean Wilentz, *The Age of Reagan: A History, 1974–2008* (New York, 2008), and Godfrey Hodgson, *More Equal Than Others* (Princeton, 2004). Overviews with a largely political focus include Michael Schaller, *Right Turn: American Life in the Reagan–Bush Era, 1980–1992* (New York, 2007) and William C. Berman, *America's Right Turn: From Nixon to Clinton* (Baltimore, 1998); an economic survey is Samuel Rosenberg, *American Economic Development Since 1945* (Basingstoke, 2003). Excellent on the political economy are Robert M. Collins, *More: The Politics of Economic Growth in Postwar America* (New York, 2000) and Lizabeth Cohen, *A Consumers' Republic: The Politics of Mass Consumption in Postwar America* (New York, 2002). On foreign policy see John Dumbrell, *American Foreign Policy: Carter to Clinton* (Basingstoke, 1997) and Melvyn P. Leffler, *For the Soul of Mankind: The United States, the Soviet Union, and the Cold War* (New York, 2007).

Very helpful on the political system is the series *Developments in American Politics*, edited by Gillian Peele, Christopher J. Bailey, Bruce Cain, and B. Guy Peters. Essential on presidential politics is Richard E. Neustadt, *Presidential Power and the Modern President* (New York, 1990) and Fred Greenstein, *The Presidential Difference: Leadership from FDR to Clinton* (New York, 2000). On parties and politics see E.J. Dionne, *Why Americans Hate Politics* (New York, 1991), Benjamin Ginsberg and Martin Shefter, *Politics By Other Means: Politicians, Prosecutors, and the Press from Watergate to Whitewater* (New York, 2002), and John B. Judis, *The Paradox of American Democracy* (New York, 2000). Invaluable on recent changes is Paul Pierson and

Contemporary America: Power, Dependency, and Globalization since 1980,
First Edition. M.J. Heale.
© 2011 M.J. Heale. Published 2011 by Blackwell Publishing Ltd.

Theda Skocpol, eds, *The Transformation of American Politics* (Princeton, 2007). Developing particular perspectives are Peter Applebome, *Dixie Rising: How the South Is Shaping American Values, Politics, and Culture* (San Diego, 1996) and Michael Kazin, *The Populist Persuasion* (Ithaca, 1998).

James Davison Hunter, *Culture Wars* (York, 1991), helped to precipitate the debate over cultural politics, appearing roughly coincidentally with Arthur Schlesinger, Jr., *The Disuniting of America* (New York, 1991). More broadly on ethnic and racial themes see David A. Hollinger, *Postethnic America: Beyond Multiculturalism* (New York, 1995) and Stephan Thernstrom and Abigail Thernstrom, *America in Black and White: One Nation, Indivisible* (New York, 1997).

Studies which have helped shape this volume's treatment of the American place in the world, in addition to Leffler cited above, have included Paul Kennedy, *The Rise and Fall of the Great Powers* (New York, 1987), Odd Arne Westad, *The Global Cold War: Third World Interventions and the Making of Our Times* (New York, 2005), Raymond Garthoff, *The Great Transition: American–Soviet Relations and the End of the Cold War* (Washington, 1994), and John Gaddis, *Now We Know: Rethinking Cold War History* (New York, 1997). Also relevant is Rhodri Jeffreys-Jones, *The CIA & American Democracy* (New Haven, 1989).

Perceptive analyses relevant to the themes of this study include Joseph S. Nye, Jr., Philip D. Zelikow, and David C. King, eds, *Why People Don't Trust Government* (Cambridge MA, 1997), Kevin Phillips, *Boiling Point: Republicans, Democrats, and the Decline of Middle-Class Prosperity* (New York, 1993), and Michael Lind, *The Next American Nation* (New York, 1996). Particularly useful is Nolan McCarty, Keith T. Poole, and Howard Rosenthal, *Polarized America: The Dance of Ideology and Unequal Riches* (Cambridge, MA, 2006).

B. The 1970s, the Carter Presidency, and the 1980 Election

For broad studies of a sometimes overlooked decade see Edward D. Berkowitz, *Something Happened: A Political and Cultural Overview of the Seventies* (New York, 2006) and Bruce J. Schulman, *The Seventies: The Great Shift in American Culture, Society, and Politics* (New York, 2002). Darker is Philip Jenkins, *Decade of Nightmares* (New York, 2006). Suggestive studies of urbanization, in addition to Lizabeth Cohen above, include Matthew D. Lassiter, *The Silent Majority: Suburban Politics in the Sunbelt South* (Princeton, 2006) and Joel Garreau, *Edge City: Life on the New Frontier* (New York, 1991).

Jimmy Carter's administration is examined in Burton Kaufman, *The Presidency of James Earl Carter, Jr.* (Lawrence, 1993), John Dumbrell, *The Carter Presidency*, 2nd edn (Manchester, 1995), Charles O. Jones, *The Trusteeship Presidency: Jimmy Carter and the United States Congress* (Baton Rouge, 1988), and Gary Fink and Hugh Davis Graham, eds, *The Carter Presidency* (Lawrence, 1998). Jimmy Carter himself published *Keeping Faith* (New York, 1982), and useful too are the memoirs of aides, including Joseph A. Califano, Jr., *Governing America: An Insider's Report from the White House and the Cabinet* (New York, 1981) and Hamilton Jordan, *Crisis: The Last Year of the Carter Presidency* (London, 1982).

The rise of conservatism is often traced to the 1970s. Major studies include Sidney Blumenthal, *The Rise of the Counter-Establishment* (New York, 1986), Godfrey Hodgson, *The*

World Turned Right Side Up (Boston, 1996), and Sara R. Diamond, *Roads to Dominion: Right-Wing Movements and Political Power in the United States* (New York, 1995). Helpful on other aspects are Theodore H. White, *America in Search of Itself* (London, 1983), Seymour Martin Lipset, *American Exceptionalism* (New York, 1996), and Jeffrey M. Berry, *The New Liberalism: The Rising Power of Citizen Groups* (Washington, 1999). Useful for the 1980 election are Jack W. Germond and Jules Witcover, *Blue Smoke and Mirrors: How Reagan Won and Why Carter Lost the Election of 1980* (New York, 1981) and Thomas Ferguson and Joel Rogers, eds, *The Hidden Election* (New York, 1981).

C. Economics and Immigration

Among sources on the US economy are the annual *Economic Report of the President* and the annual *OECD Economic Surveys: United States*, Paris. Helpful too are the regular reports on economic conditions of the Economic Policy Institute, including Lawrence Mishel, Jared Bernstein, and John Schmitt, *The State of Working America, 1998–99* (Ithaca, 1999) and Lawrence Mishel, Jared Bernstein, and Heidi Shierholz, *The State of Working America, 2008/2009* (Ithaca, 2009).

For overviews of economic change, beyond those mentioned in the Introduction, see Stanley L. Engerman and Robert E. Gallman, eds, *The Cambridge Economic History of the United States*, vol. 3 (Cambridge, 2000) and Harold G. Vatter and John F. Walker, eds, *History of the U.S. Economy Since World War II* (Armonk, NY, 1996). Placing the US economy in a global context are Henry C. Dethloff, *The United States and the Global Economy Since 1945* (Fort Worth, 1997) and Nicholas Spulber, *The American Economy: The Struggle for Supremacy in the 21st Century* (Cambridge, 1995). On free trade see Alfred E. Eckes, Jr., *Opening America's Market* (Chapel Hill, 1995). For critical studies of the broad thrust of the economy see Jeffry A. Frieden, *Global Capitalism: Its Fall and Rise in the Twentieth Century* (New York, 2006), Robert Brenner, *The Boom and the Bubble* (London, 2002) and *The Economics of Global Turbulence* (London, 2006), and Andrew Glyn, *Capitalism Unleashed: Finance, Globalization, and Welfare* (Oxford, 2007). See also Bennett Harrison and Barry Bluestone, *The Great U-Turn: Corporate Restructuring and the Polarizing of America* (New York, 1988). Valuable for their perspectives on the long 1980s are James Medoff and Andrew Harless, *The Indebted Society* (Boston, 1996), Benjamin M. Friedman, *Day of Reckoning: The Consequences of American Economic Policy Under Reagan and After* (New York, 1988), Paul Krugman, *The Age of Diminished Expectations* (Cambridge, MA, 1990), and Robert B. Reich, *The Work of Nations* (New York, 1991).

The modern United States has been shaped by its demography as well as its economy. Basic statistics can be found in the annual *Yearbook of Immigration Statistics* (Washington). The global context is provided in Stephen Castles and Mark J. Miller, *The Age of Migration*, 2nd edn (Basingstoke, 1998), Peter Stalker, *Workers Without Frontiers* (London, 1999), W.M. Spellman, *The Global Community* (Stroud, 2002), and David M. Reimers, *Other Immigrants: The Global Origins of the American People* (New York, 2005). The American perspective is offered in Leonard Dinnerstein *et al.*, *Natives and Strangers: A Multicultural History of Americans* (New York, 1996) and Roger Daniels, *Coming to America: A History of Immigration and Ethnicity in American Life*, 2nd edn (New York, 2002). Useful collections of essays are Philip Davies and Iwan Morgan, eds, *America's Americans: Population Issues in U.S. Society and Politics* (London, 2007) and William C. Fischer, David A. Gerber, Jorge M.Guitart, and Maxine S. Seller, eds, *Identity, Community, and Pluralism in American Life* (New York, 1997). The return of mass immigration is examined in Pyong Gap Min, ed., *Mass Migration to the United States* (Walnut Creek, CA, 2002). The questions it raised about the American national interest are explored in Richard Alba and Victor Nee, *Remaking the American Mainstream* (Cambridge, MA, 2003), Cheryl Shanks, *Immigration and the Politics of American Sovereignty, 1890–1990* (Ann Arbor, 2001), Leo R. Chavez, *Covering Immigration* (Berkeley, 2001), and Bill Ong Hing, *Defining America Through Immigration Policy* (Philadelphia, 2004). Issues of nationality and ethnicity are addressed in Peter H. Schuck, *Citizens, Strangers, and In-Betweens* (Boulder, CO, 1998) and David G. Gutiérrez, *Walls and Mirrors: Mexican Americans, Mexican Immigrants, and the Politics of Ethnicity* (Berkeley, 1995).

Economic dimensions are explored in James P. Smith and Barry Edmonston, eds, *The New Americans: Economic, Demographic, and Fiscal Effects of Immigration* (Washington, 1997) and George J. Borjas, *Heaven's Door: Immigration Policy and the American Economy* (Princeton, 1999). Good on the implications for immigration policy are David M. Reimers, *Unwelcome Strangers: American Identity and the Turn Against Immigration* (New York, 1998) and Roger Daniels and Otis L. Graham, *Debating American Immigration* (Lanham, MD, 2001). Helpful is James G. Gimpel and James R. Edwards, Jr., *The Congressional Politics of Immigration Reform* (Needham Heights, MA, 1999). Good on the 1990s and after is Andrew Wroe, *The Republican Party and Immigration Politics* (New York, 2008).

Helpful for the themes of this book is Edward S. Cohen, *The Politics of Globalization in the United States* (Washington, 2001). On the English Only movement see James Crawford, ed., *Language Loyalties: A Source Book on the Official English Controversy* (Chicago, 1992), Ronald Schmidt, Sr., *Language Policy and Identity Politics in the United States* (Philadelphia, 2000), and Dennis Baron, *The English-Only Question* (New Haven, 1990). See also Carol M. Swain, *The New White Nationalism in America* (Cambridge, 2002).

D. The Long 1980s (Reagan and Bush Sr.)

There is now an immense range of publications on the age of (especially) Ronald Reagan and the elder George Bush. One of the best studies of the 1980s is Robert M. Collins, *Transforming America: Politics and Culture in the Reagan Years* (New York, 2007); also offering a synoptic view is Gil Troy, *Morning in America* (Princeton, 2005). From a neoconservative perspective is John Ehrman, *The Eighties* (New Haven, 2005), and fascinating is John Patrick Diggins, *Ronald Reagan: Fate, Freedom, and the Making of History* (New York, 2007). The Reagan era has also attracted a number of valuable essay collections, among them Larry Berman, ed., *Looking Back on the Reagan Presidency* (Baltimore, 1990), W. Elliot Brownlee and Hugh Davis Graham, eds, *The Reagan Presidency: Pragmatic Conservatism and Its Legacies* (Lawrence, 2003), Kyle Longley *et al.*, *Deconstructing Reagan* (Armonk, NY, 2007), and Cheryl Hudson and Gareth Davies, eds, *Ronald Reagan and the 1980s* (New York, 2008), which contains a couple of historiographical pieces. Ronald Reagan's own writings are worth consulting. There is Ronald Reagan, *An American Life* (New York, 1990), his early radio addresses in Kiron K. Skinner, Annelise Anderson, and Martin Anderson eds, *Reagan, In His Own Hand* (New York, 2001), the same editors' collection in *Reagan: A Life in Letters* (New York, 2003), and Douglas Brinkley, ed., *The Reagan Diaries* (New York, 2007). An unusually large number of Reagan's aides, with varying degrees of loyalty, published accounts of their experiences. On the domestic front are Michael K. Deaver, *Behind the Scenes* (New York, 1987), Larry Speakes, *Speaking Out: The Reagan Presidency from Inside the White House* (New York, 1988), Donald T. Regan, *For the Record* (New York, 1989), Peggy Noonan, *What I Saw At the Revolution* (New York, 1990), and Edwin Meese III, *With Reagan: The Inside Story* (Washington, 1992). Focusing particularly on economic policy are David A. Stockman, *The Triumph of Politics* (London, 1986), Paul Craig Roberts, *The Supply-Side Revolution* (Cambridge, MA, 1984), and Martin Anderson, *Revolution: The Reagan Legacy*, expanded edn (Stanford, 1990). For those who contributed to foreign and defense policies see Alexander M. Haig, Jr., *Caveat: Realism, Reagan, and Foreign Policy* (London, 1984), George P. Shultz, *Turmoil and Triumph: My Years as Secretary of State* (New York, 1993), and Caspar Weinberger, *Fighting for Peace: Seven Critical Years at the Pentagon* (London, 1990). A few memoirs spanned the Reagan and Bush administrations, such as James A. Baker III, *"Work Hard, Study … And Keep Out of Politics!" Adventures and Lessons from An Unexpected Public Life* (New York, 2006) and Robert M. Gates, *From the Shadows: The Ultimate Insider's Story of Five Presidents and How They Won the Cold War* (New York, 1996). Alan Greenspan became Fed chair under Reagan and remained there until George W. Bush, a story he records in *The Age of Turbulence* (London, 2008).

Some perspectives of the 1980s can be gleaned from Reagan's opponents, such as Daniel Patrick Moynihan, *Came the Revolution: Argument in the Reagan Era* (San Diego, 1988) and Tip O'Neill with William Novak, *Man of the House: The Life and Political Memoirs of Speaker Tip O'Neill* (London, 1987). A major Democratic figure is examined in Adam Clymer, *Edward M. Kennedy* (New York, 1999). Some of the early journalistic accounts of the Reagan presidency were not particularly admiring, such as Haynes Johnson, *Sleepwalking Through History* (New York, 1991). The best biography of Reagan remains the three volumes published by Lou Cannon, the third of which is *President Reagan: The Role of a Lifetime* (New York, 2000). A good short study is William E Pemberton, *Exit with Honor: The Life and Presidency of Ronald Reagan* (Armonk, NY, 1997). Michael Schaller, *Reckoning with Reagan* (New York, 1992), is brief and critical, Garry Wills, *Reagan's America* (New York, 2000), is insightful, and Richard Reeves, *President Reagan* (New York, 2005), is respectful. Edmund Morris, *Dutch* (New York, 1999), is the authorized biography, undermined by poetic license. Friendly assessments include Paul Kengor and Peter Schweizer, eds, *The Reagan Presidency: Assessing the Man and His Legacy* (Lanham, MD, 2005).

For economic history in the long 1980s, in addition to those cited under section C, see Martin Feldstein, ed., *American Economic Policy in the 1980s* (Chicago, 1994). Adding to the critique of Friedman, *Day of Reckoning*, above, is Kevin Phillips, *The Politics of Rich and Poor* (New York, 1991) and Robert Kuttner, *The End of Laissez-Faire* (New York, 1991). Important for all modern presidents is Iwan Morgan, *The Age of Deficits: Presidents and Unbalanced Budgets from Jimmy Carter to George W. Bush* (Lawrence, 2009). On the rise of political conservatism see the items by Blumenthal, Hodgson, and Diamond in section B above, and Donald T. Critchlow, *The Conservative Ascendancy: How the GOP Right Made Political History* (Cambridge, MA, 2007), Allan J. Lichtman, *White Protestant Nation: The Rise of the American Conservative Movement* (New York, 2008), and Earl Black and Merle Black, *The Rise of Southern Republicans* (Cambridge, MA, 2002). Biographies of conservatives include Robert Alan Goldberg, *Barry Goldwater* (New Haven, 1995) and Joseph E. Persico, *Casey: From the OSS to the CIA* (New York, 1990). Liberals have commanded less academic attention than conservatives, but instructive are Kenneth S. Baer, *Reinventing Democrats: The Politics of*

Liberalism from Reagan to Clinton (Lawrence, 2000), focused on the Democratic Leadership Council, Jeffrey M. Berry, *The New Liberalism: The Rising Power of Citizen Groups* (Washington, 1999), and Theda Skocpol and Morris P. Fiorina, eds, *Civic Engagement in American Democracy* (Washington, 1999).

Particular episodes are examined in Paul Light, *Artful Work: The Politics of Social Security Reform* (New York, 1985) and Ethan Bronner, *Battle for Justice: How the Bork Nomination Shook America* (New York, 1989). Useful studies on racial matters include William T.M. Riches, *The Civil Rights Movement*, 3rd edn (Basingstoke, 2010), Philip A. Klinkner with Rogers M. Smith, *The Unsteady March: The Rise and Decline of Racial Equality in America* (Chicago, 1999), and Stephen Tuck, *We Ain't What We Ought To Be: The Black Freedom Struggle from Emancipation to Obama* (Cambridge, MA, 2010). For Reagan's re-election see Gerald Pomper *et al.*, *The Election of 1984* (Chatham, NJ, 1985), and the travails of his second term, Jane Mayer and Doyle McManus, *Landslide: The Unmaking of the President, 1984–1988* (Boston, 1988).

There is a rich literature on the defense and foreign policies of the Reagan years. Important are studies by Leffler, Garthoff, and Westad, cited in section A, and a valuable overview is Don Oberdorfer, *From the Cold War to a New Era: The United States and the Soviet Union, 1983–1991*, updated edn (Baltimore, 1998). Fascinating on a favorite Reagan policy is Frances FitzGerald, *Way Out There in the Blue: Reagan, Star Wars and the End of the Cold War* (New York, 2000). Jack F. Matlock Jr.'s books offer the shrewd insights of a participant in the Reagan–Bush years, *Reagan and Gorbachev: How the Cold War Ended* (New York, 2004) and *Autopsy on an Empire: The American Ambassador's Account of the Collapse of the Soviet Union* (New York, 1995). Beth A. Fischer, *The Reagan Reversal: Foreign Policy and the End of the Cold War* (Columbia, MO, 1997), focuses on a pivotal period. Also important are Bruce W. Jentleson, *With Friends Like These: Reagan, Bush, and Saddam, 1982–1990* (New York, 1994) and Theodore Draper, *A Very Thin Line: The Iran–Contra Affairs* (New York, 1991).

A president reveals something about himself in George Bush with Victor Gold, *Looking Forward* (New York, 1987) and George Bush, *All the Best, G. Bush: My Life in Letters and Other Writings* (New York, 1999). Memoirs of aides include Charles Kolb, *White House Daze: The Unmaking of Domestic Policy in the Bush Years* (New York, 1994), John Podhoretz, *Hell of a Ride: Backstage at the White House Follies, 1989–1993* (New York, 1993), Richard Darman, *Who's In Control? Polar Politics and the Sensible Center* (New York, 1996), as well as James Baker III cited above. There are a number of concise studies of the administration, including Herbert S. Parmet, *George Bush: The Life of a Lone Star Yankee* (New Brunswick, 2001), John Robert Greene, *The Presidency of George Bush* (Lawrence, 2000), and David Mervin, *George Bush and the Guardianship Presidency* (Basingstoke, 1998). For Bush elections see Gerald M. Pomper *et al.*, *The Election of 1988* (Chatham, NJ, 1989), Gerald M. Pomper *et al.*, *The Election of 1992* (Chatham, NJ, 1993), and Jack W. Germond and Jules Witcover, *Mad As Hell: Revolt at the Ballot Box, 1992* (New York, 1993). An impression of the electoral challenge Bush faced is presented in Stanley B. Greenberg, *Middle Class Dreams: The Politics and Power of the New American Majority*, revised edn (New Haven, 1996).

For foreign affairs see Steven Hurst, *The Foreign Policy of the Bush Administration* (London, 1999). The president and his National Security Adviser provide their own account in George Bush and Brent Scowcroft, *A World Transformed* (New York, 1998), and the Secretary of State in James A. Baker III, *The Politics of Diplomacy: Revolution, War and Peace 1989–1992* (New York, 1995). Valuable is Michael R. Beschloss and Strobe Talbott,

At the Highest Levels: The Inside Story of the End of the Cold War (London, 1993), as is David Halberstam, *War in a Time of Peace: Bush, Clinton and the Generals* (London, 2002). See also Strobe Talbott, *The Russia Hand: A Memoir of Presidential Diplomacy* (New York, 2002).

Morris P. Fiorina, *Culture War? The Myth of a Polarized America* (New York, 2005), is skeptical of the depth of the culture war. Several studies cited under section C indicate the economic problems facing Bush, as does Michael T. Jacobs, *Short-Term America* (Boston, 1991). Not everyone agreed that the United States was in decline, including Joseph S. Nye, *Bound to Lead: The Changing Nature of American Power* (New York, 1991) and Henry Nau, *The Myth of America's Decline* (New York, 1990).

E. Environment

For a good overview of environmental history see Richard N.L. Andrews, *Managing the Environment, Managing Ourselves*, 2nd edn (New Haven, 2006); a useful introduction is Riley E. Dunlap and Angela G. Mertig, eds, *American Environmentalism: The U.S. Environmental Movement, 1970–1990* (New York, 1992). Important for the early period is Samuel P. Hays, *Beauty, Health, and Permanence* (Cambridge, 1987), and critical of the turn of modern environmentalism is Mark Dowie, *Losing Ground: American Environmentalism at the Close of the Twentieth Century* (Cambridge, MA, 1995). There is much to be learned from the collections of essays which abound on this subject, among them Otis L. Graham Jr., ed., *Environmental Politics and Policy, 1960s–1990s* (University Park, PA, 2000), Norman J. Vig and Michael E. Kraft, eds, *Environmental Policy*, 6th edn (Washington, 2006), and Dennis L. Soden, ed., *The Environmental Presidency* (Albany, 1999). Good on recent policy are Stephen Hopgood, *American Foreign Environmental Policy and the Power of the State* (Oxford, 1998) and Christopher McGrory Klyza and David Sousa, *American Environmental Policy, 1990–2006* (Cambridge, MA, 2008). Several studies place American environmentalism in a wider international context, among them Miranda A. Schreurs and Elizabeth C. Economy, eds, *The Internationalization of Environmental Protection* (Cambridge, 1997), Norman J. Vig and Michael G. Faure, eds, *Green Giants? Environmental Policies of the United States and the European Union* (Cambridge, MA, 2004), and Matthew Paterson, *Global Warming and Global Politics* (London, 1996).

F. Globalization

Several of the titles in section C are relevant here, including those by Brenner, Glyn, and Reich. Valuable introductions include Ian R. Tyrrell, *Transnational Nation: United States History in Global Perspective since 1789* (Basingstoke, 2007), Carl Guarneri, *America in the World* (Boston, 2007), Alfred E. Eckes, Jr. and Thomas W. Zeiler, *Globalization and the American Century* (Cambridge, 2003), and Thomas L. Brewer and Gavin Boyd, eds, *Globalizing America: The USA in World Integration* (Cheltenham, 2000). The journalist Thomas L. Friedman has written supportive studies of globalization, most notably *The Lexus and the Olive Tree* (London, 2000) and *The World Is Flat*, updated edn (London, 2006). Asking a pertinent question is Dani Rodrik, *Has Globalization Gone Too Far?* (Washington, 1997), and unequivocally critical are Gary Hytrek and Kristine M. Zentgraf, *America Transformed: Globalization, Inequality, and Power* (New York, 2008). An important critique is Benjamin R. Barber, *Jihad vs. McWorld: Terrorism's Challenge to Democracy* (London, 2003), as are Joseph Stiglitz, *Globalization and Its Discontents* (London, 2002) and George Soros, *The Crisis of Global Capitalism* (London, 1998).

Relevant specialized studies on economic perspectives include Richard Stubbs and Geoffrey R.D. Underhill, eds, *Political Economy and the Changing Global Order*, 3rd edn (Oxford, 2005), Graham Dunkley, *The Free Trade Adventure* (London, 1997), and Jagdish Bhagwati, *A Stream of Windows: Unsettling Reflections on Trade, Immigration, and Democracy* (Cambridge, MA, 1998). Paul Krugman addresses the 1998 Asian crisis as well as later financial turmoil in *The Return of Depression Economics and the Crisis of 2008* (London, 2008).

G. Bill Clinton and the 1990s

Broad studies of the 1990s include Haynes Johnson, *The Best of Times* (San Diego, 2002) and William C. Berman, *From the Center to the Edge: The Politics and Policies of the Clinton Presidency* (Lanham, 2001). Helping to put the Clinton presidency in perspective is Alex Waddan, *Clinton's Legacy? A New Democrat in Governance* (Basingstoke, 2002). Helpful for understanding populist tensions are Greenberg, *Middle-Class Dreams* in section D, Susan J. Tolchin, *The Angry American*, 2nd edn (Boulder, 1999), Jacob S. Hacker, *The Great Risk Shift: The Assault on American Jobs, Families, Health Care, and Retirement and How You Can Fight Back* (New York, 2006), and Kevin Phillips, *Arrogant Capital: Washington, Wall Street, and the Frustration of American Politics* (Boston, 1994).

Bill Clinton has attracted his fair share of biographers. Substantial if not altogether satisfactory is Nigel Hamilton, *Bill Clinton, An American Journey* (New York, 2003) and *Bill Clinton, Mastering the Presidency* (New York, 2007). Focusing on the first term is Martin Walker, *The President We Deserve* (New York, 1996), while another journalist encompasses the whole eight years in Joe Klein, *The Natural: The Misunderstood Presidency of Bill Clinton* (New York, 2002); excellent is John F. Harris, *The Survivor: Bill Clinton in the White House* (New York, 2006). Critical is Rich Lowery, *Legacy: Paying the Price for the Clinton Years* (Washington, 2003). The Clintons have produced their own lengthy memoirs, Bill Clinton, *My Life* (London, 2004), and Hillary Rodham Clinton, *Living History* (London, 2004). Perhaps more instructive are the accounts of their aides and others who came into regular contact with the White House, most notably Robert B. Reich, *Locked in the Cabinet* (New York, 1998), George Stephanopoulos, *All Too Human: A Political Education* (Boston, 1999), Robert E. Rubin, *In An Uncertain World: Tough Choices from Wall Street to Washington* (New York, 2004), Sidney Blumenthal, *The Clinton Wars* (New York, 2003), Dick Morris, *Behind the Oval Office* (New York, 1997), and Benjamin R. Barber, *The Truth of Power: Intellectual Affairs in the Clinton White House* (New York, 2001).

Journalist Elizabeth Drew has written riveting accounts of the era, most notably *On the Edge: The Clinton Presidency* (New York, 1994) and *Showdown: The Struggle Between the Gingrich Congress and the Clinton White House* (New York, 1996), as has Bob Woodward in *The Agenda: Inside the Clinton White House* (New York, 1994) and *The Choice* (New York, 1996). Academic studies include Baer, *Reinventing Democrats*, cited in section D, Colin Campbell and Bert A. Rockman, eds, *The Clinton Presidency* (Chatham, NJ, 1996), and

Theodore J. Lowi and Benjamin Ginsberg, *Embattled Democracy: Politics and Policy in the Clinton Era* (New York, 1995). Electoral studies include Robert E. Denton Jr., ed., *The 1996 Presidential Campaign* (Westport, CT, 1998), Mark J. Rozell and Clyde Wilcox eds, *God at the Grassroots, 1996* (Lanham, 1997), and Jack Rakove, ed., *The Unfinished Election of 2000* (New York, 2001).

Various episodes are examined in Theda Skocpol, *Boomerang: Clinton's Health Security Effort and the Turn Against Government in U.S. Politics* (New York, 1996), Steven M. Gillon, *The Pact: Bill Clinton, Newt Gingrich, and the Rivalry That Defined a Generation* (New York, 2008), and Nicol Rae and Colton C. Campbell, *Impeaching Clinton* (Lawrence, KS, 2004). For Clinton's opponents see Dick Williams, *Newt!* (Marietta, GA, 1995), Mel Steely, *The Gentleman from Georgia: The Biography of Newt Gingrich* (Macon, GA, 2000), and Nicol C. Rae, *Conservative Reformers: The Republican Freshmen and the Lessons of the 104th Congress* (Armonk, NY, 1998).

There is a substantial literature on foreign affairs. Halberstam, noted in section D, remains relevant. The dozen years from the fall of the Berlin Wall are examined in Derek Chollet and James Goldgeier, *America Between the Wars* (New York, 2008). A critical survey is William G. Hyland, *Clinton's World: Remaking American Foreign Policy* (Westport, CT, 1999); authoritative is John Dumbrell, *Clinton's Foreign Policy: Between the Bushes* (London, 2009), the main themes of which were crisply foreshadowed in the author's *Evaluating the Foreign Policy of President Bill Clinton* (London, 2005). Helpful in understanding Clinton's foreign policy as well as that of his successor is Tony Smith, *A Pact with the Devil: Washington's Bid for World Supremacy and the Betrayal of the American Promise* (New York, 2007). Contributing valuable insights too are Trevor B. McCrisken, *American Exceptionalism and the Legacy of Vietnam* (Basingstoke, 2003), Ronald D. Asmus, *Opening NATO's Door: How the Alliance Remade Itself for a New Era* (New York, 2002), and D. Yankelovich and I.M. Destler, eds, *Beyond the Beltway* (New York, 1994). Accounts by participants include Madeleine Albright, *Madam Secretary* (London, 2004), Richard Holbrooke, *To End a War*, rev. edn (New York, 1999), and David Owen, *Balkan Odyssey* (London, 1995). Also relevant is Louise Richardson, *What Terrorists Want* (New York, 2006).

H. Since 2000

For the contemporary political system see Pierson and Skocpol, eds, *Transformation*, and McCarty, Poole, and Rosenthal, *Polarized America*, cited in section A, and Joe Soss, Jacob S. Hacker, and Suzanne Mettler, eds, *Remaking America* (New York, 2007). Also helpful are Thomas Frank, *What's the Matter with America? The Resistible Rise of the American Right* (London, 2006) and Ronald Brownstein, *The Second Civil War: How Extreme Partisanship Has Paralyzed Washington and Polarized America* (New York, 2007), though the former needs to be balanced with Fiorina, *Culture War?*, cited in section D. On social and economic problems see Hacker, *The Great Risk Shift*, in section G, and Richard Wilkinson and Kate Pickett, *The Spirit Level: Why More Equal Societies Almost Always Do Better* (London, 2009).

On the administration of the younger Bush is Colin Campbell and Bert A. Rockman, eds, *The George W. Bush Presidency* (Washington, 2004) and Iwan Morgan and Philip J. Davies, eds, *Right On? Political Change and Continuity in George Bush's America* (London, 2006). Unfriendly is Kevin P. Phillips, *American Dynasty: Aristocracy, Fortune, and the Politics of*

Deceit in the House of Bush (New York, 2004). A succinct overview is Steven E. Schier, *Panorama of a Presidency: How George W. Bush Acquired and Spent His Political Capital* (Armonk, NY, 2009). The views of Bush's first Treasury Secretary are captured in Ron Suskind, *The Price of Loyalty* (London, 2004), and of his first Environment Secretary in Christine Todd Whitman, *It's My Party Too* (New York, 2005).

There is an extensive foreign policy literature. Putting US policy in context is David Held and Mathias Koenig-Archibugi, eds, *American Power in the Twenty-First Century* (Cambridge, 2004), and critical is Chalmers Johnson, *The Sorrows of Empire: Militarism, Secrecy, and the End of the Republic* (New York, 2004). Important is Smith, *Pact with the Devil*, cited in the previous section. The president's early perceptions of the War on Terror are available in George W. Bush, *"We Will Prevail": President George W. Bush on War, Terrorism, and Freedom* (New York, 2003), and useful if unconvinced is Ivo H. Daalder and James M. Lindsay, *America Unbound: The Bush Revolution in Foreign Policy* (Washington, 2003). On the role of the neoconservatives see James Mann, *Rise of the Vulcans: The History of Bush's War Cabinet* (New York, 2003) and Stefan Halper and Jonathan Clarke, *America Alone: The Neo-Conservatives and the Global Order* (New York, 2005). Richard Crockatt, *America Embattled: September 11, Anti-Americanism, and the Global Order* (London, 2003), is incisive, while Bob Woodward examines Bush's wars at length in *Bush at War* (New York, 2002), *Plan of Attack* (New York, 2004), and *State of Denial* (New York, 2006). Critical are Richard A. Clarke, *Against All Enemies: Inside the War on Terror* (New York, 2004) and Thomas E. Ricks, *Fiasco: The American Military Adventure in Iraq* (New York, 2006). Cautioning against expectations of major change as Bush's presidency drew to a close is Timothy J. Lynch and Robert S. Singh, *After Bush: The Case for Continuity in American Foreign Policy* (Cambridge, 2008).

For the financial turmoil that marked the end of the decade see Niall Ferguson, *The Ascent of Money* (London, 2008), John Cassidy, *How Markets Fail* (London, 2009), Andrew Ross Sorkin, *Too Big to Fail: Inside the Battle to Save Wall Street* (London, 2009), and Michael Lewis, *The Big Short: Inside the Doomsday Machine* (London, 2010). On the survival of big government see Katherine S. Newman and Elisabeth S. Jacobs, *Who Cares? Public Ambivalence and Government Activism from the New Deal to the Second Gilded Age* (Princeton, 2010), and for doubts about US viability see Stephen S. Cohen and J. Bradford DeLong, *The End of Influence: What Happens When Other Countries Have the Money* (New York, 2010).

Index

Contemporary America: Power, Dependency, and Globalization since 1980,
First Edition. M.J. Heale.
© 2011 M.J. Heale. Published 2011 by Blackwell Publishing Ltd.